The Armenian Rebellion at Van

The Armenian Rebellion at Van

Justin McCarthy
Esat Arslan
Cemalettin Taşkiran
Ömer Turan

*Utah Series in Turkish
and Islamic Studies*

The University of Utah Press
Salt Lake City

Utah Series in Turkish and Islamic Studies
M. Hakan Yavuz, editor

 The Defiance House Man colophon is a registered trademark of the University of Utah Press. It is based upon a four-foot-tall, Ancient Puebloan pictograph (late PIII) near Glen Canyon, Utah.

11 10 09 08 07 06   5 4 3 2 1

LIBRARY OF CONGRESS CATALOGING-IN-PUBLICATION DATA
The Armenian rebellion at Van / Justin McCarthy...[et al.].
    p. cm. — (Utah series in Turkish and Islamic studies)
  Includes bibliographical references and index.
  ISBN-13: 978-0-87480-870-4 (pbk. : alk. paper)
  ISBN-10: 0-87480-870-7 (pbk. : alk. paper)   1. Armenians—Turkey—
Van—History—19th century.   2. Armenians—Turkey—Van—History—20th
century.   3. Van (Turkey)—History—19th century.   4. Van (Turkey)—
History—20th century.   I. McCarthy, Justin, 1945–
  DR435.A7A7556 2006
  956.6'20154—dc22   2006019190

www.uofupress.com

Contents

Maps

Acknowledgments

The financial support of the Istanbul Chamber of Commerce; the Istanbul Chamber of Industry; the Istanbul and Marmara, Aegean, Mediterranean and Black Sea Chamber of Shipping; and the Istanbul Commodity Exchange made this study possible. The authors thank them for their contribution and for their faith in the work.

The authors also wish to thank the directors and staffs of the Askeri Tarih ve Strategic Etüt Başkanlığı Archives, the British National Archives, the U.S. National Archives, the Baş Bakanlık Arşivi, the Houghton Library at Harvard University, the Inter-Library Loan Department of the University of Louisville Library, the Türk Tarih Kurumu Library, the Library of Congress, and the British Library.

Foremost among the many who aided the authors were Fügen Çamlıdere, Melih Berk, Rita Hettinger, Lee Keeling, Caitlin McCarthy, and Carolyn McCarthy. Hüsnü Dağ was instrumental in organizing and beginning the study. The project would not have begun without his efforts. Birsen Karaca provided essential translations from Armenian. We thank them all for their vital contributions.

CHAPTER I

The Ruins of Van

On July 24, 1919, two Americans, Captain Emory H. Niles and Arthur E. Sutherland, Jr., arrived by horseback at the city of Van. Niles and Sutherland were the first outsiders to see Van since the end of World War I. The region they traveled through was barren, in many places devoid of human life. "The country," they wrote, "is one of bare mountains and ruins."[1]

The two Americans estimated that there were five thousand inhabitants in the city of Van and slightly more than one hundred thousand in the entire province. Except for approximately seven hundred Armenians, the population of the city was entirely made up of Muslim refugees who had fled during the war and returned when Ottoman armies reconquered Van. From survivors' accounts, Niles and Sutherland estimated that one-half of the Muslim refugees had died. Van City was nine-tenths destroyed, as were a large majority of the province's villages. The city had no commercial life ("In the City the shops contain nothing"), no schools. The governor, praised by the Americans, was able to keep open military and civilian hospitals and an orphanage. The people were no longer starving, but only because their diminished numbers were so few that the limited amount of grain that the government was able to distribute sufficed. The refugees had been in "great want" at first but now had planted enough to guarantee a harvest that would see them through the winter.

Van's Armenians, who had been one-fourth of the province's prewar population, were gone. Only those seven hundred remained, protected by soldiers from the vengeance of the Muslims. The inhabitants told the Americans that the Armenians had destroyed everything and tortured, raped, and killed the Muslims. Niles and Sutherland, like other Americans and Europeans, had been fed on a diet of anti-Turkish propaganda that made the Armenians into saints and the Turks into devils, so at first they did not believe the claims of the Muslims. They changed their minds: "At

I

first we were most incredulous of these stories, but we finally came to believe them, since the testimony was absolutely unanimous and was corroborated by material evidence. For instance, the only quarters left at all intact in the cities of Bitlis and Van are the Armenian quarters, as was evidenced by churches and inscriptions on the houses, while the Moslem quarters were completely destroyed. Villages said to have been Armenian were still standing, whereas Musulman villages were completely destroyed."

The Muslims were living in Armenian houses and Armenian villages, because their own houses and villages had been obliterated. Less than one-third of the villages existing before the war were fit for life, and this was only because the refugees had been repairing them for more than a year before Niles and Sutherland arrived.

Before World War I and the Armenian rebellion against the Ottomans, Van had been known as a city of trees, gardens, and vineyards, remarkable in an otherwise barren landscape. Its markets and warehouses had been the center of trade for all of southeastern Anatolia. The city had been inhabited longer than history had been written. It had been filled with mosques and churches, many of them renowned for their beauty. Now it was a ruin.

The Armenians of Van had revolted against the Ottoman government, putting their trust in the Russians, who betrayed them. They and the Russians had driven the Muslims from the province. The Armenians in turn had been driven out. Theirs was the final exodus. Surviving Muslims returned. Neither side, however, can truly be said to have won the war. More than half of Van's Armenians had died, as had almost two-thirds of its Muslims.

The new Turkish Republic found it impossible to rebuild on the ruins. A new city was built to the southeast. The Ottoman city of Van had died.

NOTES

1. United States National Archives 184.021/175. The report of Niles and Sutherland was deliberately suppressed by those who did not wish their account to be seen (Justin McCarthy, "American Commissions to Anatolia and the Report of Niles and Sutherland," in *Türk Tarih Kurumu Kongresi XI, Ankara: 5–9 Eylül 1990* [Ankara: Türk Tarih Kurumu, 1994], pp. 1809–53). The only extant copy is a draft found among detritus of the American Harbord Commission. The report thus contains grammatical infelicities and intermixed usages such as "Moslem" and "Musulman." The recorded interviews of the inhabitants that were conducted by Niles and Sutherland have been lost, probably destroyed.

CHAPTER 2

The City and Province of Van

THE CITY OF VAN

To its inhabitants, the city of Van was beautiful. It was within easy walking distance of the largest lake in Anatolia. Mountains, often snow-capped, surrounded the city. The views of the mountains and the lake were spectacular. To outsiders more accustomed to trees, the surroundings of Van may have appeared a bit bleak. The only greenery consisted of scrub bushes on hillsides, crops on farms, and some trees along watercourses. Parts of the city contained tree-lined streets and gardens, although these were often behind walls, a private beauty. The stark beauty of the mountains and Lake Van represented the city's public face.

The city of Van was situated 2 kilometers east of Lake Van. The Van fortress district, the Old City of Van, stretched for 1 kilometer along the foot of a defensible outcropping of rock 200 meters above the plain. It had been a most defensible fortress and seat of government since ancient times, surrounded by a moat and thick fortification walls. The Old City had four gates: the Tabriz Gate, Palace Gate, Middle Gate, and Quay Gate. To the east, outside the Tabriz Gate, the land rose sharply to a rocky prominence. After conquering the region in 1534, Süleyman the Magnificent had built the Van Citadel (İçkale: inner fortress) on this promontory directly north of the Old City. It was used in the later nineteenth century as a garrison and site for an artillery battery.

The houses and streets of the Old City were what might be expected in a traditional Middle Eastern city. The houses were built of mud brick and wood. The streets were narrow, winding, and dark. Some estimated that there were five thousand houses in the Old City. This was surely a gross exaggeration: government figures listed only 5,400 households in the whole district of Van, which included the entire city of Van (much larger than the Old City alone) and the surrounding countryside.[1] Without doubt, however, the Old City was packed full of two-story houses,

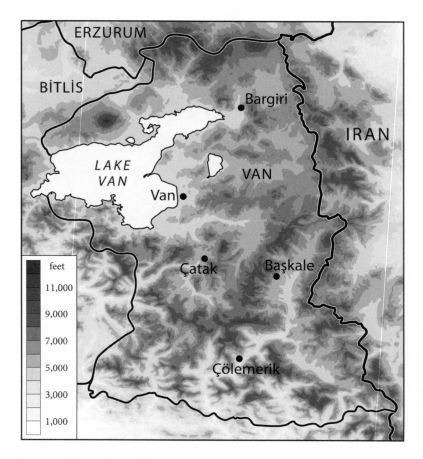

MAP 2.1. The Province of Van.

mosques, churches, and markets. Commercial buildings in the Old City included warehouses, caravanserais, markets, workplaces, and bazaars, many of which had been there for centuries. Most of the Old City would have been recognizable to inhabitants of Van in the Middle Ages.

What was new in the Old City had been created mainly by the government. The Old City was the administrative and economic center of the city and province. The Palace Gate (Saray Kapısı) neighborhood in the southeast contained the Provincial Government Headquarters, police and gendarme (rural paramilitary police) headquarters, courts, the central jail, a barracks, government health and agricultural offices, the customs office, a post and telegraph office, the Ottoman Bank, the Public Debt

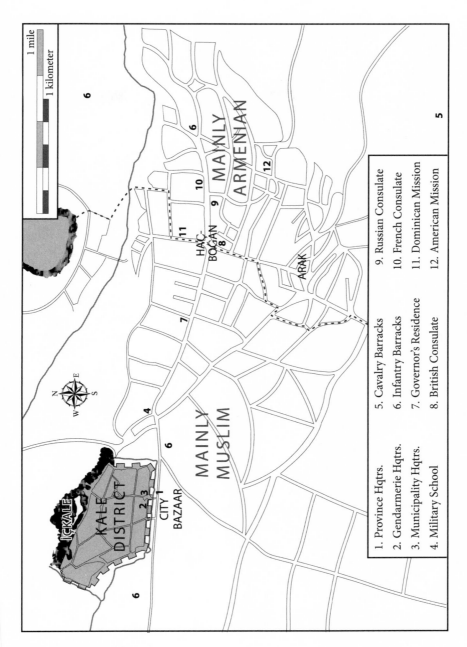

MAP 2.2. The City of Van.

and Tobacco Reji offices, and government schools. Most of these buildings were recent, built during the reign of Abdülhamit II.[2]

In the latter half of the nineteenth century the city of Van expanded considerably beyond the fortress walls. The new section of the city, called the Garden District, stretched slightly more than 3 kilometers to the east and southeast of the Old City and covered an area six times as large. Van could still not be called a big city. Outside the Old City it was more lightly settled. A great fire of 1876 and a famine in 1878–80 had dictated that houses be farther apart than was usual in the Middle East in order to keep flames from spreading and to be able to grow food.[3] Thus houses in both the Muslim and Christian Quarters of the New City were built apart from each other, centered in wide gardens surrounded by walls six feet high. Residents grew much of their own produce, in particular grapes and other fruit. The result was attractive and livable. Even the provincial governor and government officials lived in the Garden District. Consulates, foreign missionary establishments, and modern schools were found there, as well as the American missionary hospital, the military hospital, a telegraph office, the Agricultural Bank (Ziraat Bankası), and mosques and churches. Although some neighborhoods were mixed, in general Christians lived in the east of the Garden District, Muslims in the west.[4]

THE CITY'S PEOPLE

Turkish and Kurdish Muslims and Armenian and Nestorian Christians, with only a very small number of Jews and others, made up the population of Van. Evliya Çelebi, who visited Van in 1655, wrote that there were twelve neighborhoods in the city, of which three were Armenian. Orhan Kılıç estimated that 35,000–45,000 lived in the city in the seventeenth century, nearly 30 percent Armenian, the rest Muslims. The only Christians at that time were Armenian, and half the Muslim population was made up of soldiers, administrators, and Muslim pious foundation (*vakıf*) officials.[5]

No one knows exactly how many lived in Van in the late nineteenth and early twentieth century. The Ottomans kept detailed records of the city's population, but only the totals for the *kaza* (district), which included the city and its surroundings, have been found among the millions of documents yet to be searched in the Ottoman Archives. The population of the kaza was listed as 79,736 in 1912: 45,119 Muslims, 33,789 Armenians, and 828 others. The Ottomans, like similar states, underregistered women and children, so these figures probably underestimated the rural section of the kaza's population by one-fourth.[6] Soldiers, administrators native to other provinces, and temporary residents were not included. Vital Cuinet gave a low estimate for Van City in the 1890s: 16,000 Muslims, 13,500 Armenians, and 500 Jews, a total of 30,000.[7]

Although the numbers of the continuously resident population of Van probably did not change much from the 1880s to World War I, the city's actual population fluctuated greatly, depending on external conditions. Both Muslims and Armenians flooded the city in times of famine and civil unrest, looking for security and food.

THE PROVINCE OF VAN

Climate

Only in the context of Middle Eastern regional features such as the Caucasus Mountains or the Arabian Desert could Van's climate have been considered salubrious.

Van was not particularly hot in the summer, at least not by the standards of the Middle East. July was the hottest month, and its average maximum temperature was only 22° (72°F), although it might reach 38°C (100°F). Winter, however, was horrible. The coldest month in Van City, February, averaged −4°C (25°F), but −29°C (−20°F) was possible.[8] Temperatures fell below freezing on more than one-third of the days in a year. (It should be noted that these are figures for Van City, whose climate was moderated by its proximity to Lake Van. Many parts of the province, especially higher regions, were colder and generally nastier. Hakkâri, in the mountainous south, for example, averaged 4°C colder in winter than Van.) Van's average annual precipitation was 380 millimeters. In high summer it barely rained at all (3 millimeters in August).[9] Most of the precipitation was in the form of snow, which fell almost one-fourth of the year. During winter, houses in villages were connected by shoveled paths with "walls" that rose above a man's head on each side; visiting a friend was akin to walking down a tunnel. Mountain passes within the province and leading to other provinces were closed. Trade and communication were mainly shut down in winter.[10]

Muslims

The ethnic affiliations of Van's Muslims are surprisingly hard to identify. The Ottoman population registration system, the best source of most information on the people, recorded Ottoman subjects by religion, not by ethnic or language group. European commentators seem to have been eternally confused over who was a Turk or a Kurd. They often used "Turk"

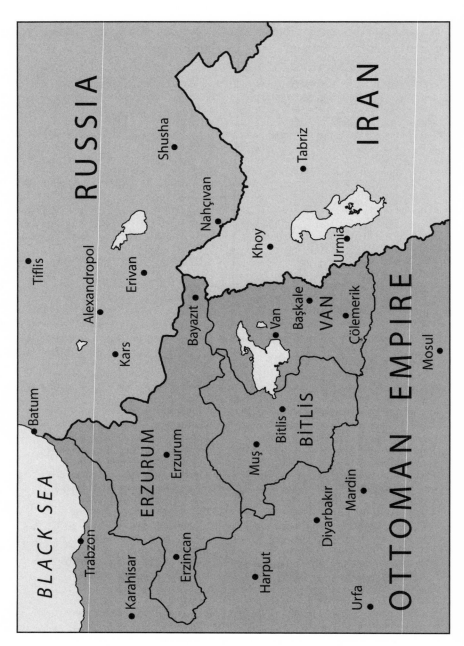

MAP 2.3. Ottoman Eastern Anatolia.

TABLE 2.1. Government Statistics for Van Province in 1897/1898.

DISTRICT NAME	VILLAGES	HOUSEHOLDS	MOSQUES, MESCIDS	MEDRESES	DERVISH LODGES	MONASTERIES, CHURCHES	SHOPS
Van District*	67 neighborhoods[†]	5,417	32	10	15	15	1,636
Erçek Subdistrict[‡]	53 villages	1,666	5	2	—	30	6
Havasor Subdistrict	48 villages	1,830	9	2	—	30	5
Timar Subdistrict	70 villages	2,580	5	3	1	35	3
Erciş District	123 villages	3,612	—	—	—	—	123
Gevaş District	66 villages	2,890	—	3	—	—	11
Müküs District	65 villages	1,797	—	5	—	—	12
Çatak District	83 villages	1,623	—	—	—	—	83
Bargiri District	104 villages	1,285	2	—	—	—	6
Adilcevaz District	62 villages	1,934	8	—	—	—	75
Karçekan District	70 villages	1,860	—	—	—	—	8
Total	811	26,494	61	25	16	110	1,968

Source: Van Vilâyeti, Van Vilâyeti Salnamesi, 1315 (Van: Matbaa-i Vilâyet,1315) p. 207.

* District = kaza.

[†] Subdistrict = mahalle.

[‡] Neighborhood = nahiye.

TABLE 2.2. Population of Van Province, 1912.

RELIGION	POPULATION	PROPORTION
Muslim	313,322	.6146
Greek	1	*
Armenian	130,500	.2560
Syrian, Chaldean, Nestorian	62,400	.1224
Jewish	1,798	.0035
Other	1776	.0036
Total	509,797	

Source: Justin McCarthy, *Muslims and Minorities* (New York: New York University Press, 1983), pp. 110–11. These population figures are based on Ottoman records, corrected for undercounts, especially undercounts of women and children. A number of estimates of the Van population have been made at different times by travelers and others. The so-called Armenian Patriarch Statistics, supposedly taken from files of the Armenian patriarch of Constantinople, were forgeries, but a real compilation of statistics was made by order of the Armenian patriarch of Echmiadzin. For 1913–14, these listed 110,897 Armenians in Van (Raymond H. Kévorkian and Paul B. Paboudjian, *Les Arméniens dans l'Empire Ottoman à la veille du génocide* [Paris: Editions d'Art et d'Histoire, 1992], appendix, p. 60). We believe the higher figures for Armenian population in the table are more accurate, because they are based on actual counts of the population, not estimates.
* Less than .0001.

to describe the settled and "Kurd" to describe the tribal, whatever the language actually spoken by the subject. As in most of the Middle East until very modern times, the identity of individuals was primarily religious, followed by local/tribal and family affiliations. Asked "What are you?" a Kurd, after reflecting on the absurdity of the question, would probably reply "a Muslim,"[11] then give the name of his or her tribe or village.

Linguistically, the Muslims of Van were overwhelmingly Kurdish. A sizable number of Kurds in Van and smaller groups in other cities had become socially a part of Ottoman civil society, speaking Turkish as well as a Kurdish dialect and adopting the general Ottoman culture, which included Turks, Kurds, Bosnians, Albanians, Circassians, and dozens of other ethnic groups. Six fairly large families in Van traced their lineage to the first Turkish tribes to arrive in Van centuries before and considered themselves to be Turks. In the countryside, the Muslims were Kurdish-speaking farmers and tribespeople. Those who were usually called "Turks" by Europeans in Van were the aforementioned Turks of ancient lineage and Ottoman officials. Sometimes the Europeans included the "Otto-manized" Kurds as "Turks." The largest number of Ottoman officials were soldiers, who were indeed primarily Turkish-speakers from Anatolia and Ottoman Europe. Their officers and other government officials might be from many backgrounds. The officials all spoke Turkish natively, but their ancestors might have spoken any number of European or Middle Eastern languages.

The tribal affiliations of Van's Kurds were too numerous to be listed here. The largest tribal confederation was the Haydaran (also called the Haydaranlı). The confederation was made up of tribes who inhabited the great high plain that stretched across southern Erzurum and northern Van Provinces into Iran—from Bayazıt in the north and Patnos in the west into Iran. The Haydaran were more or less constant enemies of the Sipikan (Sipikanlı) Kurds to their west and the Sheveli Kurds to their south. The Sheveli, part of the second largest tribal confederation in Van, the Shikaks, lived between Bargiri and Van City. The most numerous and powerful Shikak tribe was the Shekifti, whose territory crossed the Iranian border in southeastern Van Province. Judging from government and consular reports, the Shikaks and Haydaran were the most troublesome, if only because of their sheer numbers. Both of these tribes were internally divided, however, and tribes in the confederations fought each other only slightly less often than they fought others.

Very few of Van's Kurdish tribes were truly nomadic—the Herki, the Atmanikan, and some smaller tribes. Many, such as the Goyan and the Miran, were mainly seminomadic, spending winter in their villages and living in tents in summer pastures. Many tribes were mixed: some of the Jalali were nomadic, some sedentary. Some of the Shikak and Hartushi groups were sedentary, some seminomadic. Even nomadic tribes like the Herki had some sedentary subtribes.[12]

The life of the tribes was changing. Tribes like the Hasanan (Hasananlı), many of whom had been seminomadic, were becoming sedentary in the 1890s. This seems to have been generally true of the northern tribes. Moreover, the tribal structure was under great stress as the Ottoman government gradually increased its power over the tribes. The great tribes were losing their cohesion, while many smaller tribes were being subsumed into larger confederations. This resulted in a greater number of medium-sized centers of power. Given the tribes' penchant for warfare, this was not good for civil order.[13]

Kurdish tribes were led by their chiefs. Succession was not always hereditary and was not guaranteed to the oldest son. Earlier in the nineteenth century the power of the great chiefs had diminished significantly. Until Sultan Mahmud II began to extend state power into southeastern Anatolia, each Kurdish leader, called *mir* (emir), had ruled over a large stretch of the region, dividing power in the southeast among themselves. Once a renascent government asserted its powers and ended the "emirates," the local power of smaller tribal chiefs increased, as did the power of

MAP 2.4. Kurdish Tribes.

the *şeyh*s. These were leaders of dervish (Sufi mystic) fraternities. Because their position and prestige were defined by religion, not by tribal structure, they were able to attract a following from many tribes, often creating "synthetic tribes" with themselves as chief and religious leader. Two of the most important families of leaders, the şeyhs of Şemdinan and Barzan, came to power in this way.[14]

Map 2.4, drawn from contemporary British sources, indicates only the largest and most important tribes.[15] The areas indicated for each large tribe or confederation were not exclusive. Villages belonging to one tribe often

MAP 2.5. The Armenian Church in Van.

were next to villages belonging to another, and nomadic tribes traveled across the lands ascribed on the map to another tribe as they went to summer and winter pastures. The Herki, for example, wandered the southern part of the province in small groups with their flocks. The powerful chiefs were always expanding their territory, although the gains were usually lost once they died. There were hundreds of tribes and semiautonomous clans in tribes that cannot be listed on one small map.[16]

Armenians

Like the Muslims, the Armenians in the countryside were primarily subsistence farmers. The urban Armenian population, however, contained many well-to-do families—money changers/bankers and merchants, doctors and dentists, lawyers, government officials, translators in consulates,

TABLE 2.3. The Armenian Church in Van: Approximate Armenian Figures.

	DIOCESE	ECCLESIASTICAL HEAD	EXTENT	ARMENIAN CHURCH MEMBERS	PARISHES	CHURCHES	CATHOLICS	PROTESTANTS
Patriarchate of Constantinople	Van	Archbishop	Kazas of Van, Mahmudiye (Saray), Erciş, Adilcevaz	100,000	108	130	500	200
	Lim and Ktutz	Abbot	Nahiye of Timar	11,000	25	32	—	—
	Albak (Başkale)	Abbot	Sancak of Hakkâri	10,000	20	23	—	—
Catholicosate of Akhtamar	Akhtamar	Catholicos	Kazas of Gevaş, Çatak, Karçekan	70,000	130	203	—	—
	Hizan	Bishop	Kaza of Hizan	25,000	64	69	—	—

Source: Malachia Ormanian, The Church of Armenia, edited by Terenig Poladian, 2nd ed. (London: Mowbray, 1955), pp. 206–8.

artisans and craftsmen, workers, priests, teachers, and journalists.[17] All contemporary observers stated that the Armenians had control of the trade of the province. While most of the Armenians of Van City were by no means rich, as a group they were more prosperous than the city's Muslims.

The 1876 Erzurum Province Yearbook stated that the leaders of the Van Gregorian community were the bishop of Lim Island (in the northeast of Lake Van) and the catholicos of Akhtamar Island, both named Agop. Ex-patriarch Malachia Ormanian wrote that four ecclesiastical jurisdictions governed the Gregorian Church in the province: the small diocese of Lim and Ktuts Islands, which included some area on the mainland shore (the Nahiye of Timar); the extensive Catholicosate of Aghtamar (Akhtamar), which governed the region south/southwest of Van City and southeastern Bitlis Province; the Diocese of Aghbak (Albak, Başkale) in the east-southeast; and the Archdiocese of Van, which covered all the rest of the province.[18] There were very few Uniate Catholic and Protestant Armenians in the province. While Catholic and Protestant (mainly American) missionaries had made many converts among the Armenians of Western Anatolia, the Van Armenians mainly remained loyal to the Gregorian Church. The city had only a small group of Armenian Protestants, ministered to by native pastors and missionaries.

To a large extent the appointment of Armenians to government positions was a part of the diversification in government initiated by Sultan Abdülhamit II and continued by later governments. Members of minority groups rose to all but the highest positions in Istanbul (e.g., foreign minister, but not grand vezir). Government appointments in Van followed the pattern set in Istanbul, although circumstances and problems were unique. In Van, as well as in similar provinces such as Erzurum and Bitlis, the government was most anxious to enroll Christians in official positions in order to show the minorities that they were a part of the Ottoman system and to assure them fair treatment by a government that included many members of their own communities. This, it was hoped, would blunt the appeal of nationalist revolutionaries. Operating by the same logic, the revolutionaries did all they could to discourage Armenian membership in the government.

Appendix 2 lists Armenians in Ottoman service as they appeared in various Van provincial yearbooks. Perhaps reflecting their economic position in the province, most of the Armenians in the administration were in financial positions—treasurers of districts and of administrative councils—as well as high officials in the important area of land registration.

Armenians, undoubtedly members of the merchant class, sat on the administrative councils and boards of Van as well serving as judges in the provincial courts and on judicial councils. Late in the nineteenth century Armenians started to serve as deputy governors and assistants to governors or deputy governors. These were high positions of considerable power and authority. Armenians also began to appear in government lists as police officers and officials. As late as 1908 Nazareth Tcharukhdjian was police superintendent in Van. As will be seen, many of these positions, particularly police offices and administrative posts, carried considerable danger to the incumbents. They were liable to be assassinated by Armenian revolutionaries, who viewed those who took part in the government as traitors.

Nestorians

The Nestorians (also known as Assyrians) inhabited the mountainous region south of Van in the Ottoman Empire and the lowlands west of Lake Urmia in Iran. The heartland of the Ottoman Nestorians centered on the towns of Tiari, 80 miles directly south of Van City, and Koçanis, the traditional seat of the Nestorian patriarch, near Çölemerik. Those who lived in the mountains, known as Aşiret (tribal) Nestorians, had been virtually independent until the Ottomans began to extend state authority to their mountains in the middle nineteenth century. Others lived as clients of Kurdish tribes. The Nestorians were not nomadic but divided themselves into tribes, each with its own chief (*malik:* king). In fact, the highest authority among the Nestorians was held by the Nestorian patriarch, the Mar Shimun, who was both an ecclesiastical and a secular leader. The office was hereditary in the Mar Shimun family: the patriarch himself was celibate; the office was inherited by a nephew of a deceased patriarch. It was not unknown for nephews to fight over the succession.[19]

Unlike the Armenians, the Nestorians were seldom involved in the commerce and industry of Van Province. The Aşiret Nestorians remained in their mountains. Those in Iran and some of the non-Aşiret Nestorians in the Ottoman Empire might travel as far as Russia as day laborers and beggars.[20] Some were accomplished stonemasons, constructing fine homes for Kurdish chiefs in the southeast.

The lives of the Nestorians were intimately bound up with the Kurds who surrounded them. They were a constant factor in Kurdish alliances and feuds, sometimes fighting against Kurdish tribes, sometimes fighting alongside them as allies. Before World War I their greatest disaster was a slaughter by the forces of Şeyh Ubeydullah Bedirhan in 1847. After that the power of the Nestorians in their conflicts with Kurdish tribes was considerably diminished. They did have a European champion in the British, however. The archbishop of Canterbury sponsored a mission to the Nestorians that managed to make a small number of converts to Protestantism, as did an American mission among the Nestorians in Iran.[21]

Jews

Ottoman official statistics listed 1,400 Jews in the province in 1912. Most of these Jews were rural, however, living in remote and poorly registered areas, so they were greatly undercounted. Cuinet estimated 5,000,[22] which was probably closer to the truth.

Americans

Missionaries of the American Board for Foreign Missions first visited Van in 1870. The Van mission station was opened in 1872. The mission, headed by Dr. George C. Raynolds throughout its time in Van, first occupied a rented house in the Old City then opened an extensive compound in the Garden District. The first mission school for boys opened in 1875, and a new elementary and secondary boys' school in the Garden District in 1881. Mrs. Raynolds began a girls' school, offering primary and some high school courses, in the Old City in 1879. By 1910 there were boarding primary and high schools for both boys and girls, with 953 students (433 boys and 520 girls), all Armenians. In 1896 the missionaries began relief work and provided limited medical assistance in Van City. Medical work expanded to surgery and a general hospital in 1900 with the arrival of Dr. Clarence Ussher.[23]

As they did elsewhere in the Ottoman Empire, the Americans provided an excellent modern education for Van's Christians. The missionaries came to Van with the intention of drawing Armenians away from the Gregorian Church and into Protestant beliefs. They soon found this impossible. They satisfied themselves with the thought that their schools and other activities were bringing a moral change in the Armenians and causing the Armenian Church to adopt more Protestant beliefs.[24] (The accuracy of the former view is unknown, but the latter was demonstrably wishful thinking.) The labors of the missionaries were more noteworthy for their temporal than for their spiritual benefits.

Europeans

Unlike the cities of Western Anatolia and Ottoman Europe, Van was not the home to many Europeans. With the exception of Russian subjects, who were mainly Armenians from the Southern Caucasus, the European

subjects resident in Van were consular officials or missionaries. As a stra-
tegically important city, however, Van was the site of a number of foreign
consulates: Iran, Russia, Great Britain, France, and Italy.[25] German Protestants and French Catholics (Dominicans) each operated a mission, whose
efforts were directed at local Christians. The British operated a mission
among the Nestorians in the southern part of the province. Because the
missions were not very successful at gaining converts, they can properly be
considered service organizations, providing education for Christians and
relief and medical care for Christians and many Muslims. The Dominicans operated a school for Armenians. German Evangelical missionaries
of the Deutsches Hilfsbund came to Van to provide relief services to poor
Christians in 1895. By 1910 they were feeding and clothing 500 of the poor
daily. Their efforts were coordinated with those of the American missionaries. Just before World War I the Germans opened a boys' school and a
girls' school with 11 teachers and 238 students.[26]

Agriculture and Animal Husbandry

The Ottoman government attempted to draw up statistics on agricultural
production in Van Province, but these were at best informed estimates.
There were too few officials to count all the herds and visit every field.
Data on numbers of animals were particularly deficient, because taxes
were paid on each one, giving a great incentive to hide animals and lie to
the tax collector. Indeed, enumerating farms and animals was a dangerous
business. Those who went out to count sheep belonging to Kurdish tribes
had to be accompanied by soldiers in order to survive. Nevertheless, official estimates do afford a fairly accurate picture of what was produced in
Van, if not the true quantity of production.

Wheat was the most important grain crop in Van Province. Fifteen
times as much wheat was produced as the next grain crops, barley and rye.
Only very small amounts of other cereal crops were grown. Yet Van did not
actually produce much wheat; per capita wheat production was one-third
that of provinces such as Erzurum and Ankara.[27] Van did not have enough
flat land for large-scale cereal farming. Each year wheat, barley, and flour
had to be imported from other provinces. Rainfall was scarce, and farmers
were forced to use irrigation from rivers and streams to produce a variety
of fruits: melons, watermelons, grapes, apples, apricots, pears, cherries,
sour cherries (*vişne*), and quince.[28] There was a limit to what could be
produced with low-technology irrigation. The per capita production of
grapes, for example, was only one-twentieth that of the province of Aydın
in Western Anatolia, which had better weather. In regard to the produc-

tion of wine from those grapes, however, Van was a major producer in per capita terms.[29] The farms of the province grew only small amounts of vegetables, and the diet of the populace was surely deficient. The vegetables produced were of the type that will keep for long periods: onions, lentils, green beans, broad beans (*bakla*), and okra. Walnuts were a primary crop, both for local use and for export. Small amounts of hazelnuts and almonds were also produced. Other export crops included flax seed (for oil) and tobacco.[30]

The mountainous scrub land of Van Province dictated the type of animals found there: few (if any) camels, many goats. Pack animals were primarily donkeys and mules. Oxen, donkeys, mules, and water buffaloes (and perhaps some horses) did the plowing. Sheep (the most numerous animal) and goats (the second most numerous) were reared for wool for export, as well as for meat, milk, and cheese. Unlike Erzurum Province to the north, which was known for its beef, Van Province contained approximately the same number of cows per person as in the rest of Anatolia.[31] Horses were no more common than elsewhere in Anatolia, and most of these were in the hands of Kurdish tribes. The tribes depended on the horses for transport and bred them for sale. The rest of Van walked or rode on donkeys. Wool, woolen goods, skins, and live animals were the province's most valuable exports.

The agricultural state of Van was always poor. In good years there was enough to eat, but never sufficient food to put aside for the bad years. The years of famine came often. The worst famine was in 1878–80. Lesser famines came every few years, however. The government took what actions it could to aid the starving (forcing hoarders to disgorge grain, punishing price gougers, etc.), but the state did not have enough power to police such crimes outside the urban areas and their surroundings.[32] Except for the famine in 1878–80, no one starved in the cities. Villagers often went hungry.[33] Both Christians and Muslims suffered during times of famine, but considerably more aid from outside sources was given to Armenians. American and British relief funds and supplies usually were restricted to Armenians, and sometimes Nestorians, while the limited government funds went to all.[34] This cannot have endeared either the local Christians or the foreigners to the Muslims. In one case, American missionaries gave relief to Armenian families then found that some of the families had converted to the Armenian Catholic Church. They went to the British consul, who was in charge of relief distribution, and demanded that the money given to the Catholics be returned, because the relief was only to go to Gregorian and Protestant Armenians. The consul refused.[35]

Historically, Shia incursions from Iran from time to time disrupted agriculture, just as Ottoman incursions into Iran damaged agriculture there. These were not a problem in the later nineteenth century, but the unsettled state of the province, particularly battles among and raiding by Kurdish tribes, remained to plague farmers.

Education

The superior economic position of the Armenian community was evident in education.[36] Once the Armenian community began to educate its students in modern schools, Armenian schools quickly outpaced the educational opportunities available to Muslims (tables 2.4 and 2.5). Until the beginning of the twentieth century schools for Muslims were traditional and religiously based. Students in elementary schools memorized sections of the Quran and learned prayers, morals, and very basic writing. Those fortunate enough to attend the Muslim secondary schools learned to read and write properly but did not take advanced mathematics or sciences. Conditions were far superior in the Armenian schools.[37]

Comparing Armenian and Muslim student numbers leaves no doubt as to which community was foremost in education. Approximately 1 of every 250 Armenians in the province was in secondary school in 1901. The comparative figure for Muslims was 1 of every 1,500. The Armenian youths were six times as likely to attend high school. It should be noted, however, that neither group was doing particularly well. By comparison, the figure for the Turkish Republic in 2000 was 1 in 13.[38] It must also be remembered that these figures for Armenian education do not include the American missionary schools. Armenian students alone had the benefit of the modern education offered by American missionaries. The missionaries founded an elementary school and a boys' secondary school in 1872–73. The following year they began a girls' secondary school. By 1898 the boys' secondary school had eighty pupils, the girls' secondary school ninety, and the elementary school forty-one.[39]

Other religious communities sponsored their own schools. In 1900, Cuinet estimated, there were fifty students in the two Chaldean schools at Gevar. Sixty students studied in two Jewish schools, one at Başkale, the other at Diza.[40]

Hampered by limited resources, the government had nevertheless begun to improve education in the province. At the turn of the century it was reported that twenty-seven new schools had been built in the province since 1876, of which eleven were new primary schools. Construction had accelerated in later years, and nineteen schools were opened between 1890

TABLE 2.4. Schools in Van in 1871/1872.

KAZAS (DISTRICTS) AND NAHIYES (TOWNSHIPS)*	CHRISTIAN PRIMARY SCHOOLS	MUSLIM PRIMARY SCHOOLS	MUSLIM SECONDARY SCHOOLS (MEDRESES)
Van Kaza	6	30	6
Gevar Kaza	—	—	—
Çölemerik Kaza	—	3	2
Albak (Başkale) Kaza	2	1	1
Mahmudi Kaza	—	—	2
Erciş Kaza	3	3	7
Adilcevaz Kaza	5	2	—
Müküs Kaza	2	15	2
Gevaş Kaza	2	7	—
Çatak Kaza	1	1	4
Abağa Nahiye	—	—	—
Şemdinan Nahiye	—	4	8
Humaru Nahiye	—	—	1
Oramar Nahiye	—	—	—
Beytüşşebab Nahiye	—	—	—
Çal Nahiye	—	1	2
Hoşap Nahiye	—	—	1
Bargiri Nahiye	—	—	1
Karçekan Nahiye	—	—	—
Vastan Nahiye	—	—	1
Norduz Nahiye	—	—	—
Total	21	67	38

Source: Salname-i Vilâyet-i Erzurum, 1288 Hicri Senesi (Erzurum: Erzurum Vilâyeti Matbaası, 1289) , p. 148.
These statistics are for a very early period, when Ottoman data were deficient. They should be used only to indicate approximate numbers and the relative numbers of schools and other buildings. Note that Jewish schools are not included and that only registered, formal schools are listed.
* Vilâyets were made up of sancaks, which were divided into kazas, which were divided into nahiyes.

and 1900. Secondary schools were to be found in the cities of Van, Gevaş, Edremit, Erciş, Adilcevaz, Elbak, Gevar, and Çölemerik.[41] Between 1871 and 1898 the number of state (Muslim) elementary schools doubled, to 125.[42] This was an impressive achievement, but it still meant only 1 elementary school for every 2,200 Muslims in the population. (Traditional Islamic

TABLE 2.5. Armenian and Muslim Secondary Schools in Van Province.

YEARS	MUSLIM SECONDARY SCHOOLS	MUSLIM STUDENTS	ARMENIAN SECONDARY SCHOOLS	ARMENIAN STUDENTS	AMERICAN SECONDARY SCHOOLS	ARMENIAN STUDENTS
1888[a]	5	211	—	—	—	—
1897–1898[b]	8	207	—	—	—	—
1898–1899[c]	8	157	7	780	—	—
1899–1900[d]	8	205	—	—	1	390
1900–1901[e]	8	213	7	970	1	390
1901–1902[f]	8	201	9	1070	1	390
1903–1904[g]	8	201	9	1070	1	390

Sources: Ottoman imperial, provincial, and education yearbooks.

a. *Salname-i Devlet-i Aliyye-i Osmaniyye* (Istanbul: Matbaa-i Âmire, 1306), p. 210. Note that the years in the table and in other statistics given here for education are the years in which the data were published. They may be considered to represent the previous year, but the data were undoubtedly collected sporadically and were only approximate. Lack of information in the table (e.g., 1899–1900) obviously does not mean that the schools did not exist, only that the information was omitted from the official source.

b. Van Vilâyeti, *Van Vilâyeti Salnamesi, 1315* (Van: Matbaa-i Vilâyet, 1315), pp. 149–50.

c. *Salname-i Nezaret-i Maarif-i Umumiye, 1316 sene-i hicriyesine mahsustur* (Istanbul: Matbaa-i Âmire, 1316), pp. 1210–11.

d. *Salname-i Nezaret-i Maarif-i Umumiye, 1317 sene-i hicriyesine mahsustur* (Istanbul: Matbaa-i Âmire, 1317), pp. 1428–29.

e. *Salname-i Nezaret-i Maarif-i Umumiye, 1318 sene-i hicriyesine mahsustur* (Istanbul: Matbaa-i Âmire, 1318), pp. 1594–95.

f. *Salname-i Nezaret-i Maarif-i Umumiye, 1319 sene-i hicriyesine mahsustur* (Istanbul: Matbaa-i Âmire, 1319), p. 1319.

g. *Salname-i Nezaret-i Maarif-i Umumiye, 1321 sene-i hicriyesine mahsustur* (Istanbul: Matbaa-i Âmire, 1321), pp. 677–78.

education continued alongside the new schools: 105 students were studying at the nine mosque schools [*medreses*] in the province in 1900.)[43]

In practice the government schools, which educated a number of Christians in other provinces, only enrolled Muslims in the Van Province. Armenians attended their own schools. Contemporaries reported that both the Muslims and the Armenians realized the importance of education and that they were engaged in a sort of race to educate, especially after the 1908 Revolution.[44] Undoubtedly they both greatly increased their efforts, although the Armenians had a distinct economic advantage. American missionaries reported on the "race" from their own, not disinterested, perspective: "Several Armenian organizations are taking hold of the work, but unfortunately most of them are exerting an anti-religious influence which is perverting the morals of the people. The Government too is entering the field and would probably be glad to get this whole education work into its own hands and make the schools helpful for promoting a Moslem propaganda."[45]

The provincial government founded a printing press in Van City in 1889–90. At first it was a simple press that printed lithographed handwriting, not movable type. The press produced the official gazette, *Van*, in Turkish. The situation had not greatly improved ten years later.[46] Van's Armenians, however, had a much more vibrant printing and literary life. *Artsvi Vaspurakan* (The Eagle of Van) was published in 1855–56 and 1858–64. Other short-lived publications followed; by 1914 two Armenian weekly newspapers were published in the city: one by the Dashnak Party, *Ashkhatank* (Labor), and one by the liberal Armenakan Party, *Van-Tosp*. After the 1908 Revolution the Dashnaks also published a number of political pamphlets.[47]

Van had long been a center of Armenian culture.[48] Anahide Ter Minassian estimated that 70 percent of the Armenians in Van City and 30 percent in the countryside could read and write.[49] This is almost surely an exaggeration, especially for the rural areas, but indicative of a high rate of literacy for the region. No comparative estimates exist for Van's Muslims, but the figure was certainly much lower.

Van cannot be said to have been well supplied with public libraries. In addition to the library of the Great Mosque (presumably religious in character), Van City had one library: the İskender Paşa Library, with forty-three books. The Şeyh Library in Elbak held three hundred books.[50] Presumably the various schools had at least small libraries for their students.

It would be a mistake to overemphasize the effects of the educational differences between the Muslims and Armenians of Van. The contrast between Muslim and Christian educational attainments in the western and northern regions of the empire was great. That difference was not as great in Van, although it was also developing there. In urban areas of the province Armenians were much more educated and more literate than Muslims. In rural areas there was much less difference. Armenian schools in rural areas only blossomed very late and cannot have had great effect by 1914. The majority of Van Province's Armenians, and an even higher proportion of its Muslims, were functionally illiterate.

The Commercial Importance of Van

According to the Erzurum Province yearbook (*salname*) of 1871–72, the people of Van and surrounding towns used a type of pitch taken from the flat area above the Van Citadel in construction. In addition, local people used a kind of soda (called *perek*), accumulated from dried lake water, in place of soap. Van Province possessed a small number of useful minerals: some silver and lead at Çatak, iron oxide ore at Gevaş, salt near Van, coal at Akçay on the Karasu River and at Başkale, and borax at Başkale as well. A number of localities produced high-quality chalk. The government had given a concession to produce and process naphtha from the Gürzüt village of Bargiri Kaza. There were other, very small scale mines in Van as well; but in general Van was simply too remote and mining too difficult to support much exploitation of its minerals. There were sulfur springs in the Zilan Valley and iron carbonate springs at Pisan, but Van was hardly the place to develop healthful baths in a tourist industry. Plans to exploit minerals such as the yellow arsenic found in Çölemerik Kaza produced limited results. The government estimated that sixty-seven minerals were found within the Van Province borders; most were undeveloped.[51]

The Van landscape, at first glance, does not seem amenable to forestry, but there were forest resources in the province. The people of the Gevaş Kaza and Karçekan Nahiye profited from tree farms that produced oak and juniper. Likewise, inhabitants of the Çatak, Müküs, and Gevar Kazas sold lumber from forests of oak and similar woods.[52]

Ferries and commercial boats plied Lake Van. Some of the province's rivers were wide enough for limited commercial and personal travel: two streams that flowed west in Çatak; the Bendimahi Stream that flowed from the Abak Plain (west-northwest of Bargiri) to Lake Van; and the Kotur River that flowed east from Elbak Nahiye to Khoy in Iran. The Great Zap River flowed into the Tigris and Euphrates river system. In general, however, the province had very little river transportation. A hot-water sulfur spring in the Zilan Valley of Erciş Kaza was reportedly a remedy for lumbago and rheumatism.[53]

Industry

Because of Van's position on by far the largest lake in Anatolia and near the Iranian border, its traditional industry revolved around ships and weapons. In the sixteenth and seventeenth centuries Van was the garrison town for the Ottoman army in the region. Many weapons, such as swords and muskets, were made in the city. Much of the construction work done in the town was military or associated with the military, including numerous establishments for traditional military off-duty pursuits.[54]

By the middle of the nineteenth century the industrial production of Van had altered. Iran was no longer a military threat, so the garrison of soldiers was greatly diminished. Military construction was minimal until

World War I approached. In any case, weapons of modern warfare could no longer be produced in small craft shops. Industry in Van settled into the production of goods for local consumption, essentially basic goods used by townspeople, farmers, and tribespeople in ordinary life: shoes, normal clothing, pots and pans, jewelry, saddles, wagons, and the like. Except for some government buildings, which were built in more modern patterns in Abdülhamit II's time, construction was traditional work with mud brick and timber, much as it had been for millennia.

Van did produce some quality goods, primarily hand-crafted cloth and clothing. Distinctive Van overcoats, shawls, and white and red cloth were exported from the province and enjoyed a market as far away as Istanbul.[55] Erzurum was also a good market for Van's products. The export market provided jobs for weavers and merchants as well as for those who made the tools and built the buildings used in the trade. Leather goods and rugs and *kilim*s were also made and exported. Van kilims, made by Kurdish tribespeople, were highly valued throughout the empire.[56]

Table 2.6 shows Vital Cuinet's estimates of industrial production in Van. His figures are surely inaccurate, but they do give a reasonable general view of production. Cuinet's list is by no means complete, including only major production. The Van yearbook for 1897–98 listed very small-scale manufacturing, including rugs and kilims, weapons, plates, pots and utensils, wagon, carriage and phaeton construction, carpentry, saddles and leatherwork, jewelry, shoes, and other work.[57]

Transportation, Communication, and Commerce

Van's historical importance was largely a product of its position on the traditional natural highways that connected Erivan, Bitlis, Tabriz, and Mosul. Without this geographic situation or the presence of a great lake, the economic role of Van (with its mountainous terrain and awful winter climate) would have been negligible. Because of its location, however, Van had been the center of the caravan trade for centuries. Although two other caravan roads passed between the Ottoman Empire and Iran (from Diyarbakır in the south and Erzurum in the north), the most important route was the Trabzon–Erzurum–Van–Iran road, which reached Istanbul and Europe by way of the Black Sea. The north–south road between the Caucasus and the Persian Gulf (Batum–Erivan–Van–Çölemerik [Hakkâri]–Mosul–Baghdad) crossed the Trabzon–Iran road in Van. Van also had direct connections to the west and on to the Mediterranean, through Bitlis and Siirt and (in winter when snows closed the passes between Van and Bitlis) southwest to Diyarbakır.[58]

TABLE 2.6. Industrial (Craft) Production in Van Province (excluding Hakkâri), ca. 1890.

ITEM	WORKSHOPS	WORKERS	PRODUCTION	PRODUCTION EXPORTED	TOTAL VALUE (LIRA)
Cloth (inexpensive wool and cotton)	900	2,200	90,000	20,500	17,000
Clothing (made from wool and cotton)	100	300	6,000	200	11,000
Mohair Shawls	90	270	6,000	2,000	2,400
Mohair Clothing	45	135	3,000	200	3,600
Taffeta	10	20	600	—	1,200
Taffeta Women's Clothing	5	10	300	—	1,500
Kurdish Kilims	—	—	15,000	5,000	12,000
Stockings (pairs)	—	—	10,000	1,000	200
Saddles (leather)	50	100	2,000	200	800
Gold, Jewelry	100	200	5,000	1,500	6,500
Pottery	60	60	300,000	24,000	1,500
Other	—	—	—	—	3,400

Source: Vital Cuinet, *La Turquie d'Asie,* vol. 2 (Paris: E. Leroux, 1891), p. 677.

Despite its position, Van never rose to become a great transportation hub. A combination of long, cold winters, the need to cross mountain passes, and narrow roads made the province ill-fitted for nineteenth-century commerce. By the second half of the nineteenth century other routes had superseded the traditional roads through Van. According to Cuinet, at the end of the nineteenth century there were steamboats on Lake Van, but this only provided a small improvement for a bad transportation situation. Road travel between Van and Bitlis took four days, whereas the same journey would have taken one and a half days on a good road. The trip from Van to Muş, which would have taken two days on a proper road, took five days. Erzurum was seven days away, not the five days it might have been. Moreover, travelers feared attacks by bandits and tribes. Cuinet estimated that transportation deficiencies quadrupled the cost of commercial transport: transporting 120 pounds of goods the 363 kilometers between Van and Erzurum cost 200 *kuruş,* whereas on a better, safer road it would have cost 50.[59] In the years between Cuinet's publication (1891) and World War I the government made significant strides in

TABLE 2.7. Exports of Van Province (excluding Hakkâri), ca. 1890.

ITEM	AMOUNT	VALUE (LIRA)
Sheep	100,000 head	60,000
Goats	2,000 head	400
Oxen, Cows	5,000 head	10,000
Horses	1,000 head	5,000
Donkeys	500 head	750
Wool	60,000 okka	3,000
Taffeta	30,000 okka	3,000
Animal Skins	20,000 okka	1,200
Barley and Wheat	2,960 hectoliters	10,000
Borax	10,000 kg	100
Taffeta Shawls	2,000 pieces	800
Butter	5,000 okka	400
Dried Grapes	50,000 okka	750
Flax	5,000 okka	100
Flax Oil	1,500 okka	150
Walnuts	20,000 okka	600
Kilims	5,000 pieces	4,000
Buds	—	1,000
Serge	500 pieces	200
Stockings	1,000 pairs	20
Gemstones	—	1,500
Van Cloth	10,000 pieces	1,500
Clothing	400 pieces	660
Tobacco	400,000 okka	14,000
Fish	—	400
Saddles	200 pieces	80
Fur, Pelts	—	1,140
Total		120,750

Source: Vital Cuinet, La Turquie d'Asie, vol. 2 (Paris: E. Leroux, 1891), p. 679.

TABLE 2.8. Imports of Van Province (excluding Hakkâri), ca. 1890.

ORIGIN	GOODS	VALUE (LIRA)
Trabzon	Cotton goods, calico, woolen cloth, iron, "French cottons" (from Austria), black flannel, black satin, hand-dyed cloth, woolen goods, various silks, sugar, coffee, tea, iron bars, iron plates, pots and pans, steel, tin, copper, lead, candles, alcohol, spices, cigarette paper, matches, porcelain glass materials, window glass, and others	77,680
Russia	Petrol, silk, samovars, woolen goods, faience/tile/porcelain	2,000
Aleppo and Antep	Striped cloth, calico, muslin, blue silk thread, Indian cotton, silk and cotton cloth, Hama belts, handkerchiefs, hand-dyed cloth, copper, cochineal	23,890
Diyarbakır	Sheets, silk caps, various cotton goods, sesame, olive oil, okra, melon seeds, used copper, raisins, madder, walnuts, watermelons, figs, coarse woolen cloth, shawls, woolen belts/sashes, tanned sheep hides	2,458
Erzurum	Tokat dyed cloth, Riga cloth, horseshoe nails, stirrups, halters, reins, girths, foils and rapiers, iron chains/fetters, copper pots and pans	5,495
Bitlis	Walnuts, dried fruits, anise, firewood, charcoal, tar, red cotton goods, marble	3,255
Iran	Raw cotton, rice, dried fruit, tobacco (*tömbek*), shawls, rugs/kilims, silken goods, Indian cottons, alum, henna, adhesive/gum/resin, sheep	31,434
Siirt	Raisins, madder, walnuts, dates, figs, watermelons, coarse woolen cloth, shawls, belts, sheep skins/leather	2,380
Total		148,592

Source: Vital Cuinet, *La Turquie d'Asie,* vol. 2 (Paris: E. Leroux, 1891), pp. 680–84.

road-building in Eastern Anatolia. As in so many areas, however, a lack of funds kept most needed improvements from being made. A railroad connection would have been necessary, and Van was low on the list for the Ottomans' limited capability to build railroads.

Cuinet wrote that Van City had one telegraph station that transmitted international telegrams in Turkish or French and three stations that sent internal telegrams in Turkish. The entire Van Province contained eight telegraph stations: six internal and two international.[60]

According to Cuinet, the exports of Van Province (including Hakkâri, not shown in table 2.8) in 1890 were 165,750 lira;[61] its imports were 171,992 lira, a "balance of payments" deficit of 6,242 lira.[62] By far the most valuable exports were animals and animal products, followed by agricultural products, then cloth, clothing, and textiles. Van was a fine example of the raw material/handcraft–producing, finished goods–importing economic regimen.

Table 2.8 shows that about half of Van's imports came from Trabzon. These were often (probably mainly) goods from other countries, transshipped in Istanbul. It should be noted that these imports were not capital goods to be used in Van manufacturing. They were mainly consumer goods, the "extras" that make life livable (coffee, tea, sugar, cigarette paper, etc.).

The government listed 110 boats that plied Lake Van at the turn of the century. Officials wanted to increase the lake trade, and the government was planning a shipyard and new docks and facilities. The boats were small by seagoing standards,[63] but they were important in carrying passengers and bulk goods. The main boat piers were at Adilcevaz on the lake's west coast and at İskeleköy, the port of Van City, on the east. Most of the boat owners were Armenians.[64]

CONCLUSION

The proper word to describe the economic and educational life of Van is "poor." Van's poverty was largely a function of geography. The province had no seacoast, no long navigable rivers, and mountainous terrain that made road travel difficult. Winter snows, which would have closed even good roads, could last six months. There was also the significant question of what would be traded, even if conditions had been better. Van's natural trading partners were Iran and Russia. The Russian economy, though, funneled the goods of Transcaucasia north to the Russian heartland. And what was available in Iran for lucrative trade with Van? The goods in western Iran were essentially the same as the goods in Van. Political conditions (described in chapter 3) surely played a part in Van's poverty. Economic development rests on settled political conditions, and Van's situation was anything but settled.

NOTES

1. Van Vilâyeti, *Van Vilâyeti Salnamesi, 1315, Birinci Defa* (Van: Matbaa-i Vilâyet, 1315), p. 207.

2. For descriptions, see Anahide Ter Minassian, "Ermeni Kaynaklarına Göre Yüzyıl Başında Van," in *Modernleşme Sürecinde Osmanlı Kentleri,* ed. Paul Dumont and François Georgeon, trans. Ali Berktay (Istanbul: Tarih Vakfı Yurt Yayınları, 1992), pp. 117–18

(Turkish translation; original: Paul Dumont and François Georgeon, eds., *Villes ottomanes à la fin de l'Empire* [Paris: L'Harmattan, 1992]). Dickran Kouymjian, "Visual Accounts of Van through Travel Accounts," and Anahide Ter Minassian, "The City of Van at the Turn of the Twentieth Century," in *Armenian Van/Vaspurakan,* ed. Richard G. Hovannisian (Costa Mesa, Calif.: Mazda Publishers, 2000), pp. 153–93.

3. On the terrible famine of 1878–80, see Great Britain, National Archives, FO 195/1315, Clayton to Trotter, Van, February 2, 1880. Some describe the famine as continuing through 1881.

4. FO 195/2283, Dickson to O'Conor, Van, February 9, 1908; Ter Minassian, "Ermeni Kaynaklarına Göre," pp. 120–22.

5. Orhan Kılıç, *XVI. ve XVII. Yüzyıllarda Van, 1548–1648* (Van: Van Belediye Başkanlığı, 1997), pp. 255–66.

6. Dahiliye Nezâreti, Sicil-i Nüfus İdare-yi Umumiyesi Müdüriyeti, *Memalik-i Osmaniye'nin 1330 Senesi Nüfus İstatistiği* (Istanbul: Dahiliye Nezâreti, 1336 Mali). The city's population was undoubtedly better registered.

7. Vital Cuinet, *La Turquie d'Asie,* vol. 2 (Paris: E. Leroux, 1891), p. 700. Sami Bey (Frasheri), the compiler of the most complete Ottoman geographical dictionary, *Kamusülalam,* vol. 6 (Istanbul: Mihran, 1316), seems to have taken his figures from Cuinet, or else both quoted the same official resource. Sami was an Ottoman official who probably had access to the figures. Interestingly, Armenian sources do not ever seem to have listed Jews among the city's inhabitants, although they were surely present.

8. For comparison, the Van summer and winter temperatures were approximately the same as those of Kiev.

9. Las Vegas, Nevada, had three times as much rainfall in the month of August. London and Paris had twenty times as much.

10. This is partly true even today. Large buildings are constructed on the sides of roads over mountain passes in Van Province so that travelers will not freeze to death if caught in a sudden storm. Railroad trains have special long tunnels cut into mountainsides leading nowhere; trains are pulled into them to escape blizzards.

11. The vast majority of the Kurds were Muslims, although there were also Christians, Jews, and heterodox Muslims who were attached to tribes or were even members of tribes.

12. These descriptions are based on Mark Sykes, "The Kurdish Tribes of the Ottoman Empire," *Journal of the Royal Anthropological Institute of Great Britain and Ireland* 38 (July to December 1908): 451–86. For the general situation of the tribes, see Martin van Bruinessen, *Agha, Shaikh, and State: The Social and Political Structures of Kurdistan* (London: Zed Books, 1992), and "Kurdish Tribes and the State of Iran: The Case of Simko's Revolt," in *The Conflict of Tribe and State in Iran and Afghanistan,* ed. Richard Tapper (New York: St. Martin's, 1983).

13. See especially chapters 4 and 5 for numerous mentions of this.

14. See chapter 7.

15. The Barzani are the exception. The tribe was not particularly large, but its şeyh had a religious following that transcended tribal boundaries. This made them a threat to the Ottoman state and to other states even today. See chapter 7.

16. The primary sources for map 2.4 are a book by F. R. Maunsell, a military officer, British consul at Van, and a first-class spy (*Military Report on Eastern Turkey in Asia: Compiled for the Intelligence Division of the War Office* [London: War Office, 1894]), and Sykes,

"The Kurdish Tribes of the Ottoman Empire." They were compared to the 1-250,000 Maunsell maps drawn up for the British War Office, which include tribes. It is impossible to evaluate the accuracy of these designations because of changing tribal holdings and affiliations and especially because World War I altered the entire situation. We realize that the Kurdish tribes today often go under different names and even inhabit different territory. The larger ones remain. With some exceptions, spellings of the names used here follow used by Mark Sykes.

17. Ter Minassian, "Ermeni Kaynaklarına Göre," p. 131, and "The City of Van," p. 188.

18. See table 2.3. See also Robert H. Hewsen, " 'Van in This World; Paradise in the Next': The Historical Geography of Van/Vaspurakan," in *Armenian Van/Vaspurakan*, ed. Richard G. Hovannisian (Costa Mesa, Calif.: Mazda Publishers, 2000), p. 37.

19. There were two patriarchs during the period of this study, Ruwil Shimun XX (1860–1903) and Binyamin Shimun XXI (1903–18).

20. Consuls often remarked on the seasonal migration of these Nestorians, particularly noting that Nestorians made a good living as wandering holy men in the Russian Empire.

21. The largest group of Nestorian converts, the Chaldeans, were Uniate Catholics living to the south, in the Tigris Valley. They had little or no part in the history of events in Van Province.

22. Cuinet, *La Turquie d'Asie*, p. 636.

23. According to the annual reports of the American Board in 1910 and 1911, George C. Raynolds was the head of the Van station. He was responsible for general work. His wife, Mrs. Martha W. Raynolds, was responsible for women's work and rug making as a part of industrial work. Clarence D. Ussher was responsible for medical work. His wife, Mrs. Elizabeth Ussher, was responsible for lace making as a part of industrial work and for women's work. Ernest A. Yarrow was station treasurer, responsible for general work, and superintendent of the Boys' High School. Mrs. Martha T. Yarrow taught in the Boys' School. Miss E. Gertrude Rogers and Miss Caroline Siliman were together responsible for the Girls' High School and Boarding School: Rogers was responsible for the High and Intermediate Departments and Siliman responsible for the Primary and Kindergarten Departments. Miss Grisell M. McLaren was responsible for general evangelistic work for women, including touring the region (*The One Hundredth Annual Report of ABCFM* [American Board of Commissioners for Foreign Missions] *Together with the Minutes of the Centenary Meeting Held at Boston Oct. 11–14, 1910* [Boston: American Board, 1911]; and *The One Hundred and First Annual Report of ABCFM Together with the Minutes of the Meeting Held at Milwaukee, Oct. 10–13, 1911* [Boston: American Board, 1912]).

24. "We have come to believe that there are a good many converted Christians in the old church, even beyond the limits of our personal acquaintance" (ABC [American Board of Commissioners for Foreign Missions Archives, Harvard University] 16.9.7, Eastern Turkey Mission, 1910–1919, Documents, vol. 25a, no. 123, "Annual Report of Van Station for the Year 1910").

25. Depending on the country, these were considered either consulates or vice-consulates. In practice, the difference between the two was negligible. Beginning in the 1890s the British vice-consul, for example, routinely reported directly to the embassy in Istanbul, just as a consul would have done, not through the consulate in Erzurum. Non-British sources routinely referred to the British vice-consul at Van as "consul." To

avoid confusion, the vice-consuls at Van are referred to here as "consul," unless their proper title is essential to the meaning of the material.

26. ABC 16.9.7, Eastern Turkey Mission, 1910–1919, Documents, vol. 25a, no. 269, "American and German Missions in Turkey"; ABC 16.9.8, Eastern Turkey Mission, Woman's Board, vol. 01, Eastern Turkey, 1903–1909, Letters, no. 18; Otto Kley, "Der Deutsche Bildungseinfluss in der Türkei," *Beiträge zur Kenntnis des Orients* 14 (1917): 43. They had not yet begun teaching in 1910 (Grace H. Knapp, *Mission at Van* [privately published, 1916], p. 12; Clarence D. Ussher, *An American Physician in Turkey* [Boston and New York: Houghton Mifflin Company, 1917], p. 211).

27. Unless otherwise indicated, agricultural and horticultural comparisons in this section are drawn from Orman ve Maden ve Ziraat Nezâreti, Kalem-i Mahsus Müdüriyeti İstatistik Şubesi, *1325 Senesi Asya ve Afrika-yı Osmanı Ziraat İstatistiği* (Istanbul: Matbaa-yı Osmani, 1327 Mali). These statistics for Van can only be considered broad indicators, not in any way precise. For per capita comparisons, production/total population = per capita production.

28. Grapes, grape juice, and raisin production were always important in Van. Orhan Kılıç found in tax records from the early seventeenth century that Van City Muslim vineyards produced 200,000 bunches of grapes and non-Muslim vineyards produced 400,000 (Kılıç, *XVI. ve XVII. Yuzyıllarda Van, 1548–1648*, pp. 274–79). The Christians and Jews could legally drink wine; the Muslims could not.

29. What the Ottoman statistician called "wine" may have included a large amount of what should be called grape juice and grape syrup. Like other crops, grapes would have to be stored in a less perishable form, as raisins and wine.

30. Production is listed here by type and by quantity, as given in the 1876 yearbook (*Salname-i Vilâyet-i Erzurum, 1293 Hicri Senesi* [Erzurum: Erzurum Vilâyeti Matbaası, 1293], pp. 152–55). The *1325 Ziraat İstatistiği* indicates that tobacco was a considerable crop. Per capita production was very high, comparable to that of the Western Anatolian provinces.

31. The 1876 yearbook listed 14,600 bulls, 46,400 cows, and 34,550 calves in Van. That number had changed very little by 1910 (*1325 Ziraat İstatistiği*).

32. "The price of bread in Van has been and continues to be 60 paras an oke [*okka*, approximately 2.8 pounds or 1.28 kilograms], which is extremely high, and this has had a very serious effect on the poorer classes. It is mainly owing to the habit of all Armenians who have a little money investing it in wheat, which they hoard until they can force prices still higher. They seem quite regardless of the consequences of such action on their poorer compatriots. A public-spirited Turk, Jemal Bey, has opened a baker's shop and is selling bread at 45 paras, thereby tending to force down prices, but his action is too isolated to have much effect" (FO 195/2082, Maunsell to O'Conor, Van, May 2, 1900).

33. Reports of poor harvests and famine are to be found throughout the diplomatic literature. See, for example, FO 195/1315, Clayton to Trotter, Van, February 2, 1880; FO 195/2063, Maunsell to O'Conor, Van, December 29, 1899; FO 195/2063, Maunsell to O'Conor, Van, February 20, 1899; FO 424/198, Maunsell to O'Conor, Van, February 21, 1899; FO 424/208, Tyrrell to O'Conor, Van, January 10, 1905.

34. At least one British consul felt that Kurds often suffered worse than Armenians from famine (FO 195/1315, Clayton to Trotter, Van, May 25, 1880).

35. FO 195/2063, Maunsell to O'Conor, Van, April 10, 1899.

36. On education in Van, see the extensive, if somewhat jaundiced, analysis of act-

ing consul H. H. Lamb in FO 195/1521, Van, December 23, 1885, "Report on the State of Public Instruction in the Vilayet of Van."

37. Ter Minassian, "Ermeni Kaynaklarına Göre," p. 132.

38. United Nations Educational, Scientific and Cultural Organization (UNESCO) and the U.S. Census Bureau.

39. *Salname-i Nezaret-i Maarif-i Umumiye, 1316 sene-i hicriyesine mahsustur* (Istanbul: Matbaa-i Âmire), pp. 1210–11.

40. Cuinet, *La Turquie d'Asie,* p. 655. It should be noted that Cuinet tended to overstate the numbers and influence of Uniate Catholics such as the Chaldeans, of whom there were very few in Van Province.

41. *Salname-i Nezaret-i Maarif-i Umumiye, 1317 sene-i hicriyesine mahsustur,* pp. 1428–29, and *Salname-i Nezaret-i Maarif-i Umumiye, 1318 sene-i hicriyesine* (Istanbul: Matbaa-i Âmire, 1317 and 1318), pp. 1598–1601.

42. *Salname-i Vilâyet-i Erzurum, 1288 Hicri Senesi* (Erzurum: Erzurum Vilâyeti Matbaası, 1289), p. 148; *Salname-i Nezaret-i Maarif-i Umumiye, 1316 sene-i hicriyesine mahsustur,* pp. 1256–57.

43. *Salname-i Nezaret-i Maarif-i Umumiye, 1317 sene-i hicriyesine mahsustur,* pp. 1422–24.

44. See Ter Minassian, "Ermeni Kaynaklarına Göre," p. 132.

45. ABC 16.9.7, Eastern Turkey Mission, 1910–1919, Documents, vol. 25a, no. 116, "Report of Village Work in the Van Station Field, Eastern Turkey Mission, 1910."

46. *Salname-i Nezaret-i Maarif-i Umumiye, 1317 sene-i hicriyesine mahsustur,* pp. 1430–31; *Salname-i Nezaret-i Maarif-i Umumiye, 1318 sene-i hicriyesine mahsustur,* pp. 1598–99.

47. Ter Minassian, "The City of Van," p. 192; Rubina Peroomian, "The Heritage of Van Provincial Literature," in *Armenian Van/Vaspurakan,* ed. Richard G. Hovannisian (Costa Mesa, Calif.: Mazda Publishers, 2000), pp. 133–52.

48. See Nairy Hampikian, "The Architectural Heritage of Vaspurakan and the Preservation of Memory Layers," and Peroomian, "The Heritage of Van Provincial Literature," in *Armenian Van/Vaspurakan,* ed. Richard G. Hovannisian (Costa Mesa, Calif.: Mazda Publishers, 2000), pp. 87–116 and 133–52.

49. Ter Minassian, "The City of Van," pp. 191–92.

50. *Salname-i Nezaret-i Maarif-i Umumiye, 1317 sene-i hicriyesine mahsustur,* pp. 1428–29.

51. Cuinet, *La Turquie d'Asie,* pp. 659–60, 663–64; Van Vilâyeti, *Van Vilâyeti Salnamesi, 1315,* p. 210.

52. The descriptions of the size of these forests indicate that no survey had ever been taken. The Gevaş forest was "three hours long and half an hour wide," the Karçekan forest "four hours long and two hours wide," referring to the time taken to walk across them.

53. *Salname-i Vilâyet-i Erzurum, 1288 Hicri Senesi,* pp. 166–81.

54. Kılıç, *XVI. ve XVII. Yuzyıllarda Van, 1548–1648,* pp. 281–86.

55. The word "shawl" is somewhat deceptive. These shawls were not what would be considered a shawl today, a mainly decorative article of apparel. They were large, warm, and used by both sexes.

56. For lists of goods produced, see Van Vilâyeti, *Van Vilâyeti Salnamesi, 1315,* pp. 154–55; *Salname-i Vilâyet-i Erzurum, 1288 Hicri Senesi,* pp. 161–62.

57. *Van Vilâyeti Salnamesi, 1315,* pp. 154–55.

58. Kılıç, *XVI. ve XVII. Yuzyıllarda Van, 1548–1648,* pp. 286–88.

59. Cuinet, *La Turquie d'Asie,* pp. 674–75.

60. Ibid., pp. 634–35. International (Turkish and French): Van and Başkale; internal (Turkish only): Van, Erciş, Vosdan, Karçekan, Çölemerik, Dizi, Mahmudi.

61. Ibid., p. 216. Again, Cuinet's figures here and elsewhere should only be taken as general estimates, not exact figures.

62. Ibid., pp. 679 and 684. This includes Hakkâri Sancak, for which Cuinet gave separate figures, because it was at the time separated administratively from Van. Again Cuinet's figures, here and elsewhere, should only be taken as general estimates, not exact figures.

63. The boats had an average capacity of 10–15 tons.

64. Van Vilâyeti, *Van Vilâyeti Salnamesi, 1315,* p. 157; Cuinet, *La Turquie d'Asie,* pp. 668–71.

CHAPTER 3

Allegiance, Politics, and Power

Eastern Anatolia had never been completely under Ottoman control. Far from the center of authority in Istanbul, populated by independent-minded Kurds, Armenians, and Nestorians, and not a promising source of revenue, it was a most difficult region to rule directly. Süleyman the Magnificent had set a pattern of allowing local chiefs, Christian as well as Muslim, in effect to rule themselves. As long as they did not threaten commerce or overthrow their formal allegiance to the state, they were infrequently bothered by central government forces.

The situation began to change in the middle of the nineteenth century. Ottoman government reforms slowly extended to the East. More bureaucrats appeared, as did governors more intent on actually ruling. New telegraph lines connected the East to the capital. Government ability to affect events in the East was bolstered by an increased military presence, brought to the area by the threatening presence of Russia.

Property

There was a great economic gap between the urban and the rural in Van Province, but also great economic variance among villages. The poorest villages, whether Christian or Muslim, lived in a state of constant destitution. In good years they barely survived. In years of famine they starved. Others weathered bad times fairly well.

Freeholders (for lack of a better word) were at the top of the rural economy of Van Province. Most of these were Kurds and Armenians, although inhabitants of some Nestorian/Chaldean villages and some Turks can be included in the group. What distinguished them from the less fortunate was not legal ownership of their land. Some were actual freeholders; but most paid some form or rent/tax for their land, which was legally the property of the sultan.[1] What actually distinguished them was stability of land tenure, decent land, and the ability to keep a reasonable amount of the proceeds of their labor. Most of the villages that enjoyed this status were those that could be effectively protected by the government, because they were in range of Ottoman garrisons. Others were well armed and able to protect themselves from attacks by Kurdish tribes. The armed villages were inhabited by Muslims, Christians, or both together. They had always been armed. While unable to resist concerted attacks by entire tribes, they could make attacks on them an expensive proposition for tribes or bandits. There were easier targets, so the tribes and bandits left them alone. Easily defended villages in mountainous terrain, perhaps the majority of them Armenian and Nestorian, particularly fell into the well-defended category.

Lower on the economic scale, and able to survive but not prosper, were the villages "owned" by Kurdish tribes. Again, such villages were both Christian and Muslim. These villages paid a traditional "tax" to a tribe in their region. In turn, the tribe provided protection from other tribes as well as protection from the owner tribe itself. This type of arrangement was seen all over Europe and Asia in premodern times. It had been in place in Eastern Anatolia long before the Ottomans appeared. Like all such traditional "taxation" it rested on the idea that that it was more beneficial to the powerful to keep the farmers working and paying forever than it was to take all the farmers had at once, let the farmers starve, then have nothing left for anyone.[2] Occasionally the arrangement worked very well for both the Kurdish "owners" and the villagers. Armenian villages controlled by Mehmet Sadik of the Haydaranlı tribe were among the richest in Van Province. The poorest of the villagers had at least a hundred sheep, a considerable number when compared to other villagers. Yet Mehmet Sadik was a notorious raider and sometimes outright criminal who opposed both the Ottoman and Persian governments.[3]

Worst off were those villages, Muslim and Christian, that fell into neither category. They were not well armed, were too far from Ottoman garrisons to be protected by the state, and were not under continuous protection of any one tribe. Control of these villages was a prize fought over by various tribes, and it is never good to live on a battlefield. Tribes that might have long protected "their" villages would raid and steal from villages they could not control. Stronger tribes would raid the villages theoretically under the protection of weaker tribes. The raids were seldom murderous but could result in starvation and destitution among the victims, because traditional Kurdish raids largely involved the stealing of sheep.[4]

Nineteenth-century European observers usually saw the misfortunes of raided villages as purely Armenian troubles. This was never true. Tribes and bandits selected their targets by the ease of the operation and the booty to be gained. They did not discriminate among likely targets by religion. But Armenians were able to complain to European consuls and American missionaries, usually exaggerating their suffering, in the sometimes successful hope that they would be aided or compensated. Muslims did not complain to Westerners, so most Europeans and Americans did not see Muslim suffering. It must also be said that most Europeans simply did not care about the Muslims. They wrote of "the Kurds" as if the Kurds as a group attacked Armenians. In fact, it was the tribal attacking the settled. A few perspicacious and broad-minded consuls did report on tribal raids on Kurdish villages. From their reports and Ottoman records it can be seen that the suffering was not sectarian. Both mosques and churches were sacked. Muslims as well as Christians were robbed and killed.[5]

It was also not true that the sufferings of the poor were purely the fault of Kurdish tribes. Some of the difficulties of cultivators were not unlike those seen in other places and other times. Peasants, both Armenians and Muslims, borrowed heavily against future harvests, mortgaging their lands. When the harvest did not come in as well as expected, the notes were called in and the peasants lost their land.[6] Armenian merchants and moneylenders often preyed on their own. In 1900 (a famine year), for example, a syndicate of Armenian merchants "cornered the market" in wheat, driving up the price of bread. Protected as they were by Europeans, the merchants were beyond direct government action. The governor could not simply force them to disgorge their stocks of wheat or lower the price of bread. He tried instead to bring wheat from surrounding provinces, only to find that the merchant ring had been there before him. Villagers were driven deep in debt to those same merchants.[7]

Kurdish Tribes

Until the Armenian Revolution brought a greater threat, the key to the problems of the Ottoman East was the disruption caused by Kurdish tribes. The Ottoman government and the Armenians were not natural antagonists. Never strong enough on their own, Armenians could only present a real threat to the Ottoman state if they allied with foreign powers. On the contrary, it was in the Ottoman interest to safeguard the Armenians, as well as the settled Muslims, if only to continue collecting their taxes. It was not so with the tribes.

The government was unquestionably on the side of the settled population and thus was often opposed to tribal elements, such as the Kurdish and Nestorian tribes. The tribes had raided, and sometimes devastated, the settled population throughout history. The Ottoman government, like other Middle Eastern governments, wished to stop this pastime. A traditional Muslim belief held that justice was the first duty of a ruler, and religious beliefs did affect even rulers and bureaucrats, but there was also a more concrete cause for Ottoman concern for the settled population: farmers and merchants, at least potentially, paid taxes. Nomads seldom did so. Common sense dictated the Ottoman attempt to protect the settled population, no matter what the religion of farmers and city dwellers.

The Kurdish tribes and the Ottoman government were natural antagonists, as was true of the tribal-state relationship in virtually every country. There was no evidence of anything resembling "Muslim solidarity" between the Kurdish tribes and the regular army troops and gendarmerie.[8] As armed units loyal only to their chiefs, the Kurdish tribes were very difficult to control. Only a major intervention by a large army and subsequent extermination or forced sedentarization could have subdued a tribe. Even in the days of their greatest power the Ottomans did not have the wherewithal for this. The state could only employ a policy of divide-and-rule, punishing only the worst rebels and rewarding those chiefs who were loyal with honors and official positions.

The Ottoman government took seriously its duties to protect the subjects of the sultan and ensure the survival of the empire. Despite immense problems and officials who sometimes might put personal goals above the needs of either state or subject, the empire persevered in its duties; but it could not succeed without money to pay its soldiers and bureaucrats. The greatest need of the later Ottoman state was monetary. The tribes could sometimes be forced to pay minimal taxes, usually in the form of sums paid to the government for the tax farm of the villages controlled by a tribe.[9] The sums paid, however, were only a small part of the outlay necessary for the military forces that kept the tribes under some degree of control. Military force was needed. Without it, the tribes would soon have created such an anarchy that no taxes would have been paid in the East. The independent farmers, who did pay taxes, would have been ground down. The caravans of tax-paying merchants would have been constantly raided, leaving nothing on which to pay taxes. The potential development of tax-paying manufacturing and modern commerce, never much more than a dream, would never have had a chance of fulfillment.

The Ottomans also needed to keep the tribes in check because of the ever-present danger of European intervention. The Europeans were always watchful for signs of disruption in Eastern Anatolia. Unwatched, the tribes would have provided that disruption. Attacks on Armenians, in particular, always had the potential to spark Russian intervention. It was the prospect of such intervention that led the Armenian revolutionaries to attack Kurdish tribes, hoping for retaliation that would lead to European interference in the East. Only Big Power politics had kept the Russians at bay. If tribal anarchy erupted in the Ottoman East, public opinion in Western Europe might have made opposition to Russian invasion impossible.

It was therefore both natural and essential for the Ottoman state to oppose the tribes. The administration of the Van Province in the late nineteenth and early twentieth centuries fought a sometimes bloody battle to control the tribes. It was only partly successful, primarily due to a lack of government resources.

The Ottoman Bureaucracy

Ottoman officials were generally, not always, unified in their foremost desire—to save the empire—but they often disagreed on how this was to be accomplished. From the beginning of the Ottoman period of reform until the end of the empire traditionalists battled against reformers for control of the state, a battle that was reflected in Van especially after the 1908 Revolution, which brought reformers to power. Personal animosities and ambitions often thwarted this higher goal. In Van Province the civilian and military authorities frequently worked at cross purposes.

Some Ottoman officials tolerated what now can be seen to have been dangerous activities by Armenian revolutionaries but at the time appeared to be political compromise. For example, governor Tahir Paşa (1897–1906) allowed the Dashnak Party to cement its control over Van's Armenians, because he was more interested in temporary peace than in stopping potential rebellion. Most damaging to the Ottoman state was the alliance between the Committee of Union and Progress and the Armenian revolutionary parties. The alliance was forged in Europe, when both the Ottoman democrats and the Armenians found common cause against the government of Abdülhamit II. "Revolutionary brotherhood" blinded the Ottoman democrats, although perhaps not the Armenians, to the essential differences in their views. The democrats wanted a politically modernized empire. They were willing to concede a great deal of autonomy to national groups who avowedly shared the same basic ideals. The Armenian revolutionaries, however, saw autonomy as a stepping-stone to independence.

It is probable that they never thought that any Ottoman government, democratic or royal, would ever willingly cede real autonomy, which was true. The revolutionaries were more than willing, though, to use the bonds forged with the democrats to increase the power of their rebel organizations.

THE MILITARY

Most of the soldiers in Van were Turks from Anatolia and Ottoman Europe. Their life was hard. Pay was usually many months in arrears, leaving the soldiers with little to live on. Their families were mainly farmers who had no money to send to their sons serving as privates in Van. Survival depended on the meager rations distributed in their barracks, and even these were sometimes not enough to relieve their hunger. Soldiers in Van rioted in 1904 not because they had not been paid for eight months, even though that was the case, but because they had not been given enough to eat.[10]

The hard life and close quarters of the soldiers were a breeding ground for epidemic disease. In March 1910 an epidemic of typhoid began in the Erzurum garrison that was to cause twenty deaths a day. At the epidemic's height the army in Erzurum had sixteen doctors and no nurses to treat two thousand cases of typhoid.[11] Cholera struck the soldiers of the Van garrison in 1905,[12] and a "very serious" typhoid outbreak among the troops in Muş occurred in the winter of 1912–13.[13] On the eve of World War I soldiers in Van and elsewhere suffered from a typhus epidemic that reduced the fighting strength of the garrisons and influenced the fighting of the war.[14]

Major Emilius Clayton, a British consul at Van, described one outbreak of disease among the soldiers:

Tabreez, May 2, 1898
I have the honour to report that during the past winter there has been great mortality among the Turkish troops in Van.

There were five battalions in the town, whose strength I estimated at about 250 to 300 men each.

The estimates given as to the number of deaths that occurred varied from 500 to 1,000. I was told by a man who lived near the Military Hospital that several funerals left it daily, and I noticed myself a pinched and sickly look on the faces of many of the soldiers I saw in the streets.

It is difficult to ascertain the exact numbers that died, as the authorities tried to conceal the state of affairs, but 20 per cent. would probably not be an over-estimate. At Serai I was told that the battalion there had lost many men, thirty to fifty, but that the battalion at Bashkala was better off.

The cause of these deaths was put down to "typhus." Whatever it was it was undoubtedly due to exposure to cold. The men's rations appeared to me good and sufficient, but they were badly clothed, the bedding was insufficient, and the rooms were badly warmed.

The most trying of all was the sentry duty at night. Owing to an idea held by the authorities that the revolutionaries might try to cause disturbance in Van, and the unreliableness of the police, there were a large number of posts with several sentries on each, so the duty came around pretty often.

The Turkish sentry remains standing on his feet, and, though relieved hourly, the men used to get thoroughly chilled in the bitter winter nights, with the thermometer at many degrees below freezing.

The ordinary military great-coat is quite useless against cold of this description, and continued exposure to it under such conditions must be a severe strain on the human condition.[15]

THE ARMENIAN REVOLUTIONARY PARTIES

While more unified than the Kurds, the various Armenian revolutionary groups pursued different goals, using different tactics. Armenian revolutionary organization in Van began in the 1870s with two small parties: the Union of Salvation (founded in 1872) and the Black Cross Society (founded in 1878). The latter was a secret society with a platform of bloody revolution, but neither party can be said to have had any real impact. The first party that actually performed revolutionary acts was the Armenakan Party, organized by students in Van in 1885. Unlike the earlier groups, the Armenakan movement was organized along standard nineteenth-century revolutionary principles: dues, bylaws, a central organization and local branches in secondary cities, military training, a revolutionary newspaper (*Armenia*), and a cadre of sworn revolutionaries supported by auxiliary members. They were assisted in their military preparations and preparation for guerrilla warfare by the Russian consul in Van, Major Kamsaragan, himself an Armenian, who opened consular premises to them and personally assisted in their military training. The Armenakans began what was to become an essential feature of all Armenian revolutionaries—the creation of bureaus in Iran to facilitate the smuggling of weapons to Van. Other than a few small battles with soldiers and Kurds, however, the Armenakans were not to become important revolutionaries. Their one significant action was participant in the 1896 Van Rebellion.[16]

The two small parties and the Armenakans were the only revolutionary party actually founded and centered in Van. The most successful revolutionaries were imports from the Russian Empire.

The Hunchakian Revolutionary Party (founded in Geneva, Switzerland, in 1887) was a Marxist party with an ideology much like that of other Communist revolutionaries. (In an act of ideological piety the Hunchaks began to translate the *Communist Manifesto* into Armenian.) The founders were Armenian students from Russian Transcaucasia who were steeped in the revolutionary philosophy of the time and tied to the Russian revolutionary parties. Their program was described as "advanced atheistic socialism" by their detractors, and they were proudly both socialist and atheistic but also nationalistic. Their objectives were to be gained through revolution in "Turkish Armenia," chosen because more Armenians lived there and because revolution there would be easier than in "Russian Armenia." Following that revolution, they believed, would come a socialist state. In line with the policies of similar groups, their national revolution would be a part of the expected World Revolution.

Louise Nalbandian, the primary historian of the early Armenian revolutionaries, has described the Hunchak methods as "Propaganda, Agitation, Terror, Organization, and Peasant and Worker Activities."[17] The aim was Armenian revolution. The party manifesto proclaimed: "It is necessary to forcefully reshape, revolutionize the social the present social organization in Turkish Armenia, inciting popular revolt."[18] Terror was to be the basis of their plan. Ottoman officials were to be terrorized. Enemies, both Armenian and Turkish, were to be killed: "eliminate the most harmful Turkish and Armenian individuals within the government, eliminate the spies, the traitors" (party manifesto).[19] One party branch was specifically charged with terrorism. In a forecast of the revolutionary future, the Hunchaks declared that the best time for revolution in the Ottoman Empire would be when the Ottomans were at war.

Van was never a center of Hunchak activities, although the party did have its cells there. The Hunchaks concentrated their energies on the Sasun and Zeytun rebellions of 1894–95.[20] There they initiated the basic policy of the Armenian revolution: to enlist the Great Powers in creating an Armenian state by engendering sympathy for slaughtered Armenians. Armenian bands led by Hunchaks revolted against the government, murdered Muslims, and engaged in acts of brigandage. This incited the Kurds in the regions, as well as the Turkish soldiers sent to put down the rebellions. In revenge for massacres of Muslims the Kurds and soldiers massacred Armenians. This had the effect on the European press that the rebels desired. Only dead Armenians were reported, not dead Muslims. Pressure was put on governments by the public, incensed by the "Armenian massacres," but the Europeans refused to act. They sent commissions, not warships. The Hunchak strategy had failed. In 1896 the Hunchaks split into two parties. Their place at the head of the Armenian Revolution was taken by the Dashnaktsutiun.

The Armenian Revolutionary Federation (ARF or the Dashnaks, from the title Dashnaktsutiun, "federation" in Armenian) was officially founded in July or August of 1890 in Russian Transcaucasia.[21] It held its first congress in Tiflis in 1892. The "Program and Rules" passed at the congress clearly defined the purpose of the organization: "The aim of the ARF Dashnaktsutiun is to achieve political and economic liberty in Turkish Armenia by means of insurrection." The program went on to describe means to achieve this end: arming "the people," sabotage, execution of government officials and Armenian "traitors," and so forth.[22] In their founding meetings in 1890 the Dashnaks had declared a "people's war against the Turkish government."[23]

Like the Hunchaks, the Dashnaks were ideologically socialist, members of the Second International. They were more adept, however, at submerging their economic convictions and advancing their nationalistic aims.

The governing body of the Dashnaks was the ARF World Congress. In 1898 the second World Congress of the party divided Dashnak responsibilities between a Western Bureau and an Eastern Bureau. Headquarters for the Eastern Bureau were in Tiflis. It oversaw the local Dashnak committees in the Caucasus, eastern Anatolia, and Iran. The Western Bureau, headquartered in Geneva, oversaw Istanbul, Western and Central Anatolia, and the rest of the world, including Europe and the United States. A special "responsible body" for the Van-Muş region was instituted in 1907, indicating the importance of that region to the Dashnaks. Eastern Anatolia came under a separate bureau, centered in Erzurum, in 1913.[24]

The tactics of the Armenian revolutionaries were largely the same as those perfected by revolutionaries in the later twentieth century. The basic principles of Mao Tse-Tung in China, General Vo Nguyen Giap in Vietnam, and Fidel Castro in Cuba bear striking similarities to those of the Dashnaktsutiun in Anatolia. Mao declared that revolutionaries must have a "long view." Patience and slow organization were the bases of revolutionary success. At first the Armenian revolutionaries needed to learn this lesson.

Until World War I all their major attacks failed. Once they had learned, however, they slowly organized the countryside and cities, "silencing" Armenian critics and forging alliances, even with Kurdish tribes.

REBEL ADVANTAGES AND DISADVANTAGES

The revolutionaries had definite advantages in their conflict with the Ottoman state:

- The structure of society and power in the Ottoman East: The Ottomans had only a weak hold over the Kurdish tribes and often could not protect their subjects, whether Christian or Muslim, from Kurdish depredations. The Kurdish oppression of Armenians drew many to the revolutionary ranks.
- Ottoman poverty: The Ottomans could not afford to provide security in the East. The troops and police sent to Van and other eastern provinces were inadequate in number and poorly paid, often not paid at all for months at a time. There were too few soldiers to chase down either Armenian rebels or Kurdish malefactors. Unpaid soldiers were more likely to take bribes to let rebels and tribespeople escape. They were also likely to steal from the populace, driving many to the rebels.
- The perilous state of the Ottoman Empire: The resources available to the Ottomans were mainly devoted to rebellions in the Balkans and Crete and to the ever-present need to defend against Russia.
- The meager lives of the Armenians of Eastern Anatolia: Living at subsistence level, preyed on by Kurdish tribes, the Armenians might be willing to take desperate measures, including revolution, to improve their lot.
- The support of Europeans: The European public knew nothing of Muslim suffering or of Armenian attacks on Muslims, but they often read of suffering Armenians in their newspapers. Prejudice in favor of Christians, pandered to by politicians such as William Gladstone, was an effective tool in rallying Europeans to the Armenian cause.

If the revolutionaries had advantages in their struggle, they also had disadvantages: the revolutionaries could never be sure that their plans would remain secret. Both the Russians and the Ottomans had extensive spy networks among the revolutionaries. Both were willing to pay for information. Judging by Ottoman reports, the spies often gave accurate information to their masters. Disaffected revolutionaries were a serious problem. They were by definition men who were willing to use their weapons. In 1909 the head of the Dashnaks in Erzurum was assassinated by an Armenian who had been expelled from the committee.[25] In 1908 Davit (a Dashnak who had a grudge against Aram Manukian, one of the committee heads in Van) betrayed Dashnak weapons stores to the authorities. Nearly two thousand weapons were lost.

The revolutionaries were disunified. Hunchaks could not keep their own party together, much less unite with Dashnaks. Armenakans rejected both the socialism of the other parties and their plans to bring Europe to their aid. Only in the final period of their campaign, just before World War I, can the Armenian revolutionaries in Van be said to have become unified in purpose and action. But greater than the gap between the various revolutionary groups was the chasm between the revolutionaries and the Armenian "notables," primarily the Armenian merchants. The rich merchant families, as well as the church, were the traditional leaders of the Armenian community. The revolutionaries threatened to take their place as community leaders. Moreover, the revolutionaries threatened the merchants' livelihood. The merchant class had done quite well under Ottoman rule. Indeed, as the nineteenth century advanced, the Armenian merchants had increased their wealth until they far surpassed the Muslims around them. Merchants were necessarily conservative and tied to the government. They needed government permits, clearance of their goods through customs, and similar government services, as well as protection for their shops in the cities and for their caravans. They sold to the government—a good source of contracts and jobs—even if the government paid irregularly. Merchants needed civil order to maintain an environment in which they could sell their goods, and the revolutionaries were a primary source of civil disorder. In Van the merchants lived in superior houses, sent their children to Armenian community and American missionary schools better than anything available to Muslims, and controlled all the major commerce of the city. This was not fertile ground for revolution.

The poorer people also might not be amenable to revolution. Some— such as the Armenians of Zeytun, virtually independent in their mountainous villages—had long opposed the government. Most of the Armenians of the East, however, accepted their situation. They had been Ottoman subjects for centuries. It is doubtful that they had any particular love for their rulers, but they had survived for all those centuries, keeping their livelihoods, religion, and customs. Peasants are likely to be conservative, fearing with much justification that radical change might leave them worse off than they were. That was to become the case.

The process of turning the Armenian people of Van into supporters of the revolution was gradual. The revolutionaries were only the final cause that drove the Armenians from their traditional if grudging allegiance to the sultan.

It was the Russians, not the Armenian revolutionaries, who gave the first impetus to Armenian separatism. The change in Armenian sympathies began when Russian power was felt in the East. In their wars against Iran and the Ottoman Empire in 1827–29, the Russians defeated first the Persians then the Ottomans. The Russians killed or expelled 26,000 Turks from their newly won territories, including the province of Erivan (now the Armenian Republic), where Turks had been a majority. Armenian elements had supported the Russians in their conquests. The Russians, in turn, offered to Armenians the lands and farms from which the Turks had been evicted, as well as relaxation of normal taxes. More than a hundred thousand Armenians came from Iran and the Ottoman Empire. The process was repeated in the 1877–78 Russo-Turkish War, when Armenians in the Ottoman northeast supported Russian invaders, even acting as Russian police in occupied cities. When the Russians left at war's end, they were accompanied by perhaps twenty-five thousand Armenians. In turn, the Russians expelled more than a hundred thousand Muslims from their newly conquered territories.[26]

Both Muslims and Armenians began to view the Armenians and Russians as potential allies. Muslims, seeing the fate of their co-religionists, viewed the Armenians differently. The Armenians, previously no threat, were now dangerous. The age-old status quo was changing, and the Muslims were very possibly to be the losers. But the greatest change came to the Armenians. Previously they had acquiesced to the status quo, some prospering, some suffering. Now there was an opportunity for those who were unhappy as Ottoman subjects. Armenians who wished to disavow Ottoman rule now had at least a chance to do so. Alliance with Russia was undoubtedly seductive. Russia was richer and more powerful than the Ottoman Empire. Economic opportunities there were greater. While the Russian Orthodox and the Gregorian Armenians each considered the other to be heretics, both were Christians, in some sense co-religionists, a status never shared by Armenians and Muslims. The Russians also gave the Armenians the chance to reconstitute an Armenian homeland, albeit one under the rule of the tsar. For more than a millennium Armenians had scattered from their impoverished lands in Anatolia and the South Caucasus. By expelling the Muslims of Erivan and bringing in Armenians the Russians had created an "Armenia." Despite the overwhelming Muslim

majority in Eastern Anatolia, could not the Armenians hope for an extension of Armenia into the Ottoman Empire, even if it necessitated further
expulsions of Muslims? All the promises afforded by alliance with Russia
were seductive.

THE EUROPEANS

Ottoman efforts against Armenian rebels were hamstrung by Europeans.
The government was never able to act decisively against the Armenian
rebels, because of European interference. Under constant threat from
the Russians and economically attacked by all Europeans, the Ottomans
needed friends, or at least they needed to minimize the number of their
enemies. Until 1907 the British were the closest the Ottomans had to a
supporter, but the British were odd friends. They constantly interfered
in Ottoman internal affairs. In particular, they viewed themselves as pro-
tectors of the Armenians. Successive British governments faced a public
and members of Parliament who took the Armenian side in all things,
demanding diplomatic and even military action to assist Armenians.

In the nineteenth century, as today, military doctrine dictated that
governments act swiftly and decisively against rebels. If governments did
not act, rebels had time to organize and recruit. Potential converts to their
cause saw that the government was weak and joined the cause. Yet the Ottomans were kept from acting decisively by British, French, and Russian
interference. The British intervened in a number of cases for Armenian
rebels. British pressure on the government in Istanbul secured the amnesty of convicted rebels and light treatment for those who openly advo-
cated rebellion.[27] The British were responding not to the situation in the
Ottoman East but to political conditions in Britain. The Armenian cause
had influential backers in Britain, and few people in Britain ever heard
anything but the "Armenian side" of events in the Ottoman Empire.

When Kurdish tribes attacked Muslims, for example, the consuls did
nothing; but a Kurdish attack on Armenians drew letters to the ambassador in Istanbul demanding the removal of officials and lenient treatment
for Armenians. Governors and generals in the East were thus constrained
to treat rebels lightly by the actions of the consuls. Consuls in Van and
Bitlis Provinces could and did obtain the removal of governors and generals. They demanded and received amnesties for rebels. For example, after
the discovery in 1908 of two thousand guns and ammunition and dynamite hidden in Van, the murder of the Armenian who had betrayed the

weapons caches, the murder of gendarmes, and subsequent massacre of thirty-two Armenians, the *vali* (governor) was advised by the British consul to apprehend the guilty Armenian rebels and the Muslims who had killed Armenians. But the consul demanded that the Muslims be tried and punished and the Armenians be given amnesty. He pressured the government in Istanbul through the British Embassy to bring this about.[28] The government did exactly as the British wished. Muslims were indeed tried, and Ottoman officials were removed from office, whether or not they had acted inappropriately.[29] The leaders of the Armenian rebels were captured and were then freed.

The Ottomans were forced to pay particular attention to Russian demands. They knew that the Russians intended to stir up unrest in the East, but they also knew that Russia was capable of using real or manufactured difficulties of Christian minorities as an excuse for armed intervention. That is what they had done in the war of 1877–78, which resulted in great losses of Ottoman territories in both Europe and Asia. But the Russians also offered practical assistance to Armenian rebels (as will be seen in coming chapters). The Russians used their right of extraterritoriality to support rebels. The leaders of the Armenian revolutionaries in Van were all Russian subjects who were not subject to Ottoman law, because of treaties that reserved trial and punishment of their nationals to European powers.[30]

European pressure did the most damage to the Ottoman ability to wage war on rebels. As in subsequent generations, fighting guerrillas effectively involved punishing those who supported the rebels as well as fighting the rebels themselves. These were the tactics used by the British, French, and Russians against rebels in their own colonies. One need only compare Ottoman actions in Van Province with British actions against rebels in India, French actions in North Africa, or Russian actions in the Caucasus to see the double standard that was at work. The situations were indeed different, because the Europeans were imposing colonial rule on majorities, whereas the Ottomans were attempting to protect a majority, the Muslims, against a distinct minority, the Armenian rebels. The Europeans, however, would not allow the Ottomans the tools that they themselves used to put down revolt. Comparing the Ottomans and Russians reveals the inequity. The Russians in effect expelled millions of Jews from their northwest provinces. By 1878 they had murdered or expelled 1.2 million Caucasian Muslims and four hundred thousand Turks and Tatars from their Asiatic conquests and the Crimea. Yet there was no European outcry against them. The Ottomans, in contrast, were not to be allowed even to stop a rebellious minority.

PROPERTY RIGHTS

The question of property rights was a cause of conflict for all parties in the Ottoman East. In some areas Kurdish tribal leaders had for centuries functioned almost as feudal lords. Armenians on their lands paid them a percentage of each year's harvest and performed labor for the chiefs. In return, they were protected from other Kurdish chiefs. As the Ottoman world changed and reformed, Armenians naturally wanted to end this situation, and the tribal chiefs wanted to perpetuate it. The sticking point was land ownership. In raw theory, most of the land was the property of the sultan, who rented it to tax farmers. In fact, the chiefs had "owned" it. New rules were beginning to register the land as private property. Should the deeds be given to the cultivators or to the chiefs who had always been considered to be the masters of the lands? Attempts at reform had been made. Some lands had been registered in cultivators' names, but much still remained in the old system. There was much argument, legal and otherwise, over conflicting land claims. This was not unusual in the Ottoman Empire, or in the rest of the world, but it contributed to Muslim-Armenian tension.

The problems of traditional land tenure existed for Muslims as well as Christians. They too had quasi-feudal relationships with landlords. They too had conflicts over lands. It is difficult to say that one religious group suffered more than others in an archaic and ultimately unfair system that was only slowly changing. Another land tenure problem was solely Armenian. Large numbers of Armenians had left the Ottoman Empire at various times. Some had followed the Russian armies that evacuated Eastern Anatolia after the 1877–78 war. Others had fled because they feared violence or had gone to Iran or Russia in support of revolutionary ideals. Still others had gone to Russia or to the United States for work. If they were gone for more than the legal limit of years, their land was considered abandoned and was legally subject to seizure. In fact, it often was taken by neighbors or tribal leaders soon after the Armenians' departure. Returning Armenians wanted their land back. The new possessors had no wish to return it.[31] Ottoman efforts at remedying the problem were mixed in both their intentions and their success. In the late 1890s, for example, the government did nothing to retake Armenian lands seized by the powerful Haydaranlı chief Hüseyin (Husayn) of Patnos, but they did seize lands taken by weaker chieftains.[32] They could not begin to take action against Hüseyin until state power had increased more than a decade later.

The seizure of land by powerful chiefs was in fact part of a process that affected Muslim landholders as well as Armenians.[33] The powerful took land whenever they could, influenced by no feelings of Muslim brotherhood. Individual farmers, independent villages, and lands held by weaker chiefs all fell into the hands of strong tribal leaders.

Indeed, in a retrospective glance at the "agrarian question," the British consul remarked in 1911 that the Armenian land question was, in fact, "not as prominent as the more difficult question of the settlement of claims of Raya Kurds who demand the restoration of the lands taken away from them by their Chiefs and Aghas. It appears that at the time of the formation of the Hamidie cavalry the power and influence of the Kurd chiefs and Aghas became greatly increased through the favour shown them by Abdul Hamid. These chiefs then began gradually to appropriate the land and property of the Raya Kurds and to reduce them to a state of serfdom."[34]

Both Muslims and Armenians also lost lands for nonpayment of taxes. Entire villages were purchased quite legally by Kurdish chiefs and Armenian entrepreneurs when they were auctioned off for delinquent taxes.[35]

THE COMPLEXITY OF POLITICAL LIFE IN EASTERN ANATOLIA

If one is to understand the political life of the Ottoman East, it is essential to appreciate its complexity. All too often the situation in the East has been portrayed as one of two-sided conflict, although the sides change, depending on the interpreter: Turkish-Armenian, Turkish-Kurdish, Kurdish-Armenian, Ottoman-Russian, Christian-Muslim. In reality, the political situation was much more complex. There were many "sides," and each local power was always striving for its own advantage.

Kurdish tribes never presented a united front. They opposed each other and fought among themselves more often than they opposed either the government or the Armenian revolutionaries. The two largest tribal confederacies are good examples. The Haydaranlı (the largest) were divided into three subtribes, centered roughly around Patnos, Erciş, and Bargiri, and there were other clans of the Haydaranlı in Iran. They frequently fought each other, and in practice each accepted no higher tribal authority. The Shikaks (the second largest tribal grouping) dwelled from the Saray District south, in both Eastern Anatolia and western Iran. In theory the Shikaks were one organization, with a paramount chief, but in fact they were a deeply divided confederation with at least seven major and a large number of minor subtribes. Judged by the number of his followers, the paramount chief was in fact one of the weaker leaders.[36] The Shikak subtribes were as often at war with each other as with other tribes. During the Persian constitutional revolution of 1905–11, one group of the Shikaks took the side of the constitutionalists and one the side of the shah and his Russian allies.[37] It is doubtful if either was much concerned with political issues, preferring personal gain to ideology, but it is instructive that loyalty to the Shikak tribe was at best secondary.

The relationship between the Armenian revolutionaries and the Kurdish tribes was ever changing: sometimes enmity, sometimes "friendship" born of mutual self-interest. At a time when Armenian revolutionaries were attacking some Kurdish tribes in order to provoke reprisals, other Kurdish tribes were helping the revolutionaries to smuggle weapons into the Ottoman East. Armenian villages and Kurdish tribes seldom were friendly neighbors, but in at least one instance the government deliberately settled Kurdish tribes that had migrated from Iran near Armenian villages to protect the Armenians from other Kurdish tribes. The Armenians were pleased with the results.[38]

NOTES

1. Usually called "tax farming," the system had been used for centuries to collect the sums due to the government. Because of the lack of qualified bureaucrats and tax collectors, the right to collect the tax on property (and a considerable personal cut) was in theory auctioned off to the person who would provide the highest gain to the state. In fact, in provinces such as Van the tax farm had become quasi-hereditary in the hands of rich locals and tribal chiefs. This began to change late in the nineteenth century as more lands were registered in the cultivator's name and the government became more capable of collecting its own taxes. The turnover to the new system took decades, however.

2. For an example of the working of this system, see FO 424/197, Monahan to O'Conor, Bitlis, October 13, 1898.

3. FO 195/2284, Dickson to Lowther, September 22, 1908.

4. For many examples of this traditional occupation of Kurdish tribes, see FO 195/1688.

5. For example: "[Kurdish Chief] Pasha Mtran pulled down a monastery in Cizre and used the materials to construct a rather fine bazaar. He also 'remodeled' a Cizre mosque into his Hamidiye barracks. This was apparently only one of fifteen such mosques Mustafa Pasha destroyed for their building materials" (FO 195/2125, Tyrell to O'Conor, Van, October 7, 1902, quoted in Janet Klein, "Power in the Periphery: The Hamidiye Light Cavalry and the Struggle over Ottoman Kurdistan" [Ph.D. dissertation, Princeton University, 2002], p. 281). Klein (pp. 280–81) lists a number of attacks on Muslims as well as Armenians: FO 195/1728, Hampson to White, Erzurum, January 16, 1891; FO 195/22831, Safrastian to Shipley, Bitlis, June 22, 1908; MAE Nantes, AA E/113, Roqueferrier to Cambon, No. 6, Confidential, April 13, 1896. See the descriptions of tribal actions against Muslims and Christians in chapter 4.

6. See, for example, FO 424/203, Freeman to O'Conor, Bitlis, June 7, 1902.

7. FO 424/200, Maunsell to O'Conor, Van, June 20, 1900.

8. See, for example, FO 195/1688, Devey to Lloyd, Van, December 18, 1889. In one example of the lack of tribal respect for the government, a new commandant of gendarmes arrived in Bitlis Province in 1908. His baggage followed in a separate caravan, guarded by two gendarmes. The caravan was attacked by Modeki Kurds, who killed the gendarmes and took the commandant's belongings (FO 195/2283, Safrastian to Shipley, Bitlis, May 30, 1908).

9. See note 1 above on tax farming.

10. FO 424/206, Tyrrell to O'Conor, Van, January 8, 1904.

11. FO 881/9744, Lowther to Grey, Constantinople, April 10, 1910.

12. See Susan R. Norton, January 2, 1905 ABC 16.9.8, Eastern Turkey Mission, Woman's Board, vol. 01, Eastern Turkey, 1903–1909, Letters, no. 18.

13. FO 195/2450, Monahan to Marling, Erzeroum, September 29, 1913.

14. See chapter 8.

15. FO 424/196, Elliot to Currie, Tabreez, May 2, 1898.

16. Most of this material on the early history of the revolutionary groups is taken from Louise Nalbandian, *The Armenian Revolutionary Movement* (Berkeley: University of California Press, 1963), pp. 80–84, 90–178; Hratch Dasnabedian, *History of the Armenian Revolution Federation, Dashnaktsutiun,* trans. Bryan Fleming and Vaha Habeshian (hereafter *History of the ARF*) (Milan, GEMME Edizione, 1989), pp. 31–35; Hratch Dasnabedian, "The Hnchakian Party," trans. Mariné A. Arakelians, *Armenian Review* 41, no. 4 (Winter 1988): p. 22; Anahide Ter Minassian, *Nationalism and Socialism in the Armenian Revolutionary Movement,* trans. A. M. Berrett (Cambridge, Mass.: Zoryan, 1984).

17. Nalbandian, *The Armenian Revolutionary Movement,* p. 110.

18. Quoted in Dasnabedian, "The Hnchakian Party," p. 22.

19. Ibid.

20. The Sasun and Zeytun events are described quite differently in various books. See, for example, Justin McCarthy, *Death and Exile: The Ethnic Cleansing of Ottoman Muslims.* (Princeton: Darwin, 1995), pp. 119–21; Kamuran Gürün, *The Armenian File* (London: Rustem and Weidenfeld and Nicolson, 1985), pp. 137–54; Salahi Sonyel, *The Ottoman Armenians.* (London: Rustem, 1987), pp. 117–98; Richard G. Hovannisian, "The Armenian Question in the Ottoman Empire, 1876–1914," in his *The Armenian People,* vol. 2 (New York: St. Martin's, 1997), pp. 218–26; Dasnabedian, "The Hnchakian Party," pp. 27–30.

21. No one is sure of the exact date. The organization was first called the Federation of Armenian Revolutionaries, later the Armenian Revolutionary Federation. For a short while the Hunchaks united with the Dashnaks, but the two soon broke apart again.

22. *History of the ARF,* pp. 31–35.

23. Nalbandian, *The Armenian Revolutionary Movement,* p. 156.

24. Dikran Mesrob Kaligian, "The Armenian Revolutionary Federation under Ottoman Constitutional Rule, 1908–1914" (Ph.D. dissertation, Boston College, 2003), pp. 6–8, referring to Hratch Dasnabedian, *H.H. Tashnagtzutian Gazmagerbagan* (Beirut: n.p., 1974), pp. 25–29.

25. FO 195/2347, Shipley to Lowther, Erzurum, November 1, 1909.

26. McCarthy, *Death and Exile,* pp. 31–32, 113–16.

27. See, for example, FO 424/200, O'Conor to Salisbury, Constantinople, September 4, 1900; FO 424/199, Maunsell to O'Conor, Van, October 24, 1899.

28. FO 881/9433, Dickson to Barclay, April 13, 1908; FO 881/9433, Barclay to Grey, May 19, 1908; FO 881/9433, Dickson to Barclay, May 24, 1908.

29. FO 881/9433, Barclay to Grey, Constantinople, April 5, 1908.

30. The use of these Russian treaty rights was confused by the dual and even triple nationality of rebels, and the Ottomans did insist on the rights to try rebels if they held Ottoman citizenship. Thus some rebels were never tried and were simply spirited across the border by the Russians, whereas others were tried and imprisoned. See chapter 5.

31. This problem was referred to throughout the diplomatic literature. See, for example, FO 195/2375, Molyneux-Seel to Lowther, Van, October 9, 1911; and FO 195/2458, Smith to Mallet, Van, February 14, 1914. Returning lands taken from Armenians was, as might be expected, extremely unpopular with Kurdish tribes and could lead to revolt. See, for example, the case of Sait Bey of Erçek in chapter 7.

32. FO 195/2082, Maunsell to O'Conor, Van, July 24, 1900. Concerning the villages returned to Armenians because they were near government forces in Van, Maunsell reported: "The large Armenian villages near the lake in the Arjish kaza are still protected by detachments of regular troops ordered by the Vali of Van and are quite exempt from any Kurdish oppression."

33. See FO 195/2104, Satow to de Bunsen, Van, January 3, 1901; FO 195/2082, Maunsell to O'Conor, Van, May 2, 1900; MAE Nantes, AA E/119, Srabian to Constans, No. 76, Erzurum, June 7, 1906; FO 195/2104, Satow to O'Conor, Van, Jane 10, 1901; all cited in Klein, "Power in the Periphery," p. 292. Klein feels that Armenians potentially suffered more from these exactions. Because of the existence and actions of the Armenian revolutionaries, the landholders could be accused of being traitors and their lands could be seized more easily (Klein, "Power in the Periphery," p. 298). See also ABC 11.4, Barton, James L., Papers, 1877–1943, Box 11:2.

34. Klein, "Power in the Periphery," pp. 292–93, quoting FO 195/2375, Van, February 6, 1911, Molyneux-Seel, "Notes on Journey from Van to Erangan."

35. FO 424/224, Safrastian to McGregor, Bitlis, July 25, 1910, cited in Klein, p. "Power in the Periphery," p. 291.

36. FO 195/2146, Tyrrell to O'Conor, Van, September 1, 1903. The theoretical leader, Cafer Ağa, was the grandson of a truly powerful leader, Ali Khan, but his tribe had broken up after his death.

37. FO 371/540, Dickson to O'Conor, Van, January 31, 1908.

38. FO 424/202, Satow to O'Conor, Van, August 20, 1901.

CHAPTER 4

Rebellion in 1896

Immediately after the Ottoman loss in the 1877–78 Russo-Turkish War, Eastern Anatolia can be said to have been in a state of near anarchy. During the war, state power in regions such as Van and Bitlis had essentially collapsed as soldiers were drawn off to the front. With the war lost, many of the soldiers were never to return. The period was one of great disruption in Eastern Anatolia. Kurdish tribes fought among themselves in what Europeans called a war.[1] Tribal raids on the settled Muslim and Christian population, always a factor in the East, seem to have increased.[2] Murder was uncommon, but theft was everywhere.[3] Roving gangs of ten or twelve wandered the countryside, stealing sheep when they could.[4] Most of those who suffered from the anarchy were Armenian and Muslim villagers who lost sheep and harvests to the raiders.

Under such disturbed conditions the settled inhabitants of Van looked for salvation where they could find it. British Consul Clayton in Van remarked: "The Christians are profoundly discontented and ready to turn their eyes to any quarter from which they may think they can obtain some assistance."[5] Many Armenians hoped for the Russians to invade once more.[6] Many supported revolutionary tactics that might bring this about. There were substantiated, though limited, reports of "Armenian brigands" attacking Kurds,[7] and Armenians made an attempt on the life of Bahri Paşa, the governor of Van.[8] Animosity between Muslims and Armenians was increased by revolutionary Armenians in Van City who gave public speeches against the government.[9]

THE DISADVANTAGE OF LIVING NEXT TO IRAN

Perhaps the largest number of Kurdish raiders came from western Iran, which they used as a refuge from the Ottoman authorities. Western Iran was essentially without either law or government until the Russian invasion of 1910. Except for unruly small garrisons in some towns, there was no regular Iranian military in the region. The only authority came from Kurdish tribes and Armenian revolutionaries.

Major tribes such as the Haydaranlı and Shikaks had branches on both sides of the border. Individual leaders, such as Şerif of the Shekifti Shikaks, had lands and tribal followers on both sides of the border. The tribespeople owed true allegiance only to their leaders, not to either Iran or the Ottoman Empire. By the mid-1880s the Ottoman authorities in Van had been given men and supplies to begin major actions against the tribal raiders from Iran. Even earlier, in 1879, when government resources were severely limited, the state had done what it could to limit Kurdish raids. Reacting to raids in Van Province, the Ottoman gendarmerie battalion in Van crossed the Persian frontier in 1879 to punish, but primarily to warn, Kurdish tribes.[10] In 1884 Ottoman troops in Van mobilized to stop a major incursion of an entire tribe intending to move permanently from Iran.[11] But such actions were limited. The tribes were largely free to act as they wished wherever there was no nearby garrison of troops.[12]

Western Iran also provided a safe haven for Armenian revolutionaries. Without any effective government presence to restrict them or their Kurdish opponents, many, perhaps most, of the Armenian villages and towns of western Iran had long been armed and self-reliant. The ideals of the revolutionary parties found fertile ground there. The region to the northwest of Lake Urmia became a revolutionary headquarters where the parties could organize and stock weapons. Salmas (southwest of Dilman), Dilman, and their surroundings were the centers of Armenian control, as were armed and fortified villages near Khoy.[13] The Armenian population in the Khoy area was considerably augmented by refugees from the troubles of the 1890s.[14] The Salmas region was to remain a secure base for Armenian rebels until World War I.[15]

Smuggling of weapons and men through Iran was not as extensive or as well organized as it was to become after 1900,[16] but in the 1880s and 1890s western Iran was already a center for Armenian smuggling into Van Province. Weapons were brought from Russia to the "safe areas" in Iran then carried through Armenian villages and rugged terrain on both sides of the border until they reached secret depots in and around the cities in Van Province. After the 1896 Van rebellion the Ottoman authorities were to identify in more detail a number of arms smuggling routes, but they had already taken notice of main smuggling routes prior to 1896. The main weapons smugglers before 1896 were members of the Hunchak Party, although Dashnak symbols were found on weapons captured by the Ottomans as they passed from the Salmas region.[17]

Neither the Kurdish tribes nor the Armenians can be said to have controlled the entire region northwest and west of Lake Urmia. At first the two battled often for control, leaving destruction behind. In particular, fights between the revolutionaries and the Shikak tribe disrupted the region from Başkale to Kalasar (as noted below).[18] In the 1900s, however, the primary chiefs along the border made peace with the revolutionaries. Both directed their energies against the Ottoman government, freeing the energies that revolutionaries and tribes had used against each other in Iran.[19]

There was more behind the difficulties between Kurdish tribes and the settled population than the traditional tribal way of life. Compared to the settled population, tribespeople (although not always their chiefs) were poor. The Kurdish raids involved the poor stealing from the less poor.[20] Armenians were the richest, so they undoubtedly were favored targets. At the same time, incidents between Armenian nationalists (whom the consuls called "agitators") and Kurds began to be serious. The Armenians and Kurds each blamed the other. British consul C. M. Hallward in Van felt that the majority of Armenians and Muslims wanted only peace, but Kurdish tribes and "Armenian agitators" were fomenting trouble.[21] Kurds both attacked the settled population and battled among themselves, fighting small wars in the 1880s and 1890s. Either by design or because of lack of power, the government did little to stop these clashes among the tribes. The tribal leaders themselves certainly seemed to have no fear of government interference.[22]

Unsettled conditions in the countryside naturally drove many into the city of Van for protection. Although European estimates of ten thousand refugees in the city were probably exaggerations, the presence of large numbers of both Armenian and Kurdish migrants in Van undoubtedly increased the possibility of unrest in the city.[23]

All the settled people of Ottoman Eastern Anatolia had cause for complaint. It is easy to say that the Ottoman government should have done something about conditions in Van, but specific remedies were hard to find. Many of the problems of Van were insurmountable: the province was necessarily poor. No matter what steps any government might take, low rainfall, a miserable climate, and deforestation stretching back millennia meant poor harvests. Famine was always expected, appearing regularly whenever rainfall was less than normal. Those remedies that might have worked—better schools, irrigation schemes, roads and railroads, a great increase in the security forces—shared the same predicament. They all demanded great outlays of money, and the funds were never available.

With the encouragement of Russia, Nestorians increased their raids and conflicts with the Kurds. They went so far as to burn Kurdish villages and declare defiance of the government, openly petitioning the Russians for their "protection." The British consul at Van wrote that the Nestorians were at fault, pursuing a policy that could only inflame the Muslims.[24] Throughout their history the Nestorians of the mountains (the Aşirets) had been virtually independent. They had grievances against the local Kurds, who lived as they did, governed by chiefs and religious leaders. The Nestorian grievance against the Ottomans was a simple one: the Ottomans were expanding state authority. The Nestorians feared that "the government is about to make an attempt on their semi-autonomy."[25] The fear was well founded, as that was exactly the Ottoman plan. The government intended to assert its authority over all in the empire, not simply the Christians of the East. The Kurds had similar complaints.

The government's ability to enforce peace and security was severely limited. In 1880 soldiers in Van did not even have enough ammunition for their guns.[26] While they had received ammunition by the 1890s, their pay often did not arrive. There also were too few soldiers to patrol a vast territory. Rather than place troops in all regions, the Van military officials were forced to house them together for reasons of economy and lack of manpower. They were sent out to quell disturbances, but the distances that had to be crossed meant that the criminals often were gone when they arrived.[27] Nevertheless, the government did act when it could to protect the populace, sometimes in a very heavy-handed manner. When Kurdish villagers sacked Christian villages in 1879, soldiers responded immediately and punished the Kurds by destroying their villages.[28] The British consul in Erzurum, in charge of the consulates in the East, remarked that the provincial governments sincerely wished to carry out reforms but did not have the money.[29]

Under the circumstances, improvements in governance began only slowly and sporadically in 1880.[30] By 1891, however, the situation in Van Province was much improved. Sparked by untrue and unfair reports current in Britain, the British consul in Van, George Pollard Devey, wrote a "Memorandum on the misleading views respecting Armenian affairs disseminated by paragraphs recurring in current newspapers, in particular the *Daily News,* and upon the condition of Kurds and Armenians generally." Many of Devey's comments (thankfully less verbose than his title) were simple refutations of allegations of massacres of Christians and denials of assertions that the Ottoman government was planning such actions. He went on to comment, though, that illegal Kurdish tribal "exactments" from Armenians had been greatly lessened and now occurred only in isolated districts, whereas six years before they had been prevalent. By no means, he stated, were the "feudal" arrangements that remained always bad for Armenians. Devey felt that taxes were sometimes unfair but were not "cruelly executed" and did not ruin the populace: "Personally I believe the distribution and collection [of tithes] to be fairly well managed, and to be improving. To sum up, taxes are heavy and the people extremely poor, but the taxation 'grievance' is for the most part fictitious, nor is the pressure more burdensome on Armenians than on other communities." Devey felt that both the courts and provincial officials were improving, especially the financial and judicial departments. Bias in favor of Muslims still existed but was decreasing every year.[31]

THE HAMIDIYE

What was needed in Van Province was an increase in the police power of the state. One government initiative to increase its power in Eastern Anatolia, however, was to have negative consequences. In 1890 Sultan Abdülhamit II attempted to remedy certain military problems by creating an irregular cavalry from Kurdish tribes, naming it the Hamidiye. The new force was to provide cavalry in time of war and to provide security in the eastern provinces in peacetime. The model was believed to be the Cossack regiments of the Russian army, although the Hamidiye were quite different from the Cossacks, particularly in terms of military discipline.[32]

The organizational structure of the Hamidiye was tribal. Smaller tribes fielded one "regiment," larger tribes a number of regiments. The troops remained under the command of their tribal leaders. When regular army officers were assigned to the Hamidiye units, they had no real authority. Such officers, in any case, were not of high quality; assignment to a Kurdish tribe was more likely to be a punishment than a career enhancer. The Hamidiye regiments were given uniforms and modern rifles to be able to perform their duties.

In theory, the plan for the Hamidiye had many advantages for the Ottoman state. Lack of cavalry was indeed a problem for the Ottoman military in the East, as had been shown in the Crimean War and the 1877–78 Russo-Turkish War. Internally, the Ottomans did not have the resources to police Eastern Anatolia. If Kurdish tribes could be brought under military control, they could aid in defending the borders and putting down rebellions (although not even the most fervent advocates of the Hamidiye believed that they would help in collecting taxes). Independent-minded Kurdish chiefs would be brought into the Ottoman system. Provision was

made for Hamidiye chiefs and their sons to attend special schools in Istanbul and in the East, where it was hoped they would become part of the
general Ottoman political culture.[33]

Detractors of the Hamidiye have always failed to mention that they did
provide some benefit. Hamidiye tribes played a significant role in stopping
an Armenian revolutionary invasion from Iran in 1896. Hamidiye units
served in battles in both Yemen and Ottoman Europe. Some Hamidiye
tribes rallied to the Ottoman cause in World War I, fighting the Russians. They also played a large part in protecting Muslim civilians from the
depredations of the period of Russian and Armenian occupation during
and after that war.[34] The negatives of the Hamidiye system, however, out-
weighed the positive.

Government officials were especially frustrated by the Hamidiye command structure. The Hamidiye came under the command of Zeki Paşa,
the general (*müşir*) in command of the Fourth Army in Erzurum and later
Erzincan, and only through him were they under the authority of the
military command. Neither the civilian nor the military leaders in provinces such as Van had command authority over the Hamidiye. In Van in
1903 both the governor and the military leader complained that they had
great difficulty in stopping Hamidiye Kurds from occupying Armenian
villages, because they had no authority over the Hamidiye and Zeki Paşa
was no help.[35] The effectiveness of the system was not helped by the fact
that Zeki Paşa seemed to be eternally at odds with both the civilian authorities and other military leaders. Zeki, the brother-in-law of the sultan,
was in charge of the Hamidiye from its inception until the deposition of
Abdülhamit II.[36]

The central assumption of the Hamidiye system—that Kurdish tribes
could be brought under military discipline—proved to be utopian. Tribal
loyalties were never replaced by loyalty to the Hamidiye or to the state.
Tribes that became part of the Hamidiye did not stop battling each other,
but now they did so with better weapons. Tribes that had not been armed
by the government were at a new disadvantage, weakening the "balance
of power" in the East and actually encouraging disorder. From a military
standpoint, the worst problem with the Hamidiye regiments was that they
simply would not take orders.[37] This was especially true during Armenian
revolts of the 1890s, when Hamidiye units disregarded orders and punished the innocent and the guilty alike. In Van Province the government
was often forced to send regular army forces to stop Hamidiye units from
plundering villages that they believed had supported revolutionaries. It
was impossible to depend on Hamidiye tribes following orders unless the

orders were backed up by regular troops, even though the soldiers and the Hamidiye were ostensibly part of the same military—not a sign of a unified command.

THE REVOLUTIONARY PLAN

As seen in chapter 3, Van was the site for the first ineffective Armenian rebel organizations. It also was one of the first provinces to experience Armenian guerrilla attacks. Armenian partisans had begun to operate in the Van Province even before the 1877–78 war, but these were uncoordinated bands, as much bandit as rebel.[38] Groups that truly had the potential to disrupt the province, the Hunchaks and Dashnaks, did not begin to appear in any numbers in the province until the early 1890s. The Armenakan Party was the first to organize in Van, bringing weapons across the border from Iran.[39]

It was never possible that the Armenian revolutionaries could win by themselves against the Ottoman government or even against the Kurdish tribes. The intent of the revolutionaries was not to defeat the Muslims but rather to cause retaliatory atrocities against Armenians. These, they were sure, would draw European support. England and France would intervene diplomatically. Russia might go to war. The Armenians would be granted their state. This was not a far-fetched plan. It was exactly what had happened in Bulgaria. Bulgarian revolutionaries had attacked Bulgarian Muslims in 1876, killing perhaps 1,000. The Muslim response killed 3,000–12,000 Bulgarian Christians. The Russians then invaded. Ultimately 260,000 Bulgarian Muslims died and 575,000 were driven from Bulgaria. A Bulgarian principality was created.[40] The Armenian revolutionaries hoped to emulate the Bulgarian success.[41]

Revolutionary actions had their successes in antagonizing the Kurds. For example, in July 1891 two gendarmes from Başkale were escorting an Armenian revolutionary named Gharak who had been taken prisoner as he crossed from Iran with a large number of pamphlets printed in Marseilles, calling for an Armenian revolt. The gendarmes, who were Kurds, had reached the neighborhood of the Armenian monastery of Varak when they were set upon by six Armenians. One guard was wounded, the other killed. Consul Devey felt that the Armenians then went to the monastery, subsequently moving on. Devey stated: "The outcome of this fresh distressing event will be the fomentation of rancour between Armenian and Kurd and to render the work of maintaining order and harmony and justice between the different sections of the population, upon which the local Government has been so strenuously asserting itself, get [*sic*] more difficult."[42]

Ottoman lack of control over the Kurdish tribes made the revolutionary plan all the easier. The Kurds were more than willing to cooperate with the revolutionary plan by providing reprisals. In one example, early in November 1895 a Kurd near Saray saw a band of fifty-seven Armenians transporting arms from Iran. He reported the incursion to the fort at Saray, from which Hamidiye troops and gendarmes were sent to intercept the revolutionaries. In the ensuing battle, twelve Kurds and eight Armenians were killed. Half the remaining Armenians escaped to Iran; the other half were able to continue into Van Province, where they fought with local Kurds at the Armenian village of Boğazkesen. The Armenians were routed. Two were sent to Van as prisoners. The Armenian village was sacked. The events set off Kurdish raids on the Armenian villages of the region; and the Ottomans, who sent gendarmes, could do little to stop the raids. Armenians fled the region, only to return when the raids were over.[43]

Such small-scale battles were not the end of the revolutionary plan. Major revolts were to take place all over the East in the middle 1890s. In 1895, when the rebellions in Zeytun and later Van began, the Ottoman government was not completely unaware that a revolutionary action was planned, although it seemed to have no idea that it would be a major rebellion.[44] Military and police patrols were increased, but troops were not brought from elsewhere in the empire. Foreign embassies knew from their own sources that "the Armenian Revolutionary Committees are determined on provoking another massacre, and are said to be preparing insurrectionary movements in various places."[45]

By no means were all the Armenians of the city of Van and its environs supporters of the revolutionaries. In order to obtain support for their plans, the revolutionaries first had to break down resistance among Armenians. This even included the murder of Armenian clergy who did not support them. On January 18, Armenian Christmas Eve, they killed Bishop Boghos of Van, who had opposed their organization, when he went to his church to organize the worship.[46] Other Armenians who were vocal in opposing the revolutionaries (including priests, merchants, and community leaders) were also killed.[47]

It did not help that just as the revolutionaries' plans were coming to fruition Sultan Abdülhamit II curried favor with the Europeans by granting an amnesty to convicted Armenian revolutionaries, freeing more to revolt.[48]

The revolutionaries stepped up the importation of arms and men

into Van Province from Russia through Erzurum Province and through
Iran.[49] In 1895 members of the Dashnak organization came to Erzurum
from Russia and began to extort money from local Armenian notables
to buy guns. They threatened Armenian members of the Provincial Administrative Council with violence if they did not cease to serve on the
council.[50] Most of the revolutionaries who came into Van Province were
Russian Armenians, but local Van Armenians who had gone to Russia for
revolutionary training were also among those who crossed the border. In
1887 Ottoman forces captured fourteen men carrying revolutionary propaganda as they crossed the Iranian border—one was a Russian subject,
twelve were Ottoman subjects, and one had a British passport under the
name of "Harry Williams."[51] "Williams" turned out to be a Hunchak
party regular, Haroutun Ohandjian, who had lived in London and obtained a passport using false credentials.[52]

A unit of young Armenians gathered for training in large houses near
the Russian consulate in the winter of 1895–96 for training, even trying
out their weapons.[53] In the spring of 1896 the rebels gathered together to
plan their rebellion, a fact known openly in the city. Seeing that their activities went unpunished, they acted more boldly, intending to exhaust the
patience of the Muslims. Armenian rebels in the city openly began to dis-
play the determination to revolt. British Consul C. H. Williams described
their actions as "criminal folly": "I have previously called attention to the
criminal folly of these revolutionists. Parties of them constantly patrol the
streets at night in the Armenian quarters covered with guns and revolvers
which few of them know how to use. The bulk of the Armenian population have no sympathy with these men, but they are too cowardly to do
anything."[54] Kurds were killed outside the city by the rebels and hacked
to pieces, their bodies publicly exposed. The intention of the rebels was to
cause the Muslims to attack the Armenians, thus arousing the sympathy
and support of the great powers for the Armenian cause and drawing all
their Armenians to the side of the revolutionaries.[55]

Consul Williams made it clear that the excesses of the revolutionaries,
in particular their attempts to incite the Muslims, were a real obstacle to
the peace of the region. He felt that the rebels were in fact a hindrance to
true reform: "If they can be silenced, I am certain that the main obstacle
to the region's security will disappear."[56]

The question must be why the government would tolerate Armenian
rebels walking the streets "covered with guns and revolvers." Officials cannot have been ignorant of the activities of the Russian consul or of the

guerrilla training groups that he supervised. The answer must be found in international politics.

The Ottoman Empire was in real danger of forced dissolution in 1895–96. The immediate impetus was European, especially British, reaction to the Sasun-Zeytun troubles of 1894–95. The European public, which received only word of reprisals against Armenians, not initial acts against Muslims, demanded action against the Ottoman Empire. But the real cause was the belief in European government circles that the Ottoman Empire was about to dissolve.[57] Each wanted as much of the remains as it could take. Robert Cecil, Lord Salisbury, British prime minister from June 1895, led the call for action against the Ottomans.[58] At one point in 1895 Salisbury sent the British Fleet to Lemnos, immediately opposite the opening of the Dardanelles, and suggested in the cabinet that the fleet would force the straits and go on to take Istanbul, perhaps in concert with the Russians. The Russians, following long-held policy, wanted to take Istanbul, but especially to gain secure naval communication from the Black Sea to the Mediterranean.

It was a close thing. Throughout the last half of 1895 the Europeans haggled over the spoils. At various points it appeared that the Ottomans were doomed. Ottoman survival was only due to distrust among the powers: Germany would agree to Russia taking Istanbul, but only as part of a plan to draw Russia away from its French ally and into the German camp,[59] to which the French naturally objected. Italy wanted Albania as its share; the Austrians objected. The Russians contemplated attacking alone but were embroiled in north China in the Manchurian Crisis of 1895 and could not take the chance of a European war. No one really trusted Russian intentions. All the European powers fully intended that the Ottoman Empire be destroyed. The empire was only saved because they could not agree on how to go about it.

The Ottomans and all of Europe knew what was transpiring in the European cabinets. Their demise might be decided by one more act involving Armenians. The sultan's government could only watch and try to minimize disturbances. Allowing Armenian revolutionaries in Van and other cities to demonstrate, openly carry weapons, and distribute propaganda was necessary for a time, because stopping them would bring trouble, perhaps another open revolt. That might tip the scale and bring

European armed intervention. In the end, the tolerance for revolutionary bravado was prescient, or perhaps just lucky. The Van Rebellion of 1896 came after the European plans to dismember the empire had dissolved in mutual recrimination.

THE REVOLT OF 1896

The Armenian revolt of 1896 took place just as the situation was improving in the Van Province. The government had been convinced by the international reaction to the revolts in Sasun and Zeytun in 1894–95 that the security of the state depended as much on containing internal disorder as it did on stationing troops in areas of possible Russian invasion. Indeed, there was real danger that Armenian affairs might lead to Russian invasion. The Armenian revolutionary plan of revolt, reprisal, and European intervention had come very close to success in 1895. The government resolved to do what it could to remove Armenian grievances and maintain security in the East. The first steps toward including Armenians in the governing bureaucracy were taken: a post was created for a Christian deputy governor.[60] The government saw that more troops were needed in the East, to improve normal security and quickly put down revolts before they spread and led to massacre and countermassacre. A strong military leader, Sadettin Paşa, was put in charge of the military in Van and given enough troops to improve security. For the first time troops were garrisoned in outlying districts. Five battalions were delegated for the purpose.[61] Sadettin's personal ability and the danger of the situation lent him great personal authority. He reacted with vigor to security challenges.

By no means was the security situation perfect. The five extra battalions improved the situation, but many more were needed. It was often impossible to constrain a mobile force like the Kurdish tribes. When Kurds attacked four Armenian villages on March 30, 1896, twenty-six were killed and more wounded. Sadettin Paşa personally led a battalion of troops and a squadron of cavalry to the site, but he was unsuccessful in apprehending the guilty tribesmen, who were long gone when his force arrived.[62] As always, money was the problem. Still more soldiers were needed, and the forces needed to be paid regularly if they were to be expected to perform their duties properly.[63]

Despite Ottoman attempts at improving security, revolutionary tensions built in Van. British consul Williams estimated that there were approximately four hundred members of the Dashnak society and fifty members of the Hunchak society in Van, a number which must have included only the "sworn" or core members of each. He said the Dashnaks "terrorize over their countrymen, and by their outrages and follies, excite the Mahommedan population and render nugatory all efforts to carry out reforms."[64] The revolutionary committees distributed pamphlets and placed placards calling for revolt. One posted by the Dashnaks in March ended with the following sentiment:

> There can be no reconciliation; we will not put down our arms. We have a holy war, and it will be continued with greater savageness. Therefore let the Commission of the tyrant go to hell. Let there be no yielding to it. We are revolutionists, and this is our last word.
>   Death or Liberty!
>   Long live the Armenian people!
>   Long live the revolution![65]

Reports came in that the revolutionaries were planning actions in Van. Ordinary Armenians, at least those who spoke to foreign consuls, told the Europeans of the upcoming revolt at least six months before it occurred.[66] The British had word from Iran that the revolutionaries had collected money, ostensibly for relief for Sasun victims, and were using it to buy guns and smuggle them into Van for an uprising.[67] Van governor Nâzım Paşa reported to Istanbul: "All the Armenians [in the city] are armed, and they are hiding weapons."[68]

The rebels' plan was simple. It seemed to depend more on hope than on calculation. Rebels in Van were to occupy and hold Armenian sections of the city and await the arrival of a force from Iran, which would seize the entire city. The revolutionaries must have expected that this would have sparked Russian intervention. Under no other circumstances does taking the city make sense. Surely the rebels could not have believed that they could defeat the entire Ottoman army. It is also possible, however, that they had no plan for what to do if the revolt was initially successful. Their planning may not have extended so far. That had been the case in the Zeytun, Sasun, and other Armenian revolts in the 1890s. It may have been the case in Van.

The 1896 Van rebellion began on June 3, but events had actually been occurring since October 1895. The Ottoman forces were very likely prepared for the outbreak. Van army commander Sadettin Paşa, in a long report on the revolt, stated that there had been twenty-three revolutionary incidents in the region before the revolt began. His July 23 report: "Revolt was prepared before these events. The rebels made barricades from trees they had knocked down and from mud brick [adobe] up to the Dere Church, to the Protestant Missionary Building, to the Nurşin Mahalle, to Tepebaşı, to Haçboğan from the Erek Church.... In this situation the Armenian mahalle became a fortified place that might have been designed by an army officer."[69] According to very similar reports from both Sadettin Paşa and Consul Williams,[70] on the night of June 2–3 rebels began to fire on Turkish soldiers who were walking on the outskirts of the Armenian Garden District. Soldiers and officers were wounded. Armenian houses had been fortified for the attacks.[71]

Williams, the British consul in Van, wrote:

> On 6 June, accompanied by the American missionary Dr. Regnault,[72] I saw two places defended by the rebels. I was greatly astonished at their methods of defence. They themselves said that they could hold out for ten days until reinforcements arrived from Iran. They included a number of American, Russian and Bulgarian nationals. There were altogether twelve to fifteen foreigners. The rebels totaled some six hundred. The Armenians are armed with Russian rifles. The rebels say that these weapons were brought in through Iran and that they obtained them with the help of the local Armenians. The members of the various revolutionary committees wear distinctive uniforms. I mention all this in order to demonstrate that the rebels have armed themselves with these weapons not in order to "protect their children" but to prepare for an insurrection. I have documents to prove that a number of innocent Moslems have been killed for approaching, quite unwittingly, the rebel positions.[73]

Armenians who did not want to become involved with the rebellion put themselves under the protection of the English consul. On the night of June 8 the others did battle with Ottoman forces. Ottoman military observers reported that they were well armed with Russian rifles and firing from prepared positions.[74] When word came to them that the Armenian rebels had opened fire on Ottoman soldiers and civilians, Kurdish tribesmen asked if they should come to Van and join in the battle. Sadettin Paşa ordered them to draw back.[75]

It immediately became obvious that the rebels had no chance of success. Yet the soldiers, fearing a large loss of civilian lives, did not attack at first. Instead, the Sublime Porte asked the British, French, Russian, and Persian governments to appoint their consuls at Van as intermediaries between government forces and the rebels. This was done, and various schemes were drawn up. Terms were offered to the rebels. A settlement was to be overseen by European ambassadors and representatives of the sultan. A similar settlement had been offered to Armenian revolutionaries who had seized the Ottoman Bank in Istanbul earlier in 1896. That settlement allowed the rebels to go free. In the case of Van, however, the government demanded that the ringleaders receive some form of punishment. The Van rebels refused the terms.[76] Ottoman forces then took one of the Armenian outposts. The ease with which this was done seems to have convinced the rebels that they would easily be defeated.[77]

Fire from the Armenian fortifications diminished on June 9–10. The largest part of the rebel force fled.[78] The rebels had learned that the reinforcements that had been expected to come to their aid from Iran had in fact returned to Iran.[79] They had been cut down when they attacked tribes and villages on their route to Van. Other rebels had been apprehended at Çatak. Sadettin Paşa stated that 340 Muslims and 219 Armenians had been killed in the rebellion in the city. Williams estimated 500 casualties, of whom 300 were Muslims.[80] In the following days fighting continued between Armenian rebels and soldiers and tribesmen in the villages and districts of the province. The rebels were particularly active in Erciş, Abak, and Erçek regions, where Muslim villagers were killed;[81] but Armenian villagers were undoubtedly the main victims in the countryside, attacked by Kurdish tribes. Including both city and country, Sadettin Paşa listed 418 Muslim and 1,715 Armenian dead and 363 Muslim and 71 Armenian wounded. Occasional fighting between Armenian armed elements from Iran and Ottoman soldiers and tribes also continued until the fall of 1897.[82]

The Ottoman forces acted well in the rebellion, a tribute to their commander, Sadettin Paşa. Even the American missionaries (no friends to the Ottomans) admitted as much. When their mission property had come under threat from the rebels, soldiers had protected it. The missionaries naturally praised the action as well as the way in which the soldiers kept the peace during and after the rebellion.[83]

The revolutionaries obviously had not been prepared for any sort of successful rebellion. This would make sense if their sole purpose was to spark reprisals and bring European intervention. It is probably also true, however, that the naiveté and inexperience of the rebels caused them to overestimate their chances of success. Immediately before the Van rebellion, the rebels seem to have been almost intoxicated with their assumed success. Armed rebels roamed the Armenian Quarter of Van, even killing

Ottoman soldiers. Few of these rebels (probably no more than very young men with little leadership) seem to have been well trained or skilled in use of their weapons.[84]

THE COUNTRYSIDE

The troubles in Van extended throughout the province, especially to the south and west of the city.[85] As expected in the rebel plan, Kurdish tribes attacked Armenian villages, stealing sheep and murdering and terrorizing the inhabitants. The motive, as always, was gain at the villagers' expense, but there was also a strong element of revenge. The Armenian rebels had attacked Muslim villages on their retreat from Van.[86] Large numbers of Armenians were killed in the vicinity of Erciş, on the path of the retreating revolutionaries, and many Armenians of Erciş fled temporarily to Iran.[87] Armenian villages were also raided in the Çatak region, which had taken part in the rebellion. Armenians nowhere near the rebellion or the retreat also suffered.[88] The circumstances were very mixed, though: while some Kurdish chiefs raided Armenian villages, others protected them.[89] Further Armenian attacks on Kurdish tribes (see below) exacerbated the situation.

The government brought further reinforcements to Van from other provinces, both to protect against further incursions and to keep peace in the city. Şemsi Paşa, the governor, was successful in using persuasion and troops to stifle agitation among some Muslims for an attack against Armenians, who, it was felt, awaited the invaders.[90] Small bands of revolutionaries continued to roam Van Province attacking Kurds, but by the end of August the danger of invasion from Iran, massacre, and countermassacre was largely over.[91]

BORDER RAIDS AND COUNTER-RAIDS IN 1897

Armed conflict between Muslims and Armenians on the borders of Van Province continued after the failure of the Van rebellion. The concentration of revolutionaries in Iran had been defeated by Kurdish tribes. The Van revolt had failed, but the revolutionaries planned to take revenge on the Kurds. In May 1897 the British consul in Van, G. S. Elliot, visited revolutionaries who were forming in Salmas. He received information that they were to attack the Kurds in June.[92] The attacks actually came in August.

The Russians may have been involved in the 1897 attacks. It is impossible to verify the truth of the intelligence, but it was reported in April

1897 that letters from Tiflis had been intercepted, saying that the Russians would provide arms, money, and men to Armenian revolutionaries in Iran if "there is no change in the situation."[93] Events—especially the presence of Russian army officers (perhaps Russian Armenian) and modern Russian weapons in the ensuing Armenian action—indicate that this Russian support was likely.

Armenian revolutionaries from western Iran continued to harass Kurdish border settlements and attempted to mount incursions in force into Ottoman territory in early August of 1897. The number and attacks of these revolutionaries are confused in the diplomatic correspondence, but the attacks were significant. In one action a Persian force was sent to western Iran to punish Shikak Kurds for raids. Armenian revolutionary units joined the Persians, with the agreement of the Persian officers. The Persians themselves gained no significant results, but the Armenians passed over the border and attacked the Shikak Kurds on the Ottoman side. In one frontier village 40–50 Kurds were killed. The Armenians were a significant force, estimated by the Ottomans and consuls at 1,500–1,800, of whom 200 were mounted.[94] Another body of revolutionaries was expected to cross the border near Saray. Yet another group crossed the border at the same time, near Başkale. This force attacked one of the tribal clans, the Shekifti Shikaks, that had stopped the 1896 Armenian invasion in support of the Van rebellion.[95] One of their attacks, which took the encampment of Şeyh Kader by surprise, resulted in four hundred deaths (many women and children), as described by the British consul in Tabriz:

> On nearing the valley in which the encampment was situated, they stopped to tether their horses, and to partake of Holy Communion, and then proceeded to surround the Kurdish tents, which, owing to the season of the year, were open at the sides, and into which, at a concerted signal as the day broke on the 5th [of August 1897], they poured three volleys of rifle fire. Throwing down their guns, they then rushed in among the helpless Kurds with drawn swords, and put all they could reach—men, women, and children—to death, among whom the sheikh and his wife, who was dispatched by [the leader] Dr. Ohanian.
>
> It is calculated that at least 400 Kurds, of both sexes, lost their lives in this surprise....
>
> It is a fact worthy of note that the men composing the band [Armenian revolutionaries who attacked Kurds], whose desperate exploit I have just reported, are young fellows of good education, and generally of most respectable parentage.

A few belong to Tabreez, some come from Turkey, and many are from Russia.

Among those last are youths who have obtained temporary leave from the Russian army, and others deserters from the same, but all are armed with the latest pattern rifle, as I have already pointed out in past correspondence, and seem to find no difficulty in obtaining either arms or ammunition from the other side of the Arax [i.e., Russia].[96]

The Ottoman Army brought up reinforcements to fight alongside the tribal Kurds who were resisting the invaders, who were defeated and forced to withdraw into Persia. A Russian officer (possibly an Armenian officer in the Russian army) in Russian army uniform and some Persians in Persian army uniforms were found among the dead after the battle. The Persians had a significant force across the border, but they refused Ottoman requests to stop the retreating revolutionaries.[97] Şerif, the tribal overlord of the 400 massacred Kurds, gathered his forces and raided Armenian villages in Iran, killing more than 150.[98] It is doubtful if either the dead Armenians or the dead Kurds were anything but innocent villagers. Vengeance was seldom taken on those who had actually committed the crimes.

NOTES

1. FO 195/1846 Graves to Currie, Erzurum, May 3, 1894.

2. For examples from the large consular literature on the situation, see FO 195/1892, Hallward to Graves, Van, July 16, 1895; FO 195/1887, Hallward to Graves, Van, November 14, 1895; FO 424/184, Hallward to Currie, Van, November 6, 1895; FO 424/183, Hallward to Graves, Van, June 30, 1898. There is one great problem with the diplomatic literature of this time in particular, although it is found to some degree at all times: only Christian suffering is recorded, and much of that is hearsay. A good example of this is famine, for which copious evidence of Christian hunger was presented, but little or no evidence that Muslims were hungry as well. Yet famine was not selective by religion. Like famine and disease, Kurdish tribal raids were a plague for anyone who was vulnerable.

3. FO 424/184, Herbert to Salisbury, Constantinople, November 15, 1895.

4. FO 195/1376, Clayton to Trotter, Van 27 June 27, 1881.

5. FO 195/1315, Clayton to Trotter, Van, August 24, 1880. Armenians had undoubtedly turned their eyes to Russia since the 1877–78 war had demonstrated that Russia might at any time once again be in control of the Ottoman East. Consul H. C. A. Eyres was undoubtedly exaggerating, however, when he wrote that there were only two groups of Armenians in Van: those who sided with Russia and those who wanted independence (FO 195/1450, Eyres to Wyndham, Van, September 25, 1883). Eyres was given to overstatement (see note 11 below).

6. Consul Clayton felt that, although most Armenians did not wish to attach themselves to Russia, the Russian influence over the Armenians was increasing (FO 195/1376,

Clayton to Trotter, February 23, 1881; and FO 195/1376, Clayton to Trotter, March 8, 1881).

7. FO 195/1804, Devey to Fitzmaurice, Van, December 8, 1892.

8. FO 881/6447, Devey to Fitzmaurice, Van, December 8, 1892.

9. FO 195/1376, Clayton to Trotter, Van, June 27, 1881.

10. FO 195/1688, Devey to Lloyd, Van, December 6, 1880.

11. FO 195/1488, Eyres to Everett, Van, May 27, 1884. Eyres felt that ten thousand Kurds were on the move—surely a wild exaggeration.

12. One of the chief reasons why the government was able to stop raiding parties of Kurdish tribes was the engrained bravado of the tribal mentality. The tribes for centuries had been the masters of both Eastern Anatolia and western Iran. When they rode into the Ottoman Empire to raid, they rode in large groups, as they always had. Their arrival was often anticipated. Columns of horses needed roads or at least wide paths, which could be interdicted. The Armenian revolutionaries, in contrast, divided their forces, came across the border secretly in small groups on foot, then reformed. They were almost always on foot. Weapons smugglers used donkeys. Thus the Armenians could evade notice by the authorities.

13. Sami Önal, *Sadettin Paşa'nın Anıları* (Istanbul: Remzi Kitapevi, 2003), p. 83. These are Sadettin Paşa's handwritten memoirs, translated into modern Turkish by Önal.

14. FO 195/2147, Tyrrell to O'Conor, Van, September 1, 1903. Tyrrell commented, "I think there is no government here."

15. On the virtual Armenian rule of the Salmas region, see FO 881/9548, Dickson to Lowther, Van, June 15, 1909, Enclosure 5, "Report on Frontier Question round Urumia and Salmas."

16. See chapter 5.

17. Sami Önal, *Sadettin Paşa'nın Anıları*, pp. 25, 93, 97, 105. "Dâhiliye Nezâreti Celîlesi'nden Vârid Olan 5 Haziran Sene 1312 Târih ve İki Yüz Doksan Sekiz Numaralı Tezkirenin Suretidir," in Hüseyin Nâzım Paşa, *Ermeni Olayları Tarihi*, 2 vols. (Ankara: Osmanlı Arşivi Daire Başkanlığı, 1998) (hereafter *Ermeni Olayları Tarihi*), vol. 2, pp. 245–47. See also the numerous examples of arms smuggling in FO 195/1863. From the consular evidence it appears that most of the smuggling before the 1896 revolt came from the north, the Russian-Ottoman border. It may be, however, that these were only records of those who were caught and that smugglers from Iran were likely to be successful (FO 195/1863, Hallward to Cumberbatch, Van, November 13, 1895). Sadettin Paşa seemed to feel that the Iran route was the more important. *Ermeni Olayları Tarihi* is an extremely valuable collection of Ottoman documents from the period of the 1890s troubles, covering in detail both conflicts and revolutionary organization.

18. "The doings of the Armenian revolutionary parties during the last four years, as well as the general oppression exercised on any pretext by a corrupt and imbecile Administration, have brought unrest, anxiety, and despair in their train, tending to the depopulation by flight of the best part of the people, and consequent ruin of a well-favored district" (FO 424/197, Wood to Durand, Kalassar, Salmas, November 7, 1898).

19. See chapter 5.

20. See FO 195/1315, Clayton to Trotter, Van, May 25, 1880.

21. FO 195/1887, telegrams from Hallward of February 16, March 1, November 22, and other dates, 1895. Consul Hallward was not a perspicacious observer and was seldom concerned with anything but troubles experienced by Armenians. He repeatedly reported

until the 1896 revolt that the Armenians would not rebel in Van. See FO 424/181, Hallward to Graves, February 2, 1895; FO 424/182, Currie to Kimberley, Constantinople, April 22, 1895.

22. FO 195/1863, Hallward to Cumberbatch, Van, October 2, 1895. On fights between tribes, see also the enclosures in FO 195/1728, Hampson to White, Erzurum, March 14, 1891.

23. FO 195/1887, Hallward to Graves, Van, November 14, 1895.

24. FO 195/1315, Clayton to Trotter, Van, February 11, 1880; FO 195/1521, Everett to Wyndham, Erzurum, January 12 and 16, 1885; FO 195/1488, Eyres to Everett, Van, March 16, 1884.

25. FO 195/1652, Devey to Chermside (Her Majesty's consul in Erzurum), Van, December 24, 1888. See FO 195/1846 Hallward to Graves, Van, July 31, 1894, on the government and tax collecting among the Nestorians.

26. FO 195/1315, Clayton to Trotter, Van, May 25, 1880. See also FO 424/210, Shipley to O'Conor, Erzurum, June 15, 1906; FO 881/6957, Currie to Salisbury, Constantinople, October 30, 1896; FO 881/6957, Williams to Currie, Van, October 27, 1896.

27. FO 424/187, Williams to Currie, Van, April 1, 1896; Report of the Ottoman Government in FO 424/187, Herbert to Salisbury, June 3, 1896.

28. FO 195/1315, Clayton to Trotter, Van, November 7, 1879. See also FO 195/1315, Clayton to Trotter, Van, August 24, 1880; and FO 195/1766, Graves to Ford, Van, July 26, 1892.

29. FO 424/184, Cumberbatch to Currie, Erzurum, December 13, 1895.

30. FO 195/1315, Clayton to Trotter, Van, August 24, 1880.

31. FO 195/1728, Devey to Hampson, Van, January 13, 1891. See also FO 424/169, Devey to Hampson, May 5, 1891.

32. The best description of the Hamidiye history is Bayram Kodaman, "Hamidiye Hafif Süvari Alaylar: II. Abdülhamid ve Doğu-Anadolu Aşiretleri," *Tarih Dergisi* 32 (1979): 427–80. See also Janet Klein, "Power in the Periphery: The Hamidiye Light Cavalry and the Struggle over Ottoman Kurdistan" (Ph.D. dissertation, Princeton University, 2002).

33. At least one foreign observer felt that the Hamidiye could be successful, but he wrote fairly soon after they were founded (FO 881/6447, Ford to Rosebery, Constantinople, October 28, 1893, "Memorandum by Colonel Chermside").

34. See, for example, A. Rawlinson, *Adventures in the Near East* (London: Melrose, 1924), pp. 210–18. Kurdish tribes were to provide safety for some of Van's Muslims during the Armenian Rebellion of World War I (see "The End in Van" in chapter 8). The Hamidiye as such had been disbanded in 1909, replaced by regiments based on district rather than tribe, but the Kurdish units in World War I were the direct descendants of the Hamidiye.

35. FO 195/2147, Tyrrell to O'Conor, Van, April 8, 1903.

36. Many Ottoman officials were never satisfied with the entire Hamidiye scheme, feeling that they were poor soldiers whose military contribution did not justify the problems they caused. By 1899 even the sultan, who had been the main backer of the Hamidiye, was beginning to doubt their effectiveness, although he did nothing to disband them (FO 424/198, Black to O'Conor, Constantinople, May 1, 1899).

37. Consul Tyrrell commented: "The Turks say the Hamidiye are 'irregular,' which they surely are" (FO 195/2147, Tyrrell to O'Conor, Van, December 24, 1903; see also FO 2147, Tyrrell to O'Conor, Van, April 2, 1903).

38. *History of the ARF,* pp. 21–22.

39. Ibid., p. 25.

40. The principality was later joined with Eastern Rumelia to become the Bulgarian Kingdom. See Ömer Turan, *The Turkish Minority in Bulgaria (1878–1908)* (Ankara: Türk Tarih Kurumu, 1998), pp. 15–78; McCarthy, *Death and Exile*, pp. 59–108. The Bulgarians had an advantage that the Armenians of Eastern Anatolia did not share: they were a much larger proportion of the population. Turan (pp. 79–118) and McCarthy (pp. 89–90, 108, 341–43) give slightly different estimations of the population.

41. See Anahide Ter Minassian, *Nationalism and Socialism in the Armenian Revolutionary Movement*, trans. A. M. Berrett (Cambridge, Mass.: Zoryan, 1984), pp. 17–19; William Langer, *The Diplomacy of Imperialism* (New York: Knopf, 1960), pp. 157–58.

42. FO 195/1729, Devey to Hampson, Van, July 20, 1891.

43. FO 195/1863, Hallward to Cumberbatch, Van, November 13, 1895; FO 424/184, Hallward to Currie, Van, November 6, 1895. There are far too many examples of Armenian attacks on Muslims in Hüseyin Nâzım Paşa's *Ermeni Olayları Tarihi* to list them here. For the Van Province, see, for example, entries in vol. 1 on pp. 132, 154, and 213 and in vol. 2 on pp. 236–43 on attacks in Van Province before the 1896 revolt.

44. FO 424/184, Cumberbatch to Currie, Erzurum, October 19, 1895.

45. FO 424/183, Currie to Salisbury, Constantinople, July 18, 1895. Mehmed Hocaoğlu, *Arşiv Vesikalarıyla Tarihte Ermeni Mezâlimi ve Ermeniler* (Ankara: Anda, 1976), pp. 313–17, 331, 334–36, gives Sadettin Paşa's comments on some of the early attacks in Van and in the countryside from Ottoman Archives. Unfortunately, Hocaoğlu's documentation is incomplete, not listing full archival references. His quotations seem to be completely reliable, however.

46. FO 424/186, Williams to Currie, Van, January 26, 1896; FO 424/186, Currie to Salisbury, Constantinople, January 31, 1896; Ergünöz Akçora, *Van ve Çevresinde Ermeni İsyanları (1896–1916)* (Istanbul: Türk Dünyası Araştırmaları Vakfı, 1994), p. 103. The Armenian celebration of Theophany was on January 6 in the Julian Calendar, which accounts for the date.

47. See FO 424/184, Cumberbatch to Currie, Erzurum, October 21, 1895; FO 424/183, Currie to Salisbury, Constantinople, July 18, 1895; FO 424/181, Currie to Kimberely, Constantinople, January 15, 1895.

48. FO 424/184, Currie to Salisbury, Therapia, October 2, 1895; FO 424/187, Williams to Currie, Van, May 27, 1896, quoted in Muammer Demirel, *Ermeniler Hakkında İngiliz Belgeleri (1896–1918)/British Documents on Armenians* (Ankara: Yeni Türkiye, 2002), pp. 173–74.

49. FO 424/183, Halward to Graves, Van, June 4, 1895. FO 424/183 and FO 424/210 contain too many mentions of the smuggling of arms and men to list here. One interesting case was the attempt by 200 revolutionaries to cross the border into the Ottoman Empire. They came upon a Russian detachment, which tried to stop them, but the Armenians defeated the Russian soldiers and continued on (FO 424/210, O'Conor to Grey, Constantinople, May 29, 1906).

50. FO 424/184, Currie to Salisbury, Constantinople, October 9, 1895.

51. FO 195/1887, Hallward Telegram to Currie, July 25, 1887.

52. FO 424/183, Home Office to Foreign Office, London, July 6, 1895. Scotland Yard found that, while in London, Ohandjian had been living with Avedis Nazarbekian, the editor of the Hunchak newspaper *Huntchak*.

53. The complicity of the Russians in the revolutionary actions is unknown, but they

had been active in supporting rebels in Van since at least 1880. The Russian consul in Van at that time, Major Kamsaragan, himself an Armenian, was an ardent supporter of the revolutionaries. He even personally gave instruction in weapons and tactics to the rebels. It is impossible that he was acting without the approval of his government (FO 424/107, Clayton to Trotter, Van, October 12, 1880; FO 424/122, Goschen to Granville, Constantinople, March 17, 1881; FO 424/122, Biliotti to Granville, Erzurum, March 5, 1881).

54. Quoted in Demirel, *Ermeniler Hakkında İngiliz Belgeleri,* p. 125.

55. Mayewsky, *Van, Bitlis, Vilâyetleri Askerî İstatistiği* (Istanbul: Matbaa-i Askeriyye, 1330), pp. 189–90.

56. Great Britain, Parliament, *Turkey No. 8 (1896),* no. 117, enclosure 1, quoted in Kamuran Gürün, *The Armenian File* (London: Rustem and Weidenfeld and Nicolson, 1985), p. 155.

57. Information on the European plans and conflicts is found in Langer, *The Diplomacy of Imperialism,* pp. 196–210. Langer is trustworthy only on the larger events of European diplomacy, for which he is very thorough. His book was originally published in 1935, however, and little updated in later editions. The relevant archival records were not open to him, which is especially evident in his coverage of the Ottoman Empire.

58. Previously, in 1894, Archibald Primrose, Lord Rosebery, had suggested allowing the Russians to seize Eastern Anatolia.

59. The Triple Alliance of Germany, Austria-Hungary, and Italy.

60. The deputy governor took up his job just as the rebellion began. Williams commented: "His appointment has been received with complete apathy by both Muslims and Christians" (FO 424/188, Van, June 7, 1896).

61. FO 424/186, Williams to Currie, Van, March 4, 1896.

62. FO 424/187, Williams to Currie, Van, April 30, 1896.

63. FO 424/187, Williams to Currie, Van, April 1, 1896; Report of the Ottoman Government in FO 424/187, Herbert to Salisbury, June 3, 1896.

64. FO 424/186, Williams to Currie, Van, March 4, 1896.

65. Ibid. The "tyrant" was Abdülhamit II, the "Commission" the Ottoman commission sent to investigate after the Zeytun and Sasun troubles. For further examples of Armenian revolutionary poems/songs, see Hüseyin Nâzım Paşa's *Ermeni Olayları Tarihi,* vol. 2, pp. 266–67 and 285–99.

66. FO 424/210, Geary to O'Conor, Bitlis, December 26, 1905. British ambassador Philip Currie had notified the Foreign Office in July 1895 that reliable sources had told him that the Armenian Committees were "determined to provoke another massacre" (FO 424/183, Currie to Salisbury, Constantinople, July 18, 1895).

67. FO 424/182, Kimberley to Durand, Foreign Office, April 18, 1895.

68. "Van Valisi Nâzım Paşa'nın Müfettiş Şakir Paşa'ya 13 Kasım 1311," in Hocaoğlu, *Arşiv Vesikalarıyla,* p. 331.

69. Başbakanlık Osmanlı Arşivi, Hariciye Arşivi, Hazine-i Evrak, Klasör 313, Dosya 69.

70. *Turkey No 8 (1896),* no. 337, enclosure 1, quoted in Gürün, *The Armenian File,* pp. 155–56; BOA (Başbakanlık Osmanlı Arşivi, Prime Minister's Ottoman Archives), Hariciye Arşivi (HR, Ministry of Foreign Affairs), Hazine-i Evrak, Karton 313, Dosya 69. Abbreviations for Ottoman archival documents from the BOA are found at the Ottoman Archives web site: http://www.devletarsivleri.gov.tr/yayin/osmanli/rehber_osm/0002_2_belgetasn.htm.

71. "Van Vilâyeti Aliyyesinden Vârid Olup Dâhiliye Nezâreti Celîlesi'nden bâ-

Tezkire Gönderilen 3 Haziran Sene 1312 Târih ve Şifreli Telgrafnâmenin Suretidir," in *Ermeni Olayları Tarihi*, vol. 2, p. 244. The best descriptions of the 1896 rebellion are those of Sadettin Paşa and other officials. See Sami Önal, *Sadettin Paşa'nın Anıları*, and "Ferik Sa'âdetlü Sa'deddin Paşa Hazretleri Tarafından Tanzim Olunup Dâhiliye Nezâret-i Celilesi'nden Takdim Kılınan Lâyihanın Suretidir," in *Ermeni Olayları Tarihi*, vol. 2, p. 359–70. See also Hocaoğlu, *Arşiv Vesikalarıyla*, pp. 338–45.

72. This should be Raynolds, not Regnault.

73. Esat Uras, *The Armenians in History and the Armenian Question* (Istanbul: Documentary Publications, 1988), p. 757. "These people were no patriots trying to defend their wives and children, but pure and simple rebels. I have ample proof that they murdered in cold blood unarmed and inoffensive Mahommedans, who were unfortunate enough to come near their positions" (*Turkey No. 6*, 1896, Williams to Herbert, Van, June 28, 1896, quoted in Salahi Sonyel, *The Ottoman Armenians* [London: Rustem, 1987], p. 207).

74. "Dâhiliye Nezâreti Celîlesi'nden Vârid Olan 5 Haziran Sene 1312 Târih ve İki Yüz Doksan Sekiz Numaralı Tezkirenin Suretidir," in *Ermeni Olayları Tarihi*, vol. 2, pp. 245–47.

75. Akçora, *Van ve Çevresinde Ermeni İsyanları*, p. 112.

76. FO 424/187, Herbert to Salisbury, Constantinople, June 21, 1896 (nos. 225, 226). Unfortunately the British chargé d'affaires in Istanbul, Michael H. Herbert, was generally ignorant of both the workings of the Ottoman government and the situation in Van, preferring to rely on his "sources" in Istanbul rather than on his consul in Van. He gave little support to the efforts of Consul Williams to conciliate, at first forbidding him any role whatsoever. On June 19 Herbert first telegraphed London that the Porte would never accept Great Power mediation then had to telegraph again the same day, stating that the Porte had asked for that mediation (FO 424/187, Herbert to Salisbury, Constantinople, June 19, 1896 [nos. 217, 218, 222]). Herbert showed his misunderstanding of the Van situation by telegraphing London of the imminent danger in Van. One reason for this, as Herbert's private sources told him, was that Sadettin Paşa had been bought off by "the Kurds" for 500 lira! Three days later the Armenians left the town, and the rebellion was over (FO 424/187, Herbert to Salisbury, Constantinople, June 17, 1896; FO 424/187, Herbert to Salisbury, Constantinople, June 22, 1896).

77. FO 881/6958, Williams to Currie, Van, March 14, 1897. Williams commented that the report of Consul-General Cecil Wood published in the British *Blue Book* on the troubles was wrong in many particulars.

78. The Armenian districts of the Van Garden City were honeycombed with tunnels and holes in the walls that surrounded the houses. These facilitated the escape of rebels in both 1896 and 1908. See FO 195/2147, Tyrrell to O'Conor, Van, January 31, 1903.

79. Although the main group of revolutionaries was stopped, small groups successfully crossed the border and made it to Van (FO 424/195, Elliot to Curry, Van, January 10, 1898). While most of this report is hearsay, it does appear that small groups did pass.

80. Gürün (*The Armenian File*, p. 155–56) and Salahi Sonyel (*The Ottoman Armenians*, p. 208) list the same source for the statements by Sadettin Paşa and Consul Williams: BOA, Hazine-i Evrak, carton 313, document no 69, August 9, 1986; and *Turkey No. 8 (1896)*, no. 337, enclosure 1.

81. For example, see the following entries in *Ermeni Olayları Tarihi*, vol. 2: "Dâhiliye Nezâreti Celîlesi'nden Vârid Olan 6 Haziran Sene 1312 Târih ve Üç Yüz İki Numaralı Tezkirenin Suretidir" (p. 248); "Dâhiliye Nezâreti Celîlesi'nden Vârid Olan 24 Haziran

Sene 1312 Târih ve Üç Yüz Altmış Altı Numaralı Tezkirenin Suretidir" (p. 300); "Dâhiliye Nezâreti Celîlesi'nden Vârid Olan 9 Temmuz Sene 1312 Târih ve Dört Yüz Kırk Dört Numarah Tezkirenin Suretidir" (p. 304); "Ferik Sa'âdetlü Sa'deddîn Paşa Hazretleri Tarafından Tanzim Olunup Dâhiliye Nezâret-i Celîlesi'nden Takdîm Kılınan Lâyihanın Suretidir" (pp. 359–70). See also Hocaoğlu, *Arşiv Vesikalarıyla,* pp. 345–48, for a more complete list of the troubles in the various regions of the province.

82. Akçora, *Van ve Çevresinde Ermeni İsyanları,* pp. 115–22.

83. ABC 16.10.1, Constantinople Archives, vols. 5–6, Papers on Religious Freedom and the Armenian Situation.

84. See FO 424/187, Williams to Currie, Van, March 11, 1896.

85. FO 881/6959, Elliot to Currie, Van, November 2, 1897.

86. FO 424/187, Herbert to Salisbury, Constantinople, June 24, 1896. Williams was of the opinion that the revolutionaries who had escaped from Van all were killed in battles with Ottoman troops, including Hamidiye, before they reached safety but gave no evidence to support this (FO 881/6957, Williams to Currie, Van, September 15, 1896). The *History of the ARF* (pp. 25–27) states that a thousand combatants were killed at the Iranian border, again giving no source. That estimate seems incredibly high.

87. FO 881/6957, Williams to Currie, Van, September 15, 1896. Williams estimated that 3,500 Armenian villagers were massacred by Kurds but gave no explanation for his figures. Judging from similar estimates, this was probably a large exaggeration, but the mortality was surely high.

88. FO 881/6957, Williams to Currie, Van, November 11, 1896.

89. FO 881/6957, Williams to Currie, Van, September 15, 1896.

90. FO 881/6959, Elliot to Currie, Van, August 11, 1897.

91. FO 881/6959, Elliot to Currie, Van, August 24, 1897; FO 881/6957, Williams to Currie, Van, October 6, 1896.

92. FO 424/191, Currie to Salisbury, Constantinople, June 2, 1897.

93. FO 424/191, Williams to Currie, Van, April 5, 1897.

94. FO 881/6959, telegram from Elliot in Van in Currie to Salisbury, Constantinople, August 8, 1897; see also FO 881/6959, Currie to Salisbury, Constantinople, August 18, 1897, which forwards a telegram from Elliot in Van giving slightly smaller numbers. The situation was extremely confused, and Elliot may have been describing other incursions. The British had been advised earlier that the incursion was in the offing (FO 881/6958, Currie to Salisbury, Constantinople, June 2, 1897).

95. Missionaries in Iran had reported that the tribe had killed eight hundred Armenians fleeing Iran, but their report seems to have been based on hearsay and was very unreliable (FO 424/188, Woods to Durand, Tabriz, July 16, 1896).

96. FO 881/6959, Wood to Hardinge, Tabreez, August 15, 1897. Wood reported that the Armenians were "adherents of the two Armenian Societies, the 'Tashnacsagan' and 'Hunchakian.' " Wood's account from the Persian side of the border was corroborated from the Ottoman side by the consul at Van (FO 881/6959, Elliot to Currie, Van, August 11, 1897) and by an Ottoman Commission of Inquiry (in FO 881/6959, Currie to Salisbury, Constantinople, September 23, 1897). See also *History of the ARF,* pp. 49–51, which states that the Armenian unit had 253 men, of whom 20 were killed.

97. FO 881/6959, Currie to Salisbury, Constantinople, August 10, 1897. See also FO 881/6959, Currie to Salisbury, August 12, 1897; FO 881/6959, Currie to Salisbury, August 13, 1897. The Ottomans sent a strong protest to the Persian government, which promised

to punish the officers and stop the Armenian revolutionaries; but there is no record of anything being done except the arrest of seven of the raiders (FO 881/6959, Hardinge to Salisbury, Gulhek, August 17, 1897; FO 881/6959, Wood to Hardinge, Tabreez, August 26, 1897). For an Ottoman view, see the "Circular from the Sublime Porte," in FO 881/6959, Currie to Salisbury, Constantinople, August 16, 1897.

98. FO 424/196, Elliot to Currie, Tabreez, May 5, 1898.

CHAPTER 5

Development of the Revolution, 1897–1908

After the 1896 rebellion Van governor Bahri Paşa requested substantial funds and reforms from the central government. He asked for enough money to place the province on a sound financial footing. In his plan, the cavalry regiment that had been sent to Van during the 1896 revolt was to be permanently stationed there, and the governor was to be given control over the troops. The Hamidiye, in particular, were to be controlled. They were to be put under civilian control unless they were mobilized in time of war.[1] The central government allowed Bahri Paşa to keep some of the cavalry. His other requests were not successful. Few soldiers and only limited funds were available for Van. The empire fought against an insurrection in Crete in 1896–97 and a war with Greece in 1897. Defense was needed, as always, on the border with Russia. The Hamidiye had powerful supporters in the palace and the military who protected its independence. And the centuries-old Ottoman policy of dividing power in the provinces between the military and the civilian was not easily changed. A new governor, Şemsettin Bey, was appointed to replace Bahri Paşa in May 1897, but he resigned on his way to take up his post when the central government notified him that he would not be receiving the support that he felt was essential.[2]

Nevertheless, by 1900 conditions had improved throughout the province. This was partly the result of government action. Even though the numbers of additional soldiers sent to Van were limited, they were enough to make some headway in limiting tribal raids on the settled, especially in the regions closest to Van City. Many animals taken from villagers during the 1896 troubles were restored.[3] Troops had been sent to new outposts near the camps of some notorious tribes, such as the Haydaranlı under their chief, Hüseyin, in Patnos. The weather had cooperated, and a good harvest was expected. Van suffered somewhat from an inflated price of bread,[4] but agricultural conditions were as good as could be expected.

Some progress was made on reform of the provincial administration. An Armenian assistant to the governor, with rank above all but the governor, was named. An attempt was made to bring Armenians into the police force. It initially foundered because the Armenians refused to serve without promptly paid salaries as the Muslims had long done, but by 1903 some Armenians had been enrolled.[5] Judicial inspectors arrived from Istanbul and made changes in the court system and prison. A dubious "reform" of amnesty for convicted rebels was promulgated.[6] The Van government did what little it could to ameliorate the suffering caused by the revolt. Taxes were remitted on the condition that villages provide animals and sheep to those who had suffered in the troubles. The animals, it was known, would be the same sheep and oxen stolen previously by the tribes, and they would more likely be loaned at high interest than donated, but the government was essentially powerless to control the tribes. Only in villages close to the city and to military outposts was the scheme a real success. These villages were also given 352 head of cattle brought from Iran by the government, as well as seed for planting and oxen to draw plows. There was no money to do more.[7]

Although the officials the government sent to Van were by no means all competent and honest, foreigners spoke well of most of the governors of Van, especially Tahir Paşa (governor from 1898 to 1906). They recognized that the governors had to deal with nearly insurmountable obstacles. Politics, particularly conflicts between the civilian and military branches of government, caused the government to speak with many voices.[8] The main problem was financial. The proceeds of richer provinces paid for defense and for the operation of the central government, and they were never sufficient for that. Van was expected to pay for itself. The province could not do so. The governor of Van Province stated in 1907 that the theoretical tax proceeds from Van were 105,000 lira and that the expenditures were 115,000 lira, leaving 10,000 lira to be made up from Istanbul, but the 10,000 was never sent. A deficit of 10,000 might have been managed, but the actual proceeds from tax collection were far short of the theoretical proceeds: 60,000 lira were actually collected, not 105,000.[9]

The governor spoke of 1906, but the situation was the same every year. The problem was intractable: although soldiers were needed to enforce tax collection, money was first needed to pay soldiers. Instead of hiring needed new soldiers, however, the government could not even pay those it had. Consul Williams wrote in 1897: "The administration is, however, most seriously crippled for want of money. Even the highest officials have not been paid for as much as eight months. The patience of the soldiers and zaptiehs [gendarmes] appears to me marvelous under the circumstances."[10] The soldiers were not always so passive. They rioted in Van in 1904 because they had not been fed, much less paid, and were hungry.[11]

The problem of collecting taxes was compounded by the difficulties of surviving in Van's harsh environment. Taxes were primarily collected from farmers and herders, who often were in the grips of famine. The greatest complaint of both Christians and Muslims was that taxes robbed them of what they needed to live. Some of this was the constant protest of taxpayers, but much of it was reality.[12] Reform measures, such as sending out salaried government tax collectors accompanied by troops, instead of entrusting tax collection to Kurdish chiefs, were successful but could not collect much when the people had so little.[13] Consul Williams in Van reported that in 1897 the governor wished to alleviate the suffering in Armenian villages (and presumably also in Muslim villages, although Williams did not mention them) that were in danger of starvation but that he had great difficulty in a climate in which officials were not paid and the government was virtually bankrupt. If the officials did not collect taxes, they themselves were likely to starve.

> The Vali issued orders that no taxes were to be taken from any family where there were no more than four measures of corn per head, as well as the necessary amount for seed. These orders were not obeyed. The zaptiehs [gendarmes] and officials are themselves in a state of the greatest penury, and it is not in human nature that they should not squeeze out all they can. Seeing the futility of this order, the Vali has, at my request, excepted absolutely the kazas of Hijish [sic] and Shattakh [Çatak], together with seven other villages, from all taxes until next harvest.[14]

The *bedel* (the military exemption tax, paid by non-Muslims in lieu of military service) was remitted for two years in both Van and Bitlis because of the poverty of the Armenians and, undoubtedly, in an attempt to restore loyalty after the recent revolts.[15] The lack of that traditional source of income, however, exacerbated an already impossible financial situation. In citing the need for further troops in Van Province to put down raiding Kurds, Consul Williams commented that the Van government had no money to pay them: "This money question is becoming terribly serious. There is no money at Van, and no prospect of any. It is all very well to remit the 'bedliat,' but its equivalent in cash should have been sent at the same time."[16] The consul did not mention where the central government was to find the funds.

KURDISH TRIBES

As always, the Kurdish tribes took advantage of government weakness. Kurdish tribes in Bitlis Province fought each other, attacked gendarmes, and raided cattle from Muslim and Christian villages.[17] Kurdish tribes in the south of Van Province and the north of Mosul Province raided and killed in Kurdish and Nestorian villages, preying on both Muslims and Christians.[18] The powerful Şemdinan şeyh Mehmet Sadik drew members of many tribes to his command through force and even attacked the Barzan tribe, which was led by another respected religious leader.[19] North and northwest of Lake Van, Armenians who had fled to Russia and returned were preyed upon by the Haydaranlı tribe.[20] As always, the tribes took advantage of the Ottoman-Iranian border, raiding in one country then escaping to the other. The Persian government's control of its western provinces only applied in larger cities, and often not even there. In 1900 seven hundred Haydaranlı Kurds under a Persian Haydaranlı chief, Tahir Khan, attempted to raid across the border into the Ottoman Empire near Saray. Tahir and two of his nephews were killed by Ottoman troops, but most of the Kurds fled back across the Iranian border. Exasperated Ottoman troops violated the border to follow them. The Persians complained but did nothing themselves to stop the Kurds (or the Ottoman troops).[21]

If the Kurdish tribes had ever united against the government, their armed force would have far outnumbered anything that could be fielded by the state; but at the end of the nineteenth century such unification was unlikely. Rather than unite, the tribes were further splintering. Various tribes engaged in internal struggles for leadership that diverted them from attacking others.[22] Adding to the anarchy of the Kurdish tribes, the old system of paramount tribes was failing, especially in the southeast. There was an ongoing process of tribal disintegration, as small "tribes" separated from larger ones. Sometimes a tribe would gather temporary strength and absorb smaller groups, but it usually would break apart again when a strong leader died or the tribe lost in battle. Fights between these small groups were almost constant.[23] This meant that any large-scale tribal threat to the state was minimal but also that the tribal conflicts increased the threat to civil order. Government attempts to curtail this disorder were ongoing. They sometimes resulted in major battles. The Ottomans fought one such series of actions in the Siirt region. Kurds who had been responsible for raids against the settled population held out against troops until the latter brought up artillery to bombard fortified villages.[24]

In the late 1890s the government began to improve the security in the Van Province with mixed but real results. Soldiers were sent to defend Armenian villages from tribes.[25] The Ottomans responded to tribal raids in southern Van Province by sending regular troops to Hakkâri Sancak to protect the Nestorians. They succeeded in keeping the area quiet, at least for the time being.[26] Troops opposed incursions by Persian Kurds.[27] They even used artillery to bombard the fortified villages of raiding tribes.[28] In 1900 the government gained a victory when regular troops captured Şerif, the leader of the Shekifti subtribe of the Shikak Kurds and long-standing plague for both the government and the Armenians, in a bloody battle in the Albak region near Başkale.[29] But Şerif was released, perhaps because of his Hamidiye connections, and went back to raiding and robbing caravans to Iran.[30] A problem that was to bedevil the province until World War I began in the late 1890s: Kurds had taken over the villages and homes of Armenians who had fled during the troubles of 1894–96, claiming, often correctly, that those who fled were rebels and that their land should be confiscated. The Van governor made a start on returning some villages, but success in the effort was to be very limited until after 1908.[31]

Beginning in 1898, the government made a start on collecting taxes from the Kurdish tribes and asserting government authority, with some success and some defeats.[32] Some tribes openly and flagrantly opposed the law. In August 1897 Kurds of Modeki in Bitlis Province killed the *kaymakam* (district governor) of Modeki, probably over the collection of taxes. Assisted by tribesmen who came to their aid, they then killed five officers, three sergeants, and eleven men of a unit sent to punish the perpetrators, scattering the rest of the troops. Their rebellion was not put down until the government sent a force with two batteries of mountain artillery.[33] More armed Kurdish villages in Bitlis refused to pay taxes in 1907 and drove away soldiers who were sent to collect them.[34] In the 1890s Şeyh Sadik of the Şemdinan District began a policy of simmering rebellion that was to continue until he died in 1907 and was then carried on by his son, Şeyh Taha.[35] He even attempted to assassinate the government's kaymakam of Şemdinan in 1900. Even though the kaymakam was able to fight off his assassins, receiving only a gunshot wound in his shoulder, the government had no choice but to reassign him.[36] The Ottomans were forced to adopt a cautious course toward Sadik and similar tribal leaders: trouble though they might be, their military services were thought to be needed in wartime. Consul Dickson commented on Sadik:

A certain sheik Saddig of Shamsdinan [Şemdinan], of whom I informed you in my No. 10 of December 1, 1906, may possibly give trouble in the future, as the Porte has telegraphed to the vali for information concerning him and asking why the Russian consuls of Urmi [Urmia] and Van have visited him. From what I gather he has been intriguing with the Russian consul of Urmi, asking for Russian protection and promising to place his money in a Russian bank, hoping through Russian influence to obtain possession of the estates in Persia forfeited from his Father sheik Obadullah [Ubeydullah]. It is probable that the vali will ask him to come to Van, and the chances are that he will then take refuge with the Russian consul at Urmi. He is now on the Persian frontier and not at his usual residence at Neri. As Your Excellency will be aware, he betrayed his father and elder brother to the Turkish government and thus usurped the succession. He is mean, avaricious and unscrupulous, a brigand, and although he enjoys a certain reputation as a sheik among people who have never met him, and who live at a distance, he is detested by his own people, and his banishment would be a good thing for the country. He does not like the Turkish government.[37]

NESTORIANS

The Nestorians took part in the troubles. Gangs of Nestorian bandits, just like Kurdish bandit gangs, disrupted the region and were beyond the control of the Nestorian leaders.[38] Different factions among the Nestorian ruling families vied for power, at least one faction being encouraged, and perhaps armed, by Russia.[39] Nestorians raided Kurdish villages, and Kurds raided Nestorian villages.[40] Each claimed that the raids were in response to past attacks by the other. It was not unusual for Nestorians and one group of Kurds to ally themselves in order to fight other Kurds.[41] In some cases each side in feuds and battles contained both Nestorians and Kurds.[42] The most violent feud was between the Nestorians and the Shekifti Shikak Kurds, led by Şeyh Sadik. Sadik's followers killed a Nestorian priest in 1897, a rare occurrence, since holy men were usually respected by all sides.[43] The Nestorians found allies in Kurdish tribes who had long been friendly with them or who had their own feuds with Sadik. One of these saved the Nestorian archbishop of Şemdinan, Sadik's home base, from murder by Sadik.[44] Nestorians even helped Kurdish tribes in battles against Ottoman troops.[45]

In 1902 and again in 1907 virtual wars erupted between the Nestorians of Tiari and certain Kurdish tribes. Sheep-stealing raids on one were followed by reprisal raids on the other. The governor attempted to bring peace in 1902. European pressure would never have allowed him to punish the Nestorian Christians, but he did arrest many Kurdish leaders. He did not have troops to stop the battles between the two sides but was able through diplomacy to bring them together and resolve their differences for a time. In 1907, though, the governor was to use troops to stop renewed fighting. The troops were routed by the Nestorians, who took their guns.[46] Forces sent against the Kurds were more successful.[47] Once again, peace was eventually restored. The governor in Van attempted repeatedly, and with little success, to bring the Nestorians and Kurds together for a "peace conference."[48]

Despite their state as generally unsophisticated mountaineers, the Nestorians proved to be particularly capable of exploiting European politics to gain support. They welcomed both British and Russian diplomats and spies, promising alliances that never occurred. Nestorians "converted" or threatened to convert to both Catholicism and Russian Orthodoxy. This happened so often that the same Nestorians must have been involved in various conversions.[49] The British were particularly anxious over the "conversions," as reported to the consuls by the archbishop of Canterbury's Mission to the Nestorians, who much preferred that the Nestorians remain Nestorian until they could be properly converted to Protestant Christianity. The British viewed the conversions as giving a foothold in the region to other European powers. The result was pressure from Britain on the side of the Nestorians in their eternal battles with the Kurds.[50] In one illustrative episode, Nestorians who had ostensibly converted to Russian Orthodoxy notified the British consul at Van that they could be convinced to reconvert to Nestorian Christianity if they were paid 200 lira. Both the consul and the British missionaries to the Nestorians felt this was an excellent idea, but the British ambassador refused to pay.[51]

ARMENIAN REVOLUTIONARIES

Consul Elliot wrote in 1898:

> As regards the revolutionists themselves, those who take an active part in what they consider the crusade against Turkey, may, I think, be justly divided into two classes. The professional Askaser (patriot) who dislikes regular honest work, and prefers a life of excitement and the role of a hero, while living on the funds of the Society, and the young man or lad who is induced by the story of his peoples' wrongs and a desire to emulate

the brave deeds which he hears of and which lose nothing in the telling, to devote himself to his country's cause.

Many of the former class are unscrupulous rascals, capable of any excess or ruffianism. They are more of a terror to their people than Kurds or Mahommedan officials. They quarter themselves on Christian villages, live on the best to be had, exact contributions to their funds, and make the younger women and girls submit to their will. Those who incur their displeasure are murdered in cold blood. The latter class deserves perhaps some pity, but when they place themselves in the power of the revolutionists they cease to be their own masters. They often belong to respectable and well-to-do families.

Many merchants and others who have no sympathy with the revolutionists and their wars are obliged to contribute to their funds, and would rejoice to see these societies broken up.[52]

The failure of the First Van Rebellion forced the revolutionaries to reevaluate.[53] Their attempt at rebellion naturally had drawn the attention of the European states, but it had in no sense been otherwise successful. Preparations for the earlier revolt had been made in secret by a small number of leaders confident that the people would rally to their cause, and this had proved unsatisfactory. The rebels had neither recruited widely nor transported a sufficient quantity of weapons to supporters. They had, however, learned their lesson.[54]

Even before the 1896 revolt the Dashnaktsutiun organization had been strongest among the Van revolutionaries,[55] although the Hunchak organization had been a force. Now, due to the failure of the rebellions in the 1890s and splits within the party, the Hunchaks dissolved into a minor force in Van and elsewhere in Anatolia, keeping their preeminence only in Cilicia. Leadership of the Armenian Revolution had passed definitively to the Dashnaks.

After the 1896 defeat the revolutionaries in Van were in disarray until the arrival of the Dashnak organizer Kisag (Vartkes Serengiulian) in 1901. He began to rebuild the Dashnak organization in the city. Vartan Shahbaz arrived in 1902 and Ishkhan (also called Vana Ishkhan, birth name Nigol Odabashian) and Goms ("The Doctor," Vahan Papazian) in 1903. Shahbaz and Ishkhan began to organize the region around Çatak. Aram Manukian (Sergei Hovhannisian) came in 1904. By 1905 they had been joined by other Dashnak organizers/officials: Roupen Der Minassian, Dikran, Maguetsi Mesrob, and Malkhas (Ardashes Hovsepian), as well as two Armenakans who joined the Dashnaks—Salman (Sarkis Parseghian) and Ghevond Meloian.[56] The Dashnak leaders divided operations: Aram, Dikran, and Sarkis organized Van City and the region to its north and east. Ishkhan, Shahbaz, and, for a brief time, Roupen Der Minassian organized the region to the south.[57] They were joined in 1908 by Arshak Vramian.

THE DASHNAK LEADERS

As revolutionaries left Van for other assignments and positions and duties in the cities were defined, leadership of the Dashnak organization in Van settled in the hands of those who were to lead it until World War I: Aram, Ishkhan, Vramian, and Papazian.[58]

Aram Manukian was born in Karabağ in the Russian Empire in 1879. He served the Dashnak Party as a labor organizer in 1902 then went to Kars, where he was a leader in a short-lived uprising against the Russians. Forced to flee Russia, he went to the Ottoman Empire. The party assigned him to Van in 1904. Manukian was a born leader and superb organizer and a committed nationalist. Aram's identity was uncompromisingly Armenian. Despite his years in the Ottoman Empire, he seems never to have learned to read and write Turkish.[59]

Ishkhan (Nicol Boghossian,[60] also known as Bayendour) was born in Karabağ in 1883. He was a Dashnak militant from an early age, studying with Aram Manukian in Shusha and Erivan. Ishkhan was active in Alexandropol and Kars before fighting in Sasun.

Arshak Vramian (Onnik Derdzakian, also known by the *noms de guerre* and pen names Vehab, Vahab of Vishab, Vahab-Varaz, Nerr, and Socrat) was unique among the Van leaders in that he was born in the Ottoman Empire, in Istanbul in 1871. He studied in a seminary in Echmiadzin and became a member of the Dashnak Central Committee, later becoming a Dashnak Party organizer in Bulgaria and Romania, a member of the Western Bureau of the party, and editor of the Dashnak newspaper, *Droshak*. From 1899 to 1907 Vramian organized the party in America, becoming an American citizen.[61] He came to Van in 1908.

Vahan Papazian (also known as Goms and "The Doctor") had been a Dashnak operative in the Caucasus. From 1900 to 1902 he stayed in Finland as a fugitive from the Russian authorities.

Bertram Dickson, the British consul in Van in 1908, was a great friend of the Armenians, although he wrote to his superiors that the revolutionaries did much more harm than good for the Armenian people. Dickson seems to have had excellent sources of information on the Dashnak revolutionaries. He met with them often, was sympathetic with their aims, if not their methods, and gave the best descriptions of their organization:

The Eastern Committee is at Tiflis, Place Erivan, next door to the "Typographie Georgienne" and the "Eglise Etchmiadzin." The principal members of this Committee are Dr. Hanno Auganginian, Yadishi Topgian, Abaak Vramian, and Armen Karo.

This Committee spreads the revolutionist propaganda in Russia, enrolls young Armenians for service if required, collects money, buys and steals arms and ammunition and passes them through to Turkey. As it also has charge of the Russian revolutionary movement in the Caucasus, to which, many of the terrorist atrocities and assassinations are due, it leaves the local Committee at Van a fairly free hand in Turkish affairs, except in questions of high policy, which are decided by the Eastern and Western Committees. It would appear that the permission of the Eastern Committee has to be obtained before assassinating Turkish officials.

In connection with the Eastern Committee, there are four local Committees in Turkey, with their head-quarters at Van, Moush, Erzeroum, and Trebizond. The two latter are pacific, and confine themselves to spreading the propaganda and collecting funds. At Moush there are two chiefs, one a Russian and one a Turkish Armenian.

Van is the most important revolutionary centre in Turkey, and here there are seven members of the Committee—four active, Aram, the Doctor, Sarkis, and Ishkhan; the other three are passive. The Committees of Moush, Erzurum, and Trebizond are subservient to the Van one.

In addition to the four chiefs above mentioned, there are at Van thirty armed revolutionary soldiers, of whom twenty-five are Russian and five are Turkish Armenians. During the winter, the whole of these "fedai" ["volunteers"][62] reside in Van, distributing themselves among the various in the Armenian quarter of the garden town, moving about only at night, and then only by the gardens and the by-paths, it is said that they never sleep two days running in the same house. Although practically every Armenian sympathizes in secret with them, many of the richer Armenians in Van find their presence inconvenient and compromising.

When spring makes the roads and hills practicable for traveling, unless they have any special object in hand, like the Moush and Sassun rebellion, the active "fedai" divide into bands under their four chiefs, each taking a district, which they tour, spreading their propaganda in the villages, enrolling names, collecting money, *selling* arms and ammunition to the villagers, teaching them to handle and shoot with the rifle, &c. Usually one of the chiefs remains at Van, and they keep up a constant communication by means of couriers between the bands of Van and Tiflis and thus can always concentrate if required.

In addition to these thirty soldiers, practically the whole male

Armenian population are enrolled as members of the Society, the younger as active members some with a rifle and cartridges hidden in their houses, the others to be supplied with them by the Committee when called out. The remainder are enrolled as passive members, and are made to contribute in various ways to the cause.

From statistics, which I have reason to believe are as accurate as can be obtained, I learn that at present the "fedai" Committee have hidden in and around Van sufficient arms for 1,000 men. At Salmas, on the Persian frontier, they count on 600 armed men. From Russia, in case of necessity, they count on 2,000 armed men. Thus altogether they have in Turkey, Persia, and Russia sufficient arms and ammunition for 3,000 men, while their supply of men to carry these arms is almost unlimited.[63]

Aram and Ishkhan, the two most prominent leaders of the Van Dashnak Committee, proved to be particularly good at organizing smuggling operations. Ishkhan developed a rapport with and understanding of the rural Armenians in the Çatak region, an area that was to become the center of Armenian rebellion during World War I.[64] Ishkhan was more an organizer and politician than a fighter, but Aram was proficient in both organization and battle. He led a band that fought with Ottoman troops at the Varak Monastery in 1907.[65] But his greatest contribution was the spread of the revolution throughout the province. As a necessary first step Aram organized what might be called "revolutionary education." He and his followers essentially took over the traditional teaching function of the Armenian Church and turned it to the purpose of revolutionary indoctrination and organization.

The Dashnak plan for Van included conquering the Armenian Gregorian Church. Many churchmen already were committed to the revolution.[66] The monastery at Derik, just across the Persian border, had for some time been a revolutionary stronghold and arms depot. Its abbot, Bagrat Vardapet Tavakalian, was himself a revolutionary with the *nom de guerre* Zakki.[67] Among the most noted revolutionaries was the priest Vartan (superior of the monastery of St. Garabed), who was a Dashnak worker in Sasun. The Armenian bishop of Bitlis in 1899 was a revolutionary sympathizer who (both the government and Consul Maunsell believed) had diverted relief funds to the revolutionaries.[68] As will be seen below, Van was also not without its revolutionary clergymen. Yet initially the clerical supporters of the Revolution were relatively few.[69] In fact, the Armenian Church leaders in Van were originally very much against the revolutionaries. As an integral part of the Ottoman system, the churchmen and merchants were naturally politically conservative. The avowed atheism of the revolutionaries cannot have appealed to them. Moreover, the revolutionaries were a potential power in the Armenian community, a new authority that would necessarily draw power from the traditional leaders of the community—the church and the merchants. When the Dashnak Party began to reassert itself in Van after the 1896 debacle, with threats to bankers and others to gain funds, the bishop and "several notables" approached the British consul to ask for advice on how to keep the revolutionaries from returning. His advice was useless, but the approach shows the intent of the traditional Armenian leaders.[70]

As seen in chapter 2, the Catholicosate of Akhtamar, centered on the island of the same name, included an extensive area to the south and southeast of the city of Van. The position of catholicos became vacant in 1895 and was never filled. The assets and activities of the catholicosate, including its educational system, remained in place until World War I. Authority passed to a priest who was nominally the deputy (*vekil*) of the nonexistent catholicos. Thus, until 1905, the religious situation in the region remained much as it had been.[71]

Early in November 1905 an armed band of revolutionaries, led by Ishkan of Van, climbed over the wall of the Hakkavank Monastery. They terrorized the monks and took away Arsen Vartabed (the vekil of Akhtamar) and his secretary. Their bodies were found the next morning. Arsen was killed because he had supported the government against the revolutionaries and because his position had great value to the Dashnaks. He had been particularly important as an intermediary between the government and the Armenian populace. Consul Tyrrell remarked: "His [Arsen's] real crime was that he recognized that the revolutionists are doing more harm than good, and that he would have nothing to do with them."[72] The lesson was learned by the religious authorities. In 1906 Daniel, a member of the Dashnak organization, was appointed vekil. He named Ishkhan and Aram as his deputies.[73] Aram became the inspector of Armenian schools. After their appointment the Akhtamar seminary abandoned religion as its primary purpose. Those who had led religious instruction were discharged and replaced with Dashnak sympathizers. Classes abandoned theology and became revolutionary training courses. Educators sent out from the seminary supposedly taught religion but in fact taught insurrection.[74] The American missionaries in Van were incensed that religion had come under the control of the Dashnaks, who as a group were avowedly atheistic. The mission head, Dr. Raynolds, stated in 1911: "A considerable part of this vilayet belongs to the Akhtamar Catholicate. For a long time that institution has been under the control of the infidel Tashnagists, who have had a school at that center, where the instruction has excluded all religious teaching and church attendance, and even been actively anti-religious."[75]

The revolutionaries had paid limited attention to the rural Armenians before the arrival of Aram and his comrades. A "weapons tax" had been collected from some Armenian villagers before the 1896 revolt, but there had been little attempt to organize them.[76] The "religious instructors" now became the spearhead of Dashnak rural organization. The system was inspired. The Ottomans would naturally interfere as little as possible with the "teachers," because of both their traditions of religious autonomy and fear of European pressure if they prosecuted men of religion. Dashnak organizers spent the years between 1906 and World War I in effective organization of the Armenian villages in the province. This control did not come without a certain amount of strife with traditional village leaders, but the Dashnaks won their internal battles.[77]

Assassination was a key part of the Dashnak Revolution. It served two purposes. First, it rid the Dashnaks of enemies who were a real or potential threat to their operations. These included Ottoman officials who were too effective (especially Armenians who by their very presence in the government demonstrated that Armenians could work within the state apparatus) and those who would, out of patriotism or self-interest, betray Dashnak plans. The chief of police in Bitlis was assassinated in 1898 by the revolutionaries;[78] and the head of the judiciary in Van was killed in 1907,[79] as were others (discussed below). The second purpose was perhaps more important. Assassination was a warning to those who wanted to support the government in the future or who did not want to support the revolutionaries. Assassination and threats of assassination were particularly effective as a tool to gain "revolutionary donations" from rich Armenians. They were by nature not fighters and could be swayed by threats. This was especially true after some who refused to pay were killed, *pour encourager les autres.*[80]

The Dashnaks began their assassinations in the 1890s in Istanbul. As the basic history of the Armenian Revolutionary Federation (hereafter *History of the ARF*) states:

Constantinople, the capital of the Ottoman Empire and a semi-European city, was of fundamental importance to the Dashnaktsutiun as a theater of operation for demonstrative activities and propaganda. It is in this light that we should view the "terrorist" activity that evolved from 1894 to 1896, when the Dashnaktsutiun assassinated Armenians who served the

Sultan and the Turkish government. Included among those were Maksoud Simon Bey, the spy Ardashes, police chief Haji Dikran, defrocked celibate priest Mampre Benlian, the surgeon M. Tutunjiev, and others.[81]

The most prominent Dashnak attempt at assassination failed when Sultan Abdülhamit II escaped a Dashnak bomb.

Revolutionary solidarity was enforced ruthlessly. Those who defected from the rebels' cause or created difficulties for them were killed. The *History of the ARF* comments that "the fedayees executed many Armenian informers and government collaborators."[82] For example, near Lake Van offenders were hanged, their bodies left by the road with signs indicating that they were traitors.[83] When the activities of a Russian Armenian band (led by a certain Kevork) in the Bitlis area were opposed by Armenian priests in villages, two priests were killed by the rebels.[84] In 1903 an Armenian informer in Van was assassinated.[85] An Armenian police agent in Van was assassinated by the revolutionaries in 1907 for the help that he had given the government in identifying weapons caches.[86] Of course only the murders of the prominent were recorded. The British consul in Van in 1903, Captain G. E. Tyrrell, felt that the assassinations were effective. Many hated the revolutionaries and would have informed on their organization and weapons caches if they had not been afraid for their lives.[87]

Consul Dickson in Van described the official and organized nature of revolutionary enforcement. The Dashnak Committee leaders in Van were empowered to conduct assassinations of Armenians or Muslims, except for government officials. Before killing an official, permission had to be received from the Central Committee in Tiflis.[88]

The revolutionaries did provide the Armenians with a psychological feeling of what today would be called "empowerment." There had not been an Armenian army for centuries. Now there was an Armenian armed force that drew the attention of the world. The Armenians had long been the subjects of great empires in which they were only one among many minorities. Now revolutionaries put first what they defined as the interests of the Armenians. The revolutionary definition of the Armenian national interest, however, looked to the future. In the present, revolutionary actions often resulted in increased suffering for village Armenians. Indeed, drawing the intervention of Europe through such suffering was the revolutionaries' intention.[89]

Like all other aspects of the Armenian revolt in the East, the picture of Armenian popular support for the rebels was confused. The revolutionaries in Van, now dominated by the Dashnak Party, were led by foreign subjects, directed from Tiflis in the Russian Empire.[90] However, they increasingly gained local support. Many of the Armenian youths in Van City had been largely committed to revolution since the 1870s.[91] By 1905, British observers felt, villagers were often in sympathy with the revolutionaries and offered their support willingly. Many other Armenian villages undoubtedly harbored the revolutionaries because they had no choice. If they did not support the rebels, they would suffer, because the rebels punished those who did not exhibit "solidarity."[92] In some cases, villagers fought alongside the rebels against Ottoman troops. In others they were silent bystanders. In either case the villagers suffered. When troops fought with the rebels, both innocent and guilty might be killed. Although it did not become government policy until World War I, villages that supported rebels were sometimes (not often) burned. This was especially true when troops had lost large numbers of men fighting the rebels in a village. At other times, the villagers were only called upon to feed and house soldiers fighting rebels in their area—a heavy enough price for those who were called upon to provision both the rebels and the soldiers. Offending villages might be looted, particularly if the rebels had been fighting Kurdish tribesmen.[93]

The Weapons of the Revolutionaries

The justification for arming Ottoman Armenians was open to interpretation: a matter of self-defense or rebellion, depending on the observer. While city dwellers had little real need of guns, villagers undoubtedly had uses for weapons. Armed villages were able to protect themselves and their sheep against bandits and Kurdish tribes. Many unarmed villages were dependent on the protection provided by the state (which in practice only applied to villages close to cities and military encampments) or on the protection of tribal overlords who "owned" the villages. Other unarmed villages, Muslim and Christian, were prey.

In this context, it was reasonable for the revolutionaries to provide weapons to Armenian villagers. The villagers who purchased weapons from the revolutionaries were indeed better able to defend themselves and sometimes even able to attack others against whom they had grievances. It must be noted, however, that even Armenian villagers who did not feel that they needed weapons were forced to buy them—and the weapons were expensive. With the weapons came de facto enrollment in the revolutionary cause. The revolutionaries did not provide the weapons without the commitment that the guns would be used someday for revolutionary purposes. "Self-defense" was a concept that had broad implications for the revolutionaries. In their eyes, the ultimate self-defense for Armenians was Armenian rebellion leading to Armenian rule, completely ignoring the deaths, both Armenian and Muslim, that would be necessary to attain the goal.

While there was an element of actual self-defense in the arming of villagers, the stockpiling of thousands of weapons in cities such as Van and depots throughout the Ottoman East was quite a different matter. Those weapons could only be the essentials of a bloody revolution. Given the worst scenario predicted by Armenians, if Muslims rose up in one or many regions and slaughtered Armenians, how could the weapons in Van be delivered in time to defend the helpless? Could the revolutionaries quickly have broken out their stores of weapons, carried them on carts or on their backs through cordons of Ottoman soldiers and gendarmes, and delivered them to Sasun, Başkale, or Muş? That was an impossibility. The weapons in the depots could only have been used as part of a planned uprising. They were to be used where they were stored.

In any case, the real massacres of Armenians in the 1890s had only begun when Muslims reacted to revolutionary actions—the killing of Muslims. The revolutionaries knew this, because they had been the instigators.

SMUGGLING ROUTES

The *History of the ARF* notes:

> Beginning with the time of the "Federation of Armenian Revolutionaries" [direct predecessor of the Dashnaktsutiun], Adrbadagan [Western Iran], especially the Tabriz-Salmasd-Makou triangle, was the main relay station for arms and armed bands in transit to Turkish Armenia, to Vasbouragan [Van]. Only later did the Kars-Pasen and Yerevan-Surmalu routes, especially the former, become equally significant. The advantage of Adrbadagan may be partly explained by the generally favorable attitude of the Persian authorities.
>
> Initially, the core of the "Tabriz Bureau" consisted of Hovnan Tavtian, Hovsep Ishkhan Arghoutian, and Nigol-Douman (Nigoghayos Der Hovhannisian), who had settled there as teachers. These main figures were assisted by Satenig Madinian (Dzaghig), Vartan (Sarkis Mehrabian), the father-superior of the monastery of Derik—Rev. Pakrad Tavakalian (Zakki)—Sevkaretsi Sako, Sarkis Ohanjanian (Farhad), Kalousd Aloyan (Darvish, Toros), Garo (Arisdakes Zorian), and others. In subsequent

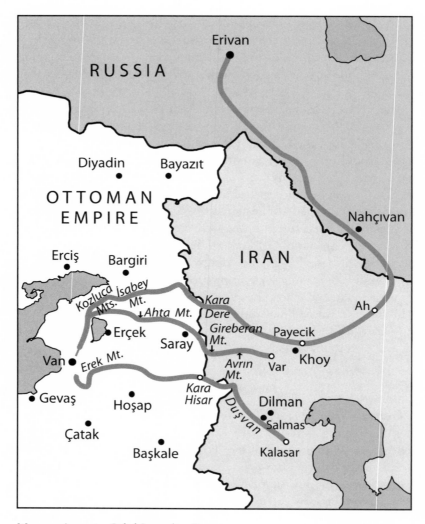

MAP 5.1. Armenian Rebel Smuggling Routes.

years, other notable Dashnak workers operated in Adrbadagan, including Stepan Stepanian (Balajan), Dr. Garabed Pashayan (Taparig), Samson Tadeosian (Karekin) and Armenag Okhigian (Slak).

Some of these workers (especially Toros, Garo, and Sako) constantly traveled to Russia to purchase gun parts and ammunition and transport them to Tabriz and Salmasd, where, in the ARF's workshops, the weapons would be assembled. Others (especially Hovsep Arghoutian, Nigol-Douman, Vartan; Farhad) often traveled as far as Van, personally carrying out the work of transporting arms and ammunition, usually at the head of arms-transport and fedayee bands. They frequently engaged Turkish forces and bands of Kurds in battle; of these encounters, the battles of Boghaz-Kyasan and Derik, led by Nigol-Douman, are well-known.[94]

Ensuring the security of the weapons smuggling routes was one of the most important conditions, perhaps the most important condition, for the success of the Armenian Revolution.

The weapons that were used by the Armenian revolutionaries primarily came from the Russian Empire.[95] Rifles, pistols, cartridges, and dynamite entered the Ottoman Empire from the north, into Erzurum Province, and from the east, through Iran into Van Province. The Iranian route, although much longer, was by far the safer one. Russians patrolled the Ottoman border much more carefully than they did the border with Iran, and the Iranians barely patrolled their border at all. The revolutionaries had virtual control of parts of the Salmas-Dilman region, where they could store weapons and plan their forays into the Ottoman Empire.

In later periods rifles, pistols, and ammunition were brought intact and in large numbers directly from Russia through Iran and into Van Province. In the 1890s, however, the smugglers were forced to be more circumspect. Arms and ammunition were freely sold in the bazaars of Russian Transcaucasia. Armenians were especially able to purchase them in Tula and Tiflis, sites of Russian armories. Because there were laws against the exporting of weapons, rifles were broken down and smuggled across the Russian-Iranian border in carts under merchandise or produce. Russian border guards were bribed or perhaps told by officials to look the other way, as it is difficult to believe such a ploy could otherwise have been successful. Armenian craftsmen who had worked in the Tula weapons plant reassembled the weapons in weapons factories in Tabriz, Salmas, and elsewhere. They were then stored or sent on for use in Eastern Anatolia.[96]

Armenian weapons smugglers encountered the first real danger as they crossed the Ottoman border. Kurdish tribes on both sides of the border were a potential threat to the smugglers. Weapons were valuable, well worth fighting the smugglers, and the Armenian revolutionaries were enemies of many but by no means all of the tribes.[97] Also, unlike the Iranians, the Ottomans did patrol their borders. They were particularly watchful for incursions by revolutionaries. In light of the danger, the revolutionaries adopted two policies to protect their shipments. The first was to enforce strict security measures. The smugglers used Armenian villages as outposts and depots. Villagers were their eyes and ears in the region, reporting on movements of troops and tribes. Smugglers waited in border villages until night then crossed with the help of local guides to the nearest Armenian village on the Ottoman side. They would pass from Armenian village to Armenian village, always traveling by night, dressed incognito in Kurdish garb.

Based on the sites of skirmishes with smugglers and reports of spies, the Ottoman security forces identified three main smuggling routes through Iran to Van City:

> Erivan to Ah to the Iranian village of Payecik, from there to Karadere, to İsa Bey Mountain, to the Kozluca Mountains, and from there to Van.
>
> Weapons brought to Western Iran, then from Var to the Avrın Mountain, to the Gireberan Mountain, to the Ahta Mountain, to the Arkav Mountain, then to Van.
>
> Weapons brought to Western Iran, then from Hukanvan and Kalasar in Iran, up the Duşvan Stream to Karahisar Abdullah, to the Keşişgöl village, crossing the Erek Mountain to reach Van.[98]

In addition to these three routes, the Ottoman security forces knew that three other secret routes existed but had not properly identified them. These must have included routes to the north and the south of the three known routes. As described below, weapons were smuggled into the Başkale-Hoşap-Çatak region from farther south in Iran. Variations on the routes must have been common.[99] According to the *History of the ARF*, a direct northern route from Erivan to Bayazıt to Van was opened in the 1890s. Weapons were smuggled into the Sasun region using the southern route to Van, then on to Sasun and to Sasun from Kars in the north.[100]

The second policy of the revolutionary smugglers was to foster Kurdish-Armenian cooperation. Kurdish tribal leaders who themselves opposed the Ottoman government were willing to facilitate Armenian smuggling in return for weapons and bribes. Kop Mehmet of the Haydaranlı, whose territory was in the far south of the Erzurum province on the Iranian border, assisted in the movement of weapons. In return for arms and ammunition for his own men, he allowed the revolutionaries to use the large village of Kaçan as a stage on the importation route and as an arms depot.[101] Farther to the south, the Shekifti branch of the Shikak tribe also made smuggling arrangements with the revolutionaries. This was particularly odd. As described in chapter 4, Şerif, the leader of the Shekifti, had engaged in a bloody feud with the revolutionaries in 1897. Yet in 1908 all was friendly between them. Şerif sent his son, Abdullah, to meet in Iran with the Armenian rebels to arrange arms shipments.[102]

The Kurdish-Armenian alliance demanded diplomacy and a certain degree of trust. In 1903 an Armenian-American doctor named Malkhas met as a representative of the Dashnaks with Şeyh Sadik, the younger son of Şeyh Ubeydullah, and requested that the Armenian porters and messengers carrying weapons and ammunition be able to travel to the region of Hoşap in security.[103] The şeyh indicated that the Armenian messengers would be secure and the goods that needed to be transported would be taken to Hoşap by his own men. He said that at this point he did not feel it was appropriate for armed groups of revolutionaries to come and go through his territory but that later he would allow this as well. The Armenians were forced to trust the şeyh, which must have raised doubts. It is instructive, however, that after 1903 Ottoman and diplomatic records contain no reports of the sorts of conflicts between Sadik and the revolutionaries that raged between other chiefs and the Armenians. The division of labor between the şeyh and the rebels seems to have been successful.[104]

In 1898, two years after the First Van Rebellion, Consul Williams did a detailed study on Armenian armaments in Van and in Iran. He estimated that there were at least a thousand rifles in the hands of Armenians in Van, most of them Berdan rifles that had previously been standard Russian equipment. There were also Martinis, the type of gun then used by the Ottoman army, and an unknown number of newer Russian-issue weapons. Williams believed that the revolutionaries themselves always had "the new Russian magazine rifle."[105] Older weapons were sold to other Armenians.

In addition to smuggling, some of the rifles in Armenian hands had come to them through sales by Kurds. The Ottoman government had outfitted the Hamidiye units with Martinis during the widespread Armenian rebellions of the 1890s. Some Hamidiye Kurds sold them to Armenian revolutionaries. These Kurds seemed to have preferred money in hand to future security from the revolutionaries. Persian Kurds had a lucrative trade in buying older Russian rifles in Iran, taking them across the border, and selling them to the revolutionaries. At one time, some Ottoman reservists (*redif*) had been known to sell rifles to anyone who would buy, although such sales had stopped by 1898.[106] Undoubtedly the smuggling sometimes had been facilitated by Ottoman officials, especially by the gendarmerie in rural areas, who had not been paid for months or who received very low salaries. Aram Manukian had been able to work with ease due to lavish bribes, both to smuggle the weapons and to learn in advance measures that the state intended to take against the revolutionaries.

Revolutionary Action

The intent of the Armenian revolutionaries did not change, despite their failures in the revolts of the 1890s. It remained a policy of sparking reprisals that would bring European intervention.[107] The leadership of the revolution did change. The Armenakans had been local—Ottoman Armenians pursuing their own cause. The earlier revolts, mainly led by the Hunchak Party, had enlisted considerable local Armenian support, particularly in the Zeytun and Sasun regions. After the failures and the loss of so many Armenian lives, Armenian villagers in many regions seem to have been less willing, at least for a while, to support such enterprises. There surely had been a failure of leadership from both the Armenakans and the Hunchaks. The Dashnak Party took over as the standard-bearer of revolution. It realized that careful planning and coordination, which had been lacking in the earlier efforts, were needed. Thus the Dashnaks brought organizers such as Aram Manukian from Russia to create a unified force from the rabble that had battled in the 1890s. These people supplanted local leaders. They were supported by a cadre of Russian Armenians. In fact, the leaders and the "sergeants" who organized and trained the Anatolian Armenians were almost all Russian Armenians. The British consul in Van, Captain Tyrrell, traveled to Muş to investigate the Armenian rebellion in the Muş-Sasun region. In the Muş hospital he interviewed one of the many revolutionary fighters who had come to the region from Russia. He reported:

> In answer to my inquiries he said that he was very well treated, and that he was very grateful for all that had been done for him in hospital. His name is Krikor Mirzabegoff, and he comes from Alexandropol, where his father is a priest. He is almost 25 years of age, and is a typical Armenian, not Russian, in looks.
>
> I understand that he served in the Karbarzkinsky Regiment at Alexandropol, and, by passing examinations, was allowed to pass into the reserve sooner than he would otherwise have done. He described himself as a commander of fifty men in the reserve. The Turks translate this as "Mulazim"—lieutenant, but he is probably only a non-commissioned officer. He said that when he was eighteen he allowed himself to be "written" as a revolutionist by a member of a committee called Korum; that, last year, having completed his military service, this Korum came and told him he

must go to Turkey to take part with the other revolutionists. He did not want to do so, and offered money to be let off. But the reply was that men of his stamp, who had a military training, were wanted, and not money.

I said that I was surprised to hear of this compulsion, as in Russia he had a Government and police who could protect him, to which he replied that the police could give him no protection against the revolutionists, and that he would have been killed if he had disobeyed the summons.

He could or would tell nothing about the revolutionists' plan of campaign, and seemed to know very little about the details of the fighting. He said, "Though I was an officer of the Russian reserve, I was only a simple soldier among the revolutionists. I fired my rifle and did what I was told, and know nothing of the plans of our leaders, or of what was going on beyond my immediate ken."

He was wounded in the second fight, the attack on Gelli Guzan, on the 3rd May. I finally asked him what was his object and that of the other revolutionists in coming into Turkey to fight. He said, "You know quite well—our object is to die."[108]

Unlike the widespread rebellions of the earlier period, the Dashnaks at first concentrated their forces on one area that appeared most likely to rebel and draw reprisals—the Muş-Sasun region. The 1896–97 Dashnak Congress in Tiflis set two tactical objectives that were carried out in subsequent years: "to build up a concentration of Dashnak forces in Sasoun and to arm its population; to organize a punitive expedition from Adrbadagan [Salmas region of Iran] to Vasbouragan [Van]."[109] As seen in chapter 4, the second objective was carried out immediately. Infiltration and arming the Armenians of Sasun were also accomplished but took six years.

Both European and Ottoman accounts indicate that revolutionaries crossed from Russia to the Ottoman Empire in great numbers at the turn of the century, passing directly south over the border into Erzurum Province or through Iran into Van Province.[110] In the north rebels crossed the Russian border of the Erzurum Province. From there the rebels went south into Bitlis Province. After 1898 skirmishes and full-scale battles between revolutionaries and troops and tribes greatly increased. Local Armenians in the Muş, Bitlis, and Sasun area often joined with the intruders.[111] Ottoman troops frequently interdicted the rebel crossings (in some cases being forced to bring up battalions that fought pitched battles with the rebels), but the bulk of the Armenians were usually able to escape back across the Russian border to cross again later.[112] Battles followed in the Bitlis Province.[113]

The frontier between the Ottoman Empire and Iran in the late 1890s can be viewed as a war zone in which Armenian revolutionaries and their followers fought against the Ottoman army and border guards and against some Kurdish tribes. Other Kurdish tribes and sometimes Persian soldiers functioned as allies of the revolutionaries. The Khoy-Salmas district, which they virtually controlled, served as the staging area for the rebels.[114] Anecdotal evidence of what actually occurred in the fights between soldiers and revolutionaries and tribesmen is scarce, but existing evidence indicates a bloody battle in which all sides often gave no quarter.[115] Crossings from Russia to the Erzurum Province seem to have been even more prevalent or at least were more often reported.

When they were discovered, the revolutionaries fought with Ottoman troops or Kurdish tribesmen.[116] It is not possible here to give accounts of the hundreds of incursions recorded in the diplomatic literature. Some examples follow.

In September 1898 fifty-five Armenian revolutionaries coming from Russia were pursued by Hamidiye cavalry and regular infantry near Malazgirt, and most were killed. In the same month more than fifty who had entered from the north were killed in battles near Muş, and another band was apprehended in Tutak. A captured prisoner at Malazgirt stated that his band was one of three that had crossed the border.[117]

Three groups of revolutionaries (bands of, respectively, eighty to a hundred, sixty, and fifty) crossed the Russian border at separate places in early October 1903. Each came into conflict with Ottoman troops and was defeated. Survivors either fled back across the border or hid in Armenian villages. The fighting spread to those villages, where Kurdish irregulars took part; undoubtedly a number of innocent suffered.[118]

In 1902 Lieutenant Colonel Maunsell, British consul in Van, reported that an Armenian band of 300 had passed the Russian border: "These men, as well as other bands in recent years, must have passed with the connivance of the Russian border guards, as they have numerous posts and the frontier is far too well watched for such a large band to pass unnoticed.... The sole object of these bands is to keep the country disturbed, to keep the Armenian Question alive, and afford Russia an excuse at some moment favourable to her of stepping in to interfere." Maunsell further noted that when the Ottomans managed to battle the bands, "endeavours are then made to make these occurrences appear as Armenian massacres, and the Russian object of making the country disturbed is accomplished."[119]

Maunsell's point was accurate. The revolutionaries crossing the border were planning to foment major rebellion, as they had in 1894–96, but their purposes were also served by reports of massacres. In 1903 a column of 130 armed revolutionaries crossed the border, intending to move south. They ambushed a detachment of Ottoman cavalry, killing two captains, one lieutenant, and seven men. As the Ottoman unit called up reinforcements, the rebels mutilated the bodies of those they had killed, expecting that this, according to British consul Tyrrell, would "rouse the Turks to ferocity, and make them retaliate on harmless villages and to commit atrocities, and so attract outside attention." The Turks, in fact, did not retaliate on the villages. They brought up more troops and killed the rebels. Reports immediately circulated, however, that the soldiers had destroyed the Armenian village of Delibaba. Consul Tyrrell stated that all the reports of atrocities were false. Nothing had happened to the villagers or the village. Tyrrell himself slept in the village days after it had supposedly been destroyed.[120] The Armenians had Russian rifles and Russian passports, and their horses were branded with Russian army brands.[121]

Larger groups were not uncommon (as seen above), but usually the bands were small, in order to pass more easily across the border. Government spies sometimes reported on planned crossings of revolutionaries. Soldiers waited to kill or capture them,[122] though by no means were all of the groups invading from Iran and Russia interdicted. Later events in both Bitlis and Van Provinces indicate that most must have passed the border unnoticed. The British consul estimated that there were five thousand to six thousand armed revolutionaries in the Sasun mountains in 1903, well drilled and trained under their leader, Andranik Ozanian. The number may have been a gross exaggeration, and surely included local Armenians, but it is certainly evidence that many had made it across the border.[123] There was one benefit to the villagers in the areas of incursion: the Ottomans were forced to send regular troops to interdict the intruders, which made the region safer. The Ottoman general İbrahim Paşa, for example, in 1898 interpreted his orders to include protection of villagers from both revolutionaries and tribesmen. He stationed soldiers in threatened villages and recovered stolen livestock from tribes, returning them to their owners.[124]

Sasun

In the early 1900s the concentration of Armenian revolutionaries was fixed on the Muş-Sasun region.[125] Numerous reports of revolutionaries coming to the area from the Russian and Iranian borders indicated that the leaders of the revolt had come from Russian territory and were joined by local rebels. The insurgents, under a blue flag with an eagle, were under the leadership of the Armenian guerrilla leader Andranik. They obviously intended their revolt to cause reprisals that would draw European intervention. Muslim villages on the outskirts of the Sasun area were attacked, as were tax collectors and officials. The attempt to draw reprisals was to some extent successful: members of the village of Hunan, for example, attacked and killed gendarmes. Most of the villagers fled to the mountains, but some were killed by the gendarmes in revenge.[126] Mindful of possible European intervention, the government sent strict instructions that soldiers and Kurdish irregulars be kept in check.[127]

In early May 1904 the Ottoman army attacked an estimated fifteen hundred rebels at Kelikozan (Ghelieguzan) and routed them. The fleeing rebels were pursued. Twenty-five villages were burned, for which the Europeans at first blamed soldiers and Kurds; the Ottoman government strenuously denied this.[128] As always, massacres of Armenians were alleged.[129] When the reports of British consuls who visited the area arrived, however, a different picture was seen. Consul Tyrrell reported: "I believe that, considering all the circumstances, it would be difficult to sustain charges of massacre and atrocities."[130]

VAN PROVINCE

Compared to the Sasun-Muş Region, Van was relatively quiet in the early 1900s. Revolutionary fervor had not died, but the slow organization and training by Aram Manukian channeled that fervor into constructive organization. Actual battles between government forces and Armenian revolutionaries in Van Province itself in the period from 1900 to 1907 were far fewer than might be expected. Van was primarily a transit point for the revolutionaries. Most of the skirmishes between troops and revolutionaries in the province resulted from interdictions of weapons and men infiltrating from Iran. Most of the men were probably on their way to the Muş-Sasun region of Bitlis Province; but, as it turned out, a large number of the weapons were to remain in Van. Other fights came as rebels escaping from the failed Sasun Rebellion passed through Van Province. The largest of the battles came as a band of revolutionaries under the rebel leader Andranik was pursued eastward from Bitlis.[131] Akhtamar Island in Lake Van was twice occupied by rebels who had fled south of Lake Van, probably planning to escape to the Armenian-controlled region of western Iran. Ottoman troops eventually dislodged the rebels, but with difficulty. The Ottomans were at a disadvantage, because the rebels had better rifles than the soldiers; at the long range between the island and the shore the Armenians could hit the soldiers, but the soldiers could not hit the Armenians. Therefore the Ottomans used their cannon, damaging some church buildings. The rebels managed to escape at night by boat. According to the government version, the revolutionaries took with them a sacred cross and other holy objects when they fled. Armenians claimed that the soldiers had done the looting.[132]

Blood feuds between Christians and Muslims, Christians and Christians, and Muslims and Muslims continued. For example, Armenians of the village of Narek, near Gevaş, who had harbored revolutionaries, were killed by the convicted (and escaped) bandit Abdulgafur, whose brother had been killed by the revolutionaries.[133]

Kurdish tribes and government forces, often enough at odds, cooperated in fighting incoming rebels, especially in southeastern Van, where the feud between the revolutionaries and some tribes (discussed in chapter 4) continued.[134] In 1899 an estimated fifty revolutionaries crossed the border east of Başkale and attacked Şerif Bey.[135] He drove them off, losing one Kurd and killing three revolutionaries. They reached "Zinis two hours east of Khoshun, where they were met by a company of regular infantry. Three revolutionaries were killed and one taken prisoner. Strict orders sent by the Vali to stop Kurds joining in fight or pillaging villages."[136]

THE RUSSIANS

The attitude of the Russians toward the Armenian revolutionaries was ambiguous. On the one hand, the tsarist government abhorred the philosophy of revolution, rightly fearing that it might itself become a victim of revolution. The Russians also strongly opposed Armenian separatism within the Russian Empire, seizing Armenian Church schools, for example, and making them state schools.[137] They had their own problems with Armenian revolutionaries, particularly in the Kars region.[138] On the other hand, Russia could only gain from the disruption caused by Armenian revolutionaries in the Ottoman Empire.

Claiming "Turkish Armenia" and its access to the Mediterranean Sea remained a fixed purpose of the Russian Empire until its demise. Armenians or Kurds who disrupted the Ottoman polity in Eastern Anatolia could only assist the Russian plan. It was not always politically expedient, though, to be seen as encouraging revolution in the Ottoman Empire. Russian political and tactical support for the Armenians waxed and waned. On the border, Russian patrols sometimes stopped Armenian revolutionaries' incursions and weapons smuggling. At other times they allowed them to pass. Some Russian consuls in Van gave very active support to the revolutionaries (training revolutionary youth, securing the release of captured rebels, giving other rebels sanctuary in Russian consulates, etc.), although this was primarily true before the 1896 revolt.

Spurred by complaints from Britain and France that they were aiding the revolutionaries, the Russians increased security on their border with the Ottoman Empire, sometimes stopping small groups of revolutionaries from crossing the Russian-Ottoman border. At such times, although very seldom, Armenian bands even battled with Russian border guards. Usually the guards allowed the bands, even groups of hundreds of armed revolutionaries, to pass without hindrance.[139] Nothing seems to have been done at any time to impede the revolutionaries from passing from Russia to Iran. They were freely given Russian passports and exit visas. Revolutionaries, even in large bands, passed from Russian to Persian Azerbaijan and back without hindrance.[140] Once the Russians took control of western Iran in 1910, the Armenian revolutionaries and their weapons traveled freely through Russian-controlled territory.

The revolutionaries' shipments of arms from Russia to Iran were in theory illegal in Russia, but from the large amount of weapons and ammunition that crossed the border it would appear that this rule was seldom enforced. Anyone with knowledge (or experience) of the Middle East and Caucasus can imagine what occurred. In the absence of direct orders to interdict arms, poorly paid border guards could be expected to take the bribes offered by smugglers to let their carts pass. As long as the weapons were not flaunted, they passed checkpoints, covered by merchandise or produce. It cannot have been difficult for Russian inspectors to have searched under bundles of merchandise for weapons, but this was not done. The guards did not actually see rifles, so no law appeared to be broken, but no one was fooled. There are some records of the Russians stopping such shipments on the northern border, but no records of shipments interdicted on the border with Iran.

The Russians were also active in drawing Kurdish tribes and Nestorians into the confusion in the Ottoman East.[141] They sent their agents, including Nestorian priests who trained in Russia, among the Nestorians to foster Russian interests, even trying for a time to sponsor mass conversion to Russian Orthodoxy. This was not an impossible task, because similar movements to convert Nestorians to Catholicism had been partially successful in the past. As noted above, the Nestorians were glad to be seen to cooperate. The main success of the conversion movement was to divide and cause dissension, which probably was the Russian plan. The Russians surely caused strife by sponsoring rebel claimants to the office of Mar Shimun, episcopal and civil leader of the Nestorians (see below).[142]

The Russians rendered one great assistance to the rebels by applying the rules of extraterritoriality in their favor. The Ottomans had long been forced by the European powers to accept the principle that subjects of European states could not be tried in Ottoman courts. They were to be tried by their own national legal systems. As the law was practiced in the Ottoman East, this usually meant that revolutionaries who were Russian subjects were not punished for their crimes. In 1897 in Van, for example, three revolutionaries—Feramoz, Arshag, and Vartan—were arrested by the Ottomans for attacks on soldiers and Muslim civilians. The Russian consul immediately claimed them as Russian nationals. They were kept in the Russian Consulate, where they were allowed to communicate with other revolutionaries. Every Sunday they went to an Armenian Church and delivered revolutionary speeches. Finally, in 1899, the Russians sent them to Russia.[143]

THE REVOLT OF 1906: A CONJECTURE

Although this is a matter of speculation, it seems likely that the revolutionaries intended a major outbreak in Van in the spring of 1906. The Council of the Dashnaktsutiun, meeting in Geneva in February–April 1905, decided to prepare "large-scale movements" in Van.[144] Reports of an upcoming revolt had been surfacing for two years. The American missionaries felt as early as the summer of 1904 that revolutionary trouble was imminent. Their sources told them that six different revolutionary bands were active in Van Province and that help was preparing to arrive from across the border. According to the missionaries, the revolutionaries were threatening to blow up the military barracks with gunpowder. Muslims in the city expected trouble, and "gunsmiths are busy putting guns in order."[145] The Dashnaks in Van Province had stockpiled thousands of weapons in depots in Van and in the countryside (see the discussion below). Large numbers of revolutionaries came into the city from outlying areas in the winter of 1905–6. Consul Arthur E. Geary reported: "They intend to continue with the utmost vigour their revolutionary propaganda during the winter in the hope that their efforts will be brought to fruition by the outbreak of serious trouble in the spring."[146] This would explain the large collection of guns and ammunition that would be found in the city in 1908.

One can only conjecture as to why no uprising took place in 1906.

The most likely cause was the opposition of Russia, which was feeling the effects of the Russo-Japanese War of 1904–5 and the Russian Revolution of 1905–6. The Revolution caused upheaval in the Southern Caucasus,[147] which would have affected any Russian plans for intervening in the Ottoman East; but the Japanese war was the most likely cause for Russian reticence. British consul Tyrrell in Van felt that Armenian plans to revolt, which he believed had been supported by Russia, were set back by the Russo-Japanese War. The Russians wanted no trouble on their western borders while they had so many problems in the East.[148] It is surely true that the Russians' major defeats by the Japanese on sea and land damaged their ability to project their power beyond their borders. The psychological effects of the losses on the Russian populace—a factor that contributed to the 1905 Revolution—must have made further military actions politically unwise. Whatever the cause, the Russians stepped up their border patrols in 1906 and stopped large group of revolutionaries from entering the Ottoman Empire.[149]

Another factor in the delay or cancellation of a Van uprising may have been the failure of the uprising in Bitlis Province. In 1903, as the Sasun troubles were growing, an Armenian informant in Bitlis told the British Consul, F. G. Freeman, that revolutionaries had plans to seize strategic points in Sasun, Van, and elsewhere in the East. Armenians would also cross the frontier from Russia. The rebels would slaughter Muslims to provoke retaliation, so that the European powers would intervene.[150] This is surely limited evidence, but it makes strategic sense and fits events in Bitlis Province and the preparations in Van. If it is true, the plan would have been to begin a major uprising in the Sasun-Muş Region, draw in Ottoman troops, then revolt behind the lines in Van. All evidence indicates that a small army of Dashnaks did exist in Iran and that they were prepared to march across the border.[151] Rebels coming from Iran would come to assist a Van revolt but would have had a difficult time passing in large numbers through Van on the way to Bitlis. It was one thing to smuggle through small groups over a long period and reassemble them as units in Bitlis, quite another to march hundreds (consuls felt "thousands" would be more accurate) across Van through high passes held by the Ottoman army. Attacking from Iran, however, would have drawn pressure from revolts elsewhere. Such a plan would have failed when the Sasun rebellion was put down relatively quickly, leaving the rebels in Van to decide whether or not to attempt rebellion on their own.

ALI RIZA PAŞA, THE GOVERNOR OF VAN

By 1907, in the wake of the Sasun troubles, the attitude of the Ottoman government toward the Armenian rebels had begun to change. The government reacted to the growing power of the revolutionaries with a "carrot and stick" approach: loyal Armenians were to be integrated into the state apparatus and given positions of authority. At the same time, officials who had temporized with the Armenian threat would be replaced by men willing to confront the revolutionaries. Revolutionaries would be vigorously pursued and punished. This risked incurring the displeasure of Europe; but the times were desperate, and Europe had not seemed to respond favorably to a policy of conciliation. Who could honestly say that allowing the rebels who seized the Ottoman Bank to go free, tolerating Dashnak organization and propaganda, or acting leniently in Sasun had improved the Ottoman image in Europe or enhanced the empire's chance for survival? The Ottomans were damned in the European press and European chancelleries no matter which approach they took, so they might as well fight their enemies.

On March 18, 1907, the *mutasarrıf* (in charge of a subprovince: *sancak*) of Hakkâri (capital: Çölemerik) Ali Rıza Bey was appointed governor of Van.[152] His appointment came at a time of increased Armenian revolutionary activity in the city, in the nearby area, and especially along the Iranian border in the southern region of the province. In June 1907 a strong Armenian band had even fought gendarmes, cavalry, and a company of regular infantry in the mountains within sight of Van City.[153]

Ali Rıza had not actually been in command in Van when these disturbances erupted. He had been delayed for four months because of illness.[154] The Sublime Porte sent an Investigation Committee led by Tahir Paşa (the ex-governor of Van) to conduct investigations in the southern region of the province, where Ali Rıza had been mutasarrıf, to ascertain if Ali Rıza had acquitted himself well there and was indeed the man to be governor in difficult times. The delegation carefully examined the area and completed its task in two months.[155] The investigations showed that Ali Rıza had not only represented the state successfully but also had gained the respect of both the Turks and Armenians. Tahir Paşa indicated in a telegram to the government in Istanbul that the permanent appointment of Ali Rıza to Van was essential.[156] The work of the Investigation Committee had been wholly beneficial. It ensured that the former governor would be able to transmit his knowledge to the new governor, a very unusual occurrence.

With the appointment of Ali Rıza the government attempted to reform the administrative problems that had plagued previous provincial administrations. Some of the remedies had been suggested ten years earlier by Governor Bahri Paşa immediately after the 1896 Van rebellion. In particular, the political infighting and confusion of authority that had resulted from the separate authority of the civil and military commanders was remedied. The government appointed Ali Rıza both as a brigadier general in charge of the military and as governor in charge of the civil administration, an unusual concentration of power in a governor's hands.[157] The appointment of a governor who already knew his province was also an unusual and welcome innovation. Most governors were appointed from service elsewhere and took quite a while to become acquainted with their provinces. Ali Rıza, however, has served for years in the region. He had extensive experience with both the Kurdish tribes and the development of the Armenian separatist movement.[158]

Ali Rıza benefited from the advice of Tahir, who had served eight years as governor, but he approached the main problems of Van quite differently. Tahir Paşa had been a conciliator. He had treated the actions of the Armenian revolutionaries primarily as a normal security event, working through the court system with the concurrence of the head of provincial judicial affairs, Ali Bey, and the police and gendarmes. He was well liked by European consuls, and the Armenians spoke well of him, but the strength of the rebels had increased markedly during his tenure in office. Ali Rıza was a different sort of administrator.

Ali Rıza Paşa does not seem to have constructed a theoretical plan of action or to have followed any "counterinsurgency doctrine" in opposing the revolutionaries. His actions, however, indicate an innate understanding of what was needed to defeat insurgents. Military power was essential, of course, because ultimately the state had to be able to defeat rebels and bandits militarily; but military power was never enough. Whether or not the people felt loyalty to the regime, they would be satisfied and pacific if they were able to lead normal lives, free from bandit attacks, revolutionaries' demands for money, and inefficient and corrupt officials. They would more likely accept even an imperfect government if it contained members of their group, both Muslims and Armenians. Those members, in turn, could represent the wishes of their group better than government officials from other groups could. In short, military power, civil order, and a sense of inclusion in the state were needed.

Consul Dickson summarized the situation in Van and Ali Rıza's character in 1907:

I am afraid he [Governor Ali Rıza] will fall foul of the revolutionists here. He has arrived here under the firm conviction, that the country was on the point of open insurrection, which was only stopped by his arrival, and he is greatly distressed by the fact that most of the arms and ammunition obtained by the revolutionists is brought over the frontier by Kurds. As I mentioned in my No. 14 of December 31, 1906, the revolutionary committee had appointed themselves a sort of governing power over the Armenians, enforcing their ideas of justice on the Armenians in some cases even, to the point of death. The late vali overlooked this saying that it relieved him of a lot of trouble and worry, Ali Bey however will not stand it, and an Armenian merchant having lately been kidnapped by the revolutionaries, he has issued orders to allow no one to be out between sunset and ten p.m. without a lantern, and anyone found out after ten p.m. is to be arrested. The streets are all strongly picketed and patrolled by some four hundred troops, I am informed, being so employed each night. I do not think this will stop the revolutionaries moving about when they want to, as they will now take to the gardens. These revolutionaries have been making themselves very obnoxious lately. They find the American school here the best recruiting ground for their purposes and have appointed themselves guardians of all the Armenian orphans, and are tyrannising the teachers and the missionaries with threats against discouraging the pupils from becoming revolutionaries. They have forced the Armenian superintendent of the orphanage to resign under threats of death.[159]

Once he was confirmed as governor, Ali Rıza immediately set upon the reorganization of the provincial government and strengthening the authority of the state. Knowing that the surest way to gain the trust of the people would be to end the oppression by the bandits, he began to apprehend both Armenian and Kurdish bandits.[160]

Ali Rıza began to attack the most pressing problem of the provincial administration: the lack of financial resources and subsequent failure to pay salaries. The provincial government was in effect bankrupt. Civil servants, security forces, and pensioners had not been paid for ten to twenty months. Official positions had been left vacant because those appointed were not able to leave their towns due to lack of resources. The first priority was the collection of taxes that had not been collected since the First Van Rebellion. Arrears had reached great amounts, sometimes for as much as twenty years.[161] Armenians who held commerce in their hands had not been paying their taxes to the state, especially after the First Van Rebellion, for various reasons, some of them justifiable. The main complaint of the merchants was that they in essence had been forced to pay taxes to the revolutionaries, who had increased their "taxes" when the state was unable to collect its own. They agreed to pay past taxes in installments, but only if the governor could protect them from the revolutionary exactments. Ali Rıza did this with some success. The government was able to collect its taxes, and salaries began to be paid.[162]

Taxes were also collected rigorously in the countryside. Traditionally, Kurdish tribes had paid taxes on their sheep based on their own estimation of the number in the flocks. In the short time he served as governor Ali Rıza began to send out tax collectors to count the sheep.[163] The tribal chiefs were not pleased; nor were the farmers, both Muslim and Armenian, who found themselves with large and often unpayable tax bills. Much was collected, but there was also injustice.[164] On the whole, collections in the cities and towns were much more successful.

Bringing Armenians into his administration was an essential element of Ali Rıza's program, but here his success was limited by the tactics of the revolutionaries. The revolutionaries hated the governor's activities.[165] They correctly viewed his reforms as drawing support from their cause. Their plans depended on intercommunal conflict, and the last thing they wanted was the integration of Armenians into the power structure.

Ali Rıza appointed a well-liked Armenian, Ohannes Effendi, to the position of deputy governor, and his brother, Armarak Effendi, as kaymakam of the Gevaş Kaza.[166] While the image of the appointment of an Armenian as deputy governor was of obvious significance, it had been done before. Ohannes was a personal friend of Ali Rıza, however, so there was reason to believe he would have a real say in the province's affairs. The appointment in Gevaş was perhaps more important, because it carried legal authority. The geographical position of the kaza of Gevaş gave it great importance in the fight against the revolutionaries. The district contained the center of Armenian revolutionary activity: the island of Akhtamar. Obstructing revolutionary activities on Akhtamar would disrupt all rebel actions. Armarak Effendi potentially could hinder the use of the island as a revolutionary base.

Like the Ottomans, the rebels realized the centrality of Akhtamar and the danger that Armarak Effendi posed for them. They were willing to take extreme action to thwart the governor's plans. They assassinated Armarak, removing a great obstacle to their cause.[167] After his brother was killed, Ohannes Effendi believed it was no longer safe for him to stay in

Van. He asked Ali Rıza to secure his appointment as deputy governor of Mamuretülaziz. He had been forced to leave Van.[168]

In the face of this setback, but still wanting to secure the loyalty of the people, Ali Rıza requested that the central government appoint the former translator (*tercüman,* a position of more authority than the name indicates) of Erzurum, the Armenian Mikail Effendi, as deputy governor of Van. The government did so.[169] It was later announced, however, that Mikail Effendi would not come to Van, undoubtedly because of his fear of the Revolutionary Committee. Leon Effendi, another Armenian and a former kaymakam, was appointed.[170]

Armenians remained in the provincial administration,[171] but the assassination of Armarak and decamping of Ohannes can only be viewed as a significant defeat for Ali Rıza's plans.

DAVIT THE INFORMER

Despite the evidence gleaned by spies and the occasional Armenian informer, the Ottoman government did not really know the extent of the Armenian preparation for revolution. The government of Abdülhamit II, always fearful of revolutionaries, saw the constant skirmishes with revolutionaries and the outbreaks in Bitlis Province primarily in diplomatic terms—dangerous because they might bring foreign intervention. There is no evidence that they realized just how ready the Dashnaks were for a major eruption. It was a story worthy of a romance novel that proved the depth of the Dashnak preparations.

Davit (also known as Davo or David), a member of the Dashnak revolutionary group in Van, loved a girl named Vatan and wished to marry her.[172] Aram also had feelings for the girl, however, and his revolutionary beliefs did not preclude him from using his position to advance his own interest. Aram forbade Davit's marriage to Vatan. Davit refused to accept the situation. Understanding that the Armenian notables in the city would never take his side, Davit went to Tiflis to obtain the permission to marry from superiors in the Dashnak Committee. He failed. In the meantime, Aram had convinced Vatan to repudiate Davit. Seeking revenge, Davit went to the governor, Ali Rıza Paşa, and told him all he knew about the Dashnaks.

Acting on Davit's information, the governor made a series of raids in February 1908, with Davit personally leading soldiers to arms caches. On February 5 two hundred rounds of ammunition were discovered in the

Surb Krikor Monastery, eight miles from Van. Soldiers seized nearly two hundred thousand more rounds and five hundred guns in the Garden District the same day. Further searches the next day revealed three hundred packages of dynamite. At that point the revolutionaries in the Garden District began to resist, firing on the troops from houses and wounding or killing seventeen soldiers and gendarmes in a brief battle in the streets. Ultimately the Ottomans estimated that they had confiscated approximately two thousand weapons, five thousand bombs, hundreds of thousands of cartridges, and much other military material.[173] Ottoman officials were amazed to discover that the weapons found would be sufficient to arm a brigade and that many of them were of a quality not found in the state forces. The weapons smuggling had obviously been successful.

Although the weapons had been seized, no member of the revolutionary committee had been caught, and large caches of weapons still remained unfound. The revolutionaries had dug cellars and passages under Armenian houses. After the brief street battle with the troops, they were able to escape further raids through interconnecting passages under the houses that connected with ancient water and drainage tunnels.[174]

Davit knew that his life was threatened. He began residence under guard in the house of Ahmet Bey, a gendarmerie major, in the Hamamönü neighborhood in the center of the Garden District.[175] Another way to aid his survival was to become Muslim, which is what he did, changing his name to Mehmet. Plans were made for him to join the army in order to ensure his safety. But boredom led to Davit's demise. After not leaving the major's house for a month, he decided to go to the Haçboğan Market (next to the major's house) on March 23, together with a gendarmerie officer and two guards.[176] A Dashnak named Dacat Terlimazian (or Tirlamasian), probably acting on the orders of the revolutionary committee,[177] took advantage of his opportunity. He fired two weapons in the market, hitting both Davit and a number of bystanders. Davit was seriously wounded and later died.[178] Eight individuals who were in the market also died; Dacat was able to make his escape.[179]

The Muslim population of Van had lived in a tense atmosphere for the past month (since the finding of the weapons caches and killing of the seventeen soldiers) and had lionized Davit as a hero. Attacks on Armenians began immediately after Davit's murder. Rioters, including some gendarmes, began to catch and beat Armenians in the market and on the roads to the Garden District. The government estimated that twenty to thirty Armenians were killed in the incident; the British consul said that forty-two died.[180] The governor and the military forces were instrumental in containing the situation, calming passions and protecting Armenians.

Mahmud Paşa, the *ferik,* and Tahir Bey, colonel in charge of the cavalry, were especially notable in this regard. The situation would have become much worse without their intervention.

Ali Rıza immediately sent soldiers to the area to contain the incident. He tried to calm down the uneducated Muslim mob and used military force to awe those who would not listen to reason. The governor visited leading Armenians who had not been involved in the incident to thank them for their loyalty to the state. Fearing that he did not have sufficient forces to contain further violence, he ordered the Fourth Battalion of the Twenty-sixth Regiment to be dispatched to Van. Very importantly, he did not allow tribal Hamidiye forces, who were called up when a general insurrection was feared, to enter the city.

As word of the assault on Davit spread, Armenians vacated their homes in the neighborhoods adjoining Muslim neighborhoods and sensibly shut themselves up in their quarters in the Garden District. The main bazaar, largely in the hands of Armenian merchants, closed. The Armenian merchants did not start to return slowly to the bazaar until April 3, so Van residents, who were dependent on the bazaar for their food, began to go hungry. Ali Rıza arranged for food to be delivered to both Armenians and Muslims. The Armenian districts were protected by soldiers, who turned away potential Muslim attackers.[181]

Rumor, always the mainstay of what passed for information among the Van populace, was a weapon against civil order and against the government. The Russian, British, and French consuls had officially approved of the measures taken by the government.[182] Unofficially, however, the Russian consul spread word of an impending massacre of Armenians. Ottoman intelligence sources believed that his purpose was to drive previously neutral Armenians into the revolutionary camp,[183] but rumors would undoubtedly have spread without his assistance. According to the rumor, reserve units and the Muslim populace would join to bring about a general massacre in the Christian neighborhoods. This rumor was spread among the Armenians and to officials of European governments. The gendarmerie believed reports that Armenians under the committee's control would attack the Muslim Quarter and themselves engage in massacre.[184] In order to prevent either scenario, more soldiers were dispatched to Van from neighboring provinces. These brought the situation under control.[185]

The revolutionaries in the city appear to have decided at first to fortify the Armenian Quarter, much as had occurred in 1896. Despite the seizure of weapons, obviously enough remained to open an actual rebellion. Revolutionaries in Iran began to mass on the border. Muslims in and near the Armenian Quarters fled, leaving the city completely divided into zones of Armenian and Muslim occupation. The Armenian notables, however, prevailed upon the rebels to abandon their plans and leave the city.[186] The Dashnak leadership disappeared. Aram and others at first left the city but eventually returned secretly to the Garden District. Once conditions had quieted in the city, on May 19, soldiers surrounded the Garden District and began a search for the leaders and weapons caches. Troops were posted all around the district, as well as in the districts in which it was feared that Muslim fanatics might take advantage of the situation to attack Armenians. Aram and twelve others, including Dacat, were found in an underground hiding place and were arrested. Other rebels were found in subsequent days, along with weapons, dynamite bombs, and tens of thousands of cartridges.[187]

The French, Russian, and British consuls in Van and their embassies in Istanbul demanded that a full amnesty be given to all Armenians who had been involved in the concealment of weapons or the murder of Davit and other Muslims. They also demanded that Muslims who had killed or threatened Armenians, as well as officials accused of complicity, be tried and punished.[188]

Despite setbacks, the administration of Ali Rıza had at least made a start at improving conditions in Van. The government was firmly in charge, as it had not been before. The events of the 1908 Revolution and European intervention were to bring Ali Rıza's reforms to a halt.

Events in Ottoman Europe and Istanbul were to have a great effect on Van. Beginning in 1907, members of the Third Army in Macedonia began to revolt, taking to the mountains. In 1908 the unrest spread to the cities of Macedonia, and revolt became general throughout the Third Army. Before the revolution could spread further, Sultan Abdülhamit II surprised the rebels by reinstituting the constitution and calling for elections to Parliament (official proclamation, July 23, 1908). The rebels did not formally take power, but it quickly became obvious in the provinces that major changes in government were underway. Conservative forces that had supported the sultan's regime were in disarray. Rebels in the military and provincial administrations, most of whom had kept their allegiance secret, came into the open. Governors, such as Ali Rıza, who had been tied to the old administration saw their influence disappear. The Armenian revolutionaries had close ties to factions in the revolutionary Committee of Union and Progress (CUP).[189] Almost overnight the Armenian revolutionaries went from being hunted outlaws, proven to be arming for revolution, to being influential friends of the "new men" who would soon rule.

In Van the immediate effect of the revolution was to free the rebels who had recently been arrested. An amnesty was declared. Aram and his colleagues were freed even before their trial was concluded. Rebels who were still hiding emerged. "The Doctor" and Sarkis went through the formality of surrendering to the authorities with their bands. They were immediately freed. The Van branch of the CUP, mainly made up of military officers, publicly supported the Armenians, as if recent events had never occurred.[190] (Once Ali Rıza was removed from office, the new governor, Mahmud Bey, still felt the revolutionaries to be a danger, however, and planned to deport the leaders, who were Russian subjects. He was "convinced" by the British consul not to do so.)[191]

Supported by the European consuls, the revolutionaries and the CUP leaders in Van immediately began to agitate for Ali Rıza's removal. Members of the military went so far as to raid the governor's house, seizing weapons and money. Ali Rıza was reassigned as governor of Kastamonu.[192] He had been popular in many circles in Van, just as the CUP and the Armenian revolutionaries were unpopular. The populace cabled Istanbul, asking for the return of Ali Rıza to the governorship. All they received in reply was the assurance that an even better governor would be named in his place.[193]

THE ASSASSINATION OF ALI RIZA PAŞA

Ali Rıza realized that he would be killed by Armenian revolutionary bands if he took the usual road through Muş and Sivas to Kastamonu. He knew that an assassination attempt had been made on a previous governor of Van, Bahri Paşa, in Trabzon. For this reason, he preferred to keep his route hidden. He said his good-byes to the population of Van, whom he had served for a year and a half.[194] In order to escape the revolutionaries, Ali Rıza traveled by an unlikely route that took him through Erzurum and Batum, where he planned to take a ship bound for Sinop or İnebolu.[195] He was killed by an Armenian revolutionary named Alev Bashian,[196] as he was about to embark on a ship in Batum.[197] Ali Rıza's body was interred in the garden of the Seyid Bilal Camii in Sinop.

NOTES

1. Faiz Demiroğlu, *Van'da Ermeni mezâlimi, 1895–1920* (Ankara: Türk Kültürü Araştırma Enstitüsü, 1985), p. 191.

2. FO 881/6958, Graves to Currie, Erzurum, May 28, 1897. On reforms and the need for money, see also FO 881/6957, Williams to Currie, Van, November 24, 1896.

3. FO 424/198, Maunsell to O'Conor, Van, December 7, 1898.

4. "The price of bread in Van has been and continues to be 60 paras an oke, which is extremely high, and this has had a very serious effect on the poorer classes. It is mainly owing to the habit of all Armenians who have a little money investing it in wheat, which they hoard until they can force prices still higher. They seem quite regardless of the consequences of such action on their poorer compatriots. A public-spirited Turk, Jemal Bey, has opened a baker's shop and is selling bread at 45 paras, therebye tending to force down prices, but his action is too isolated to have much effect" (FO 195/2082, Maunsell to O'Conor, Van, May 2, 1900).

5. There is almost no mention of these police in the literature, but Consul Tyrrell states that they were present in 1903 (FO 195/2147, Tyrrell to O'Conor, Van, April 2, 1903).

6. FO 424/188, Williams to Herbert, Van, June 7, 1896. Armenian inspectors were enrolled in the neighboring provinces of Erzurum and Bitlis. Istanbul found money to pay them, but not those in Van, which may indicate Van's place in imperial thinking. Bitlis Province had sixty Armenian gendarmes by 1897, seventy by 1898. Hard feelings arose, because the Christian gendarmes received their pay, whereas the Muslim gendarmes did not (FO 881/6958, Monahan to Currie, Bitlis, January 16, 1897; FO 424/197, Monahan to O'Conor, Bitlis, October 16, 1898). See also FO 424/191, Monahan to Currie, Bitlis, December 22, 1896, which listed a higher number of Armenian gendarmes (ninety).

7. FO 881/6958, Elliot to Currie, Van, May 10, 1897.

8. See FO 424/199, Maunsell to O'Conor, Van, June 20, 1899; and FO 424/199, Maunsell to O'Conor, Van, July 7, 1899, on the conflict between Tahir and Zeki Paşa, military commander and Hamidiye leader.

9. FO 881/9305, Dickson to O'Conor, Van, August 4, 1907. Consul Bertram Dickson felt the governor was exaggerating, but the fiscal situation was obviously not good. See also FO 424/191, Williams to Currie, Van, January 24, 1897; and FO 424/195, Elliot to Currie, Van, January 10, 1899. It should be noted that Captain Dickson, the British consul in Van, was a reliable source only when he had direct knowledge of the facts, such as when he saw events himself or had trustworthy sources in Van City (seldom in the countryside). At other times he seems to have relied almost exclusively on what he was told by Armenians and missionaries. When Ottoman and local Armenian sources differed, he assumed that the officials were lying. He could not be said, however, to be sympathetic to the Armenian revolutionary movement, with which he had much personal contact. For an excellent example of Dickson's prejudices, see FO 195/2284, Dickson to Lowther, Van, August 13, 1908, on disturbances in the Çatak region, where Kurds and Armenians were fighting. Dickson traveled to the region after the fact, accompanied by an American missionary Raynolds. He accepted all he was told by the Armenians, including incredible statistics (1,500 Kurds defeated by 38 Armenians), and discounted any official or Kurdish evidence. Dickson stated that Kurds "intended to pillage the town [Çatak] and massacre the inhabitants." How he gained his information on their intentions was not stated, but he characteristically believed that the Kurdish plan was averted only because he arrived on the scene.

10. FO 424/191, Williams to Currie, Van, May 10, 1897. For an analysis of tax abuses, see FO 881/6959, Crow to Currie, Bitlis, August 14, 1897.

11. FO 424/206, Tyrrell to O'Conor, Van, January 8, 1904. See also FO 424/108, Maunsell to O'Conor, Van, December 7, 1898. A mobilization of Hamidiye troops in 1907

had to be cancelled due to lack of funds (FO 881/9305, O'Conor to Grey, Constantinople, September 5, 1907).

12. FO 424/9050, Safrastian to Shipley, Bitlis, May 11, 1907. It is extremely unfortunate that the British Vice-Consulate in Bitlis was for a number of years left in the hands of Safrastian, who was hired in 1903 as a nineteen-year-old translator then put in charge when the British did not send out a regular diplomat to Bitlis. Safrastian's reports reflect his personal biases and lack of experience.

13. Tahir Paşa began this system. Previously the collection of many taxes was a "tax farm," in which individuals bid in an auction-like system for the right to collect taxes in many areas. Tribal chiefs were used to winning the bids (FO 195/2063, Maunsell to O'Conor, Van, April 10, 1899; FO 424/199, Maunsell to O'Conor, Van, September 10, 1899; FO 424/199, Maunsell to O'Conor, Van, October 24, 1899). The provincial government also tried a scheme to forgive the taxes of those who would work building roads. It foundered because no one wanted to do the hard work, which perhaps shows another problem (FO 195/2147, Tyrrell to O'Conor, Van, July 1, 1903).

14. FO 424/191, Williams to Currie, Van, January 24, 1897.

15. FO 424/191, Williams to Currie, Van, February 22, 1897; FO 424/191, Monahan to Currie, Bitlis, April 3, 1897.

16. FO 424/191, Williams to Currie, Van, March 12, 1897.

17. FO 881/9305, Heard to O'Conor, Bitlis, August 25, 1907; FO 881/8202, Tyrrell to O'Conor, Van, September 1, 1903.

18. FO 195/2082, Maunsell to O'Conor, Van, May 23, 1900. Maunsell stated that the tribes were the "herki and Zebari Kurds."

19. FO 195/2147, Tyrrell to O'Conor, Van, March 31, 1903; FO 195/2147, Tyrrell to O'Conor, Van, March 31, 1903. Both were leaders of the same Nakşbendi *tarikat* (Sufi order).

20. FO 424/197, Elliot to O'Conor, Van, October 14, 1898.

21. FO 424/200, Spring-Rice to Salisbury, Gulhek, April 21, 1900; FO 424/200, O'Conor to Salisbury, Constantinople, June 30, 1900; FO 424/200, Maunsell to O'Conor, Van, July 1, 1900. On conditions in western Iran, see also FO 881/8202, Tyrrell to O'Conor, Van, September 1, 1903; and FO 195/2222, Dickson to O'Conor, Van, December 1, 1906.

22. FO 195/2082, Maunsell to O'Conor, Van, July 24, 1900.

23. FO 881/8202, Tyrrell to O'Conor, Van, September 1, 1903; FO 242/199, Maunsell to O'Conor, Van, October 24, 1899; FO 424/202, Satow to O'Conor, Van, April 29, 1901; FO 195/2147, Tyrrell to O'Conor, Van, July 1, 1903.

24. FO 881/9432, O'Conor to Grey, Van, February 4, 1908.

25. FO 195/2147, Tyrrell to O'Conor, Van, May 16, 1903.

26. FO 195/2082, Maunsell to O'Conor, Van, July 24, 1900.

27. FO 424/199, Maunsell to O'Conor, September 10, 1899.

28. FO 881/9432, O'Conor to Grey, Van, February 4, 1908.

29. FO 195/2063, Maunsell to O'Conor, Van, April 10, 1899; FO 424/198, Maunsell to O'Conor, April 30, 1899. Maunsell commented that this showed the sincerity of the government in opposing tribal excesses, since Şerif was a Hamidiye commander.

30. FO 195/2147, Tyrrell to O'Conor, Van, April 2, 1903. Tyrrell said that the raiding of caravans was an annual event for Şerif. For the arrests of Muslims who were "leading men and well-known fanatics," see FO 424/191, Monahan to Currie, Bitlis, April 2, 1897.

31. FO 195/2147, Tyrrell to O'Conor, Van, May 12, 1903. On this issue, see chapter 6. For a list of Armenian villages occupied by Kurdish tribes in Erciş Kaza, see FO 424/191, Williams to Currie, Van, March 12, 1897. Williams gave no source, but it was probably an Armenian one. It is impossible to tell how reliable this and other such evidence was.

32. FO 424/197, Elliot to de Bunsen, Van, June 22, 1898.

33. FO 424/191, Crowe to Currie, Bitlis, May 25, 1897; FO 424/191, Crowe to Currie, Bitlis, June 6, 1897; FO 881/6959, Crow to Currie, Bitlis, August 9, 1897.

34. FO 881/9305, Heard to O'Conor, Bitlis, August 25, 1907.

35. The diplomatic literature on Sadik is voluminous. See, for example, FO 424/196, Elliot to Currie, Tabreez, May 17, 1898, and the reference to Sadik in chapter 7.

36. FO 195/2082, Maunsell to O'Conor, Van, May 2, 1900.

37. FO 195/2250, Dickson to O'Conor, Van, March 31, 1907.

38. One Nestorian gang robbed the American missionary W. H. Browne, for which they were excommunicated by the Nestorian patriarch (FO 424/199, Maunsell to O'Conor, November 27, 1899).

39. FO 195/2063, Maunsell to O'Conor, Van, December 29, 1899. On internecine conflicts among the Nestorians, see FO 195/2147, Tyrrell to O'Conor, Van, August 26 1903; FO 195/2147, Tyrrell to O'Conor, Van, April 1, 1903; FO 195/2147, Tyrrell to O'Conor, Van, April 8, 1903; FO 195/2147, Tyrrell to O'Conor, Van, November 12, 1903; and FO 195/2147, Tyrrell to O'Conor, Van, November 30, 1903.

40. FO 195/2063, Maunsell to O'Conor, Van, December 29, 1899; FO 424/200, Maunsell to O'Conor, Van, December 29, 1899. Maunsell commented that "the Christians [Nestorians] are every whit as quarrelsome, ignorant and reckless as their Kurdish neighbors, and they are mixed up in the inter-tribal quarrels and blood-feuds of the latter" (FO 424/200, Maunsell to de Bunsen, Van, November 18, 1900).

41. See the examples given by Maunsell in FO 424/200, Maunsell to de Bunsen, Van, November 18, 1900.

42. For example, see FO 195/2458, Smith to Mallet, Van, May 29, 1914 (Lt. Ian M. Smith).

43. FO 424/191, Williams to Currie, Van, February 8, 1897.

44. FO 881/6959, Elliot to Currie, Van, July 6, 1897. Elliot identified the Kurdish leader as the "Kurdish Chief living at Khoumaroo."

45. FO 424/199, Maunsell to O'Conor, Van, November 27, 1899. The Nestorians seem to have easily risen above old feuds to gain benefit. In 1908 they sheltered an old enemy, Şakir Ağa of the Hartushi tribe, who was fleeing from Ottoman forces (FO 195/2284, Dickson to Lowther, Van, September 30, 1908).

46. Satow to O'Conor, Van, January 30, 1902; FO 424/203; Satow to O'Conor, Van, February 11, 1902; FO 424/203, Satow to O'Conor, Van, February 28, 1902; FO 881/9305, Dickson to O'Conor, Van, October 29, 1907.

47. FO 195/2250, Dickson to O'Conor, Van, March 31, 1907.

48. FO 371/774, Morgan to Lowther, Van, October 2, 1909.

49. Nestorians on the Urmia Plain in Iran seem to have converted to Russian Orthodoxy in large numbers at one time (FO 195/2147, Tyrrell to O'Conor, Van, September 1, 1903). How long they remained Orthodox is unknown, but they were surely back to Nestorian allegiance by World War I.

50. There are too many such reports, spanning thirty years of the diplomatic litera-

ture, to mention here. Most were rumors. See, for example, FO 195/1315, Clayton to Trotter, Van, February 11, 1880; FO 195/1488, Eyres to Everrett, Van, March 16, 1884; FO 424/197, Elliot to de Bunsen, Van, September 13, 1898; and FO 424/199, Maunsell to O'Conor, Van, October 24, 1899.

51. FO 424/200, O'Conor to Salisbury, Constantinople, June 6, 1900.

52. FO 424/196, Elliot to Currie, Tabreez, May 5, 1898. Extortion of funds for the Armenian revolution was an old tradition. See FO 195/1688, Devey to Lloyd, Van, December 6, 1880.

53. Hüseyin Nâzım Paşa, *Ermeni Olayları Tarihi,* 2 vols. (Ankara: TC Başbakanlık Devlet Arşivleri Genel Müdürlüğü, Osmanlı Arşivi Daire Başkanlığı, 1994).

54. Ali Karaca, "Tehcire Giden Yolda Ermeni Meselesine Bir Çözüm Projesi ve Reform Müfettişliği (1878–1915)," in *Ermeni Meselesi Üzerine Araştırmalar* (Istanbul: Tarih ve Tabiat Vakfı, 2001), pp. 9–90; Ali Karaca, "Türkiye'de Ermeniler İçin Yapılan Reformlar (Örtülü Bir İşgale Doğru) ve Tehcir Gerçeği (1878–1915)," in *Uluslar arası Türk-Ermeni İlişkileri Sempozyumu* (Istanbul: Tarih ve Tabiat Vakfı, 2001), pp. 107–70.

55. Before the 1896 revolt Dashnak workers had frequently come to Van from Iran, and Dashnak leaders had been resident in the province, concentrated in the Van City and Çatak regions. Hratch Dasnabedian, *History of the Armenian Revolution Federation, Dashnaktsutiun,* trans. Bryan Fleming and Vaha Habeshian (hereafter *History of the ARF*) (Milan: GEMME Edizione, 1989), p. 53, gives their names. They included Vartan (Arshag Tadeosian), a member of the first Dashnak Bureau (1892–96).

56. Before arriving in Van, Kisag had received Dashnak training in Istanbul, been imprisoned there briefly, and then gone to Bulgaria and the Caucasus. Shahbaz had taken part in the occupation of the Ottoman Bank, had served the Dashnaks in the Caucasus and Bulgaria, and had worked in the armaments factory in Tabriz. Like Aram and Ishkhan, Der Minassian had trained in Kars. (He only remained in Van for a short while in 1905.) Parseghian, also usually known as Sarkis, had been part of the Dashnak extortion operation and was a veteran of Dashnak activities in Bulgaria, the Caucasus, and Switzerland. Both Salman and Meloian were Armenakans who joined the Dashnak Organization. The *History of the ARF* (pp. 67, 83, 185–214) lists three "local leaders" as well (Teos, Ales, and Panos), but the fact that so little is known about them may indicate a certain lack of importance.

57. *History of the ARF,* p. 83.

58. The following descriptions are drawn from the *History of the ARF;* Anahide Ter Minassian, "Van, 1915," in *Armenian Van/Vaspurakan,* ed. Richard G. Hovannisian (Costa Mesa, Calif.: Mazda Publishers, 2000), pp. 209–44; and Yervant Khatanassian, "Two Glossaries for the Assistance of Researchers," *Armenian Review* 32, no. 3 (September 1979): 267–79.

59. Dikran Mesrob Kaligian, "The Armenian Revolutionary Federation under Ottoman Constitutional Rule, 1908–1914" (Ph.D. dissertation, Boston College, 2003), p. 188, referring to a document from the Dashnak Eastern Bureau.

60. Khatanassian ("Two Glossaries") gives his birth name as Nicol Boghossian; Ter Minassian ("Van, 1915") gives it as Nikoghayos Poghosi Mikayelian.

61. Although this is not mentioned in the sources listed above, Vramian produced American naturalization papers in 1909 (FO 195/2318, Morgan to Lowther, Van, October 20, 1909).

62. *Fedai* is from the Turkish, originally Arabic, meaning "one willing to sacrifice his life." The term was in general use for Armenian guerrillas. It is still used for guerrillas in the Middle East today.

63. FO 881/9433, Dickson to Sir N. O'Conor, Van, March 2, 1908. See also FO 881/9432, Dickson to O'Conor, Van, February 17, 1908. It must be noted that Dickson made this assessment after the weapons were seized (see below). He estimated in 1907 that the Dashnaks had "2,000 armed men in Van" and could expect 3,000 more from villages "in a few days" (FO 881/9305, Dickson to O'Conor, Van, August 4, 1907).

64. See chapter 8.

65. FO 881/9305, Dickson to O'Conor, Van, August 4, 1907.

66. See, for example, FO 195/1804, Devey to Fitzmaurice, Van, December 8, 1892.

67. Louise Nalbandian, *The Armenian Revolutionary Movement* (Berkeley: University of California Press, 1963), p. 174.

68. FO 195/2063, Maunsell to O'Conor, Van June 16, 1899.

69. Nalbandian, *The Armenian Revolutionary Movement,* p. 183.

70. FO 424/191, Williams to Currie, Van, January 24, 1897.

71. Canan Seyfeli, *Istanbul Ermeni Patrikliği kuruluş ve tarihten günümüze idari yapısı* (Ankara: Aziz Andaç Yayınları, 2005), p. 44.

72. FO 424/208, Tyrrell to O'Conor, Van, January 10, 1905. It is interesting that the Americans felt at one point that Arsen had cooperated with the revolutionaries (C. D. Ussher, letter of August 8, 1904, ABC 11.4, Barton, James L., Papers, 1877–1943, Box 11:2). This may have been a falling-out among the revolutionaries.

73. Hüsamettin Yıldırım, *Rus-Türk Ermeni Münasebetleri 1914–1918* (Ankara: Kök, 1990), p. 64.

74. Ottoman Empire, *Aspirations et agissements révolutionnaires des Comités Arméniens avant et après la proclamation de la Constitution Ottomane* (Istanbul: n.p., 1917), p. 263; Hasan Oktay, "Taşnak Partisinin Van Şubesinin V. Kongresi (Vasparugan Ermeni İhtilal Komitesi Meclis-i Meşveretinin Müzâkerât Fezlekesi)," *Yeni Türkiye Dergisi* 38 (2001): 824.

75. ABC 16.9.7, Eastern Turkey Mission, 1910–1919, Documents, vol. 25a, no. 123, "Annual Report of Van Station for the Year 1911." The Dashnaks actively and successfully opposed the expansion of American missionary instruction in the villages. ("Annual Report of Van Station for the Year 1911"). They saw the Americans, who had a very different view of the use of schools, as opposition. Dashnaks threatened native pastors and even disrupted missionary meetings in Van City itself (ABC 16.9.7, Eastern Turkey Mission, 1910–1919, Documents, vol. 25a, no. 117, "Annual Report of Van Station, Eastern Turkey Mission, the Year 1910"). "The political situation has been changed somewhat by the appointment of a new governor. The delicacy of the situation is very much increased by the presence and activity of the revolutionists, whose influence has greatly extended and who assume to control the conduct of all the Armenians both in the city and in the villages. This increases the difficulty of our own work. One of the most regrettable things about the presence of the revolutionists is the open and decided influence against religion and morality which they exercise" (*The Ninety-seventh Annual Report of ABCFM Presented at the Meeting Held at Cleveland, Ohio, Oct. 9–11, 1907* [Boston: American Board, 1908], p. 81).

76. The Hunchaks, very much a spent force in the early 1900s, had operated in rural regions (especially in Zeytun and Sasun) in the 1890s but do not seem to have done much

with the Van villagers. Dashnak rural organization began in earnest in the Sasun-Muş region before it began in Van.

77. G. C. Raynolds, ABC 16.9.7, Eastern Turkey Mission, 1910–1919, Documents, vol. 25a, no. 111, "Report of the Village Work in the Van Station Field, Eastern Turkey Mission, 1910."

78. FO 424/196, Currie to Salisbury, Constantinople, April 15, 1898; FO 424/196, Monahan to Currie, Bitlis, March 28, 1898.

79. FO 881/9305, Dickson to O'Conor, Van, October 29, 1907.

80. Although extortion had been used before, the decision to use extortion and exemplary murder to gain Dashnak funds was formally taken by "The Body Representing the Will of the Dashnaktsutiun" in 1901. See *History of the ARF,* pp. 62–63, which gives the decision to implement the policy and some of those murders. It states that the policy was successful: "in implementing the project the ARF lost a few of its men; nevertheless, it also carried out several dramatic assassinations" (p. 63). The Hunchaks also carried out assassinations (Hratch Dasnabedian, "The Hnchakian Party," trans. Mariné A. Arakelians, *Armenian Review* 41, no. 4 [Winter 1988]: 26–77). Altan Deliorman, *Türklere Karşı Ermeni Komitecileri* (Istanbul: Boğaziçi Üniversitesi, 1975), p. 31, lists some of the Armenians murdered.

81. *History of the ARF*, p. 47.

82. Ibid., p. 67.

83. FO 424/206, Heathcote to O'Conor, Bitlis, August 3, 1904.

84. FO 424/208, Heathcote to O'Conor, Bitlis, June 4, 1905. For earlier examples of the murder of priests and others by the revolutionaries, see FO 424/184, Cumberbatch to Currie, Erzurum, October 21, 1895. The "enforcement" reached the highest levels. A revolutionary attempted to kill the Armenian patriarch of Constantinople, Malachia Ormanian, during a church service in 1903. Ormanian, considered by the revolutionaries too conciliatory toward the government, was wounded (FO 881/8202, Whitebread to Lansdowne, Constantinople, January 26, 1903).

85. FO 195/2147, Tyrrell to O'Conor, Van, April 2, 1903.

86. FO 881/9305, Dickson to O'Conor, Van, August 4, 1907.

87. FO 195/2147, Tyrrell to O'Conor, Van, April 2, 1903.

88. FO 195/2283, Dickson to O'Conor, Van, March 2, 1898.

89. The only concrete assistance that the revolutionaries provided to Armenian villagers lay in sometimes assisting the villagers in their fights with the Kurds. See Consul Dickson's report on the disturbances in the Çatak region in 1908, for example. The report, drawn entirely from Armenian and missionary statements after the facts, was completely one-sided, but it did indicate that the "fedai" had participated in the fights on the side of the Armenian villagers (FO 195/2284, Dickson to Lowther, Van, August 18, 1908).

90. See FO 424/191, Williams to Currie, Van, January 24, 1897.

91. See Hasan Oktay, "Ermeniler ve Van İhtilal Örgütü 1896–1915," *Ermeni Araştırmaları Dergisi* 5 (2002): 87; M. Kalman, *Batı Ermenistan Kürt İlişkileri ve Jenosit* (Istanbul: Zel, 1994), pp. 40–41; Türkkaya Ataöv, "Ermeni Terörizminde silah Sağlanması: Osmanlı Belgelerine Dayalı Gerçekler," *Uluslararası Terörizm ve Uyuşturucu Madde Kaçakçılığı Sempozyumu* (Ankara: Ankara Üniversitesi 1984), pp. 163–71.

92. Ussher, September 10, 1904, ABC 11.4, Barton, James L., Papers, 1877–1943, Box 11:2.

93. For a typical incident, see FO 424/208, Heathcote to O'Conor, Bitlis, May 14, 1905, which describes a battle between rebels sheltering in a village and troops in which seven Armenian revolutionaries from Russia, sixteen villagers, and twelve soldiers died. The village was not burned, but Kurds looted it.

94. *History of the ARF,* p. 49.

95. Although it seems likely that the Russian government sometimes provided weapons to the revolutionaries, especially immediately before World War I, no proof of this has surfaced. Consul Dickson felt that the weapons smuggled into the Ottoman Empire were bought or stolen from Russian armories. He cited one instance in which the Dashnaks stole 1,000,000 rounds of ammunition from the Alexandropol Armory by bribing some guards and drugging others (FO 881/9433, Dickson to Sir N. O'Conor, Van, March 2, 1908). This incident is also mentioned in the *History of the ARF,* p. 69.

96. FO 424/196, no. 17, Elliot to Currie, Tabreez, May 2, 1898; Nalbandian, *The Armenian Revolutionary Movement,* pp. 173–174; Sami Önal, *Sadettin Paşa'nın Anıları* (Istanbul: Remzi Kitapevi, 2003), p. 105.

97. For example, in 1908 two of the chiefs of the three Haydaranlı subtribes, Hüseyin and Emin, were enemies of the revolutionaries, while the third, Mehmet, was their ally.

98. Ali Karaca, ed., *Anadolu Islahatı ve Ahmet Şâkir Paşa* (Istanbul: Eren, 1993), p. 130. See also FO 195, 2147, Freeman to O'Conor, Bitlis, January 10, 1903.

99. For example, the depot at Kaçan, mentioned below, was slightly north of the first route.

100. *History of the ARF,* pp. 65–66. The *History of the ARF* also lists a route from Kars and one from Batum to Erzurum. In 1913 guns came from the north and may have used this route earlier. See "Rebellion in the City of Van" in chapter 8.

101. FO 195/2284, Dickson to Lowther, Van, September 22, 1908. Kop Mehmet also cooperated politically with the revolutionaries. After the 1908 Revolution they united in an attempt to secure the dismissal of Cevdet Bey, the kaymakam of Saray, who was deemed too efficient by both Kurdish tribesmen and Armenian rebels (FO 195/2284, Dickson to Lowther, Van, September 30, 1908).

102. "Dilman and Salmas are used as a base by the Fedai to pass arms and men into Turkey. The have a strong Committee there, of which one Muggerditch is the head. Formerly they were on bad terms with the neighboring Kurds, but this year they have been the best of friends" (FO 371/540, Dickson to O'Conor, Van, January 31, 1908).

103. Malkhas: Ardashes Hovsepian, a prominent Dashnak in Van. See the section "Armenian Revolutionaries" above.

104. Malhas, "Yaşantılar," *Hayrenik Aylık Dergi* 2 (1926), cited in Kalman, *Batı Ermenistan Kürt İlişkileri ve Jenosit,* appendix 68; FO 881/8202, Freeman to O'Conor, Bitlis, January 24, 1903; *History of the ARF,* p. 65.

105. FO 424/196, no. 17, Elliot to Currie, Tabreez, May 2, 1898.

106. See Önal, *Sadettin Paşa'nın Anıları,* p. 163. There were, however, unsubstantiated rumors of soldiers selling rifles to revolutionaries as late as 1911. See FO 195/2375, Molyneux-Seel to Lowther, Van, April 8, 1911.

107. See FO 424/206, Tyrrell to O'Conor, Moush, August 4, 1904.

108. FO 424/206, Tyrrell to O'Conor, Moush, August 4, 1904.

109. *History of the ARF,* pp. 46–47. The Sasun rebellion cannot be described here for reasons of space and because it had limited direct impact on Van Province. For information on the rebellion, see the extended entries in FO 424/202, Hocaoğlu, Gürun, and

other entries in the bibliography. For the most relevant comments by Consul Maunsell in Van, see FO 195/2063, Maunsell to O'Conor, Van, June 16, 1899; FO 195/2063, Maunsell to O'Conor, Van, June 16, 1899; FO 195/2063, Maunsell to O'Conor, Van, June 16, 1899; FO 195/2063, Maunsell to O'Conor, Bitlis, May 21, 1899; FO 195/2063, Maunsell to O'Conor, Van, June 16, 1899; FO 195/2063, Maunsell to O'Conor, Van, June 16, 1899. The American missionaries commented: "As the station [Van] is not far from both the Russian and the Persian borders, it is necessarily troubled by the ill-guided efforts of Armenian revolutionarists, so called, whose only mission seems to be to create disturbances and bring trouble upon their own people" ("July 7, 1904, Van Station Secret Report," *The Ninety-Fourth Annual Report of ABCFM Presented at the Meeting Held at Grinnell, Iowa, Oct. 11–13, 1904* [Boston: American Board, 1905], p. 69).

110. Reports of Armenian incursions were so frequent that they can be found throughout the diplomatic records of the time. For example, see FO 424/196, Elliot to Currie, Tabreez, May 17, 1898; FO 424/200, Maunsell to O'Conor, Van, April 26, 1900; FO 881/8202, Freeman to O'Conor, Bitlis, January 10, 1903; FO 881/8202, Hampson to O'Conor, Erzeroum, September 2, 1903; FO 881/8202, O'Conor to Landsdowne, Therapia, October 9, 1903; and FO 881/8202, Tyrrell to O'Conor, Van, October 27, 1903.

111. These battles were too numerous to cite individually. For examples, see FO 424/197, O'Conor to Salisbury, Constantinople, November 23, 1898; FO 424/197, Mirzoyan to O'Conor, Bitlis, November 18, 1898; FO 424/197, Massey to O'Conor, Erzurum, November 21, 1898; and Massey to O'Conor, Erzurum, November 28, 1898; and FO 424/199, Lamb to O'Conor, Erzurum, November 9, 1899. Some of the incursions are described briefly in *History of the ARF*, pp. 67–69. The British pointed out that the Ottomans were making all possible efforts to protect the Armenian border villagers from attacks. This was not always successful (FO 424/199, O'Conor to Salisbury, Constantinople, July 12, 1899).

112. See, for example, FO 424/199, Lamb to O'Conor, Erzurum, November 13, 1899; FO 424/199, O'Conor to Salisbury, Constantinople, November 22, 1899; FO 424/205, Hampson to O'Conor, Erzurum, October 2, 1903; FO 424/205, Hampson to O'Conor, Erzurum, October 3, 1903; FO 424/205, Hampson to O'Conor, Erzurum, October 4, 1903; FO 424/205, Hampson to O'Conor, Erzurum, October 9, 1903; and FO 424/205, Hampson to O'Conor, Erzurum, October 13, 1903. In addition to guns, the rebels brought with them large amounts of dynamite (FO 424/205, Hampson to O'Conor, Erzurum, September 2, 1903).

113. The examples are too numerous to cite, but see FO 424/202, de Bunsen to Landsdowne, Constantinople, November 23, 1901, on one battle in which revolutionaries seized the Arakh Monastery. The Ottomans were thwarted in attacking them because they could not fire on the monastery, in which there were many children. See also FO 424/197, O'Conor to Salisbury, Constantinople, November 10, 1898; and FO 424/208, Heathcote to O'Conor, Bitlis, August 1, 1905.

114. The government in Iran was satisfied to accept large bribes to leave the revolutionaries alone. See FO 424/196, Elliot to Currie, Tabreez, May 17, 1898.

115. See, for example, FO 424/196, Elliot to Currie, Van, March 12, 1898; FO 881/6958, Currie to Salisbury, June 3, 1897; and FO 881/6958, Williams to Currie, April 5, 1897.

116. See, for example, FO 424/203, O'Conor to Landsdowne, Constantinople, December 17, 1902; and FO 424/206, Tyrrell to O'Conor, Van, May 7, 1904.

117. FO 424/107, O'Conor to Salisbury, September 28, 1898; FO 424/197, Graves to de Bunsen, Erzurum, September 23, 1898; and FO 424/197, Graves to de Bunsen, Erzurum, September 29, 1898.

118. FO 881/8202, Hampson to O'Conor, Erzurum, October 5, 1903; FO 881/8202, Hampson to O'Conor, Erzurum, October 6, 1903; FO 881/8202, Hampson to O'Conor, Erzurum, October 23, 1903; and FO 881/8202, Shipley to O'Conor, Erzeroum, November 4, 1903.

119. FO 424/203, Maunsell to O'Conor, Constantinople, February 12, 1902.

120. FO 424/204, Tyrrell to O'Conor, Van, October 27, 1903. False accusations of abuse of Armenians by soldiers and others, which did not stand up under investigation by European consuls, were common. For example, see FO 196/1617, Devey Telegram, Van, May 29, 1890; FO 881/6447, Devey to Graves, Van, October 3, 1893; FO 881/6447, Devey to Graves, Van, November 6, 1893; FO 424/200, Maunsell to de Bunsen, Van, November 10, 1900; FO 424/208, Townley to Landsdowne, Constantinople, January 24, 1905; FO 195/2284, Dickson to Lowther, Van, September 22, 1908; FO 424/210, Hagopian to Foreign Office, September 26, 1906; and FO 424/210, Dickson to O'Conor, Van, September 30, 1906; and FO 881/10401, Marling to Grey, Constantinople, July 6, 1913.

121. FO 195/2147, Tyrrell to O'Conor, Van, October 27, 1903.

122. FO 195/2082, Maunsell to O'Conor, Van, December 19, 1899.

123. FO 424/205, Hampson to O'Conor, October 19, 1903. For a lower estimate see FO 424/205, Shipley to O'Conor, Erzerum, November 16, 1903.

124. FO 424/197, Monahan to O'Conor, Bitlis, October 13, 1898.

125. One British consul estimated that five thousand to six thousand "fedai" there were "all well armed, drilled, and organized" (Hampson to O'Conor, Erzeroum, October 19, 1903). Another (Maunsell to O'Conor, Constantinople, November 6, 1903) estimated five hundred. Both were far from the seat of the action. The actual number probably fell somewhere between the two estimates, perhaps near the Ottoman estimate of eight hundred to fifteen hundred. The Sasun troubles are not considered here in any detail. There is extensive mention of them in FO 195/2172.

126. FO 424/206: O'Conor to Landsdowne, Constantinople, March 1, 1904; Heathcote to O'Conor, Bitlis, February 13, 1904; and Heathcote to O'Conor, Bitlis, February 20, 1904.

127. FO 424/206, Shipley to O'Conor, Erzeroum, March 12, 1904.

128. The Ottoman government instead listed Muslim homes burned and Muslim villagers killed. See, for example, BOA, HR. SYS (Political) 2865/11 Hariciye Nezaretine 27 Haziran 1904, no. 187, Ambassador in Paris to the Interior Ministry; BOA, A.MKT. MHM. 673/25, telegram of the Bitlis Governor Ferit to the Grand Vezir on 8 Haziran 1905.

129. FO 424/206, O'Conor to Landsdowne, Constantinople, May 9, 1904; "Memorandum of Mr. Lamb" in FO 424/206, O'Conor, Constantinople, May 24, 1904; June 20, 1904; and June 25, 1904.

130. FO 424/206, O'Conor to Landsdowne, Constantinople, July 9, 1904.

131. Andranik's band was wide ranging. In 1902 it had occupied the Arakh Monastery near Muş, from which it escaped, pursued by troops (FO 424/203, Freeman to O'Conor, Bitlis, January 7, 1902).

132. FO 881/9050, O'Conor to Grey, Constantinople, May 7, 1907; "Note by Sublime Porte," in FO 881/9050, O'Conor to Grey, Constantinople, May 27, 1907; Ussher,

September 12, 1904, ABC 11.4, Barton, James L., Papers, 1877–1943, Box 11:2. The incident in 1904 caused a stir in Van out of proportion to its importance, but the governor kept any trouble in check (September 13, 1904, ABC 11.4, Barton, James L., Papers, 1877–1943, Box 11:2).

133. FO 424/206, Tyrrell to O'Conor, Van, October 17, 1904.

134. On the general history of Armenians in the Russian Empire, see Ronald Grigor Suny, "Eastern Armenia under Tsarist Rule," in *The Armenian People from Ancient to Modern Times,* ed. Richard G. Hovannisian (New York: Palgrave/St. Martin's, 1997), vol. 2, pp. 109–37.

135. This was the same Şerif who would soon be in alliance with the Armenian rebels to smuggle weapons into Van, an indication of the confusing and changeable situation in the province.

136. FO 195/2063, Maunsell to O'Conor (telegram), Van, July 23, 1899.

137. This seizure was a major conflict between the Russians and the Armenians, resulting in riots and even guerrilla actions. See FO 424/205, Stevens to Landsdowne, Batum, numerous dispatches in September and October 1903; FO 424/205, Scott to Landsdowne, St. Petersburg, September 17, 1903; FO 424/186, Stevens to Salisbury, Batoum, January 23, 1896; the entries in FO 881/8202, Scott to Landsdowne, St. Petersburgh and Batum, September 15, 17, 18, 19, 23, 24, 25, 26, and October 1, 29, 1903; and *History of the ARF,* p. 70. There had been earlier seizures. For a general picture, see Anahide Ter Minassian, *Nationalism and Socialism in the Armenian Revolutionary Movement,* trans. A. M. Berrett (Cambridge Mass.: Zoryan, 1984), pp. 7, 31, 32; and Suny, "Eastern Armenia under Tsarist Rule," pp. 131–37.

138. See *History of the ARF,* pp. 69–70.

139. Consul R. W. Graves felt that the revolutionaries were aided by Armenians in the Russian service: "a large number of the smaller police officials in the Caucasus are Armenians, and in sympathy with revolutionary movements in Turkey" (FO 424/197, Constantinople, December 2, 1898, comment on Elliot's memorandum of November 30, 1898).

140. FO 424/196, Elliot to Currie, Tabreez, May 5, 1898.

141. See chapter 7.

142. The British were particularly interested in the conversion problem, because British missionaries were important in the Nestorian country. Among the many documents on the civil and religious conflicts and Russian spies among the Nestorians (etc.), see FO 424/200, Maunsell to O'Conor, Van, November 13, 1899; FO 424/200, Maunsell to O'Conor, Van, December 20, 1899; FO 424/200, Maunsell to O'Conor, Van, December 29, 1899; and FO 424/200, Lamb to O'Conor, Erzurum, February 24, 1900.

143. FO 195/2063, Maunsell to O'Conor, Van, March 20, 1899. Maunsell did not give any names or further identification of the three; nor did he know what happened to them once they reached Russia. Rebels named Arshag and Vartan appear later, but the names were not uncommon, so it is impossible to know if they were the same men. It was not only Russian citizenship that protected the revolutionaries. When one of the leaders of the Dashnaks in Van (Arshak Vramian) was summoned before the prosecutor in 1909, it was found that he could not even be questioned, because he held naturalization papers as an American citizen and was in fact immune to Ottoman law (FO 195/2318, Morgan to Lowther, Van, October 20, 1909).

144. *History of the ARF,* pp. 77–79.

145. ABC 11.4, Barton, James L., Papers, 1877–1943, Box 11:2, Confidential Statement, Bitlis and Van Vilayets, June 7, 1904. See also Ussher, September 12, 1904, ABC 11.4, Barton, James L., Papers, 1877–1943, Box 11:2.

146. FO 424/210, Geary to O'Conor, December 26, 1905.

147. See Justin McCarthy, *Death and Exile: The Ethnic Cleansing of Ottoman Muslims* (Princeton: Darwin, 1995), pp. 123–26.

148. FO 424/206, Tyrrell to O'Conor, Van, April 8, 1904.

149. FO 424/210, O'Conor to Grey, Constantinople, May 29, 1906.

150. FO 195/2147, Freeman to O'Conor, Bitlis, January 10, 1903.

151. See "The Disadvantage of Living Next to Iran" in chapter 4.

152. Ali Rıza had a reputation in the bureaucracy as a strong man who could handle difficult assignments. He had been assigned as the kaymakam to both Şemdinan, seat of Mehmet Sadik, and the dangerous border region of Saray, home of İsmail Simko (see chapter 7). When he was assigned to Saray, the Kurdish tribes complained that he was too hard a man (FO 195/2147, Tyrrell to O'Conor, Van, January 31, 1903).

153. FO 881/9305, Sbordone to Shipley, Van, June 24, 1907.

154. BOA İrade-i Dahiliye (Ministry of the Interior) 14, 23, 25.

155. BOA İrade-i Dahiliye, 46/1. The commission was not actually disbanded until immediately after the 1908 Revolution. Tahir Paşa became governor of Erzurum (FO 195/2284, Dickson to Lowther, September 30, 1908).

156. BOA İrade-i Dahiliye, 46/1; BOA İrade-i Dahiliye, 46/2.

157. Hüseyin Çelik, *Görenlerin Gözüyle Van'da Ermeni Mezalimi* (Van: Yüzüncü Yıl Üniversitesi, 1996), p. 77.

158. BOA İrade-i Dahiliye, 25.

159. FO 195/2250, Dickson to O'Conor, Van, March 31, 1907.

160. *Ermeni Komitelerinin Amal ve Harekât-i İhtilâliyesi* (Istanbul: Matbaa-i Amire, 1332), p. 256; Demiroğlu, *Van'da Ermeni mezâlimi, 1895–1920,* p. 53; FO 195/2250, Dickson to O'Conor, Van, March 31, 1907.

161. FO 195/2250, Dickson to O'Conor, Van, March 31, 1907.

162. Demiroğlu, *Van'da Ermeni mezâlimi, 1895–1920,* p. 53.

163. FO 195/2250, Dickson to O'Conor, Van, March 31, 1907.

164. FO 195/2250, Dickson to O'Conor, Van, June 1, 1907.

165. Ali Rıza received a number of death threats (FO 881/9305, Dickson to O'Conor, Van, August 4, 1907).

166. Demiroğlu, *Van'da Ermeni mezâlimi, 1895–1920,* p. 54.

167. BOA İrade-i Dahiliye, 55. Consul Dickson had an unfavorable opinion of Armarak (FO 881/9305, Dickson to O'Conor, Van, August 4, 1907).

168. BOA İrade-i Dahiliye, 55.

169. BOA İrade-i Dahiliye, 35.

170. BOA İrade-i Dahiliye, 72/1.

171. See appendix 2.

172. Descriptions of these events have been drawn from the Ottoman Archives (as noted) and from FO 881/9432, Dickson to O'Conor, Van, February 9, 1908; FO 881/9432, Barclay to Grey, Constantinople, March 27, 1908; FO 881/9433, Dickson to Barclay, Van, April 6, 1908; FO 881/9433, Barclay to Grey, Constantinople, May 17, 1908; FO 881/9433, Dickson to Barclay, Van, April 20, 1908; FO 881/9433, Dickson to Barclay, Van, May 18,

1908; FO 881/9433, Dickson to Barclay, Van, May 24, 1908; Çelik, *Görenlerin Gözüyle Van'da Ermeni Mezalimi,* p. 78; Demiroğlu, *Van'da Ermeni mezâlimi, 1895–1920,* pp. 55, 565; Ergünöz Akçora, "Yaşayanların Diliyle Van ve Çevresinde Ermeni Mezalimi," in *Yakın Tarihimizde Van Uluslararası Sempozyumu* (Van: Van Yüzüncü Yıl Üniversitesi, 1990), p. 157; Hasan Oktay, "Ermeni Komitecilerini Katlettiği Van Valisi Ali Rıza Paşa ve Türküsü," *Yeni Türkiye Dergisi* 38 (2001): 835. There are alternative versions of the story, of which the most common is the contention by anti-Dashnak Armenians that Aram raped Vatan and Davit was seeking revenge (see K. S. Papazian, *Patriotism Perverted* [Boston, Baikar Press, 1934], p. 69).

173. The British consul gave a smaller estimate in his "Approximate List of guns ammunition etc. belonging to the fedai seized by the government in Van up to 30 June 08":

Rifles	1300
Cartridges	450,000
Mauser Pistols	50
Gunpowder	120 lbs.
Dynamite	800 lbs.
Bombs	19
Infernal Machines	3
Various machines instruments + electric batteries	
Money forger's implements + molds	
Huge quantities of lead and chemicals	
Printing presses. Archives, letters	
Revolutionary flag	
Committee's seal.	

(FO 195/2283, Dickson to Barclay, Van, June 29, 1908). See also FO 881/9432, Dickson to O'Conor, Van, February 9, 1908; and FO 195/2283, Dickson Telegram to Barclay, Van, June 9, 1908. For praise of Ali Rıza's handling of the situation, see FO 881/9432, Dickson to O'Conor, Van, February 17, 1908. For a thoroughly fanciful account of these events, drawn exclusively from the Dashnak paper in Paris, *Pro-Armenia,* see Aykut Kansu, *The Revolution of 1908 in Turkey* (Leiden: Brill, 1997), pp. 61–62, which contends that the revolutionaries in question were "a thousand Turkish [!] revolutionaries armed with two cannons" and claims that the fedai were members of the Committee of Union and Progress. Kansu's bibliography lists the appropriate British records, but she seems not to have read them or to have ignored them.

174. FO 881/9433, Dickson to Barclay, May 24, 1908; FO 195/2283, Dickson to O'Conor, Van, February 9, 1908.

175. BOA Y. MTV, 307/152, lef 4.

176. "About three miles from the [old] city a large cross-road comes in, and at the junction is a small bazaar. This spot is called Hach Poghan (The Cross Place), and is about the center of the 'garden city.' Roughly, it may be said, that west of Hach Poghan is a Moslem quarter, and east of it a Christian. A native of Van can pass from one end of the garden to another, without going along the roads, by means of holes in walls, &c., but troops almost invariably keep in the streets" (FO 195/2283, Dickson to O'Conor, Van, February 9, 1908).

177. The Dashnaks denied they had ordered the murder. According to local reminiscences, Aram, who was concerned that his work of many years would be destroyed,

summoned the members of the Van Dashnak committee to an emergency meeting and imprinted a black cross (the traditional mark of assassination) on Davit's name. An Armenian ironworker's apprentice named Dacat was selected to kill Davit.

178. BOA Y. MTV, 307/152, lef 2; FO 881/9432, Barclay to Grey, Constantinople, March 27, 1908.

179. BOA Y. MTV, 307/152, lef 3.

180. BOA Y. MTV, 307/152, lef 4; FO 881/9433, Dickson to Barclay, Van, April 6, 1903. Consul Dickson reported that the revolutionaries distributed the remaining guns to young Armenians and planned a more general revolt that did not transpire: "The fedai committee had decided that if the perquisitions were continued, they would resist, and that in that event they would mobilize all their available resources in this country, Persia, and Russia for a general Armenian revolt" (FO 195/2284, Dickson to Lowther, Van, September 7, 1908).

181. BOA Y. MTV, 307/164, lef 1. BOA Y. MTV, 308/2, lef 2; FO 881/9433, Barclay to Grey, Constantinople, April 5, 1908, "Summary of a Telegram Address by the Governor-General of the Vilayet of Van to the Grand Vezir"; FO 881/9433, Dickson to Barclay, Van, April 6, 1903. The bazaar was not completely opened for more than a month.

182. BOA Y. MTV, 307/152, lef 1.

183. BOA Y. MTV, 307/164, lef 2.

184. Ibid.

185. Ibid.

186. FO 881/9433, Dickson to Barclay, Van, April 6, 1903; FO 881/9433, Barclay to Grey, Pera, May 4, 1908, "Telegrams from the Governor of Van."

187. "Among the captured twelve were Aram, the Commander-in-Chief of all the 'fedai'; Theos, the chief native 'fedai,' and quite the most dangerous and influential among them—he might be called the Chief of the Intelligence and Staff; Terlimazian, the assassin of the traitor David, whose death caused the massacre of the 23rd March; Krikor, who with Theos murdered Armenak Effendi last year; Meloyan, the head Professor at the Armenian school in Van; two other 'fedai' soldiers, the remainder being natives of Van of lesser importance" (FO 881/9433, Dickson to Barclay, Van, May 24, 1908). Dickson believed that an informer had betrayed the Dashnak leaders (FO 195/2283, Dickson telegram to Barclay, Van, May 20, 1908). See also FO 195/2283, Dickson Telegram to Barclay, May 19, 1908; and FO 195/2283, Dickson Telegram to Barclay, May 26, 1908. The Russian consul asked instructions from his ambassador as to what he should do, because Aram and others were Russian subjects (Russian Foreign Affairs Archive, Political Section, No. 113, 7/20 May 1908, p. 51, quoted in Yusuf Halaçoğlu, *Ermeni Tehciri ve Gerçekler/1914–1918* [Ankara: Türk Tarih Kurumu, 2001], p. 37).

188. FO 881/9433, Barclay to Grey, Pera, May 10, 1908, FO 881/9433, Dickson to Barclay, Van, April 6, 1903; FO 881/9433, Dickson to Barclay, Van, May 10, 1903.

189. See chapter 6. Elements of the Turkish revolutionaries in Van had cooperated with the Dashnaks against Ali Rıza and were to be responsible for his dismissal (M. Şükrü Hanioğlu, *Preparation for a Revolution: The Young Turks, 1902–1908* [Oxford: Oxford University Press, 2001], p. 108, referring to British, Armenian, and German sources on the cooperation).

190. Aykut Kansu, *1908 Devrimi* (Istanbul: İletişim, 1995), pp. 79–80. In an indication of the situation, a requiem service for the souls of Armenians who had died in the

recent events was attended by the local CUP, the military band, and military officers and men.

191. FO 195/2284, Dickson to Lowther, Van, November 3, 1908.

192. FO 195/2284, Dickson to Lowther, September 7, 1908; Akçora, "Yaşayanların Diliyle Van ve Çevresinde Ermeni Mezalimi," p. 157.

193. Demiroğlu, *Van'da Ermeni mezâlimi, 1895–1920,* p. 54. Despite earlier statements of support, Consul Dickson did not evince a high opinion of Ali Rıza at the end. See FO 881/9433, Dickson to Barclay, May 24, 1908.

194. Those who remembered those days said that the population of Van was in tears (Çelik, *Görenlerin Gözüyle Van'da Ermeni Mezalimi,* p. 77; Akçora, "Yaşayanların diliyle Van ve Çevresinde Ermeni Mezalimi," p. 157).

195. *Cumhuriyetin Ellinci Yılında Van* (Istanbul: n.p., 1973), p. 116.

196. Aydın Talay, *Yıkılan Bir Şehrin Anatomisi* (Van: Van Belediye Başkanlığı, 1996), p. 120.

197. Hüseyin Çelik, "Ali Paşayı Vurdular," in *Van Turizm ve İş Rehberi* (Istanbul: İhlâl Finans, 1998), p. 59; BOA YEE; 36/131/152 lef 127; BOA YEE, 36/131/152 lef 231.

CHAPTER 6

The Committee of Union and Progress
and the Armenians, 1908–1912

The years 1907 and 1908 saw a sea change in the Armenian revolution in Van. Before then, the revolution had one main plan—to attack Muslims and bring about reprisals that would lead to European intervention. The model was Bulgaria, in which events had occurred exactly in that fashion, leaving in the end an independent Bulgaria. This had not worked for the revolutionaries in Eastern Anatolia. The massacres of Muslims in the rebellions of the 1890s and early 1900s had indeed led to massacres of Armenians, but the European powers had not intervened. After 1908 the revolutionary plan was to cooperate with the Russians in the conquest of Eastern Anatolia, in the hope that this would at least lead to autonomy. Great Power politics played a part in the transformation of the plan, as did internal affairs in the province.

The Anglo-Russian Agreement of 1907, shifting the balance of power in Europe, had great effect on the situation in Van and the plans of the revolutionaries. In the agreement Russia and Britain put aside their previously conflicting interests in the Middle East by dividing Iran into "spheres of influence." Britain was to have control over the southwestern Iran, where it had developing oil interests. Russia was to control northern Iran, a region that included the territory directly east of Ottoman Anatolia. All of Van Province bordered on the Russian sphere. British opposition to Russian action in western Iran, which had effectively kept the Russians from outright control of the region, ended.

In 1909 the Russians sent an army into northwestern Iran, ostensibly to put down constitutionalist government in Tabriz. By 1910 there were eight battalions of infantry and a division of Cossacks in northwestern Iran, along with twenty-four cannon. They were stationed at Tabriz, Urmia, Khoy, Dilman, Maku, Maragha, and Savuçbulak (Mehabad).[1] Unlike Persian rule in the past, the Russians actually controlled western Iran.

The Armenian rebels, like all other reasonable observers, could see that Russian power was dominant in the East. Russia had defeated the Ottomans in each of their nineteenth-century wars. In those wars Russia had possessed a far worse strategic position than it enjoyed in 1910. The Russians now threatened Ottoman Anatolia in both the north and the east. Never had Russia been in a better position to attack the Ottoman Empire. In the Crimean War Britain had been an ally of the Ottomans. In the 1877–78 war it had at least supported the Ottomans diplomatically. Now Britain was on the side of the Ottomans' enemy. Also, like all other reasonable observers, the Armenians could not foresee to what an extent Germany would later assist the Ottomans. The Ottomans appeared to be without real support. To the rebels, the situation was clear: Russia would win, and the best chance for the Armenian cause was alliance with Russia.[2]

For the government of Van and the Muslim people of the province, 1908 was a year of revelation and change. The discovery of thousands of rifles, hundreds of thousands of cartridges, and hundreds of pounds of dynamite indicated to anyone whose eyes were open that the revolutionaries were intent on more than self-defense. Unfortunately, the eyes of the new government of the Committee of Union and Progress were not open (as discussed below). In Van itself the triumph of the Ottoman revolutionaries was the all but final step in dividing the Armenians and Muslims into two antagonistic communities.

Viewing all the Armenians, not only the revolutionaries, as a threat to the state and to the lives of the Muslims was not a matter of prejudice or poor judgment. The Armenians of Van themselves had begun to be unified in their opposition to the Ottomans and the Muslims. The careful work of the revolutionaries in the countryside and cities had been successful. Those Armenians who stood up to the revolutionaries had been, or soon would be, silenced. Only the very bravest Armenians would in the future take the Ottoman side, with grave consequences for the Armenians.[3] But Armenian solidarity with the revolutionaries was not simply a matter of fear. Many Armenians, perhaps a majority of them, wanted an Armenian state. European-style nationalism had worked on their consciousnesses, just as it previously had entered the minds of Serbs, Bulgarians, and Greeks. Given a choice, most of the Armenians surely would have preferred a peaceful life under Ottoman rule to an awful war in the name of nationalism, but it did not appear that they would be given that choice. The revolutionaries would attack Muslims and spark reprisals on innocent Armenians—few Armenians could have doubted that. Nor could they have doubted that the Russians would ultimately attack and win. If they were to suffer, the logic must have been: try to ensure that their side would win by joining and supporting the revolutionaries.

ARMENIAN REVOLUTIONARIES AND THE COMMITTEE OF UNION AND PROGRESS

The association between the Armenian revolutionary movement and the Committee of Union and Progress began in the 1890s.[4] The two shared a goal—the deposition of Sultan Abdülhamit II—and both were part of the heady revolutionary atmosphere of nineteenth-century Europe. At first the cooperation between the two groups was minimal, primarily expressions of common interest. The Armenians, especially the Dashnaks in Europe, were at first the most interested in some form of alliance.[5] Many members of the CUP opposed cooperation with the Armenians. They were committed to a unified Ottoman Empire under constitutional rule, with common citizenship, whereas the Armenian committees were dedicated to autonomy and perhaps independence for Armenians. The CUP, however, was a stew of conflicting ideologies. Members of another faction, themselves favorable to the idea of an empire made up of autonomous regions, supported cooperation with the Armenians.[6] They also had a practical purpose in wanting Armenian contacts: They felt, largely correctly, that the British supported the Armenian cause. Alliance with the Armenians would draw British support to the CUP.[7] These "decentralizers" at first negotiated secretly with the Dashnak Committee. Later, assured that the majority of the CUP would support them, they published open letters suggesting alliance.

The Dashnak and Reformed Hunchak Committees agreed to take part in the convention of Ottoman opposition groups convened by the CUP in Paris in 1902, but only on the condition that their terms, supporting Armenian autonomy, were met.[8] The delegates to the convention were not elected. They were primarily selected by those who favored decentralization, and the majority of those delegates unsurprisingly accepted the Armenian conditions. At the convention, after days of wrangling, the majority of delegates accepted the concept of separate treatment for the "six provinces" that were claimed as Armenia,[9] the idea of autonomy, and the benefit of European intervention to topple the regime. A significant minority of delegates, however, with sizable support led by Ahmed Rıza and other Old Guard members of the CUP (the centralizers), completely opposed all those points.[10] Indeed, the "minority" at the meeting may have been an actual majority of CUP supporters, because the delegates had mainly been chosen by the decentralizers. Many of the centralizers had begun to espouse forms of Turkish nationalism, but their main objection was that revolutionary groups such as the Macedonians and Armenians wanted independence, not a reformed Ottoman Empire.[11]

The conflict between the two positions continued until the triumph of the Ottoman revolutionaries in 1908 and beyond. In 1907 a Congress of Ottoman Opposition Parties in Paris brought the Dashnaktsutiun and the Ottoman rebels into a "tactical alliance" to depose Abdülhamit II and bring back the Ottoman Constitution, but only did so by submerging real differences.[12] The CUP still contained both those who accepted the autonomy of Armenians and other groups and those who wanted a unified empire.

In terms of the ultimate effect of the Dashnak-CUP collaboration on the Armenian Question, the most important factors may have been the CUP's acceptance of the Dashnaks as the representatives of the Armenians in the empire and the political connections that developed between the two parties.[13] After the revolution, it was not ideology but rather practical politics that dictated the CUP alliance with the Dashnaks. Simply put, the Dashnaks were a necessarily element in the electoral and parliamentary coalition that kept the CUP in power. Even those who had opposed decentralization were willing to temporize with the Dashnaks in order to retain power. The European approbation of the Armenians was also a major factor underlying Dashnak political influence. The Ottoman Empire remained at the edge of a precipice: traditional British support against Russian intentions had disappeared, and German support for the Ottomans was only beginning. The European powers kept up strong pressure in favor of the Armenians. An alliance with the dominant Armenian political power seemed to be one way to hold off European dissolution of the empire.

THE CUP AND THE DASHNAKS IN VAN

The CUP already seems to have been in contact with the Dashnaks in Van in 1907. It was common knowledge there that the two revolutionary committees had an understanding. Secret meetings between the two were reportedly held in the city.[14]

After the revolution, although it was not yet a part of the legal administrative apparatus of the state, the CUP had what amounted to control over the Van government. In November 1908 Major Vehib of the Salonica

Committee of Union and Progress was in Van, reorganizing the CUP there and deciding which government officials would be promoted and which exiled. He created a "secret committee" that was to act as watchdog over officials: representatives from the army, local Muslims, and local Armenians were selected, then a secret "active and responsible committee" was chosen. Members of the secret committee were known only to each other and, of all people, to the British consul.[15] Van even became an open meeting place for revolutionaries. After the revolution, agents from the CUP met there with Armenian, Russian, and Persian revolutionaries.[16] Three senior CUP members came to Van in 1911 and stayed for nearly a month. They held conferences with what were described as "various Armenian political parties."[17]

With the removal of Ali Rıza and the advent of the new regime, the Armenian revolutionaries came out in the open. The Dashnak Party, led by those who had been pardoned by the new government, rapidly turned itself into a very public political force. Aram, Ishkhan, "The Doctor," and Sarkis became politicians. Public speeches and pamphlets, filled with accusations against the state, became the norm for Armenian political life in the province.[18]

The three Armenian political parties—Dashnak, Hunchak, and Armenakan—did not easily relinquish their conflicts. Immediately before the triumph of the 1908 Revolution they had held competing public meetings and bickered among themselves. By March 1908, however, the Dashnaks in Van had easily established their supremacy. The Hunchaks submerged themselves under Dashnak authority. The Armenakans, by then transmogrified into the more conservative voice of the merchant class, settled into impotent opposition.[19] In the 1908 elections the Dashnaks, now in electoral alliance with the Hunchaks and supported by the Committee of Union and Progress, dominated the electoral process. The main public platform of the Dashnak Party was appealing—all taxes in arrears were to be forgiven.[20] For a penurious government this was clearly impossible, but it was good politics.

The election was a two-step process in which delegates were elected to an "electoral college" that chose the parliamentary representatives. The Dashnaks advanced their candidates for the electoral college and the Doctor (Vahan Papazian) as the "Armenian Candidate" for the parliament. They did not hesitate to use threats to achieve this result,[21] but his selection was probably a popular choice among Armenians. By 1908 the Armenian Church in Van, the revolutionaries' only potential rival for popular support, was under Dashnak control. The church distributed Dashnak electoral and revolutionary propaganda and supported Papazian's candidacy.[22] The Armenakan Party, supported primarily by the rich merchant class, was not popular in any sense of the word and had little sway over poorer Armenians. Their candidate, Terzibashian, was vilified and easily defeated in meetings that decided who would be the Armenian candidate.[23] Even some Kurdish tribes, although not the largest ones, were temporarily convinced to support the Armenians politically, because the Dashnaks were obviously in ascendancy.[24]

The benefits for the Dashnaks of their alliance with the Committee of Union and Progress were evident from the start of the new era in government. In the first election for the new Ottoman Parliament, after all the electoral machinery had been completed, two Muslims were elected from Van Province. Alleging voting irregularities in Erciş Kaza, Armenians went not to the law but to the CUP, which nullified the election and sent the local CUP head, Colonel Tahir, to arrange a more satisfactory result. Vahan Papazian was finally selected.[25] While not quite possessing a veto over bureaucratic appointments, the Dashnak Committee was able to dispose of officials who opposed it. At one point Nâzim Bey, the acting governor of Van, was removed from his position because of complaints from the Dashnaks. This was done despite furious complaints, especially from the military, that the government was giving in to Dashnak pressure and removing a capable leader.[26]

Despite their participation in the electoral process, there was never a question of the Dashnaks' disbanding their revolutionary bands and ending their smuggling of arms. The Van Dashnak leader Ishkhan categorically refused to do so.[27] If anything, the freedoms brought by the new regime encouraged such activity, because it was obvious that the Dashnak leaders who organized them would not be punished. The policies that had freed those who had stockpiled weapons in 1908 also ensured that those who once again brought in arms also went unpunished. A large number of militants began to arrive in Van from Russia and Iran. Armenian preparation for revolt and the importation of weapons continued.[28]

Futile attempts to arrest rebels proved their virtual invulnerability; intervention by the CUP and the Russian consulate assured that they would be freed.[29] In such an atmosphere it was natural that what the British described as the "systematic importation of arms" continued.[30] Consul Dickson wrote that by the beginning of 1909 hundreds of guns had already passed to the Van Armenians.[31] After the Russians occupied western Iran in 1909, the Iranian smuggling route for arms and ammunition became more secure. More than ever, western Iran had become a stronghold for the revolutionaries. The Ottoman government estimated that the rebels had formed four battalions there—four thousand men, with leaders who held ranks from corporal to major.[32] The Armenians undoubtedly showed a new militancy. In July 1912 Armenians of Voizim attacked the Kurds of the Müküs district (east of Çatak) and engaged in a two-day battle until troops arrived to put an end to the fighting.[33]

The new freedoms were a boon for revolutionary organization. Village revolutionary organization had previously been illegal and necessarily clandestine; now it was "political campaigning" that was not only tolerated but encouraged. Dashnak activities in the rural areas naturally increased, causing unease and bitterness among the Muslim populace. In 1911 British consul J. Molyneux-Seel analyzed the Dashnak position in Van Province. He was no friend to the Ottomans, whom he blamed for not properly addressing Armenian property rights and not properly punishing the Kurdish tribes. Yet he saw the Armenian revolutionaries as the main cause of discontent in the province:

> From what I have seen in the parts of the country I have visited I have become more convinced than ever of the baneful influence of the Taschnak Committee on the welfare of the Armenians and generally of this part of Turkey. It is impossible to overlook the fact in that in all places where there are no Armenian political organisations or where such organisations are imperfectly developed, the Armenians live in comparative harmony with the Turks and Kurds.[34]

The consul believed that the difficulties in regions where the revolutionaries were active went beyond the disruption caused by the rebels themselves. He felt that in those regions the government was less likely to address real Armenian grievances, because problems and complaints were ascribed to Dashnak agitation. Molyneux-Seel stated that the rebels kept the Armenian population in "a certain amount of alarm either well-founded or not" to advance their cause and to sell weapons lucratively to villagers: "They buy rifles at say £10 and force the villagers to buy from them at £20."[35]

THE BENEFIT FOR VAN'S CHRISTIANS

The changes in Van Province after the 1908 Revolution were not purely political. The advent of the CUP government brought tangible benefits to the Van Christians, who would naturally have attributed their improved situation to the Dashnaks. The army officers who made up part of the

CUP were willing to seek military solutions to the problems in the East. The "politicians" of the CUP, however, were friendly with the Armenian revolutionaries, so the military force was directed at the Kurds alone. Armenian villages that had been seized by Kurds were returned by force to their original owners.[36] Even though they had only limited success, troops were sent out to harry Kurdish bandits.[37] In one incident the Armenian bishop reported to the mutasarrıf of Başkale that tribes were threatening Christians in parts of Hakkâri Sancak. The mutasarrıf sent two companies of soldiers to protect them.[38] A large-scale disarmament of the Kurdish Hamidiye regiments began, with two thousand rifles collected from the Kurds in 1908 alone.[39] The Hamidiye as such were disbanded, turned into a militia, and reconstituted on a territorial rather than tribal basis. The army also intervened in the ongoing conflicts between the Kurds and the Nestorians, taking the Nestorian side. Troops, sometimes with cannon, were sent to attack Kurds who had raided Nestorian villages.[40] In one instance the Kurdish Jerikli tribe raided the Nestorian village of Ashita, killed ten people, and stole sheep. The Van governor sent three battalions after the Kurds. These surrounded the tribesmen, seized the stolen sheep, returned them to the Nestorians, and arrested the leaders of the tribe.[41] Powerful Kurdish chiefs were brought to Van, sometimes under arrest, to assert the power of the state over them. Europeans, who were unconcerned on the situation of the Muslims under the chiefs' control, commented that this had a salutary effect on the situation of the Armenians.[42] Any actions that hindered tribal aggression, even one-sided actions, made the province safer.

THE RESULTS OF THE ALLIANCE

Although the electoral alliance of the Committee of Union and Progress and the Dashnaktsutiun continued through the election of 1912, it was already beginning to dissolve. The Dashnak Arshak Vramian was elected a deputy from Van in 1912, but the many Dashnaks were dissatisfied with CUP efforts to help elect Dashnak deputies in other parts of the empire.[43]

On August 5, 1912, the CUP lost power in Istanbul. The Liberal Union, which (under various party names) had been the main opposition to the CUP, took power. The Liberals preferred alliance with more conservative Armenian groups. They were no friends of the Dashnaks, but their tenure in office saw little change in the political situation in Van. In the nearly six months of their government the Liberals were too busy losing the Tripolitanian War and the First Balkan War to devote much concern to the East. It was their traditional allies in the Committee of Union and Progress who were to begin questioning the alliance with the Dashnaks. After the CUP returned to power in the coup d'état of January 23, 1913, its tolerance of revolutionary separatism soon ended. The ruling triumvirate (Talat, Enver, and Cemal) consisted of practical men who labored to save what was left of the empire. The CUP leaders began to distance themselves from Dashnaks.[44]

The end of the CUP-Dashnak alliance came too late for Van. In Van the alliance had produced the dual effect of empowering the Armenian revolutionaries and alienating the Muslims. The government's actions would ultimately contribute to Kurdish revolt.[45] Unfortunately, the actions seem to have had no effect in lessening Armenian revolutionary aspirations.

The CUP-Dashnak alliance was the culmination of the gradual ascendancy of the Dashnaks in Van. Their revolutionary organization, their obvious power to enforce their wishes ruthlessly, and the spread of nationalism in the Armenian community had already made the Dashnaks the accepted representatives of most Armenians even before the CUP took power in Istanbul. On March 26, 1908, immediately after the 1908 troubles in Van, Consul Elliot met with Armenian "notables," the merchants, and other nonrevolutionary leaders of the Van Armenian community. What he heard in that meeting convinced him that even those who had once been opposed to the revolutionaries now saw the Armenians as a separate "nation" in opposition to the Ottomans:

> Even these better educated Armenians have the idea that in their present struggle with the Turks, they are entitled to rights analogous to those of a belligerent power. They hold, that is, (and in all good faith,) that the Fedais are in the position of an Armenian army, engaged in war with the Ottoman Empire, and therefore, though the Turks have a right to use force against avowed Fedais, (even this is barely acknowledged by some,) they have no such right to molest "civilian" Armenians, no matter what assistance in the way of shelter, information, &c, these may give to the "active army."
>
> This absolutely ridiculous idea was propounded to me also by the Fedai leaders during my interviews with them, and it is probably from them that the others imbibed it. Of course I pointed out to them that the "Societies" are not an independent power, but at best rebels against a recognized government, and that no government would admit that shelter-

ing rebels and conspirators was anything but a criminal offense. Further, I urged that on their own showing the Fedais were breaking the laws of civilized war, in that they wear no uniform, and pass whenever possible as peaceful citizens. Naturally, my arguments quite failed to convince them.[46]

The discovery of the Dashnak arms depots and the subsequent unpunished murder of Davit ultimately strengthened the revolutionaries' power in Van. Not only did those responsible for the act escape unpunished: they were elected to Parliament. The ties between the Dashnak Party and the new government had the effect of cementing the government's power over the Van Armenians. Previously, those few who opposed the Dashnaks were necessarily allied, however grudgingly, with the state. Now the state was the friend of the Dashnaks. The Armenian clergy, which had initially opposed the revolutionaries in all things, was increasingly seen by foreign observers as an ally of the revolutionaries.[47] The Armenian opponents of the revolutionaries were left with nowhere to turn.[48]

After 1908 the Dashnaks were seen by both Armenians and Muslims as the representatives of the Armenians, an attitude fostered by the CUP government. The old ideal of creating an Ottoman nationality to replace sectarian loyalties had failed, at least in Van Province. In the old millet system, Armenians would have brought their requests and complaints to the clergy or (from the middle of the nineteenth century) to the merchant class that dominated the community. Now they brought their complaints to the Dashnaks. This was demonstrated by an incident in Saray. Consul Dickson reported:

A band of Armenian "fedai" from Russia came over the frontier, fully armed and in broad daylight, and swaggered through the Kurd country into the town of Serai and so on to Van. This greatly incensed the Kurds at Sarai, and on the occasion of some quarrel in the market, when some Armenians had been insolent to a Turk, they took the opportunity of reading them a lesson by sacking the Armenian shops and beating their owners. The Armenian men of Serai on this left their families and came to Van *en bloc* to complain, not to the Government, but to the "fedai."[49]

The deposition of Sultan Abdülhamit II and institution of the constitutional regime were not met with euphoria among the Muslims of Van. Many publicly expressed their conviction that the new government would take the side of the Armenian revolutionaries. In Van, where the intentions of the revolutionaries had so recently been demonstrated, anything that advanced Armenian separatism was anathema to the Muslim populace. The revolutionaries did nothing to allay the fears of the majority. The consuls reported that the newly powerful Dashnak leaders acted insolently toward Muslims and exerted pressure on Muslim leaders and tribal chiefs, warning them that they would be punished if they did not obey orders.[50] Tribal chiefs and urban Muslims both obviously believed that the Dashnaks were the new power in Van. Consul Dickson even reported that "[s]everal Kurdish Aghas, who have been summoned to Van by the Acting Vali to answer for their misdeeds, have actually asked Aram (a Dashnak leader) on what terms he will secure their pardon."[51] This perhaps shows the resiliency of the Kurdish leaders, but their resentment must have been great. The urban Muslims showed their resentment by posting anti-Armenian signs on the walls of Van City, where posting placards had previously been an Armenian preserve. The two communities were more divided than ever before.

NOTES

1. W. E. D. Allen and Paul Muratoff, *Caucasian Battlefields* (Cambridge: Cambridge University Press, 1953), p. 230.

2. On changes in the Dashnak calculations, see Anahide Ter Minassian, *Nationalism and Socialism in the Armenian Revolutionary Movement,* trans A. M. Berrett (Cambridge, Mass.: Zoryan), pp. 45–47. Ter Minassian and other Armenian scholars seldom mention cooperation with the Russians.

3. See the case of Bedros Kapamacıyan in chapter 7.

4. The organizations of the Ottoman revolutionaries had various names in addition to the Committee of Union and Progress (İttihad ve Terraki Cemiyeti), and these organizations were often in conflict. "CUP" has been used here as a generic term, because it would be impossible to delineate in a few paragraphs what M. Şükrü Hanioğlu describes completely in two large books. The very brief summary given here necessarily conflates great differences in ideology, political maneuverings, and so forth.

5. M. Şükrü Hanioğlu, *The Young Turks in Opposition* (Oxford: Oxford University Press, 1995), pp. 86, 87, 90, 107, 116.

6. The faction included Damad Mahmud Paşa, at the time leader of the CUP, and Prince Sabahaddin.

7. The attempt at drawing official British support was unsuccessful.

8. The Hunchaks had broken into two conflicting parties (the Hunchaks and the Reformed Hunchaks) in 1896, with further division later. (Hratch Dasnabedian, "The Hnchakian Party," trans. Mariné A. Arakelians, *Armenian Review* 41, no. 4 [Winter 1988]: 32–34; Louise Nalbandian, *The Armenian Revolutionary Movement* [Berkeley: University of California Press, 1963], pp. 128–31).

9. Van, Erzurum, Bitlis, Mamuretülaziz, Diyarbakır, and Sivas.

10. Hanioğlu, *The Young Turks in Opposition,* pp. 116, 149, 166, 182, 193–97. See also

Hratch Dasnabedian, *History of the Armenian Revolution Federation, Dashnaktsutiun,* trans. Bryan Fleming and Vaha Habeshian (Milan: GEMME Edizione, 1989) (hereafter *History of the ARF*), p. 56.

11. M. Şükrü Hanioğlu, *Preparation for a Revolution: The Young Turks, 1902–1908* (Oxford: Oxford University Press, 1995), pp. 34–49, 69.

12. Ibid., pp. 191–204.

13. Hanioğlu correctly describes the "tactical alliance" between Turkish and Armenian revolutionaries immediately before the revolution as "almost worthless" in advancing the demise of the Old Regime (*Preparation for a Revolution*, p. 209). It is a fact that the Armenian rebels had nothing to do with the success of the 1908 Revolution.

14. FO 881/9305, Heard to O'Conor, Bitlis, August 25, 1907; FO 881/9305, Dickson to O'Conor, August 4, 1907. For the view of the Dashnaks on the alliance, see Dikran Mesrob Kaligian, "The Armenian Revolutionary Federation under Ottoman Constitutional Rule, 1908–1914" (Ph.D. dissertation, Boston College, 2003).

15. FO 195/2284, Dickson to Lowther, Van, November 3, 1908.

16. FO 195/2284, Dickson to Lowther, Van, September 30, 1908.

17. FO 195/2475, Molyneux-Seel to Marling, Van, January 9, 1911.

18. Consul Dickson, not one who politely suppressed his feelings, commented that "the Armenian has become a noisy, blatant, overbearing and insolent imitation of the worst type of politician" (FO 195/2284, Dickson to Lowther, Van, September 30, 1908).

19. FO 881/9532, Dickson to Lowther, Van, March 31, 1908.

20. FO 195/2284, Dickson to Lowther, Van, November 3, 1908.

21. "In their first campaign, which has for its object the election of 'Tashnak,' as opposed to 'Armenist' or Mussulman delegates to the 'Electoral College,' they [the Dashnaks] have been completely successful, securing the election of all their candidates. This result is due partly to the threats &c., which they have not scrupled to use" (FO 195/2284, Dickson to Lowther, Van, September 30, 1908).

22. FO 195/2347, Morgan to Lowther, Van, July 21, 1909.

23. The electoral laws contained no quotas by religion, but election of an Armenian was in fact guaranteed by the CUP-Dashnak "alliance," as seen below.

24. FO 195/2284, Dickson to Lowther, Van, September 30, 1908. On the activities and feelings of the Dashnaks at the time, see FO 195/2284, Dickson to Lowther, Van, November 3, 1908. The candidacy of an Armenian was aided by the requirement that only those who paid taxes could vote for members of the electoral selection body. This body then selected the parliamentary representatives, a system that allowed a great deal of political pressure to be brought to bear on the electors, who were not bound to support any particular candidates. See Hasan Kayalı, "Elections and the Electoral Process in the Ottoman Empire, 1876–1919," *International Journal of Middle East Studies* 27, no. 3 (August 1995): 265–86.

25. FO 881/9532, Dickson to Lowther, Van, March 31, 1908.

26. FO 195/2375, Molyneux-Seel to Lowther, Van, November 22, 1911.

27. "After the Ottoman Constitution was proclaimed, Vana Iskhan refused to leave his post and disperse his fedayee formations" (*History of the ARF*, p. 202).

28. FO 371/560/37689, Dickson to Lowther, Van, September 30, 1908, quoted in Salahi Sonyel, "The Turco-Armenian 'Adana Incidents' in the Light of Secret British Documents," *Belleten* 201 (December 1987): 1296.

29. FO 195/2318, Morgan to Lowther, Van, October 20, 1909.

30. FO 371/774, Shipley to Lowther, Erzurum, April 1, 1909. See also FO 195/2375, Molyneux-Seel to Lowther, Van, October 9, 1911.

31. FO 371/774/15584, Lowther to Grey, confidential dispatch, Istanbul, March 20, 1909, enclosing copy of dispatch from Captain Bertram Dickson, Van, March 3, 1909.

32. BOA, YEE, A/22-II/22-a /131, cited in Ali Karaca, ed., *Anadolu Islahatı ve Ahmet Şâkir Paşa* (Istanbul: Eren, 1993), p. 129.

33. FO 881/10164, Molyneux-Seel to Lowther, Van, July 10, 1912. Molyneux-Seel stated: "These Armenians are all Taschnakists and are well armed."

34. FO 195/2375, Molyneux-Seel to Lowther, Van, October 9, 1911.

35. Ibid.

36. See FO 881/9746, Molyneux-Seel to Lowther, Van, July 12, 1910. For similar improvements in Armenian conditions, see FO 881/9618, Safrastian to Shipley, Bitlis, September 9, 1909. The military was not always happy with its position. There was a lack of sympathy in the government and military for many of the land claims of the Armenians. Müşir Osman Paşa met a delegation from the village of Hasköy, whose inhabitants had revolted against the government and fled to Russia. In an unguarded moment, "He pointed out to them, and with considerable truth, that the Kurds [at least those Kurds] had never risen in revolt against the Government, whereas they, the Armenians (they are all ex-fedais in this village), after rising in arms, fled to Russia to escape the consequences of their acts, and when on their return they find Kurds in occupation of their lands they proceed to cry out loudly for their restoration" (FO 371/1263, Molyneux-Seel to Lowther, Van, October 9, 1911). See also FO 881/9618, Safrastian to Shipley, September 9, 1909; FO 881/9744, Lowther to Grey, Constantinople, April 20, 1910; *The Ninety-ninth Annual Report of the ABCFM Presented at the Meeting Held at Minneapolis, Minnesota, Oct. 13–15, 1909* (Boston: American Board, 1910), p. 79.

37. FO 195/2318, "Quarterly Report of Mr. Morgan," Van, October 2, 1909.

38. FO 881/9744, Lowther to Grey, Constantinople, April 20, 1910.

39. FO 881/9532, Dickson to Lowther, Van, March 31, 1908; FO 195/2347, Morgan to Lowther, Van, November 17, 1909.

40. FO 195/2318, Morgan to Lowther, Van, October 27, 1909.

41. FO 881/10074, Molyneux-Seel to Lowther, Van, September 21, 1911.

42. FO 195/2284, Dickson to Lowther, Van, November 3, 1908. On the difficulties of the land tenure problem, see Janet Klein, "Power in the Periphery: The Hamidiye Light Cavalry and the Struggle over Ottoman Kurdistan" (Ph.D. dissertation, Princeton University, 2002), pp. 305–28.

43. Kaligian, "The Armenian Revolutionary Federation under Ottoman Constitutional Rule, 1908–1914," pp. 192–99.

44. FO 881/10376, Lowther to Grey, Constantinople, May 6, 1913.

45. Sait Bey, from whom villages were taken and returned to Armenians, became an implacable enemy of the government and eventually led his own rebellion (FO 195/2375, Molyneux-Seel to Marling, Van, January 30, 1911). See chapter 7. Kurdish attacks on Turkish troops indicated a marked hostility in the region west of Lake Van (FO 881/9923, Safrastian to McGregor, Bitlis, December 16, 1910).

46. FO 195/2283, Dickson to Barclay, Van, April 6, 1908.

47. The Armenian bishop of Bitlis was reportedly preparing to open a school jointly with the Dashnaks (FO 881/9618, Safrastian to Shipley, September 9, 1909). Much was transpiring at Bitlis at this time, but the British unfortunately did not have an official

representative there. They were represented by an Armenian translator (*dragoman*), Arshag Safrastian, who was a Dashnak sympathizer. Safrastian, for example, saw nothing odd about the alliance between the church and the avowedly atheistic Dashnaks. For an example of his feelings, see FO 881/9931, Safrastian to McGregor, Bitlis, February 24, 1911. The British seem to have taken Safrastian's feelings into account and in numerous cases referred to the prejudice in his reports.

48. See the comments of Consul Morgan in FO 195/3218, "Quarterly Report of Mr. Morgan," Van, October 2, 1909.

49. FO 195/2284, Dickson to Lowther, Van, September 30, 1908.

50. Consul Dickson described the Dashnak attitude as "their uppishness and insolence, and their habit of dictating to all and sundry" (FO 371/560, Dickson to Lowther, Van, September 9, 1908, quoted in Sonyel, "The Turco-Armenian 'Adana Incidents' in the Light of Secret British Documents," p. 1296).

51. Great Britain, National Archives, CAB 37/95/137, Dickson to Lowther, Van, September 30, 1908, cited in Klein, "Power in the Periphery," p. 315.

CHAPTER 7

Kurdish Revolts and the Inspectorates, 1912–1914

The Ottoman government was in an impossible situation in Eastern Anatolia, partly because of the CUP-Dashnak alliance and partly because of political and military events far from Van Province. Armenian participation in the political process and real improvements in living conditions in the East had not caused the Armenian revolutionaries to abandon their guerrilla forces, their weapons smuggling, or their anti-Ottoman propaganda in Europe. No matter how much the Ottomans labored to improve the lives of Armenians, it was never enough for the Europeans. Indeed, European demands for Armenian autonomy reached their climax just as Armenian life in the East was better than ever before.

The situation of Armenians and settled Kurds in the East in the years just before the outbreak of war was unquestionably better than it had been earlier. There were still tribal raids and fights between Kurdish tribes,[1] but these were much diminished, a result of increased government military presence in the region. The most often discussed problem was individual murder of both Armenians and Kurds. Both groups took part and killed members of their own group as well as of the other. By the standards of the twenty-first century, especially in American cities, the numbers were small. Nevertheless, the deaths kept up tensions.[2]

Under the leadership of Governor Tahsin Bey numerous reforms were made in Van: suppression of Kurdish tribal disorders,[3] expeditions to punish rebellious chiefs and successfully collect taxes from them,[4] a reorganization of the district administrative structure in the province, a financial commission studying financial reforms, the construction of Kurdish schools, a commission for settling land disputes between Armenians and Kurds, reorganization of the gendarmerie, mounted patrols in all neighborhoods, lighting the streets of Van City at night, and so forth. The government of the Committee of Union and Progress was anxious to make reforms to forestall European-imposed changes (ultimately a failed effort), so Tahsin was given strong political support. He brought his own officials with him—men he could trust and, more importantly, men with connections to power in Istanbul. For example, Halil Bey (later Paşa), the uncle of the minister of war, Enver Paşa, was put in charge of the gendarmerie.[5] It was rare for the consuls to praise the provincial government, though they did so in this case.[6] Even the American missionaries agreed that things were better than ever before.[7] It was all for naught. Larger problems were soon to envelop Van Province.

No amount of reform in the Ottoman provinces could compensate for the disastrous effects of the First Balkan War. Greece, Bulgaria, Serbia, and Montenegro—all former parts of the Ottoman Empire—defeated Ottoman armies swiftly in 1912. This was not defeat by Russia or another great power. It was viewed both within and outside the empire as an ignoble loss at the hands of former subjects. The Ottoman reconquest of a small part of the lost territory from Bulgaria in the Second Balkan War did little to increase confidence in the Ottoman military; it had only been possible because Bulgaria and its erstwhile allies had fallen out, allowing the Ottomans to reoccupy eastern Thrace. Worse, and a most significant point for the Muslims of the Ottoman East, the Ottomans had not been able to protect the Muslims of Ottoman Europe from their Christian conquerors. In the Balkan Wars 27 percent of the Muslims of Ottoman Europe had died. Another 18 percent had fled immediately to Western Anatolia and what remained of Ottoman Europe.[8]

The lessons of the Balkan Wars were not lost on the peoples of the Ottoman East. The Ottomans were militarily weak. Everyone, Muslim or Christian, expected that Russian invasion was imminent and that it would be successful. For the Armenian revolutionaries, this meant that the time to strike was near. In concert with the Russians, they would finally end Ottoman rule in their homeland. The Kurdish tribes also began to make plans. Some felt that accommodation would have to be made with the Russians. Others believed that the Russians would never tolerate any degree of Kurdish autonomy, so the Russians had to be opposed, even if it meant close cooperation with the Ottoman government. They assumed that a Russian victory was an Armenian victory and, to a greater or lesser degree, a Kurdish loss. Some adopted a watchful position, ready to take the winning side.

Diplomatic Negotiations to End
Ottoman Sovereignty in the East

It was obviously impossible to change overnight the centuries-old political and social system in Eastern Anatolia, but that was what the Europeans increasingly demanded. The Europeans finally threatened the dissolution of the empire unless the Ottomans in essence gave up their sovereignty over Eastern Anatolia and created autonomous European enclaves that were to be managed in the interest of the Armenians.

Had World War I not intervened, the Armenian revolutionaries would have achieved their aims without bloody revolution. Eastern Anatolia would have been detached from the empire. Christians would have ruled over the Muslim majority even if, in the end, those Christians were Russian imperialists. Ironically, success would have been the product of the sort of European intervention that had been the centerpiece of Armenian revolutionary plans until 1907–8. The earlier rebels had planned to attack Muslims then spark reprisals on Armenians that would bring European intervention. Now there was no need for massacre and countermassacre: the Europeans would intervene without instigation.

In the aftermath of the Balkan Wars, Russia began a campaign to alter the status quo in Eastern Anatolia. The immediate impetus for change came from Boghos Nubar,[9] acting as the agent of the Armenian patriarch of Echmiadzin. Boghos Nubar, stationed in Paris, began to contact the European powers with plans for a virtually autonomous "Armenia" in the Six Provinces of the Ottoman East. Although he publicly disavowed any intention of separating the provinces from the Ottoman Empire, both he and the patriarch advanced proposals that would do exactly that. While Nubar was proclaiming benign intentions toward the Ottoman Empire in Paris, the patriarch was suggesting to the tsar's government that the Eastern Anatolian provinces be placed directly under Russian control. It is impossible to believe that the patriarch, completely under Russian control himself, was acting without the approbation of the Russians. Boghos Nubar stated that "the Armenians placed their hopes completely on Russian support and that they would follow the directions of the Russian government."[10]

The Ottoman government realized its perilous state. Even before the debacle of the Balkan Wars it would not have been able to resist united pressure from Russia and the other European states. Its only hope was to play upon the disunity of the European powers. The Ottomans therefore proposed their own reform plan, communicated to the British through the Ottoman ambassador in London, Tevfik Paşa. They asked Britain in April 1913 to supply seventeen advisors who would oversee reforms throughout the empire, carefully rejecting the concept of separate treatment for Eastern Anatolia. The advisors would include inspectors for domestic departments such as justice, the gendarmerie, public works, and agriculture. Most importantly, a British inspector-general would be appointed to investigate needed reforms. The Ottoman government undertook to implement the inspector-general's suggestions.[11] Although Britain was its ally, Russia refused to accept a plan that favored Britain and excluded Russia. Diplomatic wrangling ensued. Russia suggested that Russia and its Entente allies, Britain and France, decide what reforms would be implemented. Germany, well on its way to becoming the Ottoman Empire's sole friend in Europe, found this unacceptable.

The fate of the reform scheme was settled in meetings among the European ambassadors in Istanbul that began in June 1913. The Germans suggested that the Ottoman government have a representative at the meetings but gave in when faced with strong opposition from the others. Matters were to be decided by the European powers then imposed on the Ottomans without their input. The Russians proposed that the Six Provinces of Van, Erzurum, Diyarbakır, Bitlis, Mamuretülaziz (Harput), and Sivas be made one province, governed either by an Ottoman Christian or by a European. The governor would have authority over the administration, the gendarmerie, and, if needed, the military. An assembly would have equal representation for Christians and Muslims. After more debate and dissension among the European powers, a slightly modified program was enacted. The Ottoman government did what it could to amend the program, suggesting that European advisors rather than governors be appointed, but the Ottoman wishes were ignored.

On June 25, 1913, the government of Sait Halim Paşa accepted a sixteen-article "circular" on the Eastern Anatolian Reform Project. Russia objected to the terms but eventually agreed to the project on February 8, 1914.[12] The final program was essentially the one suggested earlier by the Russians. The main changes were the inclusion of Trabzon Province along with the Six Provinces and the division of the Ottoman East into two "inspectorates," not the single inspectorate envisioned by the Russians. One inspectorate, which included Erzurum, Sivas, and Trabzon, was to be headquartered at Erzurum; the other, which included Van, Bitlis, Mamuretülaziz, and Diyarbakır, at Van. The program included a complete transformation of Ottoman rule in the inspectorates:

- A European inspector would be named to govern each of the two new provinces. He would be a European chosen from lists presented to the Ottoman government by the European powers.
- The inspectors would control the administration, judicial machinery,

police, and gendarmerie in their inspectorates. They were empowered to conduct investigations of the governors and civil servants and to dismiss officials.

- Disagreements regarding lands that were claimed to have been taken from Armenians would be decided by the inspectors.
- Official communiqués would be published in the local languages, and all would be able to use their own language in courts and government offices.
- If he felt it necessary, the military forces would also come under the inspector's command. All would be able to do their military service within the borders of the inspectorate in which they lived. The Hamidiye regiments would be turned into reserve cavalry units, their weapons kept in military depots and given out only when needed.
- Elections would be held for a General Assembly in each inspectorate. Half of the members of each Assembly would be Muslim, half Christian.
- Bureaucrats and administrative personnel would be hired on the basis of Christian-Muslim parity, half Muslim and half Christian.

The inspectorates, had they been implemented, would have been the end of Ottoman sovereignty in Eastern Anatolia. Both the symbols and substance of rule would have been taken from the Ottoman government. The police force, the military, the administration, the courts—all the most important instruments of government—would have been in the hands of outsiders. More importantly, the majority would have been effectively excluded from governance. The Reform Project was described by European officials and the European press as "Armenian Reforms," and they were indeed that. In electing members of the assemblies, each Christian vote was worth three Muslim votes (table 7.1).

No one—not the Armenians, the Muslims, or the Europeans—could have doubted that the inspectorates were the first step in the dismemberment of Ottoman Anatolia. The Eastern Anatolian Reform Project was in essence no different from the similar projects in eastern Rumelia (southern Bulgaria), Cebel-i Lübnan (the Mount Lebanon region), and the island of Crete. In all three, Europeans had forced the Ottomans to accept "reforms" and great deal of autonomy for the area, then the territory was lost. Eastern Rumelia was ultimately annexed by Bulgaria. Crete was annexed by Greece. Cebel-i Lübnan in effect became independent. The Inspectorate Agreement laid the foundation for yet another region to be taken away from the Ottomans.

TABLE 7.1. Population and Representation in the Inspectorates.

PROVINCE	MUSLIM POPULATION	TOTAL POPULATION	PERCENT MUSLIM	PERCENT MUSLIMS IN THE ASSEMBLY	PERCENT MUSLIMS IN THE BUREAUCRACY
Trabzon	1,178,655	1,505,490	78	50	50
Sivas	1,196,300	1,472,838	81	50	50
Erzurum	804,388	974,196	83	50	50
Northern Inspectorate Total	3,179,343	3,952,524	80	50	50
Van	313,322	509,717	61	50	50
Bitlis	408,703	611,391	67	50	50
Mamuretülaziz	564,164	680,241	83	50	50
Diyarbakır	598,985	754,451	79	50	50
Southern Inspectorate Total	1,885,174	2,555,800	74	50	50
Total	5,064,517	6,508,324	78	50	50

Source: Justin McCarthy, *Muslims and Minorities* (New York: New York University Press, 1983), p. 112.

THE KURDISH REACTION

The Kurdish populace may have been largely illiterate and unschooled in international politics, but the tribal leaders were intelligent men who understood the events occurring around them. They could see that Ottoman losses were forcing the government to accept a regime in the East that would lessen and perhaps destroy the tribal leaders' power. In their own interest, the chiefs could only oppose the changes being forced on the Ottoman state. But there was more than the personal advantage of tribal leaders behind Kurdish opposition to change. Ordinary Kurdish subjects in provinces such as Van saw a progression that would end in their downfall:

- A "godless" CUP government had taken power.
- The Armenians, especially the Dashnak enemies of the Kurds, had been favored by the new government.
- The government had acted against the Kurds but not against the Armenian rebels.
- Changes in the government had apparently made the Ottomans weak. They had lost much of the empire's richest land in war to former subjects, which had never happened under Sultan Abdülhamit.

- The Europeans were forcing the government to give control over the Kurds to Europeans and Armenians.

Kurds in the East might not understand the political and diplomatic machinations behind the Ottoman catastrophe, but they could see its effects in their own provinces. If they did not understand their situation, Kurdish propagandists would explain all to them.[13]

THE TRIBES AND THE COMMITTEE OF UNION AND PROGRESS GOVERNMENT

Although they had never been strong supporters of the central government, Kurdish tribal leaders were especially outraged by the new government of the Committee of Union and Progress. Part of this opposition was religious. The new Turkish leaders were viewed as irreligious, often described by the Kurds as "infidels" who had adopted European ways, abandoning what the Kurds viewed as true Islam.[14] Out of more practical considerations, the chiefs naturally opposed actions of the CUP government that were intended to centralize power in the hands of the state. For the tribal chiefs, the ideal government was one that was satisfied to let the chiefs rule largely as they wished, short of outright rebellion. That form of governing had been disappearing in the East for some time before the new constitutional government began. The change to new ways accelerated under the CUP. Now the government intended to govern.[15] Battalions were sent to Van, Erzurum, and Mosul and from there into the hinterland, to assert the authority of the state. The tax collector was obviously not far behind.

The chiefs saw changes in the structure of the Hamidiye regiments as symbolic of the changes that were overtaking their power. Formed by Sultan Abdülhamit II, the Hamidiye were intended to organize Kurdish horsemen into cavalry units that would rival the Cossacks of the Russian army. Each of the sixty-six "regiments" reflected its tribal affiliation and in fact functioned more as a government-armed extension of each chief's power than as an organized cavalry. The rifles distributed to the Hamidiye modernized tribal arsenals. In addition, the Ottoman military titles granted to the chiefs brought with them honor and respect. Even those of rebellious mind esteemed honors granted by the sultan/caliph. Yet the military discipline of the Hamidiye regiments was abysmal. The new government rightly attributed much of the Hamidiye's poor performance to their tribal character. It attempted to reorganize the units into twenty-four new regiments defined by regions, consolidating smaller tribal units under new commanders. This infuriated the chiefs, who refused to cooperate with the new system, effectively killing the Hamidiye. With the demise of the Hamidiye units went a goodly amount of the chiefs' legal authority and some of their weapons supply. Once again they saw the government as inimical to their power and their traditions.[16]

One particular cause of Kurdish aggravation was the government's defense of the rights of Armenians. The new government had begun aggressive opposition to tribal seizure of Armenian lands. Occasionally these lands had been taken in payment for debts, and both tribal chiefs and the Armenian and Muslim rich had claimed them,[17] but most of the lands had been taken illegally. The lands of Armenians who had fled to Russia and elsewhere during the rebellions of the 1890s were considered by the Kurds to have been justly and legally seized, because the holders were considered (rightly or wrongly) to be traitors. Ottoman soldiers and gendarmes now began to occupy villages previously seized by Kurds and forcibly return them to their original Armenian owners. Even the most powerful Kurdish clans, such as the Haydaranlı, were forced to return villages seized from Armenians, in some cases generations earlier than the 1890s revolts.[18] Sait Bey, a large landowner in Erçek (twenty miles from Van), had been similarly forced to return lands he had taken, which led to rebellion.[19] Much confiscated land still remained in the hands of tribal leaders, but the government was obviously beginning to enforce a change in the tradition "rights" of the chiefs to seize what they wished.

Consul Smith in Van on January 10, 1914, described the situation during the governorship of Tahsin Bey, the penultimate governor before the Armenian rebellion:

> Since the arrival of the present Vali, Tahsin Bey, strong measures have been taken against various Kurdish brigands, so that at present the Armenians have little to complain of in this respect [i.e., the seizing of land and animals]. The Vali's policy seems to be one of justice towards the Armenians, though the latter, by their carping remarks and unsympathetic newspaper criticisms of his measures make his task a difficult one. During his recent tour in the Hekkiari Sancak, he dealt with the question of the two thousand Manhoran Kurds, who four months ago immigrated from Persia and settled in Armenian villages. These he removed, and distributed amongst Kurdish villages near the frontier.[20]

Tribal leaders did not see government actions in favor of the Armenians as what they were in fact—small losses of land. They interpreted what they saw as evidence that the Armenians, led by the revolutionaries, were

gaining the upper hand. By 1912 many of the tribes were led by relatively
sophisticated men who had been educated in Istanbul or elsewhere. They
were not naive country bumpkins without knowledge of world politics.
The leaders' analysis of the political situation was essentially correct: the
perception of Ottoman weakness would indeed bring the Europeans to
press upon the Ottomans a system that inexorably would have led to pro-
Armenian government in the East and perhaps to Armenian autonomy or
independence. The chiefs fully realized who would be the loser.

KURDISH REVOLTS

The rebellion of Sait Bey was an example of the difficulties encountered
by the Ottomans as they attempted to address the problem of the Kurdish
seizure of Armenian lands. On the one hand, returning lands to Armenians pleased the Europeans and the Armenians, although the Dashnaks
never ceased to declare that the government was not doing enough to assist the Armenians. On the other hand, government actions made powerful enemies. It was undoubtedly legally and morally correct to return the
seized property, but Kurdish tribal leaders and landlords who lost property
did not see the seizures in the same light. All Kurds could not help but
notice that it was only the illegal seizures of Armenian property that were
addressed. Lands seized from Kurds were untouched. The Kurds could
also see the new political power and triumphalism of the Dashnak leaders
as well as European intervention to secure power for the Armenians. The
result was both rebellion and the dissemination of antigovernment and
anti-Armenian propaganda that was well received by ordinary Kurds, not
just tribal leaders.

Sait Bey's brigandage and rebellion were directly caused by the government's policy of returning property taken from Armenian cultivators.
When gendarmes came to his seat in Erçek to order him to return illegally
seized Armenian lands, Sait resisted, killing the gendarmes. Rather than
await retribution, Sait became an outlaw. He led a band of fifty to seventy
men himself and called on the forces of his followers, Haydaranlı Yusuf
and İsmail (Sait's cousin), as well as those of a bandit, Mir Mehe. Sait's
forces regularly raided or took "tribute" from both Christian and Muslim
villages. He once raided the sizable town of Gevaş. Troops at one point surrounded him, but he escaped.[21] Sait Bey and his followers were killed by
Ottoman forces in northwestern Iran, near the Turkish border, in 1914.[22]

Sait Bey cannot be viewed as simply one more in a long line of Kurdish brigands. He had become a rebel against the state, not a simple bandit.

There is no way to know if the land seized from him by the government truly had been stolen from Armenians, but Sait proclaimed that he had been a victim of a policy designed to placate the Armenians at the expense of the Kurds. He accompanied his raids with a steady propaganda against the government. This often fell on receptive ears. Kurds, particularly Kurdish tribesmen, felt that the government had taken the side of the Armenians against them. Sait thus expressed a view that was held by many.

Of course, some rebels primarily were willing to use Ottoman weakness to personal advantage. Tribal chiefs who fought for independent rule and expanded power were not an unusual phenomenon. What changed in the years immediately before World War I was the support given to such rebels by the Russians. Russian occupation of western Iran provided a secure zone for the rebels, a region in which they could organize and threaten the Ottoman Empire. Before the Russian 1909 invasion of Iran, the Ottomans had sometimes followed such rebels in "hot pursuit" into Iran. The Persian government had even successfully, if rarely, defeated the rebels. Now the Persian government was effectively in the hands of the Russians, and the Ottomans could not invade, for fear of war with Russia.

İsmail Simko was a Shikak tribal chief and leader of the Iranian Shikaks whose home region stretched across the border near Saray.[23] In 1911 Simko and his men had fought a serious battle with Ottoman troops as the tribesmen tried to cross the border on the Khoy-Saray road in order to raid in Van Province. They were turned back, but not without significant losses on both sides. Simko collected his troops for a major incursion in 1913 but was stopped by an Ottoman military buildup on the Iranian border. The Ottomans complained that the Russians, who were in control of western Iran, were supporting Simko.[24] They surely were doing nothing to stop him.[25]

Simko had higher ambitions than to succeed as a traditional raiding chief. His plan, which he carried out for decades, was to unite the various Kurdish tribes under his leadership and oppose both the Persian and Ottoman governments. Whether he actually thought of creating a true Kurdish state is unknown, but he certainly wished to concentrate power in his own hands.

Simko was quite willing to take advantage of Russian support to gain his ends. In the Iranian Revolution he had at first taken the side of the revolutionaries against the government then turned to side with the Russians. The Russians not only aided Simko but appointed him to administrative positions. He first resided at Kotur; but in the summer of 1912 he was invited to Tiflis, where the Russian government gave him a decoration "in recognition of his services to the Russian government. He was then given an official post at Chari whither he repaired with his men, his place at Kotur being taken by his brother."[26]

After his abortive 1913 invasion, İsmail Simko remained a threat to the Ottomans on the Iranian border but took little direct action against them (and did little to help the Russians). His followers raided but did not take part in the rebellious actions of others. Simko's major negative effects on the Ottoman polity may have been in serving as an example of success through cooperation with the Russians and later in keeping Shikak tribesmen from aiding the Ottomans in the war.[27]

Şeyh Taha of the Şemdinan family came from a line of religiously respected tribal leaders. His great-grandfather, Şeyh Taha of Neri, had been a much revered leader of the Nakşbendi dervishes who was instrumental in spreading the Nakşbendi practice throughout southeastern Anatolia.[28] His grandfather, Şeyh Ubeydullah, had a following that spread from Lake Van to Lake Urmia. He had gained the allegiance of much of western Iran, as well as that of his followers in the Ottoman Empire, but was ultimately defeated in 1881 by the Persians and arrested by the Ottomans.[29] Ubeydullah's son, Mehmet Sadik, had been a continuous trouble to the Ottomans, attacking Nestorians, aiding Armenian arms smugglers, and constantly raiding settled populations. When Mehmet Sadik died in 1907, he named his son Taha as his heir; but Taha was forced initially to contest the rule within his own family. Once assured of his own position, Taha's revolt against the Ottomans then began in earnest. He was ultimately driven to Iran by troops and was at Urmia in Russian-controlled territory in April 1913. He reputedly had thirty thousand to forty thousand armed Kurds who would answer his call. This was surely a gross exaggeration, but his force was nevertheless sizable. The Ottomans granted Taha a pardon, but he remained in Iran and in revolt.[30] All Ottoman efforts at making peace with Taha and bringing him back into the empire failed. Commissions were sent to negotiate with him, with no result. Significantly, the Russians refused to cooperate with the Ottomans' attempt to pacify the situation.[31]

The Barzan tribe was not particularly large. Its importance derived from the position of its chief as a revered şeyh of the Nakşbendi order of dervishes.[32] Many of the members of the Barzan tribe were in fact descended from Kurds who had come to Barzan in the 1840s, attracted by the religious reputation of the first famous Barzan şeyh, Abdürrahman. When the Ottomans ended the autonomy of the Kurdish *mir*s, authority among the Kurds gravitated to leaders such as the Barzan family, who matched religious prestige with political acumen.

The Barzan şeyh in 1910, Abdüsselam, was accepted by his tribal followers as both a political and religious authority in his tribe's homeland, a region east of Amadiya, on the border of the provinces of Mosul and Van. Abdüsselam and his followers had extensive relations with Kurds and Christians in that region, both as allies and as enemies. The government had great difficulty in controlling the region, because of a mountainous terrain in which villages were often connected only by trails that not even a donkey could use.

The revolt of Şeyh Abdüsselam began before the Balkan Wars. Ostensibly, Abdüsselam acted against the secularist changes of the CUP government, although the extension of government power and tax collectors into his domain played no small part in his revolt. He refused to accept Ottoman authority or pay taxes. In 1910 Ottoman forces moved against Abdüsselam from Mosul, but he and his followers took refuge with the largely autonomous Nestorians in Tiari. Unwilling or unable to fight the Nestorians as well as the Barzani forces,[33] the Ottoman forces withdrew. A later expedition against Abdüsselam in March 1913 was more successful. An Ottoman military detachment consisting of twenty cavalrymen, the 1st and 2nd Battalions of the 97th Regiment, two mountain guns, and two machine guns set out from Van. The units were much smaller than might appear; the force was much under strength due to sickness and numbered perhaps five hundred in all.[34] The Ottoman force, however, was reinforced by Kurdish opponents of Abdüsselam. In fact, Kurdish fighters predominated on the Ottoman side in both expeditions against Abdüsselam. The Barzan şeyh lost to the Ottoman forces in a battle on the Zap River then fled to Russian-controlled Iran, along with many of his followers.[35] For a time he resided in Tiflis, the capital of the Russian Caucasus, but eventually returned to Iran. Abdüsselam was captured in 1914 by enemies from the Shikak tribe and handed over to the Ottoman government for execution.[36]

RELIGION AND KURDISH REBELLION

The perception of the CUP government as "Godless" and "infidel" melded well with the perception of the government as a tool of the Christians—Europeans and Armenians. The prestige of Şeyh Taha and Şeyh Abdüsselam was based on their religious position. When they and other şeyhs

revolted, they were not only making a political statement. They were im-
plicitly, and sometimes explicitly, stating that the sultan/caliph was not
properly representing Islam. The grand şeyhs, such as Taha and Abdüsselam, were only the most visible part of an antigovernment sentiment that
spread through the extensive network of Sufi religious orders in southeastern Anatolia. While calls for Kurdish unity might, and usually did, go
unheeded, calls for Muslim unity against the "infidel" CUP government
by honored şeyhs were respected.[37] Potentially, the şeyhs could mobilize
supporters across tribal lines. This was the intention of Şeyh Sait Ali of
Hizan, who organized a meeting of şeyhs in Dohuk to plan opposition to
the government.[38] Another religious leader, Molla Selim, organized the
şeyhs near Bitlis to revolt.

Bitlis Province had a long history of revolt. Most well known and
dangerous were the Armenian rebellions in the Sasun-Muş region, but
Kurds had engaged in a near rebellion in 1907. The Sufi religious leaders of
Bitlis were particularly powerful, and they hated government reforms. Led
by their şeyhs in 1907, Kurds in Bitlis had seized public buildings and attacked Ferid Paşa, the provincial governor, pillaging his house, wounding
him, and killing the chief of police. The central government had bought
off the rebels by replacing the governor and purchasing seed corn for the
populace.[39] In 1913 şeyhs of Bitlis began to call for a demonstration against
the introduction of officials and gendarmes from the European provinces
lost in the Balkan Wars (both "Godless" and "foreign"), but police patrols
stopped them.[40]

In the spring of 1914 the government received word of plans for a more
serious revolt in Bitlis. Molla Selim, the leader of the rebels, was arrested
by the Çatak kaymakam but escaped, perhaps by bribing officials. He
then made his first attempt at revolt, arriving in Bitlis at the beginning of
March 1914 and setting up his command center near the Russian consulate
and the Armenian monastery. There was no element of surprise. When the
Bitlis governor invited Molla Selim "to discuss the situation" with him,
Selim felt that his forces were insufficient. It is possible that expected reinforcements had not yet arrived. Selim left the city to gather further support from other religious leaders. Only when he had met with and ensured
the cooperation of Şeyh Sait Ali of Hizan and şeyhs from Gevaş, Karçekan,
Mutki, and Varto did he return. The rebels eluded a military detachment
that had been sent out to meet them. They entered the city on March 19,
1914, with a tribal force of approximately two thousand men, once again
making camp near the Armenian monastery and the Russian consulate.[41]

The rebels' plan to seize the government buildings in the city center was thwarted by the foresight of the governor, Mustafa Abdülhalik Bey,[42] who had requested additional forces from Van, Siirt, Muş, and Trabzon in order to stop the rebellion. Abdülhalik himself and Major Kâzim (Özalp),[43] the commander of the Van gendarmerie force, were notable in leading the defense. Fighting lasted from March 19 to 21. The rebels were unable to take their objectives—the provincial government building, the telegraph office, and the jail. On March 21 the rebels dispersed. Molla Selim and three companions took refuge in the Russian consulate and indicated that they wished to become Russian citizens. Some of the rebels were caught by Ottoman forces just as they were about to cross the border and take refuge in Russia.[44] The remaining chief rebels were tried in a military court under martial law. Eleven were sentenced to death and were executed. Nearly a hundred followers were either imprisoned or exiled in Haifa or Yemen. Selim and his colleagues, protected in the Russian Consulate, were also sentenced to death in absentia.[45] They remained in the Russian Consulate until the war began in November 191~~5~~ 1914, when they were apprehended and executed.

Siding with the Russians

Kurdish tribal support for the Ottoman state had always been ambiguous. The paramount Kurdish leaders had been largely autonomous during most of Ottoman history. The Ottomans always had more pressing matters than Kurdish tribal affairs. The British consul in Van, Ian M. Smith, commented: "As the chiefs were generally at enmity with each other, they were kept too busy with their tribal quarrels to cause any serious annoyance to the Government, and as there was little in the country worth taxing, the latter did not interfere."[46]

In past wars with the Russians most tribal leaders had resolutely remained with the Ottoman cause. For some of them, it can be assumed, Islamic solidarity was the most important factor in political allegiance. That may have been coupled with a reasonably sophisticated view of Russian long-term intentions and the cold calculation that they would do better with the Turks than with the Russians. Some tribal leaders had been willing to cooperate with Russia, however, if the cooperation seemed to match their own and their tribes' immediate interests. It was to become easier to consider siding with the Russians after the Ottoman defeats in the Balkan Wars.

To some Kurdish leaders the only rational choice seemed to be cooperation with the Russians. The Russians seemed poised to conquer Eastern
Anatolia. They were already in control of western Iran. Russian consuls
were making overtures to Kurdish chiefs. It might be better to be on the
winning side. Some leaders indeed made that calculation. There is no way
to know if other rebellious chiefs who accepted Russian assistance agreed;
they left no records of policy planning meetings. Cooperating with Russia,
however, might indeed have been a good way to resist Armenian takeover
of Eastern Anatolia. For Russian purposes it would have been much better
to divide and conquer, leaving Kurdish power to balance Armenian power.
The Russians, after all, had never shown any desire to allow Armenian
political power in any region that they had conquered.

The Bedirhan family had a long history of rebellion. Bedir Han (Badr
Khan) amassed a large territory under his personal rule, centered on the
town of Cizre, in the 1840s. He fought the Ottoman government until
1847, perhaps only defeated because parts of his own family turned against
him.[47] The Ottomans crushed the outright rebellion, but they were satisfied to leave the Bedirhan family in charge of their tribe and region, which
spread over largely inaccessible areas. The area would have been nearly impossible for the Ottomans actually to govern and could offer little income
to the state.

The leader of the Bedirhan tribe, Hüseyin, rebelled against the government in 1913. Bedirhan tribesmen became active in disruptive tactics, such
as attacking boats on the Tigris River and killing their passengers. Hüseyin himself toured the mountainous region of northern Mosul, southern Bitlis, and southern Diyarbakır Provinces to gain support of other
tribal chiefs, even allegedly attempting to forge an alliance with the Mar
Shimun, the Nestorian leader. Hüseyin preached independence to other
Kurdish chiefs, but with limited success. The Bedirhan forces were never
powerful enough to attack cities or become a serious threat to the government, but they did disrupt their region.[48]

By itself, the Bedirhan revolt would have posed only a small threat
to the Ottomans. The initial area of revolt was remote, and the government had sufficient force to defeat the rebels. The danger increased when
Abdürrezzak, representative of Chief Hüseyin, made common cause with
Şeyh Taha and moved Bedirhan forces to the Iranian border. Both Abdürrezzak and Taha allied themselves with the Russians, which made their
revolt a significant threat on the Ottoman border. Moreover, Abdürrezzak
had a vision of Kurdish union and autonomy under Russian sovereignty

that posed a danger beyond the scope of any tribal revolt. He seems to have been the only Kurdish rebel who had an actual plan.[49]

Abdürrezzak's message was one of resistance to the Armenians and the Europeans; he felt that they would soon take over the Ottoman East, disarm the Kurds, give Kurdish lands to Armenians, and reduce the Kurds to slavery. He declared in a manifesto addressed to all Kurds that the Ottoman Empire was so completely under control of the Europeans that the sultan had been forced to trade the rights of the Kurds in exchange for the empire's survival. In the face of this, the only hope for the Kurds was united military opposition.[50] This was not to be direct opposition to the Europeans, however, for what could the Kurds do to Europe? And what could they do to convince the Ottoman government to consider the Kurds in its dealings with Europe? No, the only hope for the Kurds, Abdürrezzak proclaimed, was to eject the Ottomans from the East.

Abdürrezzak was what might be called a realist. He felt the empire was doomed to lose Eastern Anatolia. The question was whether any Kurdish rights and traditions would survive or whether the Kurds would be overwhelmed by the Armenians. If the Kurds did not want the Russians and other Europeans to grant Armenian autonomy and control over the Kurds, he declared, the Kurds had to unite, showing the Europeans that it would be too difficult to try to destroy them and that it would be against the Europeans' interests as well. Abdürrezzak recognized, as the Armenians did not, that the Russians had no desire to create an Armenia. In his plan, Kurds would have to accept Russian overlordship but could keep their autonomy and continue to live their lives as they wished. The actions he called for were revolt and cooperation with Russian invaders—in essence the same actions planned by Armenian revolutionaries.[51] Given the Russian influence on both the Armenian revolutionaries and the Kurdish rebels, this is not surprising. Abdürrezzak's analysis of the situation of the Kurds was perspicacious: the Eastern Anatolian inspectorates (see below), had they been allowed to function, would probably have led to Armenian autonomy, and the Russians would soon have taken over Eastern Anatolia.

As early as 1910 Abdürrezzak was in Iran, rallying the Kurdish tribes in the border region to his cause, although his activities were not significant until the Ottoman loss in the First Balkan War. In April 1913, under the patronage of the Russian consuls in Iran, he was organizing his followers and distributing anti-Ottoman propaganda.[52] Fortunately for the Ottomans, Abdürrezzak proved to be better at revolutionary philosophy than he was at either drawing other leaders to his cause or fighting the Ottomans himself. The Russians were able to convince others to join a formal alliance with Abdürrezzak but not to cooperate with him militarily. Although those who fought for him were always members of the Bedirhan forces, he lost much Bedirhan family support when Hüseyin died in 1913. His successor made formal peace with the government.[53] Abdürrezzak's revolt continued sporadically until the last week of May 1914. In a final conflict near Siirt between Ottoman forces and his followers the Ottomans defeated Abdürrezzak's men. Members of the Bedirhan family were taken prisoner.[54] Abdürrezzak himself and many followers escaped to Russian protection in Iran. The Russians ultimately rewarded him for his services by naming him as governor of Russian-occupied Bitlis Province during World War I.[55]

The Failure of the Rebellions

The main factors in the failure of the revolts of the Kurdish chiefs were the lack of uniform support and the disunity of the rebels. Despite a Russian-brokered agreement to cooperate with the other rebels, the Bedirhan and Barzan followers never joined forces.[56] Simko always played a lone game. Personal ambition, tribal rivalries, and some loyalty to their Islamic state kept other Kurds from uniting in opposition to the government. Powerful tribes, such as the Haydaranlı, took no part. The religious leaders of the Bitlis Rebellion acted without the support of any major tribe. Despite all the reasons to oppose the Ottoman government or to support the Russians, and despite the Kurdish revolts that did occur, it must be stressed that the Kurds as a whole remained loyal to the Ottoman state. Few major tribal chiefs did revolt. Those şeyhs who revolted never attracted enough of a following to be a serious threat, though they definitely caused difficulties. Most of the Kurds remained loyal subjects, or at least as loyal as they had ever been.

Although they failed, the Kurdish rebellions had a large and negative effect on Van Province and the Ottoman Empire. Through much of 1913 and 1914 large sections of southeastern Anatolia were disordered by the Kurdish rebels. Battles raged between Ottoman troops and Kurdish rebels, as well as among various tribes themselves. Coming as they did just as the Europeans were deciding on the inspectorates and the fate of Eastern Anatolia, they could only have worsened European perceptions of the Ottoman ability to secure civil order.

The Ottomans were able to defeat the rebels whenever they actually fought them: Abdüsselam in the battle on the Zap River, Sait in northwestern Iran, Abdürrezzak near Siirt, and Molla Selim and Sait Ali in Bitlis. They were never able to put down the rebels completely, however. Simko, Taha, Abdüsselam, and Abdürrezzak all remained in Iran under Russian protection. Ottoman resources and diplomacy were deflected to deal with the potential danger that the Kurdish rebels presented before and during World War I. When the war came, the Ottomans were deprived of what should have been the support of large numbers of Kurdish tribesmen.

THE RUSSIANS AND THE KURDS

The Russians had taken note of Ottoman weakness after the Balkan Wars. As seen above, they took diplomatic advantage of the perilous state of the Ottoman Empire to bring about the dissolution of Ottoman power in Eastern Anatolia under the inspectorates. They also did whatever possible to weaken Ottoman rule there. The Russians had long supported (in varying degrees at various times) the Armenian revolutionaries. Now the Russians turned their attention to the Kurds as well. Russian consuls in the Ottoman Empire and Iran began openly to support rebellious Kurds: proving safe havens for individual rebels and tribes in Russian-controlled western Iran, shielding insurgents from the law in their Bitlis consulate, and gathering together rebels in the attempt to create an anti-Ottoman alliance among Kurds. It seems odd that the Russians supported both the Armenian revolutionaries and the Kurdish tribes who were the revolutionaries' enemies, unless one considers the Russian motive. It is doubtful if the Russians ever expected the Kurdish revolt to be successful. The disruption that would accompany any such revolt, however, had significant potential benefit for the Russians: Ottoman energy would be expended in putting it down. The loyalty of the Kurdish chiefs to the Ottoman state, never great, would be further sundered by a conflict in which chiefs and revered religious leaders were killed in battle or perhaps executed for treason. Christians would probably suffer in the anarchy of civil war, which would facilitate ultimate Russian intervention to pacify the region. Any increase in disorder in the Ottoman East, anything that would weaken Ottoman control, paved the way for Russian conquest.

There is little doubt that the Russians at least encouraged the various Kurdish rebels. The Russian government arranged for stipends to be paid from the Russian-controlled government of Persian Azerbaijan to Şeyh Taha of Şemdinan, İsmail Simko, and perhaps others.[57] As seen above, İsmail Simko actually functioned for a time as a Russian official.

Abdürrezzak Bedirhan and Simko were both awarded Russian imperial decorations, presumably for their assistance to the Russian cause.[58] The Ottoman government accused the Russians of supporting the Kurdish rebellion. The British ambassador agreed:

> The honors given to Abd-ul-Rezzak and Simko and the good relations existing between all three conspirators and the Persian authorities of Azerbaijan ["whose subservience to Russia is well known"], as instanced above and by the cordial welcome always extended by them to Kurdish refugees from Turkish justice, such as the Sheikh of Barzan, lend color to the Turkish view that some of the Turkish malcontents stand well with Russia.[59]

The Russians were successful in fomenting rebellion and causing disruption, but no more. In order to defeat the government, the leaders of the various Kurdish factions would have had to unite. Despite common interest and personal ties, they proved unable to do so.[60] Whatever united organization existed among them was provided by the Russians. In May 1914 the Russian consul at Khoy, M. Charikoff, organized a meeting of Simko, Sait Ali, Abdürrezzak, Mecit (an agent of Şeyh Taha), and one Arsanlı Hasan Ağa—representing most of the leading Kurdish rebel elements. They agreed to conduct disruptive raids in the Ottoman Empire and to coordinate their efforts. They were reportedly given five hundred rifles from Russian stores in Iran.[61] Given personal rivalries, however, Russian coordination was to have little success in uniting the Kurds. It was successful, though, in creating a state of disorder and danger in the Ottoman East at the very time when the Europeans were declaring that only European government could bring peace to the region.

THE ARMENIAN REVOLUTIONARIES

After the debacle of the First Balkan War, Armenians in Van openly expected and welcomed the demise of the Ottoman Empire. Consul J. Molyneux-Seel reported that the large majority of Armenians in the Van Province hoped not for reforms but for the end of Ottoman rule. He stated that the Armenians "have thrown off any pretense of loyalty they may once have shown, and openly welcome a prospect of a Russian occupation of the Armenian vilayets."[62] Armenian delegates refused to take part in the Van Provincial Council, perhaps out of conviction, perhaps out of fear.[63]

The real power in the Armenian community was the Dashnak Party.

The Dashnaks had taken control of the Armenian Church and the Armenian schools in the province and were in the midst of overcoming all resistance. The French Dominican school at Van, which was very popular with the city's Armenians, lost most of its students because the priests had been forced (perhaps by the government) to fire a Dashnak teacher, prompting the Dashnaks to impose a boycott of the school.[64] On a trip to Van the British consul at Erzurum observed that the Dashnaks held more real authority than the government: "The most powerful man [in Van] seems to be Ishan, the Tashnagist organizer of bands and assassinations, often mentioned by Captains Seele and Dickson [consuls at Van]. At Akhtamar I found his satellite, a layman name of Aram, in apparent virtual charge of the see of the Catholicos which has for many years been vacant."[65]

The years immediately prior to World War I were a time of planning and arming for the Armenian revolutionaries. All activity of any importance had passed into the hands of the Dashnaks.[66] The Van Hunchaks, while they still existed, only partook of power as part of "revolutionary alliances" with the Dashnaks.

The outbreak of the First Balkan War signaled an increase in the distribution of arms throughout the province. The American missionaries reported that "the Armenian Revolutionists are again compelling the people to buy arms at high prices, for example the Russian army rifle is sold to them at LT [Turkish Lira] 18½."[67] The missionaries felt that only a small number of the arms being brought in from Iran were being stopped by the authorities.[68] In February 1913 the Dashnak Party officially put a new emphasis on buying and distributing weapons. An arms fundraising campaign was begun among Armenians in Anatolian cities, the Caucasus, and the United States.[69] The Dashnak Central Committees felt it to be an opportune time to purchase weapons, because they were cheap. The Balkan Wars had provided a vast stockpile of surplus weapons. There seems to have been no question that, once purchased, the weapons would be delivered to the Ottoman East. The Dashnaks stated that every shipment was reaching its destination. This was not true, but later events were to demonstrate that most of the weapons did arrive in Van and elsewhere in the East.[70]

Consul Molyneux-Seel reported:

The Taschnakists are now busy arming the Armenian population of the vilayet. They tell the villagers that the Turks will revenge themselves for the loss of their European provinces by a general massacre of the Christian inhabitants and that they must therefore put themselves in a position to defend their homes and families. The majority of the arms supplied are ten-shot automatic Mauser pistols. The price these pistols now fetch is £12, so that the Taschnakist trade of smuggling them in from Russia and obliging the villagers to buy them must prove a lucrative business.

The following story related to me by a Gendarmerie Officer is illustrative of the Taschnakist agents' methods:

An agent arrived in a certain village and informed a villager that he must buy a Mauser pistol. The villager replied that he had no money, whereupon the agent retorted, "You must sell your oxen." The wretched villager then proceeded to explain that the sowing season would soon arrive and asked how a Mauser pistol would enable him to plough his fields. For reply the agent proceeded to destroy the poor man's oxen with his pistol and then departed.[71]

A few Armenians, usually men of the merchant class, still remained loyal to the government. The fate of Bedros Kapamacıyan was a lesson to them.

THE ASSASSINATION OF BEDROS KAPAMACIYAN, THE MAYOR OF VAN

Bedros Kapamacıyan, a textile importer, was one of the principal merchants of Van and a member of the Van Executive Council.[72] He was twice elected mayor of the city (the first time in 1909) on the strength of both Muslim and Armenian votes. As mayor he proved himself to be conscientious and capable, reforming the administration and improving the municipal economy through measures such as putting municipal boats in the Lake Van transit trade. Kapamacıyan stood as a representative of the Armenians, particularly the Armenian merchant class, who were willing to cooperate with the Ottoman power structure and support gradual reform. His political stand was steadfastly Ottoman, supporting the governor and the central government. Kapamacıyan refused to sign Dashnak-inspired petitions for the removal of the governor and successfully lobbied the other merchants to disassociate themselves from the removal effort. The petitions (unlike those so often successful in the past) failed, primarily because the Kapamacıyan position demonstrated that the petitions obviously did not reflect universal Armenian opinion.

Both his success as an agent of the government and his politics brought Kapamacıyan into conflict with the Dashnaks. Their opposition to the mayor came to a head in April 1912, when a series of fires erupted in Van. Armenian houses were burned. As usual in such cases, blame was put on the Muslims of the city. The Armenian patriarch in Istanbul pressured the European ambassadors to take action. He also sent an investigating committee to Van that blamed everything on the Muslims.[73] Mayor Kapamacıyan opposed both the revolutionaries and the patriarch. He prepared a report stating that the events in Van had not occurred as the patriarch claimed but that the fires had been set as a provocation by members of the Dashnak Committee. Neither the patriarch nor his delegation was able to shake the mayor's resolve. All realized that the official report of an Armenian mayor would carry weight with Europeans who customarily and routinely doubted Ottoman assertions.[74]

For the Dashnaks there was only one possible solution: the removal of the mayor. The death sentence was given for Kapamacıyan.[75] The revolutionaries, whose platform was based on Armenian-Muslim conflict, could not tolerate such an important Armenian supporter of the government. Terror had long been their weapon against such Armenians.[76] With the terror and fear they created they could not only intimidate their rivals in the Armenian community but also put forth the propaganda that those they had assassinated had in fact been killed by the Ottoman security forces—assertions that were readily believed in Europe and America.

There was no end to the threats received by the mayor of Van. Foolishly, Kapamacıyan did not want his government protection to increase, perhaps feeling that a constant police presence would indicate he did not trust his fellow Armenians. He ignored the threats and continued his old habits. On the evening of December 10, 1912, together with his wife and daughter, Kapamacıyan left his house to travel to the house of his son-in-law. As he boarded his sled, a young member of the Van revolutionary organization began firing. The mayor (who was unarmed, unprepared, and without any protection) was killed with two bullets. He was sixty-five years old.[77]

A Van judiciary investigation identified the murderers of Kapamacıyan—a jeweler named Karakin and his associates—and ordered their arrest.[78] The murderers had fled, but they were soon apprehended in the village of Karagündüz: the murderer Karakin, the wagon driver Potur, Saraç Osep, and an unnamed leader of the Dashnak Committee. Others were apprehended soon after.[79] It was unusual in Van for perpetrators to be apprehended with such speed. Kapamacıyan's popularity and the fear that the murder could lead to further unrest, however, pushed the security forces to solve the murder quickly. Preliminary hearings identified

Dashnak leaders—Vramian, Aram Manukian, and others—as being behind the murder. Warrants were issued for their arrest.[80]

The Office of the Governor was in charge of enforcing judicial decisions. Despite repeated petitions to the governor and to Istanbul, the murderers and the Dashnak leaders remained free,[81] a reprise of the political interference that had freed the Dashnaks arrested in 1908. Once again the Dashnaks had been able to act with impunity, notifying any remaining government supporters among the merchant class that opposition to the Dashnaks was suicidal. After Kapamacıyan's death, even the limited Armenian support for the government disappeared.[82]

Mayor Kapamacıyan's funeral was so large that it seemed that most of the population of Van was present. The speeches at the funeral described the services that Kapamacıyan rendered to the city of Van and also showed how much he was loved by both the Armenian and Muslim populations. The British, Russian, and French consuls, together with foreign missionaries, participated in the funeral.[83] Representatives of neither the Dashnak Party nor the Van security forces attended. The funeral took place in the Armenian cemetery in the Bağlar District. Kapamacıyan was interred as evening approached.

THE INSPECTORATES

The Europeans had their difficulties in creating the Eastern Anatolian Inspectorates. None of the great powers would accept an inspector from any of the other powers, so it was decided to look to smaller countries for the inspectors. The Armenian patriarch of Istanbul told the Russian ambassador that he wished to see inspectors from Holland, Denmark, Norway, or Sweden, not Belgium or Switzerland, which had important trading relations with the Ottoman Empire.[84] Boghos Nubar was told by the patriarch and the Russians to look first in Holland.[85] Louis C. Westenenk, the inspector ultimately assigned to Erzurum, recorded the method of his selection in his diary:

> Wednesday, 4 March. The [Dutch] minister now informed me that a certain Boghos Nubar Pasha, who had pleaded for the Armenian cause with various European governments, had approached H.E. with the request that the Netherlands should also propose two candidates for the above-mentioned post of inspector-general; for that purpose he had also gone to Brussels, where 10 candidates were already proposed.
>
> Nubar Pasha, pursuing the views of the Russian government, acted as

the representative of the catholicos at Tiflis [*sic*] (spiritual head of the Armenians), and of the patriarch, official head of the Armenians at Constantinople, and therefore as the representative of the Christian-Armenians. He did not come as the delegate of Turkey; the Turkish envoy at The Hague was accordingly provisionally kept out of the affair at that time. Russia, which had kept the lead with regard to the reforms, was preparing these at present.[86]

Westenenk, an officer of the Dutch East India Colony, was chosen as inspector for Erzurum. A Norwegian major (made lieutenant colonel upon his appointment), Nicholas Hoff, was appointed inspector in Van.[87] The inspectors wasted no time in associating themselves with the Armenian revolutionaries. Four days after he was notified of his appointment Westenenk met with "the Armenian Dr. Zavriev and the mining engineer Pastermajian,[88] former deputy of Erzurum and one of the leaders of the revolutionary party Dashnaktsutiun." He discussed Armenian problems with "these civilized and intelligent men, who would do anything for the 'cause'" and received literature from them.[89] Westenenk met with them again before he left Holland. His writings indicate sympathy with their cause as well as distrust of German intentions. He felt that Russia, in contrast, wanted only "peaceful borders."[90]

Westenenk joined Hoff in Paris to meet with Garegin Pasdermadjian, Zavriev, and Boghos Nubar then traveled to Istanbul. Before meeting with Ottoman officials they received "briefings" from Dashnaks and officials of the Patriarchate. The Dashnaks also presented the inspectors with lists of Armenian candidates for official positions. The Dashnaks in their official correspondence indicated complete satisfaction with the choice of inspectors and their hopes for the future situation.[91]

Major Hoff arrived in Van on August 17, 1914.[92] After his arrival, Cevdet Bey (later Van governor himself) wrote that Hoff received a very cold welcome from the governor of Van, Tahsin Bey.[93] The Armenians gave him a much warmer welcome. At a reception given by the Armenian bishop of Van in honor of the new inspector, a leader of the Dashnaks (Ishkhan) directed his welcoming oration to Hoff: "You are the Messiah we have been waiting for the past 5–6 years."[94] But the messiah was not to save anyone. World War I intervened. Hoff was recalled by Talat Paşa, the interior minister, on August 27, 1914.[95] Once war was declared, Westenenk was not able to leave Istanbul for Erzurum. With the outbreak of the war, the Ottoman state unilaterally canceled the inspectorates (December 31, 1914).[96]

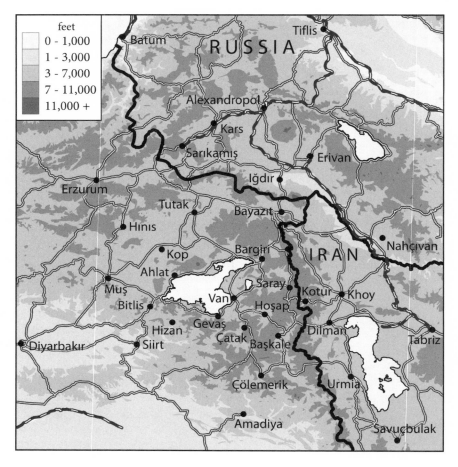

MAP 7.1. Roads and Railroads.

THE SITUATION IN 1914

By 1914 the Ottoman Empire had been defeated in the Italian War and the Balkan Wars. Its finances were in disarray. Politics in Istanbul were in a mess typical of countries that are taking the first steps to democracy. Yet, despite universal anticipation of the empire's demise, events in the Ottoman East immediately before World War I proved that the empire would have survived if left on its own. The Kurdish rebellion, fostered by Russia and fueled by resentment of expected Armenian supremacy, was defeated relatively easily. Unlike its immediate predecessors, the new government of the CUP Triumvirate was unwilling to cooperate with revolutionary separatism. It was soon to prove itself capable of reinvigorating the Ottoman military into a force that could easily defeat insurgents. The government was steadily improving life in Van, especially by effectively opposing Kurdish tribal depredations.

Of course, the Ottoman Empire was not to be left on its own. The Inspectorates Plan proved that. Nor had the Russians abandoned their intention to occupy the Ottoman East. Support for Kurdish and Armenian rebels as well as the Russian intentions for the inspectorates proved that. Had the Russians had their way, the "reforms" would have created a single Eastern Anatolian province under Russian control. They were stopped, at least temporarily, by the other European powers, yet they remained the force behind setting the terms of the inspectorates agreement and the selection of inspectors. Once Eastern Anatolia was effectively detached from the Ottoman Empire, it could not long have stood on its own. The eastern provinces did not have, and never had, sufficient local resources to keep civil order, much less build railroads and encourage industry. The Kurds would not easily have tolerated what they would rightly have seen as Armenian domination. When trouble boiled over, Russia would have intervened.

NOTES

1. FO 195/2450, Monahan to Marling, Erzeroum, September 29, 1913; FO 195/2450, Monahan to Marling, Erzeroum, September 23, 1913; FO 881/10164, Molyneux-Seel to Lowther, Van, July 10, 1912.

2. The bishop of Bitlis, for example, listed nine murders of Armenians in 1913. He did not include figures for murders of Muslims (FO 195/2450, Monahan to Marling, Erzeroum, September 29, 1913). See FO 195/2450, Monahan to Marling, Erzeroum, September 23, 1913, for instances of Kurds killing Kurds and Armenians killing Kurds; and FO 195/2450, Monahan to Marling, Erzeroum, September 29, 1913, for mention of mutual murders of Kurds and Armenians in Karçekan.

3. FO 881/10339, Molyneux-Seel to Lowther, Van, January 22, 1913.

4. FO 195/2450, Monahan to Lowther, Erzeroum, October 13, 1913; ABC 16.9.8, *The One Hundred and Fourth Annual Report of ABCFM, Together with the Minutes of the Meeting Held at Detroit, Michigan, Oct. 13–16, 1914* (Boston: American Board, 1915), pp. 88–89.

5. FO 195/2450, Molyneux-Seel to Lowther, Van, July 9, 1913. For a view of the changes in Van, see FO 195/2450, Monahan to Marling, Erzeroum, September 29, 1913; FO 195/2450, Monahan to Lowther, Erzeroum, October 13, 1913; FO 195/2450, Molyneux-Seel to Lowther, Van, July 9, 1913; and FO 881/10339, Molyneux-Seel to Lowther, Van, January 22, 1913.

6. FO 195/2450, Molyneux-Seel to Lowther, Van, July 9, 1913.

7. Ussher, October 28, 1913. ABC 16.9.7, Eastern Turkey Mission, 1910–1919, Letters, T–Z, vol. 25e, no. 81.

8. Justin McCarthy, *Death and Exile: The Ethnic Cleansing of Ottoman Muslims* (Princeton: Darwin, 1995), pp. 161–64. Another 17 percent were to follow later.

9. Boghos Nubar (1851–1930), the son of Boghos Nubar Pasha, prime minister of Egypt, was an engineer and civil servant before taking up Armenian politics. He was one of the founders of the Armenian General Benevolent Union. From 1912 he served the Armenian catholicos as propagandist and informal diplomat in Paris and as president of one of the Armenian delegations at the Paris peace conference in 1919. He was also one of the creators of Armenian Legion during World War I.

10. W. J. van der Dussen, "The Question of Armenian Reforms in 1913–1914," *Armenian Review* 39 (Spring 1986): 17, quoting *Der diplomatische Schriftwechsel Iswolskis 1911–1914*, ed. F. Stieve, vol. 3 (Berlin: Deutsche Verlagsgesellschaft für Politik und Geschichte, 1924), pp. 91–92.

11. Halil Menteşe, *Halil Menteşe'nin Anıları* (Istanbul: Hürriyet Vakfı Yayınları, 1986), p. 168; van der Dussen, "The Question of Armenian Reforms," p. 17.

12. On the inspectorates, see Joseph Heller, *British Policy towards the Ottoman Empire* (London: Cass, 1983), pp. 107–11; FO 371/2137, Beaumont to Grey, Constantinople, December 4, 1914, "Annual Report, 1913"; van der Dussen, "The Question of Armenian Reforms in 1913–1914," pp. 11–28.

13. See appendix 6.

14. FO 195/2458, Smith to Mallet, Van, March 13, 1914.

15. See FO 195/2458, Smith to Mallet, Van, April 4, 1914. See FO 881/9923, Safrastian to McGregor, Bitlis, 1911, for an example of the sort of animosity, and even murder, that greeted the officers of the government.

16. FO 195/2458, Smith to Mallet, Van, February 14, 1914. Consul P. J. C. McGregor in Erzurum described a meeting of chiefs in Erzurum to oppose the Hamidiye changes (FO 881/10075, McGregor to Lowther, Erzeroum, January 30, 1912).

17. See FO 195/2147, Tyrrell to O'Conor, Van, May 12, 1903.

18. FO 195/2458, Smith to Mallet, Van, February 14, 1914.

19. FO 195/2458, Smith to Mallet, Van, July 11, 1914. See also FO 371/2122, Mallet to Grey, Constantinople, January 6, 1914.

20. FO 371/2130, Smith to Mallet, Van, January 10, 1914.

21. FO 371/1263, Molyneux-Seel to Lowther, Van, October 31, 1911.

22. FO 195/2458, Smith to Mallet, Van, July 11, 1914.

23. Although he unfortunately gives only limited information on Simko's early history, Martin van Bruinessen's article "Kurdish Tribes and the State of Iran: The Case of Simko's Revolt," in *The Conflict of Tribe and State in Iran and Afghanistan*, ed. Richard Tapper (New York: St. Martin's Press, 1983), offers an excellent account of the general tribal situation and of Simko's actions during and after World War I.

24. FO 371/1263, Molyneux-Seel to Lowther, Van, October 31, 1911; FO 371/2449, Molyneux-Seel to Lowther, Van, May 8, 1913.

25. In 1913 Simko had at first taken the side of Azerbaijani Turks who opposed the Russian invasion of western Iran but had changed sides in order to curry favor with the Russians. The Russians, in turn, pressured tribes to accept his leadership (van Bruinessen, "Kurdish Tribes and the State of Iran," p. 383).

26. FO 195/2450, Molyneux-Seel to Lowther, Van, March 24, 1913.

27. "Simko, another Russian protégé, was acting in combination with Abdul Ressak in organizing a Kurd revolt, his immediate object being to persuade (by force if necessary)

the Kurds of the frontier who remained loyal to Turkey to throw in their lot with him" (FO 195/2450, Molyneux-Seel to Lowther, Van, July 9, 1913). Simko had a long history of rebellion against the Ottomans, the Iranians, and the British in Iraq. See van Bruinessen, "Kurdish Tribes and the State of Iran."

28. See Hakan Özoğlu, *Kurdish Notables and the Ottoman State: Evolving Identities, Competing Loyalties, and Shifting Boundaries* (Albany: State University of New York Press, 2004), pp. 72–77. The family, often called Şemdinan as a family name, claimed descendance from the Prophet, and thus the family's chief men were called "Sayyid." Taha's uncle was the famous CUP member and later parliamentarian Abdulkadir.

29. Although he was officially considered a rebel, Ubeydullah was always treated with great respect and given honors by the Ottoman government, even though it would not let him go home. His exile was by no means durance vile. See David McDowall, *A Modern History of the Kurds* (London: I. B. Tauris, 2000), pp. 53–59.

30. FO 881/10376, Molyneux-Seel to Lowther, Van, April 4, 1913; FO 195/2458, Smith to Mallet, Van, July 11, 1914.

31. FO 195/2450, Molyneux-Seel to Lowther, Van, March 24, 1913. The Russians would not even give the Ottoman commission a letter of recommendation to the Russian authorities in Iran, in effect forcing them to travel without official protection.

32. In this the Barzan family was similar to the Şemdinans. Indeed, their first leader was a disciple of the first Şeyh Taha of Neri (see the discussion below). Like the Şemdinans, the Barzan family had a tradition of resistance to Ottoman authority. The two şeyh families (Barzan and Şemdinan) shared much. They also hated each other and were in a constant feud.

33. The Russians estimated that the Nestorians had twenty thousand men under arms.

34. FO 195/2458 Smith to Mallet, Van, March 13, 1914.

35. FO 195/2458, Smith to Mallet, Van, May 29, 1914.

36. See "Kurdish Movement," in *Kavkas*, April 15/28, 1914, translated in FO 195/2458, Monahan to Ambassador, Erzeroum, June 20, 1914; FO 195/2458, Smith to Mallet, Van, March 13, 1914; and FO 881/10376, Molyneux-Seel to Lowther, Van, April 4, 1913.

37. Şeyhs had been touring the southern Van/northern Mosul region since the CUP revolution, preaching that the Christians would be given the Kurdish lands unless the Kurds opposed the government (FO 881/9548, Dickson to Lowther, Van, June 15, 1909, enclosure number 2, "Notes on a Journey between Van and Mosul").

38. FO 371/2449, Molyneux-Seel to Lowther, Van, May 8, 1913; FO 195/2929, Molyneux-Seel to Lowther, Van, May 5, 1913. It should not be thought that the şeyhs were impractical or unsophisticated men. They realized that their revolt stood no chance if opposed by the European friends of the Armenians. Therefore Sait Ali and Molla Selim proposed to the Dashnaks that they should act together against the government. They were rebuffed; but before his forces entered Bitlis, Molla Selim still emphasized publicly that his movement was not directed against the Armenians ("Ahenk Gazetesi," March 26, 1914, cited in Bayram Bayraktar, "1914 Bitlis Ayaklanması," in *Beşinci Askeri Tarih Semineri Bildirileri I* [Ankara: n.p., 1996], p. 220).

39. FO 371/537, "Annual Report, 1907," O'Conor to Grey, Constantinople, January 13, 1908; FO 371/348, Safrastian to Shipley, Bitlis, June 25, 1907; FO 371/348, O'Conor to Grey, Therapia, June 25, 1907.

40. FO 195/2450, Monahan to Marling, Erzeroum, September 29, 1913.

41. The rebels had managed to elude soldiers who had been sent to interdict them. Some believe that the Russian consulate provided support for the rebels, including weapons hidden in an Armenian church. There is no hard evidence for this, although it is quite possible. The Russian consul surely did provide sanctuary for rebels after their attack failed.

42. Mustafa Abdülhalik (Renda) was later to be an important parliamentary deputy and minister in the Turkish Republic.

43. Kâzim (Özalp) was later to be a major figure in opposing the Armenian rebels in Van Province.

44. "Şeyh Şahabettin and his supporters, captured by Captain İdris," *Tanin Gazetesi,* May 1, 1914, p. 223.

45. FO 195/2458, Smith to Mallet, Van, April 4, 1914; FO 195/2458, Smith to Mallet, Van, May 16, 1914; FO 371/2130, Mallet to Grey, Therapia, September 4, 1914; FO 195/2458, Monahan to Ambassador, Erzeroum, June 20, 1914; FO 195/2450, Monahan to Lowther, Erzeroum, April 16, 1913. There was some confusion over the number executed. The British reported "15 to 18," but eleven is probably the correct number.

46. FO 195/2458, Smith to Mallet, Van, March 13, 1914.

47. See Özoğlu, *Kurdish Notables and the Ottoman State,* pp. 70–72, on Bedirhan. Özoğlu gives a good summary of the power equation in the region in earlier periods (chapters 1–3). See also McDowall, *A Modern History of the Kurds,* pp. 45–47; Günter Max Behrendt, "Der kurdische Nationalismus in der Türkei," in *Kurdologie: Studien zur Sprache, Geschichte, Gesellschaft und Politik Kurdistans und der Kurdinnen und Kurden* (Berlin: Bibliothek Feqîyê Teyran, 1994), pp. 83–99 (seen at http://www.turkdunya.de/de/tuerkei/verschiedenes/sehe.php3?site=kurdische_nationalismus#fn18#fn18).

48. FO 195/2450, Monahan to Lowther, Erzurum, April 18, 1913; FO 195/2450, Hony to Lowther, Mosul, April 3, 1913.

49. At first, Abdürrezzak could not have been called an idealist or a "proto-nationalist." He seems to have been willing to come to an accommodation with the Ottoman government, seeking official appointment as a mutasarrıf (district governor). Only when frustrated in this did he turn to open revolt (FO 195/2458, Monahan to Ambassador, Erzeroum, June 20, 1914; FO 195/2450, Monahan to Lowther, Erzeroum, April 16, 1913).

50. See the manifesto of Abdürrezzak in appendix 6.

51. FO 195/2450, Molyneux-Seel to Lowther, Van, July 9, 1913; FO 195/2450, Molyneux-Seel to Lowther, Van, July 9, 1913. At different times the British reported that Abdürrezzak Bedirhan had made "common cause" with Şeyh Taha and with Şeyh Abdüsselam (FO 195/2458, Smith to Mallet, Van, March 13, 1914; FO 195/2458, Smith to Mallet, Van, May 29, 1914).

52. FO 881/10376, Molyneux-Seel to Lowther, Van, April 4, 1913. Molyneux-Seel identified this as propaganda for "a Kurd autonomy under the suzerainty of Russia."

53. FO 195/2450, Molyneux-Seel to H.M. Chargé d'affaires, Van, July 22, 1913; FO 195/2450, Monahan to Lowther, Erzeroum, April 16, 1913; FO 195/2450, Hony to Lowther, Mosul, April 3, 1913.

54. FO 195/2458, Monahan to Ambassador, Erzeroum, June 20, 1914; FO 195/2450, Monahan to Lowther, Erzeroum, April 16, 1913.

55. It was a position without real authority. The Russians also named his uncle, Kâmil, governor of Erzurum (McDowall, *A Modern History of the Kurds,* p. 112).

56. The Ottomans noted, probably thankfully, that the Barzan tribe had nothing to do with the Bitlis revolt (FO 195/2458, Smith to Mallet, Van, March 22, 1914).

57. FO 371/2130, Mallet to Grey, Therapia, July 2, 1914.

58. FO 195/2458, Smith to Mallet, Van, Febrâry 14, 1914.

59. FO 371/2130, Mallet to Grey, Therapia, July 2, 1914. See also FO 371/2130, "Destitution in Kurdistan," Van, April 9, 1914; FO 195/2450, Molyneux-Seel to Lowther, Van, May 24, 1913.

60. This was true even though some of the leaders of the revolts were tied together by more than common interest. Simko was married to the sister of Şeyh Taha and was a personal friend of Abdürrezzak Bedirhan (van Bruinessen, "Kurdish Tribes and the State of Iran," p. 384).

61. Official Turkish newspaper of Van, *Çaldiran*, Van, May 1914, translated in FO 195/2458, Smith to Mallet, Van, June 14, 1914. See also FO 371/2130, Mallet to Grey, Therapia, July 2, 1914.

62. FO 881/10376, Molyneux-Seel to Lowther, Van, April 4, 1913; FO 881/10339, Molyneux-Seel to Lowther, Van, January 22, 1913. A petition signed by five thousand Armenians requesting Great Power intervention in Van to that effect was given to the European consuls.

63. FO 195/2450, Molyneux-Seel to Lowther, Van, June 11, 1913.

64. FO 195/2450, Monahan to Marling, Erzeroum, September 29, 1913.

65. FO 195/2450, Monahan to Marling, Erzeroum, September 29, 1913.

66. See Ussher, October 28, 1913, ABC 16.9.7, Eastern Turkey Mission, 1910–1919, Letters, T–Z, vol. 25e, no. 81.

67. Ussher, October 17, 1912, ABC 16.9.7, Eastern Turkey Mission, 1910–1919, Letters, T–Z, vol. 25e, no. 76.

68. G. C. Raynolds, February 22, 1913, ABC 16.10.1, Constantinople Archives, vol. 7, Letters to W. W. Peet, 1913–1914.

69. Many rich Armenian merchants in Egypt, Istanbul, and elsewhere refused to give: some out of opposition to revolution, many because they feared the Dashnaks would force a "premature" rebellion. Other notables, including even Boghos Nubar Paşa, the leader of the diplomatic front of the Armenian cause, made their donations.

70. Dikran Mesrob Kaligian, "The Armenian Revolutionary Federation under Ottoman Constitutional Rule, 1908–1914" (Ph.D. dissertation, Boston College, 2003), pp. 296–301. Kaligian made use of the Armenian Revolutionary Federation archives in Boston. He states that the weapons were to be used for self-defense, because of "the worsening situation in the provinces" (p. 296); observers at the time, however, including European consuls, felt the situation much improved, as shown above. Oddly enough, Kaligian himself wrote: "Unlike most of his peers and predecessors, the vali of Van Tahsin Bey was actively working to eliminate the brigandage in his region. Several of the most notorious brigands had been captured and some executed for their crimes" (p. 333). By "brigands" one assumes Kaligian means tribal Kurds.

71. FO 195/2949, Molyneux-Seel to Lowther, Van, February 17, 1913.

72. *Teotik Salnamesi* (Istanbul: Dahiliye Nezâreti, 1911), p. 253; BOA DH MUİ, number 23-2/23-1; Y. Çark, *Türk Devleti Hizmetinde Ermeniler* (Istanbul: Yeni Matbaa, 1953), p. 175; M. Sadi Koçaş, *Tarihte Ermeniler ve Türk Ermeni İlişkileri* (Istanbul: Kastaş, 1990), p. 124. For the municipal system of the Ottoman Empire, see İlber Ortaylı,

Tanzimattan Cumhuriyete Yerel Yönetim Geleneği (Istanbul: Hil, 1985), p. 9; Mehmet Ali Gökaçtı, *Dünyada ve Türkiye'de Belediyecilik* (Istanbul: Ozan, 1996); İlhan Tekeli, *Türkiye'de Belediyeciliğin Gelişimi* (Ankara: n.p., 1982). These sources are cited in Hasan Oktay, "On the Assassination of Van Mayor Kapamacıyan by the Tashnak Committee," *Review of Armenian Studies* 1, no. 1 (2002): 79–89. Many of the references and much of the information here on Kapamacıyan are taken from this article.

73. BOA DH SYS 109/2-1.

74. Ibid.

75. BOA DH SYS 109/2-3.

76. See "The Armenian Revolutionary Parties" in chapter 3; "The Revolt of 1876" in chapter 4; "The Dashnak Leaders" in chapter 5; and *Ermeni Komitelerinin Amal ve Harekât-i İhtilâliyesi* (Istanbul: Matbaa-i Amire, 1332), p. 3.

77. FO 371/2449, Molyneux to Lowther, Van, January 13, 1909; FO 371/772/17612: Lowther to Grey, confidential despatch, Pera, May 4, 1909, BOA DH SYS 109/2-2; FO 371-2449, Molyneux-Seel to Lowther, Van, January 9, 1913. The American missionaries reported that Kapamacıyan's murder had been only one of "several murders and assassinations" in the city lately (G. C. Raynolds, Summer Report in 1913, ABC 16.9.7, Eastern Turkey Mission, 1910–1919, Documents, vol. 25a, no. 113, "Report of Van Station, Eastern Turkey Mission, 1912–1913").

78. BOA DH SYS 109/2-2. One of the witnesses who testified was Kapamacıyan's son, a Dashnak sympathizer.

79. BOA DH SYS 109/2-3; BOA DH SYS 109/2-11.

80. BOA DH SYS 109/2-15, 16.

81. BOA DH SYS 109/2-11. For the effects of the murder and trial on popular opinion, see BOA DH SYS 109/2-4.

82. BOA DH SYS 109/2-6.

83. BOA DH SYS 109/2-7a.

84. Boghos Nubar had preferred Belgian candidates because he hoped to influence them through his son-in-law, who was the chief administrator of the Belgian cabinet, but he obeyed his orders and looked instead in Holland.

85. Van der Dussen, "The Question of Armenian Reforms," pp. 25–26.

86. L. C. Westenenk, "Diary concerning the Armenian Mission," *Armenian Review* 39, no. 1 (Spring 1986): 30.

87. Communiqué of the Ministry of the Interior, April, 1330, April 28, 1914, BOA, DH.KMS, D:2-2/5 F:20-1, Dahiliye Nezaretinin 15 Nisan 1330 tarihli atama yazısı, cited in Zekeriya Türkmen, "Birinci Dünya Savaşı Öncesinde İttihat ve Terakki Hükümetinin Doğu Anadolu Islahat Projesi ve Uygulamaları," *Yedinci Askerî Tarih Semineri Bildirileri*, vol. 2 (Ankara: Genelkurmay Basımevi, 2001), p. 258. Following their appointment, each inspector received 300 lira as a travel allowance from the Discretionary Fund (May 25, 1914, Agreement). The inspectors were considered Ottoman officials, given a house (which Westenenk called a "palace" before he had seen it), and paid a salary of 400 gold lira a month by the Ottoman government (BOA, DH.KMS, D:23/3 F:20-1, Dahiliye Nezaretinin 21 Mayıs 1330 tarihli yazısı, cited in Türkmen, p. 258). In one year the Ottoman state would be paying a salary of 67 kilos, 720 grams of gold. Calculated at today's rate, each inspector's monthly salary would be equal to $350,000.

88. Garegin (Garo) Pasdermadjian, aka Armen Garo, was later to lead bands against the Ottomans in World War I.

89. Westenenk, "Diary concerning the Armenian Mission," p. 37.

90. Ibid.

91. Kaligian, "The Armenian Revolutionary Federation," pp. 317–23.

92. Haig Gossoian, *The Epic Story of the Self Defense of Armenians in the Historic City of Van,* trans. Samuels S. Tarpinian (Detroit: General Society of Vasbouragan, Raven Publishers–AKA, 1967), p. 3.

93. Anahide Ter Minassian, "Van, 1915," in *Armenian Van/Vaspurakan,* ed. Richard G. Hovannisian (Costa Mesa, Calif.: Mazda Publishers, 2000), p. 212; and Gossoian, *The Epic Story,* p. 3.

94. Ter Minassian, "Van, 1915," p. 212.

95. Gossoian, *The Epic Story,* p. 3.

96. Y. Hikmet Bayur, *Türk İnkilâbı Tarihi,* vol. 2, section 3 (Ankara: Türk Tarih Kurumu, 1983), p. 187.

CHAPTER 8

World War I and
the Armenian Revolt in Van

*As to the matter of military responsibilities, those of the guerrillas are to
exterminate small forces of the enemy; to harass and weaken large forces;
to attack enemy lines of communications; to establish bases capable of
supporting independent operations in the enemy's rear, to force the enemy
to disperse his strength; and to co-ordinate all these activities with those of
the regular armies on distant battle fronts.*
— Mao Tse Tung, *On Guerilla Warfare*, 1937

THE MILITARY SITUATION IN THE REGION

At the beginning of World War I the Russians were unsure of their strength
in the Caucasus. Like other combatants, the Russians believed that the war
would be decided in battle with the Germans and Austrians in Europe. It
was there, they felt, that their force would be needed. The Ottoman Front
was not denuded, however, and the Russians always maintained a numerical superiority to the Ottomans in the Caucasus/Eastern Anatolian Theater. While the Russian Second and Third Caucasian Army Corps were
sent to the Russian Western Front, deficiencies were made up from the
Turkistan Corps and Cossack units. Russian forces in the Southern Caucasus numbered approximately 100,000 infantry, 15,000 cavalry, and 256
cannon just before the beginning of the war. In addition, 150,000 Caucasus reservists had been called to the colors.

Despite their numerical superiority, the Russians felt capable only of
limited action if the Ottomans entered the war. They believed that a significant force would have to remain behind in defense if they attacked into
Anatolia. This would mean that the attackers would be outnumbered by
defenders, not a militarily advantageous position. The Russians therefore
planned a limited foray into the Eleşkirt Valley (in the foothills south
of Bayazıt, Diyadin, and Karakilise) in order to consolidate their border
defenses against Ottoman raiders and seize the main east–west road. They
would take no further offensive action until reinforced. Russian forces

176

were put in defensive positions along the main possible invasion points from Anatolia, stretching from the Kars region into Iran.

The most apparent Russian danger to the Van Province came from the east. The Russians had invaded Iran in 1908. By 1914 northwestern Iran was effectively occupied, a military extension of the Russian Empire. A Russian railroad ran to Tabriz, with a spur to the northern coast of Lake Urmia. Russian troops and supplies could also make use of the relatively flat ground of the Aras (Araxes) River valley and interior Iran. Once they had seized the crossroads at Bayazıt in the early days of a war, all the main roads from Russia to western Iran would be in their hands. They could project their power to the Ottoman right flank.[1]

The Ottoman Third Army, consisting of seventy thousand to eighty thousand men, faced the Russians in the East. The original Ottoman strategic plan, like that of the Russians, was defensive. If the Russians attacked in force, the Third Army would gather on the Erzurum Plain, where it would be able to bring up superior numbers from the west to face the enemy. The Third Army would remain poised to attack into the Southern Caucasus if the Russians appeared weak. One cavalry brigade at the Bargiri Pass and the Van Mobile Gendarme Division in the Van Region were stationed near the Iran border.[2] The Mobile Gendarme Division was formed from gendarmerie units and border guard battalions. This division and similar units in other provinces were made up of excellent soldiers. In times of peace the gendarmes functioned as paramilitary police in a difficult region, of necessity staying in training. They knew the terrain better than anyone. There were, however, two difficulties in turning the gendarmes into regular troops. First, they did not have the heavy equipment (especially cannon and machine guns) necessary to stand against a well-equipped Russian force.[3] Second, they had been the backbone of security in the Van Province. When they were moved to the front, the number of gendarmes available for policing duties was much diminished.[4] Nevertheless, they were needed for war.

Compared to the Russians, the Ottomans were disadvantaged in transportation and communication. On the map, the Ottomans appear to have possessed the advantage of a centralized position. The Russians were spread on a long line from the Black Sea to Lake Urmia in Iran. Their troop and supply movements were necessarily on the periphery, whereas the Ottomans had much shorter internal connections. This advantage was somewhat negated by the lack of railroads in the Ottoman East. The nearest useful railhead to Van was in Sivas, 500 road miles away. Another rail line, which passed near the southern Anatolian city of Mardin, was somewhat closer, but road links from there to Van were unsatisfactory. In addition, goods brought by the southern line had to be transshipped near Adana because tunnels through the mountains were incomplete. Nevertheless, the advantage of internal lines of transportation was real. Ottoman military communications appeared to present a good picture: the Ottomans had satisfactory telegraph communications within most parts of Eastern Anatolia and from the East to the rest of the empire. The telegraph lines, however, were to prove to be vulnerable to Armenian guerrilla action, as were the roads.

The mountainous terrain of the East afforded both Ottoman and Russian forces defensive advantages. Although the Russians controlled western Iran, the Ottomans held the passes from western Iran into Anatolia, including parts of Iran that they had seized before the onset of war. The Russians' interior and border territories were firmly controlled. They had ensured this by moving potentially troublesome Muslim populations from the border regions at the beginning of the conflict, the first deportations of the war. The Ottomans had the dual problem of rebellious Armenians and of Kurdish tribes whose loyalty was, to say the least, conditional.

The Ottoman army suffered more than the Russian army from disease, probably because of worse sanitary practices. A typhus outbreak in the winter of 1913–14 had already depleted the Ottoman force. Estimates of the loss (for example, 2,500 men struck down by typhus in Van Province) indicate that this outbreak was serious.[5] Typhus struck the Ottoman army again as it massed on the Russian frontier in 1915; and typhus, typhoid, and cholera were to become more dangerous than weapons fire to soldiers and civilians alike throughout the coming war.[6]

Despite their disadvantages, the war in Eastern Anatolia might have developed much differently had the Ottomans been willing to remain on the defensive. With only a slightly larger commitment of men, they would have held the passes into Iran, perhaps advancing into western Iran and dislodging the Russians--a feat they were nearly to achieve with limited resources. But the Ottomans were not to remain on the defensive, because Enver Paşa, the minister of war, was a man with the dream of leading Ottoman forces against the Russians, defeating them, and sparking a general revolt among the Muslims of the Southern Caucasus.

SARIKAMIŞ

The Ottoman Empire entered World War I on November 1, 1914. The first battles between Ottoman and Russians in the East occurred according to plan. The Russians moved south, occupying the Eleşkirt Valley and the cities of Karakilise, Bayazıt, and Diyadin. They were partially beaten back by the troops of Hasan İzzet Paşa. In the southeast, though, it became obvious that more troops were needed for the Ottoman defense. In the first month of war, Russian troops in Iran seized the Kotur Pass on the road from Khoy to Van and then held their positions. Dir and Başkale were taken. These were not yet major Russian incursions. Troops were available to strengthen the Ottoman defense and perhaps drive the Russians back, but these troops were sent elsewhere.

Enver Paşa had plans that did not stress defense. In December 1914 Enver brought up units to reinforce the Third Army in northeastern Anatolia.[7] The enlarged Third Army was sent into Russian territory in an ill-advised attack. The Ottoman force of 95,000 men, more than adequate for defense, was not large enough for an expedition over high mountain passes in winter undertaken by men who had only summer uniforms and insufficient artillery. Ignoring the advice of his generals, Enver sent his men—without winter greatcoats or wood for fires, mainly shod in sandals—across the Northeastern Mountains.

Enver's plan was to surprise the Russians, who assumed that no army could pass the mountain barrier, covered in deep winter snow. The Russians were indeed surprised. The Turkish troops stolidly fought against both the winter snows and the Russians, but many of the Turkish forces simply froze to death. The Russians stopped the advance of the remainder of the Ottoman troops at the small town of Sarıkamış. The losses on the retreat were even greater than on the advance. Of the 95,000 soldiers who had attacked Russia, 75,000 died; and nearly all the artillery was lost. The Ottoman Third Army, charged with the defense of Eastern Anatolia, could only muster 18,000 men in mid-January 1915, 20 percent of its strength before the Sarıkamış debacle. Even with hasty additions of all available reinforcements from military depots, only 30,000 men faced the Russians in the northeast, and they were not the equal of the experienced troops lost at Sarıkamış.[8]

Even before Sarıkamış, Ottoman defensive forces were spread thinly across the eastern front. Poorly equipped units such as the Van Mobile Gendarme Division were left to defend against the Russians who threatened from Persia, while needed forces were instead concentrated for Enver Paşa's ill-considered attack to the north. The Sarıkamış loss meant that the men needed to protect Van Province were never to return. Russian forces in Iran took immediate advantage of the Ottoman weakness to advance. On November 29, 1914, Kâzım (Özalp), commander of the Gendarme Division, reported to Third Army headquarters on intelligence reports he had received:

Today the enemy attacked Deyr [Dir]. They are equipped with artillery and machine guns. Our defending force is very small, and I believe we will have to withdraw in the direction of Hoşap. From the testimony of two captured spies we have learned that there will soon be an uprising in Van and the Van Province. I will move in the direction of Hoşap with a detachment from the forces at Saray. Due to the weakness of our force, however, if there is an uprising in the province, we will be hard pressed. The promised units from Revandiz have not arrived.[9]

The Russians went on to take Başkale; but Ottoman forces in southeastern Van and on the Iran border gained a brief reprieve when the Russians—fearing the Sarıkamış offensive might be successful—withdrew most of their forces from Iran at the end of December 1914. Ottoman irregulars, primarily Kurdish tribesmen, seized Tabriz on January 14, 1915. To the south, the Ottomans were able to retake strategic positions in the Kotur Pass and at Dir. However, Russian forces retook Tabriz on January 30 and Dilman on January 30. The Ottomans kept a tenuous hold at Kotur and in the Dir-Başkale region.[10]

Any large Russian advance in 1914 was held up by winter, which closed passes and roads, giving the Ottomans time to bring up reinforcements in southeastern Anatolia. The Ottomans were able to divert some forces to the area. By March 1915 the Ottomans had 24,000 regulars and an uncounted number of irregulars attached to the Third Army.[11] The First Expeditionary Force (see below) was gathered from Istanbul and elsewhere at the end of December 1914, adding to Ottoman forces in the East.

When the winter snows melted, the Russians took advantage of the Ottoman losses and went on the attack in the spring of 1915. The Turkish position was not impossible. They still occupied strong defensive positions and had the advantage of shorter lines of internal communication and transportation in their own territory. That was to change, though, when the Armenian rebellion robbed the Ottomans of any advantage.

POLITICAL PREPARATIONS FOR ARMENIAN REBELLION

Armenian nationalists saw the war as an opportunity to revolt. As Louise Nalbandian, the historian of the Armenian revolutionary movements, has written: "The most opportune time [for the revolutionaries] to institute the general rebellion for carrying out the immediate objective was when

Turkey was engaged in a war."[12] Like other observers, the Armenian revolutionaries saw the Ottoman debacle in the Balkan Wars of 1912–13 as an indication that the empire would soon collapse. Russia had defeated a seemingly stronger Ottoman Empire in the 1877–78 war. The rebels confidently expected that Russia would quickly seize Eastern Anatolia and perhaps even Istanbul itself. For those who saw Ottoman defeat as their sole chance for independence, the only choice was an alliance with Russia. Given their assumptions, the logic of the revolutionaries was perfect: the Ottomans would lose to the Russians. No matter what the Ottoman government promised the Armenians—reforms, autonomy, even independence—the promises could not be redeemed, because the Ottomans would lose. Russia would be making the final decisions on the fate of the Armenians.

Of course, the Armenian revolutionaries had long-standing ties with Russia. As early as 1908 Consul Dickson in Van had reported:

> I might mention here that the Armenian revolutionaries in Van and Salmas have been informed by their Committee in Tiflis that in the event of war they will side with the Russians against Turkey. Unaided by the Russians, they could mobilize about 3,500 armed sharpshooters to harass the Turks about the frontier, and their lines of communication.[13]

In retrospect it is hard to believe that the Armenian revolutionaries were such fools as to think that the Russians would grant them either independence or even considerable autonomy. Russia had never accepted Armenian separatism in the territories it controlled. Indeed, Russia had repeatedly taken action against all separatist movements within its borders. Yet in 1914 the Armenians apparently believed that the Russians would be satisfied with an Armenian client state in a hard-to-rule region so far from Moscow. Emotional commitment to revolution must also have played a part in the Armenian decision to rebel: the emotions of Armenian nationalism had long been directed against the Ottomans. Consciously or not, the revolutionaries must have realized that the only region with an Armenian majority—the Erivan Province of the Russian Empire—would not be able to gain its independence. Thus the Hunchaks, Dashnaks, and others, led by Russian Armenians, had directed their energies south. Their revolutionary planning, past rebellions, and rhetoric had targeted Eastern Anatolia as the Armenia that was to be. The commitment was too strong to deny.

The public face of the Dashnak Party was manifested at a party congress held in Erzurum in June–July 1914. Delegates from Russia and the Ottoman Empire, including the Van deputy Vahan Papazian, attended. It has been argued that Committee of Union and Progress members went to the congress to offer the Dashnaks autonomy in Eastern Anatolia if the Dashnaks in the Ottoman and Russian Empires would take part in the war against the Russians, which the Dashnaks refused. There is no real evidence for this assertion, which is based on Armenian sources; but it is not impossible.[14] What is certain is that the Dashnak Congress did resolve that Ottoman Armenians would do their patriotic duty. This was a subterfuge, as Ottoman intelligence reports and the statement of the prominent Dashnak leader Hovhannes Katchaznouni, prime minister of the Armenian Republic, attested.[15] The actual Dashnak plan, directed by the party in the Russian Empire, was to ally themselves with the Russians. Ottoman Army Intelligence reported that the actual secret resolutions of the leaders of the congress were:

1. To preserve loyalty in tranquillity pending the declaration of war, but to carry on with the preparations for arming with weapons brought from Russia and others to be obtained locally.
2. If war is declared Armenian soldiers in the Ottoman army will join the Russian army with their arms.
3. If the Ottoman army advances, to remain calm.
4. Should the Ottoman army then retreat or come to a standstill position, to form armed guerrilla bands and begin programmed operations behind army lines.[16]

In preparation for war the Armenian revolutionary groups in Van met in the middle of 1913 and agreed to coordinate their revolutionary efforts. The British consul in Van, Molyneux-Seel, felt that their alliance resulted from the Van Dashnak leader Vramian's "interview with the Russian authorities" in Tiflis.[17] The Dashnaks were unquestionably in the lead. The party had a network of agents spread throughout Eastern Anatolia, Iran, and the Russian Caucasus. It had a considerable income from "taxes" collected from fellow Armenians. Most importantly, the Dashnaks had their own sizable military force.[18]

The Dashnaks and their fellow revolutionaries had unquestioned command over the Armenians of Van. By 1913 it was evident to Molyneux-Seel that "[the Armenians have] thrown off any pretence of loyalty they may once have shown, and openly welcome the prospect of a Russian occupation of the Armenian Vilayets."[19]

PRACTICAL PREPARATIONS FOR REBELLION

In 1910 the Armenian revolutionary committees had begun to distribute a pamphlet throughout Eastern Anatolia—the "Instructions for Personal Defense." It was a blueprint for the rebellion that was to follow.[20]

The "Instructions" set out a plan for organized battle on the village level. They included psychological preparations, individual and organizational arrangements, the criteria for organizing, the selection of weapons, how to obtain weapons locally, and the distribution of weapons in the region, as well as the strategy for skirmishes with Ottoman forces. The pamphlet was written in a simple style, intended to distill a very sophisticated military doctrine into a form usable by local cadres.

The "Instructions for Personal Defense" were detailed and practical. The rules of guerrilla and partisan warfare were effectively observed.[21] Organization and command were to be the responsibility of special units that trained the Armenians in the villages. These units formed a nucleus for village organizations and acted as leaders. Villages were divided into mobile and stationary units, each of which had a leader. All were under the authority of a village leader, chosen for his experience. He represented the village to the three-person Regional Command. Members of the Regional Commands were selected from village leaders known for their personal abilities and their influence in the region.

Regional commanders were responsible for allocating weaponry, taking weapons from those who could not use them and giving them to those who could. They were to establish a system of couriers. When a village was raided by security forces these messengers were to request assistance from surrounding villages.

Muslim villagers in the regions were considered enemies. Armenians who were a minority in mixed villages and could not expect assistance from neighboring villages were instructed to take their valuables and weapons and immediately travel to villages inhabited solely by Armenians. Muslim minorities in majority Armenian villages should be expelled or held hostage. Armenians were to open their houses to co-religionists fleeing from government forces. The entire village was to pay to replace weapons that fell into enemy hands. Enemy weapons that came into Armenian hands were to be given to those who had taken them.

Most telling of the "Instructions" was the section titled "To Attack Villages," which was far from a manual on self-defense. It documented intelligence-gathering, transportation, plan of attack, and pursuit of fleeing Muslim villagers. The tactics of the "Instructions for Personal Defense" were to become the plan of the Armenian rebellion.

The period just before the outbreak of war was a time of intense organization and arming of the Armenians in Van. Eight months before the
outbreak of the Armenian rebellion Consul Smith in Van reported:

As Your Excellency is aware, these three parties [Dashnak, Hunchak, Ar-
menakan] at Van some six months ago, agreed to sink their differences
and to unite for the purpose of dealing with such matters as concerned
the general interests of the Millet. The influence of the Dashnakist
party however far exceeds that of the other two, owing to the more active and extreme policy it pursues. It is well organized, has a regular and
apparently considerable income from subscriptions, and has its agents
throughout the Armenian villages in the Vilayet who work for the party
and keep in touch with the Central Committee in Van. This party during the past year has actively concerned itself with the secret importation
of arms and their distribution amongst its followers. Mauser pistols are
the favourite weapon; they are easily hidden and imported and can be
used as a carbine, being sighted up to 1000 metres. I have seen Armenians openly carrying these arms in the country districts, and though I
have seen no rifles in the few villages I have had the opportunity of visiting, a good number of the inhabitants displayed a familiar knowledge
of the different types of rifles and their mechanism. In Van it is said that
the Armenians are now better armed than the Kurds, and there is no
doubt that they have obtained a number of modern rifles in addition to
the few old Martinis which the Government has distributed to each village. This desire on the part of the villagers to obtain arms was the result
of the general lack of security which existed up to within a few months
ago, and to the losses which they suffered at the hands of certain Kurdish brigands; the Dashnakist party made the most of this opportunity,
their policy being to put the Armenians in the province in a position to
hold their own against the Mohammedans should the necessity arise.
Also, the selling of arms in Van is a very profitable trade—a rifle or pistol
being sold for nearly three times its real value—and this makes the arming of the villagers a not unattractive business for the Dashnakist leaders
who have taken it up.

Though the Local Government must be aware of what is going on,
it has taken no steps to put a stop to the traffic in arms, it appears on
the contrary to be the policy of the Vail to help the villagers to defend
themselves if necessary by distributing old pattern army rifles in the proportion of three to six to each village, both Kurd and Armenian. Some
four months ago one thousand rifles were sent from Van for distribu-

tion amongst the Kurdish tribes on the Persian frontier, particularly in the district which had suffered most last year from the incursions of Simko.[22]

Russian espionage in Eastern Anatolia increased in the prewar period. The spies appeared under classic "cover" as journalists, merchants, and professors on research trips. Some even arrived disguised as tribal Kurds. The government felt that their purpose was to contact both Armenian revolutionaries and Kurds as well as carry out the usual military reconnaissance.[23]

OTTOMAN INTELLIGENCE ON THE PLANNED REBELLION

While the Ottomans did not know the exact timetable of Armenian revolt, they were aware that revolt was to be expected. On September 7, 1914, the Ottoman ambassador in Tehran reported information that the Russians had distributed arms to Armenians in Iran and the Caucasus and that the Russian consul in Tabriz had promised to create a new Armenia in return for their support. The Russians, he said, were in contact with the Armenians in Van.[24] Ottoman spies in Petersburg reported: "The Russian Government aims to win the support of the Armenians so as to provoke a revolt in Eastern Anatolia any time it chooses."[25] The sense of reports received from police, the military, and intelligence officers was that that Armenian rebels would revolt with assistance from Russia.[26]

The Ottoman military considered the evidence serious enough to warn all military units. On September 19, before the beginning of hostilities, the Third Army commander notified all units to take steps to counter the danger from Armenian insurgents: "Russians, with the assistance of Armenians from Caucasia, have incited our Armenians with promises of independence, promising to give to Armenians lands which they obtain from the Ottoman nation. Furthermore, many men in the costumes of our villagers [i.e., disguised as local Kurds or Turks] have brought arms and ammunition to Armenian villages from across our borders." Army units were ordered to arrest those who attempted to pass the frontier without passports, no matter who they appeared to be. Those who tried to smuggle in arms and ammunition were also to be arrested. If they attempted to escape, they were to be shot. Armenian and other non-Muslims in the army should be watched carefully and not employed in sensitive positions. Danger did not come only from Armenian rebels: the command also ordered that "Kurds and other Muslims who have been ensnared and misled by the evil thoughts of Armenians and Russians will be persuaded of the wisdom of taking action against the Russians by explaining the goals of the Armenians and Russians."[27]

Similar instructions were given to government officials, police, and intelligence operatives:

1. Disguised secret police and other reliable persons will collect information on the groups of Armenians and other non-Muslims of this sort (i.e., rebels), their organization, their areas of operation, in which villages they can be found, and their leadership.
2. If local authorities are unable to contain the revolutionary activities they discover, to keep military activities from being disrupted, or to organize the militia, they are to obtain help from the nearest military units.
3. Anyone found with weapons and not following regulations will be apprehended and delivered to the martial law War Council.[28]

Despite their prior knowledge, the Ottomans were not very successful in their struggle to contain the plans of the rebels and their Russian supporters.

Military Service of Non-Muslim Subjects

The attitude of the Christian minorities toward military service had long been ambiguous. In the early days of the empire Christians had served in Ottoman fighting units, but for a long time the Ottomans had enforced traditional Muslim rules on military service. Non-Muslims were not allowed to serve as soldiers, instead paying a tax (the *cizye*, later called the *bedelât-ı askeriye*).[29] On the whole, this was a beneficial arrangement for non-Muslims. Life in the Ottoman military, especially during the nineteenth-century wars, was difficult and often short.[30]

Despite its advantages, minorities disliked the bedelât, because it was a sign of second-class citizenship. The reforms of the nineteenth century had gone a long way toward creating the legal equality called for in the philosophy of "Ottomanism." Minority communities were governed by their own constitutions, had their own national and regional assemblies, and fully participated in the election of delegates to the Ottoman Parliament. Christians held high office, including foreign minister. But in matters of conscription and military service, inequality remained.

A new military conscription law was prepared by the Ministry of

War in October 1908. According to the draft, all subjects between ages of twenty and forty-five were to fulfill a mandatory military service. The change seemed to draw wide support. It was sent to the leaders of all the communities by the Council of Ministers. Some Armenian bishops in Anatolia sent cables to the military commission of the Parliament, requesting that non-Muslims immediately be dispatched to military service.[31] An influential Greek deputy, Kozmidi Efendi, was the bill's most eloquent supporter.[32]

On July 12, 1909, the Assembly accepted the draft calling for cancellation of the Military Exemption Tax. Implementation was to begin that same year. Of the approximately two hundred thousand who were liable for military service in March 1911, forty thousand were non-Muslims. On March 27, 1912, the War Academy graduated its first non-Muslims. Among the 394 officer candidates were 4 Greeks, 3 Armenians, and 1 Jew.[33] Eight thousand Christians and Jews were sent to the front in the Balkan Wars of 1912–13, which erupted a few months later. Some Armenian soldiers were taken prisoner by the Bulgarian army in the First Balkan War.[34]

Desertions

None of the patriotic and reformist sentiments proclaimed by minority groups in the Assembly were evident as war approached in the Ottoman East. Armenian draftees in the East were deserting in large numbers soon after the proclamation of mobilization on August 3, 1914. Armenian youths in general were refusing to report for duty.[35] By September the situation had become very clear, as reflected in the reports of the governors, the conscription officials, and the military. At first Armenians fled unarmed before they could be conscripted, but later they fled from the Ottoman forces en masse with their weapons. Some of the deserters formed small groups, virtually bandits, who terrorized the countryside, randomly attacking Muslims. Others—far more dangerous both to the Muslims of the region and to the state—formed partisan guerrilla bands, joining with Armenians from Russian territory. Revolutionary Committee members such as the famous Armenian revolutionary Andranik from Erzurum, Sempat from Muş, and Hamazasp from Van (who had been residing in Russia) established units consisting of three hundred or four hundred men each under their leadership. They began training under the guidance of Russian officers.[36]

At first these groups proved especially dangerous to the women, children, and elders in isolated Muslim villages in which the young men had

gone off to war. Soon their activities advanced to more concrete military
objectives. More than twelve thousand Ottoman Armenians went to Russian territory, where they were trained in partisan tactics.[37] Some of these
soon returned to Ottoman territory, where they joined the fighters who
had remained behind. They began to hinder military communications
and attack isolated military units, officials, and conscription officers. These
units became the military backbone, the "enforcers" of the revolutionary
plan in the Van countryside.[38]

Some deserters were integrated with young Armenians from Russian
Armenia into the Russian imperial forces as members of *druzhiny* (literally
"fellowships": volunteer units or commandos). Each 1,000 strong, these
units were made up of Armenians from Russian and Ottoman Armenia.
At the beginning of the war there were four druzhiny; another was added
soon after, and one more late in 1915. The druzhiny were among the most
effective Russian forces. They knew the territory, were dedicated to their
cause, and had a close connection with the Armenian revolutionaries and
partisans. The druzhiny were to lead the Russian advance into Van.[39]

Armenian deserters also fled to Armenian revolutionary encampments
in Russian-controlled western Iran, where they began preparations to join
in the Russian advance into Van Province. Kâzim Bey, commander of the
Mobile Gendarmerie Division, reported intelligence gathered on site and
from captured rebels to the Third Army Commander: Armenian rebels
in Iran had organized into regiments of approximately eight hundred
men each in three battalions. There were also separate partisan bands. An
Armenian reserve battalion had been formed in Khoy. Armenian volunteers and two squadrons of rebel cavalry were also operating in the region
of Bayazıt and Maku.[40]

THE REBELLION BEGINS

Both desertions and partisan activities increased at the end of 1914. It can
be seen from their reports that Ottoman officials had begun to understand the gravity of the situation. Evidence confirmed the earlier reports of
Armenian revolutionary organization and cooperation with the Russians.
The first somewhat disorganized Armenian attacks could have been interpreted as isolated incidents; but by the beginning of 1915 the rebels had
become more well organized, their attacks more intense. They were obviously working according to method and plan.[41] This was evident from the
nature of the rebel attacks: weapons, ammunition, and bombs that had
been hidden secretly were brought forth and used against Ottoman mili-

tary units and gendarmerie outposts. The Armenians in the East attacked the army's supply trains and commissariat, cutting communications lines and ambushing and killing columns of the wounded sent from the front. Roads and communications lines needed to supply troops at the front were cut. Gendarmes, who were scattered over the eastern provinces to provide some security, were ambushed and killed. Key villages and towns at crossroads and natural defense points were burned, with increasing loss of civilian lives. Bridges and fortifications were destroyed. It was impossible to see the nature of these attacks without understanding that they had a military purpose.

Reports came into the government and the Third Army Command of rebel actions throughout the southeast. Written in the unemotional language of soldiers and bureaucrats, the reports nevertheless indicate that incidents were occurring all across the region. The earlier reports also indicate that the Ottomans still felt that they could contain the rebellion, but they had undoubtedly begun to take serious counterinsurgency measures against the rebels, including burning their villages. For example, the governor of Bitlis sent the following information to the interior minister on February 21, 1915:

1. The Armenian villages that had rebelled in Hakif Nahiye were occupied and burned, the animals seized. [Revolutionary] documents were found on the body and in the house of one of the leaders, Kalo. These have not yet reached Bitlis.

2. I have been in contact with Van. Because of strong and decisive action in Hizan they do not expect trouble from the Gevaş and Reşadiye Armenians. A strong gendarmerie unit has been sent from Gevaş to resist attacks in Karjar Buçak from Armenians who have come from neighboring and more distant regions.

3. At present, nothing is happening on the Bitlis-Gevaş road. Action may have begun in Hizan. Weapons were used against our local gendarmes at two places on the Muş Plain. A detachment went to the Serveng village of the Muş central kaza to arrest deserters. It came under fire from a mill on the outskirts of the village. A two-hour battle ensued. Only one of our horses was killed. When the engagement began, three officers brought their units from Muş. The village was besieged. By the end of the battle nine had been killed. The deserters' houses were burned.

4. On the same day, in the village of Kümes in the Akaan Nahiye a volley of bullets was directed at the house where the müdür [mayor] was

residing. He had gone there with a gendarmerie unit. In an eight-hour battle nine were killed from the gendarmes and militia. The rebels set fire to the house where the müdür was taking shelter, but he escaped with difficulty. Among those who took part in the battle against the troops were the Muş Dashnak Delegate Ropen and the Dashnak Esro, so suspicion must fall on the Committee.[42]

As the Armenian rebellion grew and actions against Ottoman officials and soldiers increased, Enver Paşa, the minister of war, took note of the intelligence reports. On September 25, 1914, he sent orders that certain precautions be taken:

> Certain Armenian brigands have appeared in Bitlis and some Armenian army deserters have begun to resort to banditry. Armenians attacked the soldiers and the gendarmerie in Halep [Aleppo] and Dörtyol. Considerable quantities of explosives as well as groups of code keys in French, Russian and Armenian were found in houses belonging to Armenians in the city of Kayseri. Although these incidents are not so important at present, they indicate that our enemies are preparing to launch a revolt inside the country. Therefore, the announcement and communication of the following articles were deemed necessary.
>
> 1. Armenian privates in mobile armies as well as mobile and stationary gendarmerie units will never be used in combat services and will never be employed in the offices of the headquarters and suites of the commanders.
> 2. Army and army corps commanders, acting commanders of army corps and divisions and commandants must be and are authorized to swiftly put down in the most rigorous way any set of opposition or armed aggression or resistance against government orders and to completely eradicate such aggression or resistance. Furthermore, the commanders are also authorized to declare martial law immediately in any place they deem necessary.
> 3. Although it is necessary to be careful and alert, the kind of oppression that would frighten the people should be avoided in places where there are no concrete signs of aggression. Hence, the view that loyal and obedient subjects will not suffer any harm should be stressed and the people must not be incited to revolt as a result of desperation.
> 4. Since all problems of defense and public order concern the Armed Forces as a result of general mobilization, civil administrators shall apply to the commanders on such matters. Only the civil administrators

of the Province of Istanbul shall apply to the General Headquarters on matters and measures related to public order.

5. The most competent authorities in matters relayed to public order are the army commanders in the Third and Fourth Armies as well as the Iraqi regions; the most competent authorities in those matters are the army commanders in the First and Second Army regions. These army corps commanders shall keep the Acting Commander-in-Chief and army commanders informed.

6. The Third and Fourth Army Commanders shall immediately inform the Acting Commander-in-Chief of the measures being taken and planned in the likelihood of incidents.[43]

It had become apparent to the Central Command that matters in the East had passed beyond the competence of the civilian authorities. A guerrilla war was being waged. Despite his wish to retain the loyalty of Armenians by asserting that "loyal and obedient subjects will not suffer any harm," Enver Paşa clearly did not feel the Armenians could be trusted.

In the early days of the war, army intelligence reports started to indicate that an Armenian revolt had begun and that the situation could become serious. Officials stressed the need for precautions, but it was too late. It is obvious that the Ottoman government did not yet realize the enormity of its problem in the East. The measures undertaken to stop the rebels were classic operations to fight small bands, protect government installations, and facilitate conscription. Martial law had been declared. Armenians who remained in the army were shifted to noncombatant duties, chiefly in labor battalions. Units of soldiers and gendarmes were dispatched to chase rebels and open roads. Where entire villages in sensitive areas such as mountain passes and crossroads had rebelled, they were destroyed. Tax collectors and conscription officers were accompanied by soldiers for their protection. Plans were laid to punish villages that harbored guerrillas, although events soon made it nearly impossible to carry these out.[44] Measures like these were suited to the type of Armenian rebellion seen in past years, but they were to prove insufficient when Armenian actions became a general revolt.

The War Begins in the Province of Van

From all intelligence reports it is plain that the Armenians in the Van region relied on upcoming Russian success and would rebel.[45] In December 1914 Cevdet, the governor of Van, attempted to alleviate the situation by dealing as in the past with the Armenian community leaders, but he was convinced that this would be futile:

> I held talks with the Armenian elite. I explained the general situation on appropriate occasions. I told them that any incident between the Armenians and the Muslims would certainly affect all the Armenians living in the Ottoman territories. I pointed out that conditions created by possible clashes in regions like this one, which would not affect the final outcome of the battles, would quickly change. I realized that it was not possible to get good results, for exaggerations made by the tribes on the current situation frighten the Muslim population. I am taking great care to prevent the Armenians from provoking incidents. Since the enemy advanced from Kotur and some tribes submitted to the foe, I do not think that the Gendarme Division will be able to put up a long resistance. Therefore, I will begin to send the families [of officials] to Bitlis.[46]

Cevdet knew that there was danger in Van City, which was the reason he sent the families of officials to Bitlis, but he underestimated that danger. The "exaggerations made by the tribes on the current situation" were in fact no exaggerations, as the tribal leaders knew. Many families remained behind. Cevdet felt the main danger came from Russian invasion from Iran, through the Kotur Pass to the east of Van.

Cevdet did not discount the danger of Armenian revolt, but he felt that the greatest cause for worry was not the Armenians of the city of Van, who seemed to remain peaceful at the end of 1914. It was the activity of Armenians and Nestorians to the east and southeast of Van and on the Iranian border that he feared. It was estimated that three thousand Nestorians (a group of Christians who had never accepted any but their own leaders, always armed and now further equipped by the Russians) fought the Ottoman forces in the southern part of Van Province. Ottoman officers reported that the entire Armenian population in the Salmas region of Iran was armed and in revolt. These Armenians were purportedly commanded by Andranik and his associates.[47] Ottoman regular and irregular units clashed with the rebels. By December 1914 the Armenians in western Iran had organized into battle units and had put themselves loosely under Russian command. Many were armed with weapons and equipment brought to the area from Russian Armenia by the rebels. Many more were now armed by the Russians, and deserters from the Ottoman army joined rebel partisan bands in Iran and Anatolia, bringing with them their weapons. In various engagements with the Armenians on the Iranian borders, the Ottoman forces were sometimes able to hold their own but were some-times defeated. The undermanned Ottoman forces gained no victories.[48]

The forces attacking on the Van borders were made up of regular Rus-sian troops, the First Armenian Legion, volunteers from Russia (whose numbers included Armenians from Anatolia), and Armenian bands from the Ottoman Empire and Iran.[49] Some tribes also joined the Russians. The Russian forces significantly outnumbered the Ottoman defenders. At Hoşap the Mobile Gendarme Division commander Kâzım Bey reported on December 5:

> An enemy force comprising 4,000 infantry, 1,000 cavalry, two field and two mountain artillery guns is in the vicinity of Saray. Reconnaissance units today arrived at Molla Hasan village between Müslihan and Saray and Ercek. A 500-strong enemy unit supported by two mountain artil-lery guns from its force in Dir occupied Başkale. The remaining part of the units remained in the vicinity of Dir. Tribe leaders went south with-out any resistance against the Russians. We are now around Akgöl, north of Hoşab, with a 2,000-strong force, which was deployed from Hoşab yesterday. Other units are still at their yesterday's positions.
>
> The enemy is seizing the weapons from local people in places that it has occupied, using these weapons to arm Armenians and form units. There are some Iranian [i.e., Iranian Kurdish] tribes among enemy units. As we were forced to disarm Armenian enlisted men, due to our losses and deserters, our forces are limited. The units that moved from Ravandiz have not yet joined our forces at Somay. The two mountain guns were returned to Ravandiz, according to information from Mosul.[50]

In a major battle with Armenians on December 17–19 to the south of Kotur the Ottomans lost four hundred dead and wounded and were forced to retreat to Saray. Kurdish nomads loyal to the Ottomans were similarly defeated and forced to withdraw.[51]

As the Russians and Armenians invaded from Iran, clashes between rebels and soldiers and gendarmes continued in the interior in December 1914. Ottoman administrators in the area reported the events to the army command and the Interior Ministry. The governor of Erzurum, Tahsin Bey, reported on December 21 that the Armenians of the Karçekan and Gevaş districts of Van Province were in revolt, cutting telegraph wires and attacking the kaymakam (district head official). Tahsin stated that the gen-darmerie forces were not sufficient to put down the revolt. More soldiers would have to be sent.[52]

Armenian attacks on gendarmerie units and the seizure of roads and strategic points intensified during January 1915. Istanbul was aware of the situation, although Armenian representatives in the capital denied any revolutionary activity, blaming all of the lack of security in the East.[53] Intelligence reports accurately portrayed the impending danger of a general Armenian revolt. Analyses stated that the Russians would attack from the north (Bayazıt to Abak). At the same time, the Armenians would stage a general uprising in the Van Region, facilitating the Russian occupation of Van Province. Cevdet in Van and other officials had written that such a revolt was expected, although they underestimated its effect in the city of Van. Cevdet attempted to organize irregular tribal forces to prepare for the revolt. It appears, however, that neither the central government nor the Third Army Command anticipated the ferocity and danger of the general guerrilla war that broke out in February 1915.

In February tax collectors and gendarmes went to the Timar Nahiye (subdistrict) to the north of Van to count sheep, which were taxed by the head. Disagreement ensued between the Armenian villagers and the tax collectors. This was not an unusual occurrence, but now the villagers were armed and ready for revolt. Resistance had been previously prepared. More than a thousand armed Armenians from Timar and surrounding areas began a revolt that soon spread. They attacked neighboring Muslim villages and killed Muslim villagers. The gendarmerie post in the village of Banat was attacked, and the gendarmes and their commandant were killed.[54] The revolt soon spread to Van's Gevaş and Çatak Kazas. In Gevaş the *kadı* (judge), İsmail Hakkı, was murdered. The rebels cut roads and telegraph lines.[55]

The drawing of Armenian villages into a general rebellion, using the tactics envisaged in the "Instructions for Personal Defense," had begun. Armenians who lived in mixed Muslim-Armenian villages left for Armenian villages. The exchange was to become general as Muslims and Armenians each fled from the other. Armenian rebels attacked Muslim villages and refugees. Kurdish tribes attacked Armenians.[56] Although no records were kept of the psychological effect on villagers, it can be assumed that both Muslims and Armenians were polarized and that both groups must have suffered high mortality. The migration of the Armenians also had the effect of increasing the forces opposing the Ottomans, because many who had no wish to rebel were now part of the war. That war was no longer a conflict between Ottoman soldiers on the one side and Russians and Armenian partisans on the other. It had become a general war between the Muslims and the Armenians.

The general Armenian rebellion had fully begun by February 1915, except in the city of Van and its immediate neighborhood. By no means was the Van Province the only site of revolt. Armenians were rebelling throughout the Van, Bitlis, Sivas, Adana, and Erzurum Provinces.[57] In February Armenians attacked in Muş, Bitlis, Elazığ, and elsewhere, killing soldiers and striking columns sent to relieve those who had been attacked. Rebel organizational meetings were held in Armenian villages throughout the region. Ottoman civil and military officials forwarded reports of killings. For example, near Hizan deserting Armenian soldiers killed two gendarmes, and a three-day battle left seven soldiers and gendarmes dead. Army reports noted that Armenians had gathered together in that region's villages from other areas.[58] Gendarmes were attacked on the Muş Plain. A two-hour battle took place near the capital of Muş. An eight-hour battle in the Kümes village of Akaan Buçağı left nine Ottoman militia and gendarmes dead.[59] Reports began to come in of deserters and rebels attacking gendarmes and soldiers and massacring civilians in numerous villages through the Van region—Kümes, Tasu, Fıkırsız, Sigor, Mergehu, Istuci....[60] On February 27 approximately three hundred Muslim volunteer soldiers traveling from Adilcevaz to the city of Van were fired upon by Armenian bands as they tried to pass the village of Arın. Eight were killed. When reinforcements arrived from Erciş, the Armenians escaped in the direction of Lake Van.[61]

By March 1915 the Eastern Anatolian countryside was completely at war. Armenian rebels and deserters increased their incursions into the neighborhood of the city of Van. Without distinction of age or sex, Muslims who met with the rebels were simply killed.[62] Districts in the north changed hands as Russians first occupied them then were evicted by Ottoman forces. The Bargiri (Mahmudiye) region, the last defense line before Van, was in contention. Much of the Bargiri district was occupied by the Russians in February 1915, but they withdrew at the end of the month.

In March the rebel attacks and murders increased in a planned and methodical manner. The rebellion began to spread throughout the Van Province, particularly in Van's southern districts, which had been selected by the Armenians as the center of their revolt. In Van's Çatak Kaza, previously the scene of numerous Armenian partisan attacks, the general revolt may have been precipitated earlier than the rebels intended by the government's discovery of rebel plans. In a short while the revolt also intensified in Gevaş Kaza. Rebels cut the Bitlis-Van-Çatak telegraph line, which was the only communication from the region. They began to attack villages, army units, and Muslims on the roads.[63] The Çatak region was especially hard pressed: rebels surrounded the Çatak government building and killed two persons. Soldiers were attacked, as were gendarmerie stations. Telegraph lines were cut. Rebels fired on military units on the roads.[64] Both Van and Bitlis Provinces saw a great escalation in the rebellion, which had spread to many districts. As the governors worked with limited means, and limited success, to contain the rebellion, the tenor of their messages sent to Istanbul changed. Military reports began to describe a full-scale war: "Armed clashes on all sides continue into the night. It appears that the rebels are more than 2,000. We are working to suppress the rebellion."[65] What previously had been described as "banditry" or "disloyalty" that would soon be crushed was now admittedly a "rebellion."

Ottoman military officials reacted to the rebellion, but their forces were limited. As the rebellion grew and attacks on Muslim villages and settled areas on the province's borders increased, Cevdet Bey, who had been with Ottoman forces in Iran, traveled to the city of Van with a 600-man gendarme battalion. He had been given two field guns and now had under his command in the city one gendarme battalion, one gendarme depot battalion, 100 regular foot soldiers, and 100 cavalry (2,300 men in all) as well as one mountain cannon and the two field guns.[66] The Third Army command had a very limited number of troops available, and Cevdet was expected to use what forces he had to put down the Armenian rebellion. In fact, even if the Russian army had not been a threat to Van, the troops would not have been adequate to put down the rebellion. At a time when the Russians were about to invade the province from the north and the east and the Armenians were in revolt, the force was pitifully insufficient. It was to prove too small even to save the city of Van itself from the rebels, much less defeat rebellion in the countryside.

Cevdet, previously less worried about the safety of the city, now began to realize that Van City itself was in danger. In a communication to the Third Army Command on March 25, 1915, he told of the perilous situation in Van Province and requested a cannon and another battalion of troops:

> The Armenians have prepared a general revolt that will aid the upcoming Russian attack from Abaak and Saray and the enemy occupation of Van. They are only waiting until the roads open [from the winter snows]. Until then, they at first engaged only in occasional and isolated incidents, fearing that our position would be completely improved if the sufficient forces for which we have waited and hoped should arrive. [Seeing the forces did not arrive,] they began to assault the Muslim villages that

were near the villages where the Armenians had gathered together. In the İrelmir Kariye near Van they attacked gendarmes and tax collectors. Unable to refrain until the time of the general rebellion, their actions showed their intentions. Although the Muslim people defended themselves and detachments sent from Van scattered the rebels, these actions will repeat in even greater number in the province center and elsewhere in the province. I see the signs of these coming events. Reports from the detachment commanders at Kotur indicate that the Russians will begin to advance into the Kotur Valley. After they have occupied the important points in the Kotur Pass they will mount an assault on Saray. When that occurs there is no doubt that the Armenians will revolt on every side.[67]

The Russians had been held up by winter conditions in the mountains. By the end of March the roads were open. Russian forces threatened to invade Van Province in three regions:

- In the north, they would invade through the passes south of the Eleşkirt Valley. In March 1915 the Russian army had retaken the valley, which it had previously held then lost to the Ottomans. It was used as a base to advance south. Farther to the west the Russians moved to the Murat River, taking Tutak.[68] The reserve cavalry brigade in Bargiri was weak, a force not even sufficient to face the Armenian partisans who were invading from Iran.
- To the east of Van City, the Ottomans held the Kotur Pass, but Russians and Armenians were threatening to overrun the defenders. Armenian partisan units had been active behind the lines and had already defeated an Ottoman force there in December 1914.[69]
- Farther to the south, a Russian force to the west of Lake Urmia threatened the Başkale region of southern Van Province.

As seen above, the systematic progress of the Van revolt started in March 1915, beginning very rapidly in the Çatak Kaza. According to a report of the Van Mobile Gendarmerie commander on April 16 the rebels had progressed from cutting the lifeline telegraph lines to attacking military stations and gendarmes in the Armenian districts of Çatak Kaza. In order to stop this, detachments of gendarmerie were sent to provide security. However, the units were met by Armenians who attacked their columns.[70] They were unable to have much effect on the rebellion. Starting on April 18 Armenians battled gendarmes and militia in the Havasor Nahiye to the east of Van City. Armenians revolted in Hoşap and Erçek. Battles continued between gendarmes and Armenians in Çatak.[71]

REBELLION IN THE CITY OF VAN

The city of Van had remained relatively quiet as the countryside erupted in rebellion. This peace was not to last. The city was poorly defended, because military units were either in defensive positions to the north and east or skirmishing with rebels. The Armenian committees had joined together under the leadership of the Dashnaks. The well-armed Armenians of the city were strengthened by deserters from the army and Armenians from nearby villages. Importation of arms had continued, including ingenious strategies such as importing bombs and weapons from Trabzon in bales of hay. The Armenian Defense Council in the Old City of Van, led by the Dashnak Party, was to be a central authority of the Van rebellion in the Old City. Its chairman, Haig Gossoian (Gassoyan), wrote a brief description of the council and its prewar preparations:

> The Armenian Revolutionary Federation in the city assumed the responsibility for the defense at the very beginning. In view of the fact that Van Vasbouragan had become one of the theatres of the war, teeming with armed Kurds, Hamidie groups and other disorderly militiamen and brigands, this organization busied itself from October, 1914, by drawing up the defense plans and the preliminary tasks connected with same. The early declaration of "Holy War" added much fuel to the fire.
>
> The seven members of the Defense Council included: David Sarkissian, store keeper, Levon Kaljian, merchant, Haig Gossoyan, teacher, Mihran Toromanian, soap maker, Mihrtad Mirzakhanian, land owner-farmer, Sarkis Shahenian, merchant and Harootiun Nergaraian, coppersmith.
>
> In consultation with higher authorities, this council was able to complete essential tasks, such as, (a) registration of arms, preparation of arms caches and procurement of firearms, (b) registration of men fit for and capable of combat duty, appointment of defense leaders, reconditioning of arms, (c) creation of first aid and hospital facilities, and procurement of drugs, (d) and a provisioning committee, to be activated as soon as demand required.[72]

It is perhaps instructive that the Defense Council began its work in October 1914, well before Van had become "one of the theatres of the war." Armenians may have seen this as a precaution, although Gossoian does not state that, but the Ottomans would have interpreted these actions quite differently, especially in light of the Armenian desertions, the Dashnak meeting with Russian officials, the consolidation of the revolution-

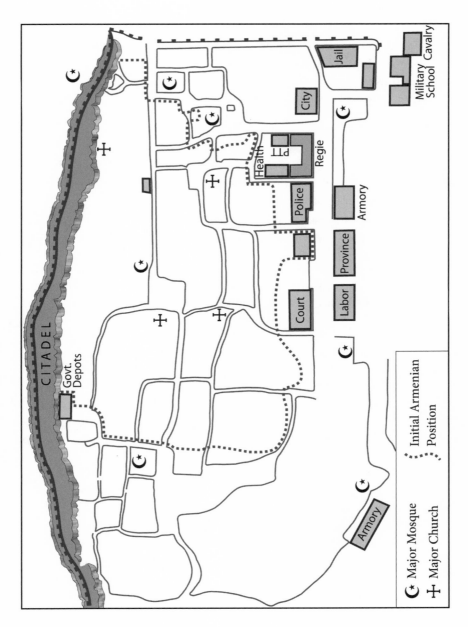

Map 8.1. Rebellion in the Old City of Van.

CITADEL

Govt.
Depots

Health

PTT

Regie

Police

Court

Labor

Province

Armory

City

Jail

Military
School

Cavalry

Armory

☾★ Major Mosque

✝ Major Church

Initial Armenian
Position

ary groups and command in Van, and the formation and first attacks of
Armenian guerrilla bands. Such preparations, made during the first days
of the revolt, long before the war came to Van and long before the government had taken any measures against Armenian rebels in Van, do appear
to be preparation for rebellion.

In April Governor Cevdet took action against the leaders of the Dashnak Party in Van. He undoubtedly expected that by killing the leaders
of the revolutionary parties he would destroy the cohesion of the rebels.
Ishkhan left Van for Çatak, ostensibly to parley with rebels there. He was
killed in the village of Hirj on the night of April 16–17. There is no proof
that the government ordered his death, but it is most likely. Vramian was
arrested on April 17 and sent under guard to Istanbul, disappearing (surely
killed) before he reached Bitlis. Of the three Dashnak leaders, only Aram
Manukian escaped.[73] Warned of Vramian's arrest, he went into hiding.
Cevdet's policy, brutal and illegal, would probably have been somewhat
successful in disorganizing the rebels had Aram not escaped. Instead it
left the Dashnaks' most capable leader in unquestioned and undivided
authority over the rebellion. It also most likely convinced the rebels that
Van City, previously a safe haven for them, was no longer safe.

The rebellion south of Van City continued, and the Ottomans found
it impossible to put it down. Despite the great need for troops on the Iranian border, units were ordered to Çatak. They encountered difficulties.
The Van Mobile Gendarme Division Commander, Kâzim Bey, reported
from Hakkâri on April 18 that his soldiers had been attacked on the roads
and still had not been able to reach Çatak. They had not received news
of the situation in Çatak, because the telegraph lines were cut. He stated:
"Van and other cities may be calm now, but when the revolt widens into a
general insurrection it is likely that all the telegraph lines will be cut."[74]

Kâzim was correct in expecting the worst. Murder and attacks on both
soldiers and civilians were now seen all over the province. Two days after
Kâzim's report, on April 20, the uprising finally came to Van City. Cevdet
Bey, the governor, reported early on April 20 to the Third Army Command:

1. The Armenian rebels opened fire on the security stations and houses
   in the vicinity of the Armenian Quarters of the city. Fire was returned
   and the area defended.
2. As a result of clashes with the bandits [the rebels] by last night a considerable number of rebels were killed. Atalan and Peltensi villages as
   well as the Akkilise Monastery, fortified as a stronghold, were burned
   down and destroyed.
3. Gevaş telegraph line has been repaired and communication resumed.

4. Today Başkale-Havasor-Mirmurtal-Reşat telegraph line was cut. Repair of this line is underway.[75]

The Van rebellion had begun.

Actually, the first phase of the rebellion had begun days before. Muslims and Armenians in mixed districts in the city had fled to purely Muslim and Armenian districts. Armenians had begun to dig trenches and construct fortifications around the Armenian districts. The Ottomans had placed guardhouses and sent patrols along the "no man's land" between the Muslim and Armenian quarters. On April 18 the three Armenian parties met and created the Military Committee of Armenian Self-Defense (also called the National Committee of Self-Defense and other names). The Dashnaks sent representatives to Iran and Russia to describe their condition in Van.[76] The Military Committee organized arms distribution, a commissariat, ammunition production, the building of fortifications, and the other functions of a wartime government. The head of the Military Committee called on the Armenians to recognize the "duty" of insurrection.[77] With the deaths of Ishkhan and Vramian, Aram Manukian was the only senior Dashnak leader remaining in Van. He was not only the titular head of the ruling Military Committee, but he took command.[78]

Some Armenian sources have claimed that the Van rebellion began with unprovoked attacks on Armenians on April 20.[79] They contend that Ottoman forces began to shell Armenian neighborhoods without reason. This seems extremely unlikely. The Armenian sources, writing after the fact for public consumption, had ample reason to proclaim that they were completely innocent. The Ottoman documents, in contrast, were purely internal reports. They had no foreseeable political or diplomatic benefit, because the authors did not expect them to be seen outside the government. These documents were simply reports sent to superiors with descriptions of events, usually written in cold and technical terminology. They must be viewed as the more reliable sources.

Given the past history of the Armenian revolutionaries in Van, it is nearly impossible to doubt that the primary impulse behind the Armenian rebellion was exactly as it had always been: the independence of the Armenians of Eastern Anatolia. Armenian sources also indicate another contributory cause for rebellion in Van City—fear. Though they never mention that Armenians were rebelling all over Van Province and elsewhere, the Armenian sources do pay much attention to the Armenian losses that accompanied those revolts. The Armenians of Van must have seen what was developing in the countryside. As will be seen in chapter 9, rebellion was rapidly developing into intercommunal war. Armenians attacked troops, and troops burned rebel villages. Both innocent Muslims and innocent Armenians suffered. Both were forced to take sides with their co-religionists.[80] There was reason for Van's Armenians to fear that the war would come to them, particularly because their leaders in the city were also the leaders of the Armenian revolt in the province. After the two Dashnak leaders, Ishkhan and Vramian, were killed, their deaths reverberated through the city's Armenian community.[81] When Cevdet ordered, quite legally, that the Armenian community turn over young men of draft age for the army, Armenians may have felt that they would lose their defenders. If the government began to station forces in the Armenian neighborhoods, might it not be planning an attack? Even Armenians who had no desire to fight may have felt it was better to act first, because the war between Muslims and Armenians seemed inevitable.[82]

Cevdet was unquestionably taking precautions against rebellion in the city. New police posts were manned. Gendarmerie units were stationed in the Muslim district that separated the Old City from the Armenian district in the Western Garden City. Armenian young men were called to serve in the army as road builders and agricultural laborers—a matter of duty and law, but also a way to remove potential rebels. These actions might indeed have caused the Armenians to fear, but what choice did the government have? Only the most foolish could have believed that there was no danger of an Armenian revolt in Van City. Precautions had to be taken.

The government could not ignore the evidence that lay before it. The Armenian revolutionaries had long ago proven their intentions. Could the government ignore the two thousand weapons that had been uncovered in Van in 1908 or the Dashnaks' steady rearming since then? Could it ignore the fact that the Dashnak organization, the same group that led the Van province's Armenians, was organizing its troops in Iran to invade the Ottoman Empire and was training Anatolian Armenians in Russia for the same purpose? Could it ignore all the intelligence reports that detailed the Dashnak plans for revolution? Could it ignore the information that the very rural Armenians who were now in revolt had been organized and trained by the "teachers" that Aram Manukian had sent out from Akhtamar? Most telling, could it ignore the Armenian revolts that had sprung up all over the province?

THE SITUATION IN THE CITY

When Cevdet wrote the Third Army Command early in the day on April 20, he was obviously growing increasingly worried by events. Unrest had begun in the Armenian section of the Garden District at dawn. Muslim neighborhoods and gendarme units near the Garden District came under fire. Cevdet still believed, however, that he could control the situation, if only he had enough force. In particular, he asked for artillery units with rapid-firing guns, an indication that he believed he would soon face a major force. By that evening (the night of April 20–21) the situation had significantly deteriorated. Armenian forces closed most of the roads into Van, fortifying them against the arrival of reinforcements. At first, only the road from Van to Gevaş remained open. It was the only lifeline to the rest of the empire, so Ottoman soldiers concentrated their limited forces to secure it. The Armenian villages near Van, which were already the scenes of attacks on officials and soldiers (in particular in the Havasor and Timar Districts), joined in the general revolt. Until reinforcements arrived from the Van Mobile Gendarme Division, the countryside was effectively in the hands of the Armenians.

The Ottomans rushed the available forces to Van: a battalion detached from the Mobile Gendarme Division, presumably the troops that had been fighting the rebels in Çatak, along with their mobile cannon. These arrived on April 23 and began to battle uprisings to the north and in the immediate north and west of the city and to patrol the borders of the Armenian-occupied Garden District.[83] They defeated the rebels in the Havasor District and elsewhere,[84] burning out rebel villages. Armenian refugees fled to Van City.[85] Other rebel villages on the hills and mountainside of Mount Erek held out against the Ottoman troops until May 8, when their fighters and others escaped to Van.

Armenian forces in Van City fought against Ottoman troops and Muslim residents in two disconnected sets of battles—in the Old City (Kale District) and in the Garden District. The battle in the Garden District was essentially a holding action by the Armenian rebels. Early in the morning of April 20 police outposts in the western section of the district were quickly overrun. The fight then became a series of skirmishes on the border of the Armenian and Muslim quarters. Both sides fortified buildings from which sharpshooters aimed at the opposition. The only successful Ottoman incursions into the rebel territory were seizures of the British Consulate and the Armenian church at Arak and the burning of some Armenian fortified houses. There were simply not enough troops and gendarmes to advance further, and the British Consulate emplacement was soon burned out by Armenian forces, forcing an Ottoman retreat.

Bombs and incendiary devices, including dynamite and incendiary grenades, were the most successful Armenian weapons in the Garden District.[86] In addition to the British Consulate, Armenians managed to destroy Ottoman emplacements all along the line. The large Hamid Ağa

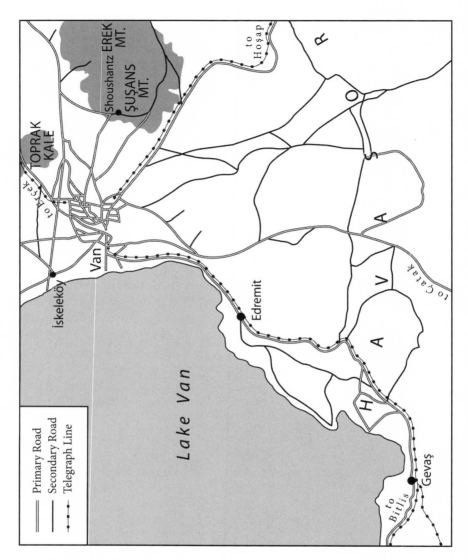

MAP 8.2. Van Roads and Telegraph Lines.

Barracks, a center of government forces, was successfully burned down. Rebels more than held their own against the soldiers, but little ground changed hands.[87]

The Ottomans bombarded the Armenian positions with shells fired from the Citadel and from Toprak Kale, to the northwest of the city. Mobile batteries fired on the rebels from the periphery of the area under their control. The shells caused great damage to the mud brick dwellings, but none of the bombardments seem to have had a significant effect on the Armenian lines or the rebels' determination.[88] Pictures of Van after the battles show a city in ruins, but how much of this was damage from cannon fire and how much from Armenian dynamite and burnings cannot be ascertained.[89] Both played a role in destroying the city.

Armenian sources describe their position as "under siege," but this should not be taken to mean that they were surrounded, with no means of ingress or egress. Armenians, both fighters and refugees, were able to enter the city.[90] They could sally forth from their territory in the Garden District, seemingly without significant opposition. On April 23 Armenian fighters from the Garden District went to the village of Darman, ten miles to the north, to assist the Armenians who were fighting there.[91] At the beginning of May a small number of men along with ammunition and supplies were sent from the Garden District to Shoushantz (southeast of Mount Erek) to aid Armenians fighting there. The ability to transport ammunition as well as "bread, sugar, soap, clothing and necessities" from the city shows that the Armenians were not surrounded by Ottoman troops.[92] This agrees with Cevdet's statements that he had relatively few troops at his disposal. It is more correct to say that the Armenians had no desire to leave, not that they were under close siege. The rebels never intended to leave the city to find greater security elsewhere.[93] The Armenians intended to hold Van until they were relieved. This, of course, is exactly what happened.

Ottoman forces held their own in the Garden District after the initial Armenian attacks. They were less successful in the Old City. Beginning on April 20,[94] battles raged through the Old City as Armenians drove back the Ottoman soldiers and gendarmes. Ottoman units in the Old City could not hold against the rebels. They were forced to withdraw first from Armenian districts in the west of the Old City then from the neighborhood of government offices to the south. The Armenians burned down the Post Office, the Ottoman Bank, the buildings of the Public Debt Commission and the Tobacco Monopoly, and other government buildings.[95] The soldiers and gendarmes were forced to flee into the Citadel (İçkale). The Muslims in the west of the Old City who could escape fled alongside troops and gendarmes into the Citadel, which became filled with Muslim refugees.[96] The Ottomans responded with cannon fire from the Citadel.

The Armenians had planned far ahead for their rebellion. They were well armed and had even prepared revolutionary flags and placards with the words "Free Armenia." Rebel units wore military headgear (*kalpak*) brought from France and Russia, some emblazoned with the word "vengeance."[97]

In the next two days Armenians burned most of the Muslim houses in the Old City of Van. The rebels selected a picked force of seven hundred men to mount a concerted attack on the Citadel, but they were driven back. Ottoman soldiers were unable to mount a successful counterattack. The battle settled into a partial rebel siege of the Citadel.[98] They were never able to surround the Citadel effectively, however. The Ottomans kept open roads to the west (to Lake Van) and to the southwest (to Gevaş).

THE OPPOSING FORCES

As in much of the history of the Van rebellion, Armenian and Ottoman sources disagree on the numbers in the Ottoman and the Armenian forces in the city. The Ottomans estimated that the original force of Armenian fighters, before the rebellion began in the city, was more than two thousand, which did not include any noncombatants. That number was increasing rapidly as civilians were armed and groups of rebels arrived from the countryside. It was felt that many of the fighters who arrived before the rebellion and during its first days were deserters from the Ottoman army, a large number of whom had military training.[99] The rebels were well armed, lacking only in artillery. They also had a supply of bombs and hand grenades.[100] By April 22, some Ottoman sources estimated, ten thousand armed Armenians were besieging the Muslims in the Van *kale* and fighting in the Garden District. Others (including the Venezuelan general Rafael de Nogales, who was serving in the Ottoman army in Van) estimated thirty thousand or more.[101]

Armenian sources tell a very different story:

The vali [governor] of Van is estimated to have had at his disposal 10,000 to 12,000 men, consisting of 6,000 infantrymen and 4,000 to 6,000 Kurdish tribesmen, chetés, and gendarmes. He also had twelve guns (light mountain artillery and short-range heavy fortress artillery), rifles and ammunition in unspecified quantity, the city arsenal, and the small flotilla on Lake Van. On the other hand, the meticulous statistics drawn up by the organizations revolving around the Military Committee make it possible to know exactly the strength of the Armenian forces. Including the refugees who arrived with the refugees of Hayots Dzor, there were in Van 1,053 Armenian combatants. This number was circumscribed by the quantity of available weapons in Aygestan [the Garden District]: 506 rifles with 74,824 cartridges and 549 revolvers, including 300 single-shot Mausers, with 39,089 bullets. The overwhelming majority of these fighters had no previous military experience, and some had never before held a weapon.[102]

In this analysis Anahide Ter Minassian appears to have drawn the statistics from Onnig Mukhitarian,[103] who took part in the rebellion but did not state that "there were in Van 1,053 Armenian Combatants." Mukhitarian in fact said that there were 1,053 in Garden City alone. Mukhitarian's figures were for those fighters alive in the Garden District on May 13, after twenty-two days of fighting, in which many must have died. The numbers of weapons and cartridges listed were for May 13, by which time there must have been some loss of weapons and a great expenditure of cartridges. These were ostensibly the numbers of men, weapons, and supplies remaining in the Garden District alone after the bulk of the fighting was over. Ter Minassian also does not include any of the Armenian fighters in the Old City in her calculation, although Armenian sources state that there were 3,500 Armenians in the Old City during the battle.[104] It should be noted that other Armenian and pro-Armenian sources gave different, even lower, numbers of combatants. For example, the historian of the Dashnak Party, Hratch Dasnabedian, wrote: "The Armenians had 800 fighters, only 400 of whom were armed with military weapons (Mausers)."[105] The missionary Grace Knapp wrote that the Armenians had "1,500 trained riflemen possessing only about 300 rifles."[106] Mukhitarian (the source of the 1,053 figure) wrote that there were only 25 to 30 Armenian fighters in the Old City![107]

It is impossible to credit the number of only 1,053 Armenian combatants in the Garden District, only half of whom had rifles. It is equally difficult to accept the highest estimate of 30,000 Armenian fighters in the city as a whole. In truth, the Ottomans had no way to make an accurate count of the number of rebels. There must have been considerably more than estimated by the Armenians, however: how else could such a small and avowedly inexperienced force have held against a force of regular Ottoman soldiers in the Garden District and defeated it in the Old City? Not even their greatest critics have ever stated that Turkish soldiers were so easily routed. On the contrary, military historians universally place Turkish soldiers among the best who have ever fought.[108] In 1896, in circumstances very similar to those described above by the Armenian analysts, Ottoman soldiers in Van had quite easily defeated Armenian rebels. And, if the Armenian analyses of the 1915 events were true, the Armenians in 1896 had been better armed.

As an explanation for the Armenian success, Anahide Ter Minassian states: "Only determination, moral fiber, organization, and effective de-fensive strategy made it possible for the Armenians to resist the combined governmental forces."[109] Without doubting any of these qualities, it seems that they would not have been enough not only "to resist" but to defeat a larger force of better-armed, equally determined professional soldiers with moral fiber of their own. A more rational assumption would be that the Armenian force must have significantly outnumbered the Ottoman force. Surely a factor of at least two or three to one in favor of the rebels, suffi-ciently armed, would be expected.

The question of the number of Armenian combatants turns on the def-inition of a combatant. There were more than thirty thousand Armenian men and boys in the Van Kaza, many or most of whom reportedly had come into the city. In addition, a large number of Armenian deserters from the Ottoman Army had come to Van, as well as thousands of refu-gees from Armenian villages.[110] This would leave many more than fif-teen thousand males who were potential combatants (i.e., not very young children or very old men).[111] All Armenian males, and quite a few of the females, were in some way engaged in the fight. Many did not have weap-ons, but they carried ammunition, built redoubts, made bullets, and so forth. When those with weapons died, their rifles or machine pistols were taken up by others.[112] The distinction between those recognized as "fight-ers" in the Armenian accounts and those who actually fought or assisted the fight may explain the difference between Ottoman and Armenian esti-mates. The true numbers of Armenian combatants will probably never be known, but an estimate of fifteen thousand or more is not unreasonable.

The question of how many Ottoman troops fought in and around Van is not difficult to settle. Although Ter Minassian does not give her source for her estimate of 10,000–12,000, the source may have been de Nogales, who gave exactly that number. It should be noted that de Nogales in-cluded in his figure "one battalion of Kurdish sharp-shooters and another of Ottoman volunteers," who were obviously not included in the very specific statement of the regular soldiers—2,300 under Governor Cevdet's command—as given in Ottoman records.[113]

Analysis reveals that the "10,000–12,000" figure of Nogales was an exaggeration, perhaps building up his importance as a commander. If the battalions of Kurdish sharpshooters and Ottoman volunteers were at regu-lar strength, which is doubtful, they would have added 2,000 men. Added to this should be the battalion sent by the Mobile Gendarme Division, at most 1,000 men. These Gendarme Division troops were not simply ac-tive at Van, however. They battled rebels near and well to the north of the city as well as at the city's borders. The 200 men sent to the Bargiri front from Van should be subtracted from the total in the city.[114] Two other battalions arrived on May 9, just before the fall of Van, although few of them seem to have gone into the city itself. At one point 1,200 Kurds did arrive.[115] They opened the roads and fought for a while in the city, but all the Kurds had deserted by May 3.[116] This means that the highest possible number of Ottoman troops in and near Van was 6,500 until May 3 and 6,200 (2,200 Kurds out, 2,000 regulars in) on May 9. These figures do not include battle deaths.

Armenian weaponry was also not what Ter Minassian avers. While there may have been some of what she calls "single-shot Mausers" in the Armenian arsenal, all Ottoman and foreign sources agree that the hand weapons most used by the rebels were C-96 Mauser Machine Pistols. As noted above, British consul Ian M. Smith described the weapon: "Mauser pistols are the favourite weapon [of the revolutionaries]; they are easily hidden and imported and can be used as a carbine, being sighted up to 1000 metres."[117] The Mauser pistols, which were decidedly not single-shot weapons, were especially effective in the sort of close combat seen in Van. De Nogales wrote: "The majority of the Armenians were well armed, above all with Mauser pistols, which, discharged at short range, are terrible weapons; the effect of them can be compared only with that of machine-guns, since instead of shooting one shot at a time they fire four, five, and sometimes six toward the same target."[118] Falsely identifying these weapons distorts even further the minimized estimates made by the Armenians who were present in Van.[119]

Numbers of weapons in the Old City should be added to the Armenian estimation of weaponry, even if those estimates are questionable. The Armenian memorialist of the fight in the Old City, Haig Gossoian, wrote: "The entire arsenal of the defensive forces consisted of 90 Mauser pistols with 13,500 rounds of ammunition, 101 rifles with 20,200 cartridges, 120 small hand revolvers with 10,800 bullets."[120]

Evaluations by the Ottomans, de Nogales, and foreign observers all indicate that the Armenians in Van were much better armed than their sources indicate. Reports of the British consuls in Van before the war corroborate the Ottoman evaluation of the firepower of the rebels. Two different British consuls wrote in 1913 and 1914 that the Dashnak Party had already armed the city's Armenians and was extensively arming the Armenians in villages.[121] Consul Smith reported in January 1914 that the Armenians were now felt to be better armed than the Kurds. The Dashnak leaders, he stated, had made a lucrative trade of selling weapons to the

Armenian villagers for nearly three times their value on the open market. Amazingly, the arms distribution was largely unopposed by the government. Indeed, according to Smith, the provincial government even helped arm the Armenians, distributing arms so that villagers could defend themselves: "Though the Local Government must be aware of what is going on, it has taken no steps to put a stop to the traffic in arms. It appears, on the contrary, to be the policy of the Vali to help the villagers to defend themselves, if necessary, by distributing old pattern army rifles in the proportion of three to six to each village, both Kurd and Armenian."[122] Nothing could be more convincing evidence that the government was taking seriously its duty to protect both Armenians and Kurds from their tribal attackers. One must wonder, however: how many of the weapons distributed by the government were eventually to be fired at Ottoman officials and soldiers?

Once again, as with manpower, it is impossible to reconcile the actions of the rebellion with the low estimates of Armenian firepower. If the Armenians' statements were true, their six hundred rifles and perhaps four hundred machine pistols defeated six thousand Ottoman fighters, all of them with rifles, supported by cannon.[123] Does this seem reasonable?

THE LAST CHANCE

The one chance for the Ottomans to save Van Province was to turn the Russian flank in western Iran. The area offered great possibilities. Unlike Eastern Anatolia, Iran had wide passes and open plains that eased any invasion from the north or south. The mainly Turkish people of Iranian Azerbaijan were no allies of the Russians. They might be counted on for support if the Ottomans arrived in force. More importantly, the Kurdish tribes in the region had shown in December 1914 that they were willing to battle the Russians, if it appeared the Ottomans were winning. Even Simko, long a rebel against the Ottomans,[124] had turned against his Russian benefactors when they appeared to be losing. Russian forces were primarily concentrated in northeastern Anatolia; their manpower in Iran was limited.

The Ottomans had just enough troops to invade Iran. The First Expeditionary Force (Kuvve-i Seferiye) had set out from Istanbul on December 24, 1914. Its leader, Halil Paşa, had been given the 36th Division and parts of the 3rd and 5th *bis* Divisions,[125] approximately ten thousand men. The force included seasoned regular troops who had not suffered at Sarıkamış and new formations of gendarmes and frontier guards (and also included

MAP 8.3. Eastern Anatolia, Azerbaijan, and Armenia.

on paper Kâzim's Van Mobile Gendarme Division). Halil had been ordered to Baghdad for attack through Iran to threaten Russian Central Asia, another of Enver's plans. Given the distances involved, this was not a reasonable objective. The dangers from the Russians after Sarıkamış, however, caused a change in plans. Arriving in Mosul on March 1, 1915, the Expeditionary Force was ordered northwest into Iran. The intent was to turn the Russian flank in western Iran and safeguard Eastern Anatolia against Russian attack from Iran. If circumstances were right, the Ottoman Force would advance north into Russia through the relatively flat, wide valleys in western Iran. Kurdish tribes and Turks in the region would join the Ottomans if they appeared to be winning. Unlike an attack into Central Asia, this was a reasonable plan with a genuine possibility of success. If successful, it would have taken much pressure from the Ottoman forces facing the Russians in the north. In the end it was not to succeed, largely due to the Armenian rebellion in the Ottoman East.

The Expeditionary Force attacked Iran, reaching and taking Dilman on April 29. The Russians rushed all their available manpower, including the 1st Armenian druzhina, to a defensive line north of Dilman.[126] The troop strengths were nearly equal. The Russians, however, had the advantage of defense. The battle was close, but the Ottomans lost. They withdrew on May 1–2.[127]

The Armenian rebellion had a deciding effect on the outcome of the Iranian campaign, and not only due to the presence of the druzhina on the Russian side. Halil Paşa should have been able to count on the Van Mobile Gendarme Division, with its three thousand men.[128] They would have been more than enough to turn the tide of battle. Instead, the Gendarme Division was in Van Province, battling the Armenian rebels.[129]

THE END IN VAN

Apprised of the situation in Van, Ottoman military commanders attempted to reinforce the city from their limited manpower resources. The force of tribal Kurds was sent to the city on April 23 and remained temporarily. On April 21 the Third Army Command sent a force to Van. It included the Erzurum and Erzincan Mobile Gendarmerie battalions and the mountain gun unit of the 28th infantry division.[130] They did not arrive in the vicinity of Van City until May 9,[131] too little and too late. They did, however, keep open the road from Van to the southwest, around Lake Van to Bitlis. This road, the only escape route from Van to the west, was to be essential to the survival of the Van garrison and Van's Muslim population.

The only nearby force that could send enough troops to put down the Van rebellion was the 1st Expeditionary Force. At the beginning of May 1915 the 1st Expeditionary Force was originally attacking at Dilman then defending the southeastern border. All of its men were needed at the front. The commander, Halil Paşa, had already allowed the entire Van Mobile Gendarmerie Division to be detached from his attack force to try to contain the rebels. Nevertheless, realizing the greater danger in the Van Rebellion but without authority to transfer a large body of troops on his own initiative, Halil sought permission from the High Command to send troops to save Van. The High Command did not yet realize the enormity of the danger. Halil was told that a sufficient force had been sent from Erzurum; there was no need for further reinforcements. By May 10 the High Command had realized its error and ordered the 1st Expeditionary Force commander to send troops to put down the rebellion. Again, it was far too late.[132] Van was lost a week after Halil received the orders to reinforce. The troops did not have time to arrive and were, in any case, too occupied by then with a Russian invasion near Başkale.

The Van Mobile Gendarme Division defended on the Başkale and Kotur fronts. It was impossible to send more forces to the city. The commander, Kâzim, did not want to leave the border completely undefended, expecting a large and effective assault by Armenian partisans, supported by Russian cavalry, across the border. In any case, his troops were too limited even for their defensive role. If the Russians were to advance from Salmas or through the Kotur Pass, a 700-man detachment without cannon defended against one Russian infantry regiment, 150 cavalry, and two cannon. The gendarme division commander had in reserve at Hoşap only one infantry battalion with one cannon.[133]

In Iranian territory Armenian partisans moved with the Russians against the Dir and Kotur units. In the Çölemerik (Hakkâri) Sancak, Nestorians were gathered together in revolt. Because it was not possible to dispatch a force to Çölemerik, the Hakkâri kaymakam was told that the Muslims would have to rely on the local gendarmes and tribes for protection. Reports arrived that Russian cavalry units had crossed the border in the Saray Region. The Muradiye Reserve Cavalry Brigade was attempting to force back the Armenian partisans and Russians who were trying to cross mountain passes north of Bargiri.

Apprised by Armenian spies of the situation in Van, the Russians sent a strong detachment of both Russian soldiers and Armenian druzhiny (the First Armenian Legion) to the Kotur Valley. The Ottoman Command expected that the Russians would send a force of Armenian partisans to raid the Ottoman interior to weaken the defense. The Russians had also reinforced their troops to the west of Lake Urmia and were advancing south of Dilman in three columns. Opposing them, the Turks had only the seven hundred men at Kotur and one thousand additional troops at Dir. Russian and Armenian units drove to the Kotur Valley, captured Kotur, and began to move west.[134]

Map 8.4. Russian Invasion.

The military situation in Van was deteriorating as the Armenians attacked the Citadel with renewed vigor. The Citadel was full of homeless Muslims who had taken refuge there. It was expected that all would be killed when the Citadel fell. Cevdet, the Van governor, evaluated the situation and requested permission from the Interior Ministry to evacuate: "The rebels have cut the roads and attacked and burned neighboring villages. Stopping them is impossible. Many homeless women and children remain [here]. It is not possible to send them to take shelter in the tribes' villages. Is it acceptable to send them to the western provinces?"[135]

On May 8 the Armenians began a general attack on Van and surrounding villages. Muslims started to flee the Western Garden District. Flames could be seen from the Citadel as what remained of the Muslim Quarter of the city and neighboring Muslim villages were set on fire. Cevdet gave the command to begin the transfer of Muslim women and children and some officials. Fourteen boats were used to transport them on Lake Van to Tatvan, across the lake, then on to Bitlis.[136] Seven of the boats were driven by bad weather to the Erciş region, where three were sunk by Armenians, with no survivors. Armenian volleys from the shore killed others. Of the twelve hundred who set out, only seven hundred survived to reach Bitlis.[137]

The Russians marched on Van from the north. The Russian commanding general, Nikolay Yudenich, ordered the Cossack brigade under General Trukhin and the four Armenian druzhiny at Bayazıt to advance through the Teperiz Pass, attack the Ottoman position at Bargiri, and move to the relief of the Armenians in Van. Danger was so imminent that Van's Governor Cevdet sent one cannon and two hundred men to the Muradiye line from Van.[138] On May 24 the Russians reached Bargiri and overcame the Turkish defenders.[139] No Turkish force stood between them and Van. The Russians had also begun to march from Kotur to Van. Armenians marched with them into Van Province.[140] Ottoman intelligence received word that the partisan leader Andranik, along with his twelve hundred men, had left Salmas and joined the Azerbaijan Russian commander Chernoroyal's division, marching in the direction of Başkale.[141] General Foma Nazarbekov's Russians advanced from Dilman, took Başkale (May 7), and slowly moved to the northwest, toward Van. Van Province was lost.

Ottoman forces were forced to withdraw to join the main army in Bitlis Province, where they could make a concerted stand against the Russians. The remains of Halil's Expeditionary Force and the Van Mobile Gendarme Division, now one-third of its original strength, retreated south of Lake Van, toward Bitlis.[142]

Cevdet sent 450 of his limited force north, to keep roads open for retreating troops, and others southwest to guarantee escape to Bitlis. On May 12 he ordered the final evacuation of Van's Muslims. Some of the Muslim population had already moved west, but many had been killed on the roads by partisan bands. Of those who had remained in Van, fearing the dangers on the roads, most now fled. Some were forced to remain, because they could not travel or because they were surrounded by Armenians. On May 16–17 the last Ottoman soldiers and civilians left the Citadel. Cevdet and his troops passed Gevaş on May 21. The troops from Van were forced to move slowly on the road to Bitlis as they attempted to protect Muslim refugees from Armenian partisans on the roads.[143]

The victorious Armenians took control of the city and burned down the remaining Muslim neighborhoods and remaining governmental or

Islamic buildings. A few days later, on May 20, Russian soldiers entered Van. Before the Russians arrived, the Armenians had set up their administration in the city, with Aram Manukian at its head (see chapter 9). The rebels welcomed General Nikolayev, presenting him with the key to the city. Two days later Nikolayev ceremoniously declared the formation of the "Van Province Armenian Government." Aram Manukian was named governor. The tsar telegraphed his congratulations.

COORDINATION WITH THE RUSSIANS

In the absence of documents, the extent to which the Armenian rebels were being directed from Russia is difficult to ascertain. Judging by both Ottoman and Armenian sources, the initial Dashnak decision to oppose the Ottoman government was primarily directed by the Russian Dashnaks. Their loyalty to the Russian cause was too often proclaimed to be questioned.

The Russians backed the Armenian revolt financially. At the Armenian Congress in Tiflis in February 1915, the Dashnak delegate announced: "As is well known, the Russian Government contributed 242,900 roubles at the beginning of the War for the provision of arms and training to the Turkish Armenians as well as for organizing revolts in Turkish Armenia. It is expected that our volunteer bands will penetrate the Turkish lines, joining up with the insurrectionists and, if possible, by creating panic in the rear of the Turkish army, help the advance of the Russian troops and facilitate their invasion of Turkish Armenia."[144] The Russian contribution to the Dashnaks was a considerable sum, the equivalent of more than $13 million in today's currency.[145]

The Russians intended to do all they could to disrupt the Ottoman war effort. In addition to fully arming and supplying rebel Armenians, the Russians also armed and assisted the organization of separatist Kurdish bands that were expected to attack from Iran against Ottoman forces in Van Province. Instructions to this effect were given to the Russian consul in Savuçbulak by the Russian Ministry of Foreign Affairs. The instructions called for the organization of small bands in the region of Khoy and Dilman in Iran. Two thousand Berdan rifles, monetary assistance, and gifts were distributed to encourage Kurdish notables to rebel.[146] It was planned that these Kurdish bands would weaken and distract the Ottomans before the Russian general attack and would oppose Ottoman forces in the Urmia region of Iran. When war came, the Kurdish tribes in Iran proved no more faithful to the Russians than they had been to the Ottomans or Persians. They did, however, cause considerable havoc in the Urmia region with their raids.[147]

In the absence of Russian planning and command documents it is not possible to ascertain exactly how closely the Armenian rebels followed Russian plans. It is impossible to believe, however, that Armenian actions were not intended to speed Russian conquest.

The best evidence for coordination between the rebels and the Russians is the actions of the rebels: the major outbreak of rebellion at the beginning of the war was to the southeast of Van, in the Çatak and Hoşap regions. A glance at map 8.3 will show the importance of the two areas. They lie on the only two roads leading to the Urmia region of Iran. Moreover, the telegraph line to the southeast ran through Hoşap. Both the roads and the telegraph line were repeatedly cut. Lines were also cut farther south, at Başkale. Ottoman units in southern Van Province often could only communicate with Third Army headquarters in Erzurum by sending messages through Mosul to Syria and from there to Istanbul and finally to Erzurum. Rebel actions in the region south of Van City were so fierce that Ottoman troops sent to battle rebels in Çatak were held up for weeks.

It was surely no coincidence that another major outbreak took place in the Gevaş area, another communications hub. Van's communications with the West passed through the telegraph line in Gevaş. The Gevaş road was the main supply route into Van and the only escape route from the city. Armenian action in Gevaş forced the Ottomans to devote considerable forces, including soldiers from Van City, to keep the Gevaş road open.

The third major center of revolt was in the Erçek-Saray-Kotur region. The telegraph from Van to the Iranian front passed through Erçek to Saray; like the others, it was cut. Officers facing the Russians at Kotur were forced to withdraw troops from the front to battle the rebels. In at least one major battle, near Saray, the rebels won.

While the subject here is Van Province, it is worth noting that the pattern of rebel actions that aided the Russian cause extended to other areas of Anatolia. In Şebinkarahisar and Sivas (regions where Armenian population was much smaller than in Van or Bitlis) Armenian rebellion broke out at the main road, railroad, and telegraph hubs leading east. Once again, Armenian attacks on the main communications lines leading from the Ottoman heartland to the Russian front cannot have been without strategic purpose.

None of this is conclusive evidence that the Armenian rebels were under Russian direction. It is, however, conclusive evidence that the rebels did significantly aid the Russian cause.

THE RESULTS OF THE ARMENIAN REVOLT

The Armenian revolt in Van Province was a pivotal component of the disaster of war in the Ottoman East. The results of the rebellion cannot easily be separated from the effects of World War I as a whole. In particular, the Ottoman losses at Sarıkamış, the Armenian revolt, and the Russian invasion of 1915 were tied together.

Had Enver Paşa's character been different—had he been willing to put the Ottoman troops in the northeast into defensive positions—it is most unlikely that the Russians would have been able to attack into Ottoman Anatolia. As the Russians themselves accepted at the beginning of the war,[148] this would have been a most difficult proposition. Russian troops were continually being taken from the Caucasus to fight in Europe, leaving too few to mount a major offensive into Ottoman Anatolia. Had the Ottoman forces dug into defensive positions, their force would have been multiplied by the natural benefits of defense in mountainous terrain. In short, the position on the northeast frontier would have been static. The Ottomans could have afforded to remove thousands of troops for use elsewhere. The Sarıkamış debacle gave the Russians their chance to invade.

After Sarıkamış the Ottomans were sorely tried by their losses. It was not an impossible situation, however. The Ottomans were able to reconstitute the Third Army, although the reservists and drafts from other army groups were not the equal of the men lost at Sarıkamış. By November 1914 the Ottomans had twelve divisions in Eastern Anatolia. Although the Russians were better equipped and better trained, with more artillery, in numbers the Ottoman force was not greatly inferior (approximately 70,000 regulars and a large number of irregular Ottoman troops against 165,000 regular Russian troops).[149] Events were to prove that they were able to defeat the Russian invaders, at least temporarily, in 1915.[150] The losses incurred in the defense and the general devastation of the Ottoman East, however, were to make the Ottomans fairly easy prey for the more massive Russian invasion of 1916. Two factors should have lessened the losses and allowed the Ottomans to throw the Russians back: interior lines of communication and an attack through Iran. Those factors were largely negated by the Armenian rebellion.

The Ottomans had one great advantage in the spring of 1915: interior lines of communication and transportation. The Russians had superior military communication in their own territory; but once they invaded the Ottoman Empire and western Iran they shared poor roads with the Turks. The Turks knew the roads. They should have been able to use them to bring up reinforcements quickly from areas that were not under attack; that was the theoretical benefit of a centralized defensive position. Most importantly, the Ottomans should have been able to make effective use of the Anatolian telegraph system to coordinate military maneuvers. The keys were the roads and the telegraph lines, as both the Ottomans and the Russians knew well. It would not have taken military genius to understand that neutralizing those two Ottoman advantages would have speeded the Russian assault. They were the focus of Armenian attack.

The military effect of the interdiction of supply and communication was obviously significant, although impossible to quantify. Even if the only revolutionary activities had been to cut lines of communication and supply and hinder the movement of troops, this would have had a major effect on the fighting of the war. Armies that do not receive their orders do not occupy their assigned positions or arrive at battles on time. Commanders denied communications and intelligence cannot evaluate their situations and act accordingly. Throughout Van, Bitlis, and Erzurum Provinces Armenian partisans focused their disruptive attacks on roads and telegraph lines. Ottoman reports (only a small selection of which have been mentioned) stressed the difficulty, often the impossibility, of military communication, because the lines had been cut by the Armenians. Defending the telegraph lines was a Herculean task. Hundreds of miles of line could be cut in thousands of undefended places by a mobile enemy, and the Armenian bands had the advantage of local knowledge. Again and again, troops were sent to repair cut lines, only to have them cut elsewhere. Coordination of troops was a nightmare in such a situation. It is no accident that the Ottomans were only able to stand against the Russians at Malazgirt,[151] once all their forces in the East had retreated until they were in actual physical contact with each other, obviating the need for long-range communication.

The assistance provided to the Russians by Armenian spies and scouts cannot be overstated. As the Russians invaded, the Ottomans should have had all the advantages of fighting on their own home ground. They should have been the only ones who knew the best mountain passes and remote paths and the only ones who could depend on the support of the local population. But the Russians were not a typical invader transversing the home territory of their enemy, hampered by a lack of local knowledge and the hostility of the local population. They were an invader that could count on the support of a sizable portion of the populace: the Armenians. Armenian intelligence shed light on battle plans. Armenian scouts led the way into what was not alien territory to them. The Russians decided to invade Van on the basis of intelligence from Armenians.[152] As the Armenian legions advanced toward the Russian conquest of Van, they were led by natives of the province.[153]

The most devastating effect of the Armenian rebellion can best be illustrated by simple statistics: the Ottomans were forced to devote six thousand men to the rebellion in Van City and an unknown number to fight the revolt in other parts of Van Province. The positive effect that a fraction of those men would have had on Halil's campaign in Iraq has already been described. They could also have been very useful in the battle to the north. The Russians attacked the Teperiz Pass and Bargiri with 5,500 men—4,000 Armenians and 1,500 Cossacks. Against them stood one Ottoman cavalry brigade of perhaps 1,700 men.[154] The defensive advantage was not enough to hold the line. The cavalry brigade was defeated, and largely annihilated, by the Russian and Armenian troops. The thousands of men at Van would surely have been enough to hold back the invaders. Given the defensive advantage in the mountains, even half the Van force would have been sufficient. The cannon used at Van would likewise have been invaluable at Bargiri and Teperiz.[155]

The effect of the Armenians on the Kurdish irregulars was also important. Some 1,800 Kurds were enrolled in the Ottoman "tribal light cavalry" at the beginning of the war, but this was only a part of the Kurdish fighters who might have aided the Ottomans.[156] Kurdish tribesmen, even including old enemies of the government such as Simko, proved willing to join against the Russians if it appeared the Russians were not winning. When the Russians appeared likely to invade, however, the Kurdish tribesmen and the Tribal Light Cavalry simply vanished. The body of Kurdish irregulars and the Kurds at Van both disappeared when the defeat seemed likely. Had the Ottoman troops at Van been available to turn the tide at Dilman and Bargiri, the Kurds would have retained their "loyalty." They were surely not the most disciplined soldiers, but they would have provided a cavalry presence, which was particularly lacking in the Ottoman regular army.

It is doubtful if Van Province would have taken such a prominent place in World War I had the Armenians not rebelled. The initial Russian plan, as stated above, was essentially defensive, but it was to be directed westward if the opportunity arose, not south. The Ottomans also had not planned to meet the Russians in Van Province. They had expected the defining battle to take place on the Erzurum Plain, which had been the site of the main battles in earlier wars. In fact, it was precisely because of the Armenian occupation of Van City that the Russians invaded the province.[157] It is not an exaggeration to say that bloody civil war, Ottoman defeat, and awful mortality were directly, but not exclusively, caused by the Armenian rebellion in the Province of Van.

NOTES

1. On the military situation before and during the first months of the war, see W. E. D. Allen and Paul Muratoff, *Caucasian Battlefields* (Cambridge: Cambridge University Press, 1953), pp. 231–92; Commandant M. Larcher, *La Guerre Turque dans la Guerre Mondiale* (Paris: E. Chiron, 1926), pp. 55–77, 81–83, 89, 106–7, 365–95; *Birinci Dünya Harbinde Türk Harbi, Kafkas Cephesi, 3üncü Ordu Harekâtı* (hereafter *Türk Harbi*, by far the best source on the Ottoman war), vol. 1 (Ankara: Genelkurmay Basımevi, 1993), pp. 97–598.

2. E. V. Maslovski, *Umumi Harpte Kafkas Cephesi, Eserinin Tenkidi* (Ankara: Genelkurmay Matbaası, 1931), p. 31 (seen in the Turkish translation; original: *Mirovaya voyna na kavkazskom fronte, 1914–1917* [Paris: Vozrozhdenie/La Renaissance, 1933]); *Türk Harbi*, pp. 63 and 73; Allen and Muratoff, *Caucasian Battlefields*, pp. 240–44. Although called a division, the Van Mobile Gendarme Division was considerably smaller than a regular division. It contained three battalions, at full strength approximately three thousand men (*Türk Harbi*, p. 47). British Intelligence erroneously listed it as having only two battalions (Great Britain, Imperial War Museum, *Handbook of the Turkish Army: Eighth Provisional Edition, February, 1916* [Nashville and Skokie: Imperial War Museum, 1996], pp. 28 and 202).

3. ATASE Arşivi, I.D.H.K. Klasör (hereafter K: file): 2809, Dosya (hereafter D: dossier): 17, Fihrist (hereafter F: catalog): 5-4/ T.D.H.; *Türk Harbi*, p. 82.

4. It is important to differentiate between ordinary gendarmes and the Gendarme Division. Gendarmes not taken by the division remained in Van City and the rest of the province. Those designated simply as gendarmes below were not part of the Van Mobile Gendarme Division.

5. U.S. National Archives, 867.00/618, pp. 5–6. The Americans had a good idea of the severity of the outbreak, called "very serious," because they treated a large number of the victims in the Van hospital (ABC 16.9.8, Eastern Turkey Mission, Woman's Board, vol. 1, Eastern Turkey, 1909–1914, Documents and Reports, Letters, A–Z, "Report of Van Station ETM ABCFM, 1913–1914").

6. "In the autumn, after the troops began to be massed in large numbers near Russian frontier, typhus fever broke out in great violence at Erzurum and Harpoot, and in greater or less degree at Mardin, Van and Bitlis. In December there were some 400 deaths a day among the soldiers and civilians in Erzurum…. At Harput the deaths were as many as 70 a day for a time" (*The One Hundred and Fifth Annual Report of the ABCFM Together with the Minutes of the Meeting Held at New Haven, Connecticut, Oct. 26, 1915* [Boston: American Board, 1916], pp. 80–81).

7. These units included forces brought from Istanbul and the 37th Division from Iraq. The loss of that division facilitated the British invasion of Basra. Hasan İzzet, commanding the Third Army, resigned rather than carry out Enver's plan.

8. *Türk Harbi*, pp. 347–562; Larcher, *La Guerre Turque dans la Guerre Mondiale*, pp. 382–87; Allen and Muratoff, *Caucasian Battlefields*, pp. 249–85. Allen and Muratoff comment on "the magnificent *élan* of the Turkish askers [soldiers] who followed with such admirable courage their foolish and incompetent leader" (p. 284).

9. ATASE Arşivi, I. Dünya Harbi Kolleksiyonu, K- 2818, D-59, F-2-54.

10. Allen and Muratoff, *Caucasian Battlefields*, pp. 261, 269, 296–300.

11. *Türk Harbi*, pp. 542, 567. See also the less informative description in Allen and Muratoff, *Caucasian Battlefields*, pp. 288–89.

12. Louise Nalbandian, The Armenian Revolutionary Movement (Berkeley: University of California Press, 1963), p. 111.

13. FO 195/2283, Dickson to O'Conor, Van, March 15, 1908.

14. Esat Uras, *The Armenians in History and the Armenian Question* (Istanbul: Documentary Publications, 1988), pp. 841–42, asserted that the only source for the offer appeared in a Dashnak book printed in Istanbul in 1920 during the period of Allied occupation and thus was unreliable propaganda. See also Kamuran Gürün, *The Armenian File* (London: Rustem and Weidenfeld and Nicolson, 1985), p. 188. Hratch Dasnabedian, *History of the Armenian Revolution Federation, Dashnaktsutiun,* trans. Bryan Fleming and Vaha Habeshian (hereafter *History of the ARF*) (Milan: GEMME Edizione, 1989), pp. 107–8, stated that the Ottoman offer was actually made to a "Commission of Nine," not to the entire congress, and that the commission refused. The commission had stayed on in Erzurum to "deal with other matters that had to be addressed" after the congress had disbanded. No actual minutes of the meetings, if they occurred, have survived.

15. Hovhannes Katchaznouni, *The Armenian Revolutionary Federation (Dashnagtzoutiun) Has Nothing to Do Anymore: The Manifesto of Hovhannes Katchaznouni, First Prime Minister of the Independent Armenian Republic,* trans. Matthew A. Callendar, ed. John Roy Carlson (Arthur A. Derounian) (New York: Armenian Information Service, 1955), p. 2. See also Gürün, *The Armenian File,* pp. 187–89; and K. S. Papazian, *Patriotism Perverted* (Boston: Baikar Press, 1934), pp. 37–38.

16. ATASE Arşivi, Cabinet No. 113, Drawer No. 4, File No. 528, Section No. 2061; Documents II, 1903. A number of these documents have been printed in *Documents on Ottoman Armenians,* vols. 1, 2, and 3 (hereafter cited as Documents 1, 2, or 3) (Ankara: Prime Ministry Directorate General of Press and Information, 1982, 1983, 1986).

17. FO 371/2449, Molyneux-Seel to Lowther, Van, May 8, 1913.

18. FO 371/2130 Smith to Mallet, Van, January 10, 1914.

19. FO 371/1783 Molyneux-Seel to Lowther, Van, April 4, 1913.

20. Ottoman Empire, *Aspirations et agissements révolutionnaires des Comités Arméniens avant et après la proclamation de la Constitution Ottomane* (Istanbul: n.p., 1917), pp. 50–53. See appendix 4, an excerpt from the "Instructions."

21. As used here, "guerrilla" means all irregular force individuals and bands. "Partisan" means large-scale bands (sometimes fifty to a hundred, often mounted). The word used in sources for the partisan bands is usually *chette* (*çete*).

22. FO 195/2456, Smith to Mallet, Van, January 10, 1914.

23. For examples of Ottoman reports on Russian spying, see Zekeriya Türkmen, "Birinci Dünya Savaşı Öncesinde İttihat ve Terakki Hükümetinin Doğu Anadolu Islahat Projesi ve Uygulamaları," in *Yedinci Askerî Tarih Semineri Bildirileri,* vol. 2 (Ankara:

Genelkurmay Basımevi, 2001), pp. 245–46; BOA, DH SYS, D 23/17 (22 Şubat 1913), D 23/10 (14 Mayıs 1913), D 23/10 (14 Mayıs 1913), D 23/13 (15 Haziran 1913), D 27/17, D 23/17 (18 Ekim 1913).

24. ATASE Arşivi, I. Dünya Harbi Kolleksiyonu, K-2818, D-59, F-2-10. Documents 1:4.

25. M. Muhtar, No. 414, September 2, 1330 (ATASE Arşivi, I. Dünya Harbi Kolleksiyonu, K-28111, D-26, F-24-1. Documents 1:5).

26. "As soon as the Armenian volunteer units commanded by Andranik approach Van, the Dashnak fighters in the area will take to the mountains and unfurl the flag of revolt. The plans for the rebellion will be implemented in April 1915. The Catholicos has informed us that 10,000 armed fighters are ready to join the action" (Dashnak decision as reported by A. Khatisian, *Hayastani Hanrapetut'ean tsagumn u zargats'ume [The Origins and Development of the Armenian Republic]*, p. 48, as quoted by Uras, *The Armenians in History and the Armenian Question,* p. 863).

27. Third Army Command to All Units, ATASE Arşivi, I. Dünya Harbi Kolleksiyonu, K-2918, D-797, F-6.

28. ATASE Arşivi, I. Dünya Harbi Kolleksiyonu, K-2918, D-797, F-6.

29. See Ufuk Gülsoy, *Gayri Müslimlerin Askerlik Macerası* (Istanbul: Simurg Yayınları, 2002).

30. Montgomery Papers, Library of Congress, c13, Letter, July 26, 1923, pp. 4–5: Before 1890 there was only one real antagonistic difference between the Christian races and the Moslems, and that was the inequality between the two. The Moslems looked down upon the Christian races as inferior races. The Christian races of course resented this but this resentment was not a strong feeling. In those days (except especially the eastern vilâyets) the Christian races lived their own lives peacefully, had as many churches and schools as they liked and by paying about $2.50 a year did not have to go to the wars. Of course when wars were on the Christian races were taxed extra but not a great extent.... There were petty annoyances but.... There was some feeling on the part of the Turks against the Christian races because the latter were able to stay at home during wars and become rich and prosperous while the Turk had to leave his family and go to war, and when returned found his property gone to rack and ruin and his family in poverty.

31. Sinan Kuneralp, "İkinci Meşrutiyet Döneminde Gayrimüslimlerin Askerlik Meselesi," *Toplumsal Tarih* (Istanbul) (December 1999): 12.

32. Speech of July 3, 1909, *Meclis-i Mebusan Ceridesi*, Devre 1, Sene 2, Oturum 105, 20 Haziran 1325/3 Temmuz 1909; Kuneralp, "İkinci Meşrutiyet Döneminde Gayrimüslimlerin Askerlik Meselesi," p. 13.

33. Kuneralp, "İkinci Meşrutiyet Döneminde Gayrimüslimlerin Askerlik Meselesi," p. 15.

34. On minority soldiers, see Esat Arslan, "Çanakkale'de Günceler Işığında Cephenin İki Tarafı," *Silahlı Kuvvetler Dergisi* (April 1997); Hüseyin Işık, *Şehitlerimiz ve Gazilerimiz* (Ankara: Jandarma Matbaası, 1995), pp. 177–78.

35. Armenian recruits were already escaping to Russia as early as March 1913—obviously to escape conscription. British consul J. H. Monahan, however, said that Armenian conscripts were well treated (FO 195/2449, Monahan to Lowther, Erzurum, March 1, 1913). Even the American missionaries stated that the Armenians were not enrolling (ABC 16.10.1 Constantinople Archives, vol. 7, Letters to W. W. Peet, 1913–1914). See A. Poharyan, "The Legendary Clash in Van," in *Van-Vaspurakani herosamarte 75*, ed. H. M. Poghosyan

and H. D. Papazyan (Erevan: Hayastan, 1990) (translated for this study by Birsen Karaca), pp. 19–21. In Erzurum Province and northern Van Province whole families followed the deserters to Russia (Général G. Korganoff, *La participation des Arméniens à la Guerre Mondiale sur le Front du Caucase (1914–1918)* [Paris: Massis, 1927], p. 17; Korganoff, an Armenian, was an officer in the Russian army and later a general in the Armenian army). Armenian sources state that the Armenians were refusing to serve out of fear of what would happen to them.

36. The Russian consul in Van had already foretold in 1913 that Armenian soldiers would join Armenian rebels and that Russia would intervene (G. C. Raynolds, February 22, 1913, ABC 16.10.1, Constantinople Archives, vol. 7, Letters to W. W. Peet, 1913–1914).

37. Justin McCarthy, *Death and Exile: The Ethnic Cleansing of Ottoman Muslims* (Princeton: Darwin, 1995), p. 186, lists intelligence sources on these movements.

38. Mustafa Bey, Governor of Bitlis, September 18, 1914, *Askeri Tarih Belgeleri Dergisi*, Sayı: 83, Belge No: 1893. Documents 2:1893; Report from the Second Cavalry Division Command to the Third Army Command. ATASE Arşivi, I. Dünya Harbi Kolleksiyonu, K-2818, D-59, F-2-37; Trabzon Governor Cemal Azmi to the High Command, October 5, 1914. ATASE Arşivi, I. Dünya Harbi Kolleksiyonu, K-2818, D-59, F-2-23, 2-24, Documents 1:6.

39. Allen and Muratoff, *Caucasian Battlefields,* pp. 242, 291, 299; Akdes Nimet Kurat, *Türkiye ve Rusya* (Ankara: Ankara Üniversitesi, 1970), p. 285; French National Archives, SHDT, Dossier: 7 N, 1649; Korganoff, *La participation des Arméniens à la Guerre Mondiale,* pp. 9–10.

40. ATASE Arşivi, K 2818, D 59, F 2-60.

41. July 28, 1330 (ATASE Arşivi, I. Dünya Harbi Kolleksiyonu, K-2911, D-26, F-15-1), Documents 1:7.

42. ATASE Arşivi, I. Dünya Harbi Kolleksiyonu, K-2287, D-32/12, F-6-2, 6-3.

43. ATASE Arşivi, I. Dünya Harbi Kolleksiyonu, K-2287, D-12, F-9, Documents 3:1999.

44. July 28, 330, ATASE Arşivi, I. Dünya Harbi Kolleksiyonu, K-2911, D-26, F-15-1, Documents 1:7.

45. On the war in Van Province, see *Türk Harbi,* pp. 575–98, 676–78; Allen and Muratoff, *Caucasian Battlefields,* pp. 231–39; Anahide Ter Minassian, "Van, 1915," in *Armenian Van/Vaspurakan,* ed. Richard G. Hovannisian (Costa Mesa, Calif.: Mazda Publishers, 2000), pp. 209–44; Ergünöz Akçora, *Van ve Çevresinde Ermeni İsyanları (1896–1916)* (Istanbul: Türk Dünyası Araştırmaları Vakfı, 1994), pp. 123–218; Larcher, *La Guerre Turque dans la Guerre Mondiale,* pp. 369–82; Onnig Mukhitarian, *An Account of the Glorious Struggle of Van-Vasbouragan,* trans. Samuels S. Tarpinian (Detroit: General Society of Vasbouragan, 1967); Haig Gossoian, *The Epic Story of the Self Defense of Armenians in the Historic City of Van,* trans. Samuels S. Tarpinian (Detroit: General Society of Vasbouragan, Raven Publishers—AKA, 1967). A-Do, *Mets depkere Vaspurakan 1914 tvakannerin* (Erevan: Loys, 1917), has not been seen for this study, but it is used extensively for the Ter Minassian article. The Gossoian volume is the more reliable of the two accounts by Armenians who were there during the rebellion. Despite some questionable statistics and statements, it is generally a straightforward description of fighting. Mukhitarian, in contrast, wrote a romantic treatise in which all Armenians were noble and all Muslims craven. His accounts are full of descriptions in which forty Armenian peasants defeat two hundred Armenian soldiers in a day-long battle in which only one Armenian dies or twenty Armenians hold

off three hundred Turkish cavalry. Mukitarian's statements on the numbers of Armenian dead and refugees add up to many more Armenians than existed in the regions described. It is perhaps needless to say that the Armenians in these accounts never rebelled and only killed in self-defense.

46. Cevdet to the Ministry of the Interior, December 1, 1914, ATASE Arşivi, I. Dünya Harbi Kolleksiyonu, K-4, D-23-A, F-4, Documents 3:1996.

47. In the first year of war Armenian chettes concentrated in the Salmas region of Iran. Andranik organized a thousand-man force of irregulars there that joined the Russian forces (Haluk Selvi, "Hangi Antranik?" *2023 Dergisi* 12 [April 2002]: 31). Born in 1865 in Şebinkarahisar, Andranik spent his life in the Armenian revolutionary cause. After killing a Turk who was fighting with Andranik's father in 1890, he fled to Istanbul. There he joined the Hunchak Committee and (under committee instructions) killed a police officer. He then fled to Batum. Dissatisfied with the lack of revolutionary fervor and activity in Batum, Andranik went to Eastern Anatolia, intending to foment revolution in Van, Bitlis, and Muş. He joined in both the first (1895) and second (1904) Sasun Rebellions.

48. ATASE Arşivi, I. Dünya Harbi Kolleksiyonu, K-520, D-2024, F-5.

49. Korganoff, *La participation des Arméniens à la Guerre Mondiale,* pp. 13–17.

50. ATASE Arşivi, I. Dünya Harbi Kolleksiyonu, K-2818, Dosya: 59, F-2-55, Documents 1:10.

51. ATASE Arşivi, I. Dünya Harbi Kolleksiyonu, K-520, D-2024, F-5.

52. ATASE Arşivi, I. Dünya Harbi Kolleksiyonu, K-4, D23-A, F-5, Documents 1:11.

53. ATASE Arşivi, I. Dünya Harbi Kolleksiyonu, K-528, D-2061, F-1-8.

54. Ottoman Empire, *Aspiration et agissements,* p. 268; Mehmed Hocaoğlu, *Arşiv Vesikalarıyla Tarihte Ermeni Mezâlimi ve Ermeniler* (Ankara: Anda, 1976), pp. 622–23.

55. Ottoman Empire, *Aspiration et agissements,* p. 268; Hocaoğlu, *Arşiv Vesikalarıyla Tarihte Ermeni Mezâlimi ve Ermeniler,* pp. 623–26.

56. Gunnar Wiessner in his *Hayoths Dzor—Xavasor* (Wiesbaden: Reichert, 1997), pp. 55–60, gives details, entirely drawn from Armenian sources, on Kurdish and army attacks on Armenians and on Armenian migration. He makes no mention of an Armenian revolt or attacks on Muslims that might have precipitated attacks, leaving the impression that he believes one day the Turks and Kurds simply decided to attack the Armenians. This, of course, reflects his sources. Wiessner bemoans the lack of available foreign reports but makes no mention of the existence of Ottoman reports.

57. The works on these rebellions are too extensive to list here. For the general history and citations, see McCarthy, *Death and Exile,* pp. 179–87; Gürün, *The Armenian File,* pp. 186–203; Ottoman Empire, *Aspirations et agissements,* pp. 221–334.

58. ATASE Arşivi, I. Dünya Harbi Kolleksiyonu, K-2287, D-12, F-6, 6-1.

59. ATASE Arşivi, I. Dünya Harbi Kolleksiyonu, K-2287, D32/12, F-6-2, 6-3.

60. ATASE Arşivi, I. Dünya Harbi Kolleksiyonu, K-2820, D-69, F-2-17, 41; ATASE Arşivi, I. Dünya Harbi Kolleksiyonu, K- 113, D-3, F-520, 11/1-3, Documents 1:15.

61. Gürün, *The Armenian File,* p. 204.

62. See chapter 9.

63. *Aspiration et agissements,* pp. 268–69. See also the quotations from the German Military archives in Celalettin Yavuz, "Ermenilerin Arkasında Hep Birileri mi Olacak?" *KÖK Araştırmalar* 3, no. 1 (Spring 2001): 20–21.

64. ATASE Arşivi, I. Dünya Harbi Kolleksiyonu, K-2818, D-59, F-1-15, Documents 1:17.

65. ATASE Arşivi, I. Dünya Harbi Kolleksiyonu, K-2818, D-59, F-17.

66. ATASE Arşivi, I. Dünya Harbi Kolleksiyonu, K-2950, D-13, F-1-44. There were also antique cannon on the walls of the citadel.

67. ATASE Arşivi, I. Dünya Harbi Kolleksiyonu, K-2818, D-59, F-1-32, 1-33.

68. Larcher, *La Guerre Turque dans la Guerre Mondiale,* p. 394; Allen and Muratoff, *Caucasian Battlefields,* pp. 303–5.

69. See the discussion above in this section.

70. ATASE Arşivi, I. Dünya Harbi Kolleksiyonu, K-2818, D-59, F-1-16.

71. ATASE Arşivi, I. Dünya Harbi Kolleksiyonu, K-2820, D-A-69, F-3-6, Documents 1:23; *Ermeni Komitelerinin Amal ve Harekât-ı İhtilâliyesi* (Istanbul: Matbaa-i Amire, 1332), p. 202.

72. Gossoian, *The Epic Story,* p. 13. Poharyan states that the Armenians in the Garden District had been trained and began final preparations to fight in March, "forecasting the calamities in the future" ("The Legendary Clash in Van," pp. 21–24). The Armenian accounts of the Van rebellion are often valuable for their information on Armenian positions and command decisions, even though they must be seen as political documents that often contain errors and omissions. For example, Haig Gossoian's account asserts that Enver Paşa's invasion on the Caucasian Front was successful! Gossoian also states that the Armenian troubles in Çatak began in April 1915, when they actually began in February, with numerous guerrilla actions before that. Nevertheless, Gossoian is useful when he describes Armenian actions in the Old City of Van.

73. Ter Minassian, "Van, 1915," pp. 217–18. It is likely that the murders of the Dashnak leaders were part of a central government policy to attack the leaders of the rebellion, because others, including Armenian leaders in Istanbul, were also executed in April. It can be argued that these were wartime killings of enemies, but it surely would have been possible to arrest and try the leaders. Evidence for court cases was not lacking. For a list of the Dashnak leaders lost, see *History of the ARF,* p. 110.

74. ATASE Arşivi, I. Dünya Harbi Kolleksiyonu, K-525, D-2050, F-4. For the Armenian statement of their successful action in the Çatak region, see Mukhitarian, *An Account,* p. 73.

75. ATASE Arşivi, I. Dünya Harbi Kolleksiyonu, K-2947, D-628, F-3-4, Documents 1:22. See the comments of Baron Max von Oppenheim on the Armenian attacks (AA MA Nr. 7253, August 29, 1915; AA MA Nr. 7253; Irmgard Farah, *Die deutsche Pressepolitik und Propagandatätigkeit im Osmanischen Reich von 1908–1918 unter besonderer Berücksichtigung des "Osmanischen Lloyd"* [Stuttgart: Steiner, 1993]).

76. Poharyan, "The Legendary Clash in Van," pp. 21–24.

77. Ter Minassian, "Van, 1915," p. 228.

78. Ibid., pp. 226–30; Mukhitarian, *An Account,* pp. 23–24, 29–31; Poharyan, "The Legendary Clash in Van," pp. 21–24. All these sources, especially Mukhitarian and Poharyan, give detailed lists of members of the Military Committee and other bodies.

79. See Gossoian, *The Epic Story,* p. 19. The American missionaries Grace Knapp and Clarence Ussher claimed that the attack began when Turkish soldiers tried to rape an Armenian woman and Armenians who intervened were killed, a story that seems too dramatic and an unlikely cause for rebellion (Grace H. Knapp, *Mission at Van,* p. 35). This book was privately printed in limited numbers but was also printed in Great Britain, Parliament, Misc. No. 31, 1916, *The Treatment of Armenians in the Ottoman Empire 1915–16* (London: H. M. Stationery Office, 1916), pp. 32–47; references here are to the British

printing; Clarence D. Ussher, *An American Physician in Turkey* (Boston and New York: Houghton Mifflin Company, 1917), p. 247.

The American missionaries in Van were generally very ill informed on events outside of the city itself. They relied on rumors told them by Armenian sources. See, for example, the missionary reports of a "great massacre" of Armenians near Muş, which was investigated by the British, who found it never happened (FO 424/200, Maunsell to O'Conor, Van, September 4, 1900). They were sometimes good sources on what they personally observed, and they often accurately reported meetings with, for example, the Russian consul or Ottoman governor. Their personal feelings were at first antirevolutionary, because the revolutionaries were avowedly atheists, whom the missionaries felt were immoral, and because the Dashnaks opposed missionary influence on the Armenians. The missionaries also refused to employ teachers who spread Dashnak propaganda (ABC 16.9.8, Eastern Turkey Mission, Woman's Board, vol. 1, 1909–1914, Documents & Reports, Letters A–Z, "Reports of Van Garden's Girls School and City Girls' School, August 4, 1909 Statistics").

During the rebellion, after the Russians had assured the missionaries of their support, the missionaries completely changed sides ("I had a long, confidential talk with Russian Consul on Saturday in which he gave the most positive assurances that, if Russia were to come in here, we may be sure that it will not interfere with our work" [ABC 16.10.1, Constantinople Archives, vol. 7, Letters to W. W. Peet, 1913–1914]). They almost never reported on any Muslim mortality and only commented on the most egregious actions by Armenians—and that in very short phrases. For example, there is no missionary mention of the well-documented slaughter of Muslims of Bitlis, except one comment on the survival of a Muslim doctor who had been kind to Armenians: "When it was understood that he had protected the Armenian women, he was saved from the fate of all the Turks found in the city" (ABC 16.9.8, Eastern Turkey Mission, Woman's Board, vol. 2, 1915–1920, Documents & Reports, Letters A–Z). Ussher devotes only a few sentences to the murders of Muslims by Armenians in Van, stating that the killings were understandable: "We remembered what they had to endure from the Turks all their lives" (*An American Physician in Turkey,* p. 285). Knapp does not make any mention of dead Muslims in *Mission at Van.*

80. See chapter 9. Ter Minassian, basing herself on A-Do's reports, lists a large number of villages destroyed, seemingly more than could conceivably have been burned in a few days (fifty-one villages "within a few days": Ter Minassian, "Van, 1915," p. 218). She never mentions any rebellion.

81. Poharyan ("The Legendary Clash in Van," pp. 19–21) and others state that the killings of Vramian and Ishkhan were the proximate cause of the rebellion.

82. Ter Minassian ("Van, 1915," p. 225) writes:

The refusal of Cevdet Bey to release Vramian and the troop movements, which as of April 5 isolated the two Armenian sectors of Van, convinced Aram that there existed no alternative to self-defense. This was not a new experience for the Armenians of Van. As the common strategy of the three Armenian revolutionary parties (Armenakan, Hnchakian, and Dashnaktsutiun), it had already been tested in June of 1896. Moreover, the Armeno-Tatar war of 1905–07, which had pitted Armenians and Muslims (Azerbaijanis) against each other in many places in the Caucasus between Baku and Tiflis, had a stirring effect on the Armenians of Van, Mush, Erzerum, and even Tabriz. The experience also seemed to demonstrate that resistance was a better gamble than submission. Finally, for the Westernized intelligentsia of Van, self-defense had become a matter of national dignity and political ethics, despite the risks of governmental reprisals.

83. Allen and Muratoff in *Caucasian Battlefields* (p. 299) state that "the Gendarme Division (formed out of militarized police battalions) under Kâzim Bey, reinforced by several regular battalions rushed up from Bitlis, held the insurgent population under siege." They are thoroughly confused. Ottoman records do not mention any battalions from Bitlis, which did not have whole battalions to send because of the Armenian revolt in Bitlis Province. Allen and Muratoff are probably confusing them with the two battalions that arrived on May 9, which did travel through Bitlis. The entire Gendarme Division was not sent, only one battalion, and Kâzim himself did not go to Van. Kâzim reported as much to his superiors on April 29 (ATASE Arşivi, I. Dünya Harbi Kolleksiyonu, K-2820, D-A 69, F-3-71, Documents 3:2005; AA No. 6/4517, Kls. 5240, H-6, F 1-23; *Türk Harbi*, p. 593). Allen and Muratoff do not identify their source.

84. "Hivasor, Timar, and Ebecik" (ATASE Arşivi, I. Dünya Harbi Kolleksiyonu, K-2820, D-A 69, F-3-71, Documents 3:2005).

85. Knapp (*Mission at Van*, p. 36) wrote that those refugees began to arrive on April 25. See note 110 below.

86. Poharyan ("The Legendary Clash in Van," pp. 34–44) and Mukhitarian (*An Account*, pp. 77–79, 82) show the effectiveness of the hand grenades, also demonstrating that the rebels had military-grade weapons.

87. Mukhitarian, *An Account*, pp. 38–57, 84–86; Poharyan, "The Legendary Clash in Van," pp. 34–44. Poharyan's account, in particular, indicates that the Turkish soldiers had little experience or training in fighting the type of urban guerrilla war seen in Van.

88. On cannon, see Rafael de Nogales, *Four Years beneath the Crescent* (New York: Scribner's, 1926), pp. 75, 81, 83–85, 94. Incredible claims were made about these cannon. Mukhitarian alleged that 400 explosive shells fell on the Armenians on May 1 alone; "More than a dozen unfortunate people were killed in the streets" (*An Account*, p. 78). This would seem to be an extremely small death toll from 400 shells. When Mukhitarian gives actual descriptions of the results of cannon fire, the effects are more reasonable (e.g., the top stories of buildings blown off, which agrees with de Nogales's descriptions). If Mukhitarian is to be believed, Ottoman forces brought cannon through the streets of Van (pp. 83–84), which indicates that they were small weapons, perhaps mountain guns. Cevdet did have under his command the two field guns that he had been given before the Van City rebellion began, as well as some guns sent by the Mobile Gendarme Division. One of these guns exploded on May 4 (Mukhitarian, *An Account*, p. 84). Gossoian wrote the Ottomans attacked the neighborhoods that the Armenians had seized in the Old City with the fortress artillery and three other cannon (*The Epic Story*, p. 31). Mukhitarian, who only spoke guardedly elsewhere of "cannons," in one place (*An Account*, p. 101) stated: "The next day, the Turks bombarded, with their two field guns, all our positions in the Arark area." It is probable that the Ottomans had their fortress artillery, two field guns, and a number of small mountain guns. Although called fortress artillery, some of these were in fact antique smooth-bore mortars, which were used despite their age (de Nogales, *Four Years beneath the Crescent*, p. 84). Gossoian (*The Epic Story*, pp. 37–38) states there were five of these mortars: "Three of these were of large caliber, two were of medium caliber." Anahide Ter Minassian states that "there were twelve guns (light mountain artillery and short-range heavy fortress artillery)" but does not note the field guns.

89. See chapter 9.

90. De Nogales (*Four Years beneath the Crescent*, p. 79) contends that Cevdet in-tended to have as many Armenian refugees enter the city as possible, in order to use up the rebels' provisions. He also states, with great indignation, that the Armenian command saw the danger in this and tried to stop it, even firing on and killing refugees trying to enter Van (p. 93). Ter Minassian ("Van, 1915," pp. 238–39) does not mention the killing: "This was also a period of high drama during which the Military Committee refused entry into the defensive ring of 'useless mouths,' a large group of Armenian refugee women and children driven there by the Turks to weaken the defenders." Poharyan ("The Legendary Clash in Van," pp. 24–31) says that Cevdet sent Armenians into the city but does not men-tion that any were turned away.

91. Mukhitarian, *An Account*, p. 67.

92. Ibid., p. 87.

93. Fighting their way to Iran if they lost Van was mentioned as an option, but this seems to have been an impossible venture.

94. Ottoman sources state that the battle began when Armenians fired on police out-posts. Armenian sources state that it began when a Turkish mob attacked the Armenian Quarter in the Old City. The battle had already begun in the Garden City before it broke out in the Old City.

95. The burnings had been previously planned for military purposes by the Armenian Council. They were not irrational outbursts: "According to our defense plans, it was imperative to destroy, at the outset of hostilities, the following buildings which could otherwise render our defense positions untenable: the building of post and telegraph, the 'Regie' [tobacco monopoly] building, the Bank, Municipal and Sanitary establishments, City Police station, the Armory and warehouse for military procurement and the Court House. In the case of the last two buildings, it was planned to try and capture them first, failing that, they were to be burned" (Gossoian, *The Epic Story*, pp. 11 and 12; see also pp. 22 and 23).

96. ATASE Arşivi, I. Dünya Harbi Kolleksiyonu, K-2820, D-A 69, F-3-41, Docu-ments 3:2003; April 20, 1915, ATASE Arşivi, I. Dünya Harbi Kolleksiyonu, K-2820, D-A-69, F-3-6, Documents 1:23. Gossoian states that Muslim refugees also fled east to the Muslim section of the Garden District, although Ottoman sources do not mention this. It seems unlikely that many Muslims could have taken this route, because most would have had to pass through Armenian lines.

97. Ottoman Empire, *Aspiration et agissements*, pp. 269–70.

98. *Türk Harbi*, p. 593. Gossoian's volume is largely a catalog and a description of the Armenian attacks in the Old City and on the Citadel.

99. ATASE Arşivi No. 4/3671, Kls. 2950, H-13, F. 1-100; *Türk Harbi*, p. 592.

100. Mukhitarian, *An Account*, pp. 77–79, 82; Gossoian, *The Epic Story*, p. 13.

101. De Nogales, *Four Years beneath the Crescent*, p. 76. From internal evidence it appears that de Nogales may simply have been taking the estimates from the *Blue Book*. He was perhaps an adequate military officer, but he also appears, in his writings, to have been paranoid with delusions of grandeur. Throughout his book, some official or another is trying to kill him, always without success. No one seems to understand proper military tactics but de Nogales. His importance, ability, and courage are exemplary, at least as he recounts them. His analyses of military situations are useful, but his analyses of the char-acter of individuals are completely unreliable.

102. Ter Minassian, "Van, 1915," p. 229.

103. Ter Minassian's exact source is not given: "The statistics are published in the principal works used in this study" ("Van, 1915," p. 229). The data, however, are exactly the same as those that appear in Mukhitarian (*An Account,* pp. 111–12) and Poharyan ("The Legendary Clash in Van," pp. 24–31). Mukhitarian may be the base source from which the others are taken.

104. Gossoian (*The Epic Story,* pp. 12, 17, 53) properly does not differentiate between "fighters" and the Armenian population as a whole. He estimates 2,500 Armenians in the Old City and speaks of an additional 1,000 Armenian refugees who entered the Old City at the start of the conflict.

105. *History of the ARF,* p. 111. He speaks of the entire Armenian force in Van.

106. Knapp, *Mission at Van,* p. 35. Knapp's distinction of "trained riflemen" is important.

107. Mukhitarian, *An Account,* p. 116.

108. See, for example, Allen and Muratoff's praise for the Ottoman fighting men, although not always their leaders, in *Caucasian Battlefields,* such as: "Sarıkamış must live in history as the most heroic manifestation of the spirit of the Turkish fighting man" (p. 285).

109. Ter Minassian, "Van, 1915," p. 229.

110. Dasnabedian wrote that 15,000–20,000 Armenian refugees were in Van (*History of the ARF,* p. 111). The American missionary Grace Knapp (*Mission at Van,* p. 35) wrote that the Armenian population of the Garden District on April 20 was "nearly 30,000" and that 10,000 refugees were later added to that number (p. 38). According to Mukhitarian (*An Account,* p. 63), 10,000 Armenian peasants arrived in the Garden District on one day, April 25. Obviously, these statements are not to be trusted, but they do indicate that large numbers of refugees were in the Garden District. Poharyan ("The Legendary Clash in Van," pp. 24–31) estimated 10,000 from the Mount Varak vicinity villages alone and "tens of thousands" total.

111. For example, 700 (the number of those who tried to take the citadel on September 22, according to both Ottoman and Armenian sources) in reality must have been the Dashnak "sworn men," deserters with military training, and other "trained riflemen" as of September 22. These were the trained core of the Armenian rebels, not the whole of the Armenian force. Calling them the "Armenian force" would be the equivalent of counting only the Special Air Service (SAS) as "the British military" or the Special Forces as "the American army."

112. "The Armenian population, from all walks of life, without discrimination of sex or age, mobilized. According to a participant, this was 'a people's war'" (Ter Minassian, "Van, 1915," p. 229). On the mobilization of the Armenian community, see Gossoian (*The Epic Story,* pp. 29–30), who describes fighting "volunteers" from the populace and the "auxiliary committees" that dealt with matters such as repairing weapons, the commissariat, and building fortifications. Even Bishop Daniel took up the fight (p. 35). Mukhitarian (*An Account,* p. 112) mentions 800 "construction laborers" who built fortifications in the Garden District and states that one-fourth of the available weapons were furnished by refugee peasants.

113. De Nogales, *Four Years beneath the Crescent,* pp. 74–76.

114. See "The End in Van" in this chapter.

115. *Türk Harbi,* p. 592; "1,200 to 1,300 Kurdish *comitadchis,* who were quite good shots and fought splendidly hand-to-hand, but were of no use whatever in organized

combat on account of their absolute lack of discipline" (de Nogales, *Four Years beneath the Crescent,* p. 75).

116. De Nogales, *Four Years beneath the Crescent,* p. 93.

117. FO 195/2456, Smith to Mallet, Van, January 10, 1914.

118. De Nogales, *Four Years beneath the Crescent,* p. 68.

119. Ter Minassian also does not mention Mukhitarian's estimate that there were 40 rifles and 36,000 cartridges (held by "men serving as bodyguards to Aram, or serving with the Defense Command and other agencies") not included in his figures of 505 rifles, 74,824 cartridges, and so forth. Nor does she include "the reserve of 30,000 cartridges at the Armenian Revolutionary Federation's arsenal" (Mukhitarian, *An Account,* p. 112).

120. Gossoian, *The Epic Story,* p. 13. Gossoian continued: "This figure was increased by 7,000 bullets later on. The munitions shop refilled 12,000 cartridges during the struggle. Also available were six large, six medium and four small bombs. About 300 pounds of powder was salvaged from Turkish shells during the conflict." Ter Minassian ("Van, 1915," p. 235), not listing her source, gives a different number of weapons: "the Armenian forces in the City, consisting of 100 rifles, 210 Mausers, and 60,000 bullets, were negligible" (p. 235).

121. FO 371/3783, Molyneux-Seel to Lowther, Van, April 4, 1913; FO 371/2130, Smith to Mallet, Van, January 10, 1914. See also FO 195/2456, Bullard to Mallet, Erzurum, January 18, 1914.

122. FO 371/2130, Smith to Mallet, Van, January 10, 1914.

123. It is impossible to tell how many of the hand weapons listed by Ter Minassian were actually machine pistols.

124. See chapter 7.

125. Bis units were made up of regular army divisions (*nizam*) with the addition of reserve units. They can be assumed to have been less effective than regular divisions.

126. One battalion and the druzhina were already in place. The Russians brought up six more battalions and two Cossack regiments (Allen and Muratoff, *Caucasian Battlefields,* p. 298).

127. *Türk Harbi,* pp. 593–99; Allen and Muratoff, *Caucasian Battlefields,* pp. 296–99.

128. The division was intended to be a part of the force (*Türk Harbi,* p. 569).

129. Not all members the Gendarme Division were fighting the rebels, but they were taking the place of Cevdet Bey's troops in their other duties, primarily guarding passes. In the Ottoman plan, those duties were to be undertaken by Cevdet's troops. Cevdet's men were otherwise occupied, however, in Van City. Had they been able to take their places on the frontier, the Gendarme Division would have been available for Halil's force.

130. ATASE Arşivi (AA) No. 4/3671, Kls. 2950, H-13, F. 1-106 and H-13, F. 1-109; *Türk Harbi,* p. 592.

131. Türk Harbi, pp. 678–79; ATASE Arşivi, I. Dünya Harbi Kolleksiyonu, K-5240, D-6, F-1-28, 1-30.

132. AA No. 6/4517, Kls. 5240. H-6, f. 1-34 and F. 1-35; AA No. 4/3671, Kls. 2950, H-13, F. 1-181, cited in *Türk Harbi,* pp. 678–79.

133. AA No. 6/4517, Kls. 5240, H-6, F 1-23; *Türk Harbi,* p. 593.

134. ATASE Arşivi, I. Dünya Harbi Kolleksiyonu, K-5240, D-6, F-1-28, 1-30; ATASE Arşivi, I. Dünya Harbi Kolleksiyonu, K-5240, D-6, F-1-8, 1-10; ATASE Arşivi No. 6/4517, Kls. 5240, H-6, F 1-10; *Türk Harbi,* p. 593.

135. ATASE Arşivi, I. Dünya Harbi Kolleksiyonu, K-44, D-207, F-2.

136. Some sources say there were twelve boats.

137. A. Süslü, G. Öğün, and T. Serdar, *Van, Bitlis, Muş ve Kars'taki Ermeni Katliamları* (Ankara: Van Yüzüncü Yıl Üniversitesi, 1994), p. 20; *Ermeniler Tarafından Yapılan
Katliam Belgeleri (1914–1919)*, vol. 1 (Ankara: Başbakanlık Devlet Arşivleri Genel Müdürlüğü, Osmanlı Arşivi Daire Başkanlığı, 2001).

138. AA No. 4/3671, Kls. 2950, H-13, F 1-163; *Türk Harbi,* p. 678.

139. Allen and Muratoff, *Caucasian Battlefields,* pp. 299–300; *Türk Harbi,* pp. 677–
78.

140. ATASE Arşivi, I. Dünya Harbi Kolleksiyonu, K-2820, D-A 69, F-3-71, Documents 3:2005.

141. ATASE Arşivi, I. Dünya Harbi Kolleksiyonu, K-2820, D-A-69, F-4, Documents
3:2006.

142. On troop movements, see the detailed description in *Türk Harbi,* pp. 676–88;
and the summary in Allen and Muratoff, *Caucasian Battlefields,* pp. 299–301.

143. ATASE Arşivi, I. Dünya Harbi Kolleksiyonu, K-2950, D-14, F-1-62.

144. Uras, *The Armenians in History,* p. 863.

145. 2003 U.S. dollars, calculated by the "GDP Per Capita" method. Other methods
would yield higher or lower sums (http://eh.net/hmit/ and http://www.roots-saknes.lv/
History/Money.htm).

146. ATASE Arşivi K-1488, D-32, F-3-5.

147. Unrest initiated by tribes in Ottoman lands was an obvious benefit to the Russians; but it is difficult to see how chaos in Iran could have aided the Russians, and it was
probably not the Russian plan. See Allen and Muratoff, *Caucasian Battlefields,* p. 295.

148. See "The Military Situation in the Region" at the beginning of this chapter.

149. Allen and Muratoff, *Caucasian Battlefields* (pp. 288–91), list twelve Ottoman
divisions in the East, but the actual numbers were far below what this suggests. For an extremely detailed view of the development of the Ottoman force after Sarıkamış, see *Türk
Harbi,* pp. 539–40, 542–84. The Ottoman manpower situation was extremely fluid, so
any general statement of numbers is very approximate. Numbers of irregulars, including
Kurdish tribes, are impossible to verify with any certainty.

150. See chapter 9.

151. See chapter 9.

152. Allen and Muratoff, *Caucasian Battlefields,* p. 299.

153. Korganoff, *La participation des Arméniens à la Guerre Mondiale,* p. 21, comments
on the great benefit of Armenian scouts to the Russians.

154. This figure includes the 200 men sent from Van. The numbers for both Russians
and Ottomans are approximate and do not include battle losses.

155. ATASE Arşivi, I. Dünya Harbi Kolleksiyonu, K-2820, D-A 69, F-3-71.

156. Abdülkadir was placed in command of the tribal light cavalry. About 1,800 had
enrolled during prewar mobilization, and more were arriving.

157. "Well informed by Armenian agents of the situation at Van, [the Russian gen-
eral] Yudenich determined to take advantage of it. Since March four of the Armenian druzhiny had been concentrated at Bayazıt. Yudenich added to this force of sturdy nationalist
volunteers the 2nd Transbaikal Cossack Brigade of General Trukhin, and he ordered this
officer to cross the Teperiz Pass over the Ala-dağ and advance on Beğrikale and Van" (Allen
and Muratoff, *Caucasian Battlefields,* p. 299).

CHAPTER 9

Destruction and Murder in Van

d wholesale destruction were seen all over Van Province from
ing of the Armenian rebellion.[1] Bloodshed had not been un-
Van before the beginning of the revolt, but the deaths during the
ad a unique ferocity. Soon after its start the revolt took on the
f an intercommunal war, not the old conflict between revolu-
nd the state or between revolutionaries and Kurdish tribes. The
ling revolutionary policy of polarizing the two communities had
ruition. The communities were even physically separated as the
concentrating the Armenian population, delineated in the "In-
for Personal Defense," was put into effect. Attack and counter-
assacre and countermassacre, were to follow.
ight be expected, in the early days of the rebellion bloodshed
ly seen in the hot beds of revolt: Başkale-Dir-Çatak, Gevaş, and
Gendarmerie outposts were attacked first, then villages. The gen-
outposts, which usually had only five to ten lightly armed men,
targets.[2] Small battles occurred between gendarmes sent to find
nd deserters or to collect taxes in Armenian villagers and armed
naries and villagers. The Armenian weaponry included rifles,
pistols, and dynamite bombs. The bombs were used on surround-
lim villages.[3] In response, government forces did not hesitate to
y force, including the destruction of the houses of families of
and destruction of entire villages that had rebelled. Gendarmes,
naries, and Muslim and Armenian villagers died.[4]
first major massacres of Muslim civilians took place when the
invaded the Dir-Başkale and Saray regions at the beginning of
In November 1914 the minor Ottoman forces in the region with-
advance of the Russian invasion. Armenian rebel bands, both local

and from Iran, attacked Kurdish villages and the civilian population of Dir and Başkale.[6] Mass rapes of females and the murder of all Muslim males took place in many occupied villages, as well as plundering and murder in the cities of Dir, Başkale, and Saray. The events in these cities foreshadowed those to come in other districts. First, officials, soldiers, and gendarmes were murdered. Robbery and extortion followed: promises—seldom kept—of survival if the Muslims gave up their hidden money and possessions. Males of fighting age were killed. Women were raped. In at least one large village near Saray the villagers were driven into the mosque, which was then burned. Numbers given by survivors are unreliable but do indicate the severity of attacks on women. For example: "More than 400 women and young girls were violated [in villages near Dir]."[7] When the Russians retreated from Dir and Başkale in December 1914, most of the Armenian population of that region fled into Iran with the Russian troops, justifiably fearing reprisals. They destroyed houses and government buildings in the cities before they withdrew. Kurdish tribes and local civilians slaughtered many of those Armenians who remained, as well as Armenians on the roads.[8]

Both Armenians and Muslims died in these border battles. No distinction was made between civilians and fighters. Most of the males—whether Kurdish and Armenian villagers, Armenian partisan band members, Kurdish tribesmen, or soldiers and gendarmes—were armed and fought. Those who could not fight were caught in the crossfire. In Dir, for example, after the Russians began their withdrawal in November 1914, Armenians built barricades and fought the Ottoman troops for a day before they too retired to Iran.[9] The rationale behind these attacks was most likely more than revolutionary. They were a part of a "softening up" plan by the Russian army. Driving refugees onto the roads disrupted administration of the Van Province and hindered the movement of troops.[10]

As the Armenian revolt progressed, the Ottoman response also escalated. By the end of February 1915 gendarmes and some minor military units were battling rebels in most areas of the province, especially in the Çatak, Havasor, and Timar regions. Government buildings were seized and entire Muslim villages destroyed, their people massacred.[11] The Ottomans were not winning, as indicated by the dispatch of a large part of the Van Mobile Gendarme Division to Çatak and later to Van. The gendarme forces, along with other troops in Van, were able to bring the revolts in Havasor and Timar under control, although the Ottomans were never successful in quelling the Çatak revolt or the revolt near Saray. The soldiers' methods, like those of the revolutionaries, were undoubtedly brutal.

The Question of Intent

Armenian sources contend that any Ottoman attacks on Armenians were unjustified because there never was a rebellion. They describe what occurred as purely Ottoman attacks on the Armenians in which any Armenian fighting was self-defense. The Ottomans, in contrast, saw a revolt and described its development in their secret documents. Only someone willing to believe that the Ottomans lied to themselves in all their orders can believe that there was no revolt. Moreover, the description of Ottoman attacks on Armenians as "mindless massacres" rests on the assumption, not reflected anywhere in Ottoman documentation, that the Ottomans had simply decided to kill Armenians, no matter what the cost. When soldiers were badly needed at the front, they were instead assigned to hunt down Armenians. When good communications were needed behind the lines, the Ottomans deliberately started a civil war that would cause them great harm. In short, if the Armenian sources are to be believed, the Ottomans decided that their first priority was to kill Armenians, even if it meant losing the war. This is absurd.

The assumption that the Ottomans were unthinking mass murderers colors the reports of Armenian deaths in the Armenian sources.[12] Ottoman forces are accused primarily of slaughtering peaceful and loyal Armenians in five regions: Havasor, Timar, Başkale, Çatak, and Saray. Ottoman documentation identifies these very areas as strongholds of the rebellion. The Ottoman accounts relate that Armenians rebelled first, killing officials, gendarmes, and Muslim villagers. Soldiers and gendarmes replied by attacking the Armenians. Not only does the Ottoman narrative have solid archival support, but it makes sense. The actions of the Van Mobile Gendarme Division demonstrate this. The division was expected to be a part of Halil Paşa's battle in Iran. It was badly needed there, and its absence likely decided the outcome of the battle. Yet the government sent a large part of the division to Çatak. The division was not ordered there until reports of the rebellion were well authenticated. Even the Armenian sources state that the Ottoman attacks on the Armenians of the Havasor and Timar regions began on April 19, well after revolts began there and one day before the revolt in Van City. In fact, contrary to what the Armenian sources allege, most of the attacks in Timar and Havasor took place days after the revolt in the city of Van began, when the Gendarme Division troops arrived. The Ottomans surely wanted to fight the rebels before that, but they did not have the troops.

The fact that the Ottomans were fighting revolts does not mean that great numbers of innocent Armenians did not die. Revenge, hatred, and ill-discipline must have affected the soldiers, just as they affected the rebels. Armenians undoubtedly fled from the soldiers and from Kurdish tribes.

THE INVASION

The first refugees in Van were Armenians and Muslims who fled from each other in the first months of the rebellion. Compared to later refugees, they went relatively short distances, each group moving to secure areas. Larger numbers of Armenians became refugees in Iran when the Russians withdrew and the Ottomans defeated rebels in the Başkale, Dir, and Saray regions in the first months of the war. At approximately the same time as the rebellion in the city of Van, Muslims were driven into the city and into safe villages by Armenian rebels to the north (Timar District) and south (Havasor District).[13] When the Gendarme Division troops arrived at Van, Armenians were then driven from the same districts by the Ottoman forces, many coming into the rebel-controlled portions of Van City. Others fled to the slopes of Mount Erek; many were later dislodged after extended battles with soldiers. The numbers of these refugees are unknown. Many made estimates, but the figures are wildly inconsistent and conflict with each other.[14]

As the Russian army approached and Ottoman soldiers retreated, Armenians who had previously not been involved in the fighting joined in the attack on Muslims. They united with Armenian partisan bands. The Muslim villages of the Bargiri region were attacked by both local partisans and Armenian bands that came with and before the Russian advance. The Muslim villagers nearest Bargiri had little time to flee. Those who did escape claimed that 300 villages had been destroyed at that time, with great loss of life. The refugees were attacked on the journey south. They said that bodies lined the road.[15]

The Muslim villagers on the Russian and Armenian line of march naturally suffered the losses expected when villages are invaded by an enemy army—rape, theft, expropriation of animals and food, and death for those who resisted the conquerors. The suffering reported by the villagers on the line of march, however, went far beyond what might ordinarily be expected in war. The attacks on villagers and refugees were not military confrontations. They were simply slaughter. Refugees were particularly defenseless. Most of the men were at the front. The refugee columns were largely made up of old men, women, and children. All were attacked. Children were not spared.[16]

The few reports that the villagers were able to send cited Cossacks and

Armenian bands as their main oppressors. Torture and rape were common, followed by mass murder, although often some villagers were only wounded and others escaped to the hills, later to relate the fate of their villages and fellow refugees.[17] One partisan band led by an Armenian from Bayazıt, Surpin, was prominently cited.

Van City

By May 20 the main centers of Van province were occupied by the Russians.[18] They did not control much of the countryside, which was in the hands of Armenian bands, sometimes accompanied by Cossack patrols.

Under the leadership of Aram Manukian the Armenians set up a short-lived government in the new Russian Province of Van.[19] From May 16 to 18 the Armenians looted and burned all that was left of the Muslim houses and governmental buildings in the city.[20] Except for some of the very old and very young, Muslim males and a large number of the females who had remained in the city were killed.[21] Survivors, almost all of them women, recorded details of the massacres, usually listing the murders of those they had known and of religious and public officials.[22] Their reports all relate the same series of events: adult males (except some of the very old) and teenaged boys were separated from the women and girls. The males were killed in various ways, many of them horrible. Some women and young children were killed at the same time as the men, some were raped, and others were simply released to wander among the rubble. From very limited evidence it also seems that some were assisted by Armenians.[23]

After the first days of the Armenian victory the remaining Muslim population of Van City was almost entirely made up of women and children. It included women who had been unable to escape the province and had come with young children into the city from burned-out villages. Some women took themselves to the American Missionary compound, looking for safety and food. Others were brought to the American Compound by Armenians. At the compound they found a small amount of food—enough bread to survive and occasionally some stew, provided by the Russians after their arrival. There was not much safety, however. Mortality from disease and deaths among the wounded were high. The American Compound was far from secure: Armenians, and later Cossacks, took women from the compound and raped them. Women and children were also taken from the compound and killed. Some women and children left the compound, feeling safer in the streets or outside the city, where they were set upon by Armenian bands. Many women were taken to the German Mission, where conditions, including rape and starvation, were worse. Others remained in the American Compound for nearly two months, until the Ottomans retook the city.[24]

Despite continuing attacks on Muslim survivors, the situation in the city improved when the Russians arrived. Aram Manukian, who had always legally remained a Russian subject, was allowed to rule in most matters, with the proviso that ultimate authority was held by the Russian military authorities. The Russians seem to have exerted a calming influence in Van, even trying to convince Muslim refugees to return to the city by providing food. A small number of Muslim males did return. The adult males who had remained in the city were already dead, but wholesale slaughter ended when the Russians arrived. The survival of the Muslim women and children left in Van was due largely to the Russians. The Russians may have acted out of a sense of common humanity, but they may also have had no wish for a city that was completely Armenian. This would fit with their policy, later evident, of making Van Russian, not Armenian.

The new administration in the city of Van was presented with a daunting task. Much of the city had been destroyed during the rebellion. Much of what remained had been burned down by the victorious Armenians. There was disease, especially typhus, but no starvation. Exact numbers are unavailable, but more than thirty thousand Armenians in Van City—both residents and refugees—needed to be fed and housed. Although the Russian army commandeered food for its own use, there seems to have been enough food available.

THE VILLAGES AND REFUGEES

During the Russian invasion and after Van City had fallen, the Armenians set about ridding the province of Muslims. Despite the flight of refugees, a sizable Muslim population still remained in the villages. Attacks on Muslim villages had been limited by the speed of the Russian and Armenian advance. Once the province had fallen, however, the attacks increased and became methodical. They followed a constant pattern: wounded and sick Muslim soldiers had been distributed to villages to recuperate; others had gone to villages when cut off from their units; some were deserters. These were always among the first to be killed, along with any officials or religious leaders.[25] Where adult male villagers were present,[26] the men and young boys were taken away and killed. In some villages the women were then raped and sometimes killed. In others they were only robbed and set on the road as refugees. This seems to have depended solely on the wishes of the Armenian commanders.[27] The Russian Regular Army seldom seems to have taken part, although villagers and officials often mentioned Cossack attacks, often in concert with the Armenians.

The inhabitants of the region to the north of Van City could not easily escape from the Russian invaders and the Armenian bands that accompanied them. Even though villagers tried to flee as soon as they heard the Russians were approaching, they did not have enough time to pass through Van City before it fell. After that, their egress point was closed. The villages were hemmed in both to the north and to the south by Russians and Armenians. They began to fill with refugees from farther north who had hoped to escape through Van City.[28] In a war noted for massacres of civilians, the villages north of Van seem to have suffered the worst mortality. Armenian bands, local Armenians, and the Armenian druzhiny from the Southern Caucasus joined together and began the slaughter in Muslim villages, advancing from one village to another. Naturally, no one kept a detailed record of the bloody Armenian advance through the villages, but the witness of survivors indicates that the slaughter was nearly complete. Survivors gave the names of villages they knew had succumbed: Zeve, Molla Kassim, Şeyh Kara, Şeyh Ayne, Ayans, Hıdır, Amuk, Zorayad, Pakes, Bağdeşan, Karaağaç, Eskele, Karacık, Molla Selim, Mındayn, Bahiz Zurafe, Gorsta, Şine…[29] Some of those who survived were saved in the brief period of Ottoman reconquest. They then fled south and west, joining those from farther south who had been able to escape earlier.

The Muslims in the south of the province were more likely to escape outright murder than were those to the north of Van. Many in the south fled to Iran and to Mosul Province. Presumably these were primarily Kurds with tribal affiliations who could find some shelter with their fellows in Mosul and Iran.[30] The route from regions such as Çatak, Hoşap, and Gurpınar was often across mountainous terrain, but the paths were not impassable to fleeing villagers in May. Some refugees had the advantage of fleeing alongside or just ahead of Ottoman forces that were taking the same routes to Bitlis. Both the Expeditionary Force and the Gendarme Division followed those routes. Refugees traveling with them would have enjoyed certain protection, as long as they could move fast. They perforce abandoned their farm animals and belongings so that they could keep up with the infantry. Thus they arrived in Bitlis Province with only what they could carry on their backs or on pack animals.[31]

The Jews of southern Van, part of the Jewish community that was mainly in Mosul Province, also suffered at the hands of the Armenian bands. Most of them, however, must have simply fled south and suffered, like all the refugees, from starvation and disease. By the end of World War I virtually no Jews remained in what had been the Ottoman Van Province. Only forty-three Jews were registered as remaining in Hakkâri Province in the 1927 Turkish census.[32]

By no means did all of the Muslim villagers flee alongside retreating Ottoman troops. The situation in the South illustrates the confusion of the time. In each village a meeting was held to decide what the villagers would do in the face of the Ottoman loss. Many, probably most, decided to take flight. Others decided to trust the Russians, believing that they would control the situation. Those who remained must have felt that life was impossible beyond the villages in which their families had lived for centuries. They were mistaken in trusting the Russians. Cossacks, the shock troop cavalry of the Russians, killed and raped throughout the South. Nearby Armenian villagers and Armenian partisan bands joined in the attacks. The survivors then became refugees themselves.

Even those refugees who decided early to flee did not necessarily immediately go west or south. They often went from their own villages, in which they felt exposed and in danger, to larger villages, where safety was in fact illusory. Some villages actually moved closer to the path of Russian invasion or to Armenian settlements. They must have had little idea of what was happening and thus made poor choices. Like the people who remained in their villages, all these were overtaken by the Russians and Armenians.[33]

Survival of the refugees from the southern part of Van Province depended to a great extent on what route they chose. Those who took the mountainous route fared better, although many were attacked by partisans near Hizan and Müküs.[34] Those who took the road through Gevaş before and after the Ottoman army's march experienced high mortality. On the Gevaş route they joined the rest of the refugees from Van Province. Refugees from the center and even the eastern part of the province had little choice but to take the road that ran along the southern shore of Lake Van.[35] Yet that road was only truly safe during the brief period when Ottoman soldiers traveled it.

Ottoman soldiers were able to patrol the Van to Bitlis route only as far as Gevaş through most of the period until Van fell. The road from Gevaş to Tatvan, however, was murderous.[36] In two portions of the journey (west of Gevaş and east of Tatvan) mountains rose near the coast, trapping refugees between the mountains and the lake, perfect for partisan attacks. Armenian partisans came to the region south of the lake from all over Van and Bitlis Provinces. Villages to the south of the lake were attacked and destroyed by local Armenians and partisans, later helped by Russian

Armenians, with attendant massacres.[37] Ottoman forces were fighting in Van Province and on the northern border of Bitlis Province and had no troops available to patrol the Gevaş-Tatvan Road adequately. The depot battalion from Van and parts of the Expeditionary Force passed along the road as they retreated and provided what protection they could for the refugees. The Russians were in pursuit, however, and the soldiers did not stop until they reached Tatvan.[38] There, at the request of the Bitlis governor, they stopped to protect the refugees and guard the approach to Bitlis City. Troops from the Expeditionary Force were assigned to assist.[39]

A very small number of refugees returned when the Ottomans triumphed briefly; but when the Russians advanced in 1916, the refugees were driven out once again.

The roads were filled with thousands of refugees. They had only the food they were able to carry with them. Nevertheless, starvation was not an immediate threat. Aside from Armenian raids, the greatest peril was lack of drinking water. Water from Lake Van was never potable. The springs and rivers on the refugees' march were soon tainted with blood and rotting corpses. Corpses also filled the roads. First dysentery then worse diseases, especially typhus and cholera, became common. As food supplies dwindled, the weakened villagers became more susceptible to disease.

For a while the refugees from Van found some safety in Bitlis, although Armenian partisan attacks continued in that province.[40] They were forced to set out again when the Russians conquered Bitlis in 1916. One part of the exodus went toward Siirt, another toward Diyarbakır. Those who survived settled in cities such as Siirt, Diyarbakır, Mardin, Urfa, Harput, Antep, Silvan, Siverek, and Adana.

The Ottoman Return and Defeat

After the fall of Van, the retreating Ottoman armies made their stand west of Lake Van, in Bitlis Province.[41] They concentrated their forces in the Kop-Muş-Malazgirt region. Halil's Expeditionary Force was forced to delay east of Bitlis to control the roads into Bitlis and to protect refugees from Armenian bands, but eventually it joined in defeating the Russians (the Battle of Malazgirt, July 10–26, and subsidiary battles). The Ottomans, moving south of Lake Van, then advanced on Van City.[42] On July 31 the Russians ordered the Armenians of Van Province to evacuate the province and march north. As Ottoman forces approached Van, the Russian army itself left Van City on August 4, moving to defensive positions at Bargiri, Saray, and Hoşap.[43]

The Armenian refugees now suffered the same sort of starvation and attacks on roads that had been the fate of the Muslims fleeing Van. Armenian sources estimate, probably fairly accurately, that one hundred thousand Armenian villagers and city dwellers took to the roads north with little warning or time to collect belongings or food. Columns of Russian and Armenian soldiers and Armenian refugees were interdicted by Kurdish forces north of Bargiri as they crossed mountain passes. Reliable evidence of what happened to the refugees there is almost nonexistent, but it has been estimated that more than five thousand refugees died in the fighting and from tribal attacks in the mountains.[44] Once the refugees reached the Russian border, they were assisted by Armenian agencies; but the relief services were overwhelmed. Aid from the Russian government was limited.[45]

The Ottoman army reclaimed the city of Van then lost it again at the end of the month. Van was to be taken and retaken until the final Russian conquest on September 29, 1915.[46] The Ottomans lost the Battle of Köprüköy (January 10–19, 1916) and ceded the East to the Russians. Erzurum fell on February 16, 1916; Bitlis on March 3.

Once the Ottomans had been defeated, the Armenians might have expected to return home. The Russians would not let them do so. Only a small number of Armenians were allowed to return, primarily to bring in the harvest for the Russians. Some Armenian partisan bands also remained. The Russians had no intention of creating an "Armenia" in Ottoman Anatolia. The Armenians were valuable allies in wartime but were easily forgotten when it seemed the war had been won. In March and April of 1915 Russian officials were already suggesting plans to settle Cossacks in Van and Erzurum Provinces.[47] "This region [Erzurum, Van, and part of Bitlis Provinces] is mostly high above sea level and is completely suitable for Russian colonists."[48] Russia concurred in the Sykes-Picot Agreement, which gave Van to Russia, not to an Armenia. Once Russia had driven back the Ottomans in 1916, all of Eastern Anatolia was put under a military governor. All administrators of occupied territories were to be Russian officers. Armenians were no longer to be governors of Van.[49]

Russia began to disarm Armenians. Armenian fighters were no longer needed, and armed Armenians might just as easily fight the Russians as they had the Ottomans. In December 1915 the Armenian Legions (druzhiny) were dissolved. Legion soldiers were put into regular army units or, if they refused those appointments, were mustered out of Russian service. The Russians had more than imperialist reasons to dissolve the legions. Complaints of the legionnaires' behavior in Anatolia had reached the highest levels in the Russian army. General Nikolayev sent this telegram to the commander of the Caucasian Army on July 1, 1915:

> When Russian officials tried to prevent Armenian volunteers from carrying away spoils, the Armenians fired on Russian soldiers. Aside from this, the Volunteers continued to set fires. They enjoy committing every sort of murder. In order to put an end to the increasing number of murders we have instituted a Court-Martial. It was necessary to organize separate discipline units to stop these [actions].[50]

Apprised of the situation, General Bolhovitinov wrote to the viceroy of the Caucasus, Count M. Vorontsov-Dashkov, that the enrollment of any more Armenian Volunteer units was being forbidden:

> July 9, 1915
>
> Your Lordship,
>
> You entrusted me with the duty of organizing the Armenian militia before the outbreak of the war.
>
> During the following eleven months we did our best to perform this duty. Our own efforts, as well as the activities of the militia, proceeded satisfactorily in accordance with your orders, and there were no complaints.
>
> However, after the capture of Van, at the time when our militia was most intensely active, A. I. Hadisov, a delegate with the military administration, received the following communiqué:
>
> The Military Commander to the Commander General:
>
> General Nikolayev informs us from Van that our soldiers have fired on Armenian volunteers carrying off booty, as well as other volunteers also engaged in pillaging and robbery. In order to put an end to such crimes a court martial has been set up in Van.
>
> For this reason the Commander General has forbidden the formation of new militia units before order can be established among the existing men. I communicate this to you on the orders of his lordship.
>
> The Commander General Bolhovitinov[51]

Whether the Russians were truly concerned for the Muslims or only wished to end an independent Armenian military force can be debated.

With the coming of the Russian Revolution the Russian army in Eastern Anatolia began to walk home. Except for Armenian units and a few

Russian officers, they were gone from Van Province by the early summer of 1917.[52] Rule in Van passed to the Armenians, who briefly created a second Armenian government in Van, complete with ministries of state and its own currency (overwritten Russian notes). The small state was situated on the shores of Lake Van and extended to Erciş in the north.[53]

Freed of Russian control, Armenian refugees from Van began to return to the province. By late 1917, according to Richard Hovannisian, 150,000 Armenians were in Van, Bitlis, and Erzurum.[54] This cannot be more than a rough estimate, but it does indicate that the Armenian numbers were too small to have a chance at controlling Eastern Anatolia. Joined with the Armenians who had been in Erzurum Province already in 1917, the Armenians were less than one-half the number of Armenians who had lived in those provinces before the war. At most, the Armenians in Van Province in 1917 could have made up 10 percent of the number of Van's prewar inhabitants of all religions. The number of Armenian fighters was small. All men from twenty to thirty-five were drafted and given some training. By January the Armenian force in Van was estimated at two hundred cavalry and two thousand foot soldiers, but they could not be said to have been a potent military force.

The Ottomans were at first occupied with losing their war elsewhere; but on April 6, 1918, they retook Van City.[55] The Armenians of Van became refugees once again. The surviving Muslim refugees returned.

DESTRUCTION

It is impossible to calculate how many Muslim and Armenian villages were forcibly evacuated, destroyed, or simply abandoned during the rebellion. The Ottomans had no time to keep count. After the Russian invasion, Armenians did make lists, which may or may not be reliable. In any case, one cannot tell from lists of empty Armenian villages which were abandoned as part of the concentration of forces policy of the rebels and which were attacked by tribesmen or soldiers.[56] It is known that Ottoman soldiers did destroy houses of draft resisters and destroyed some entire villages in their counterinsurgency program. Armenians engaged in mass destruction of villages when they made their final retreat. So little of Van Province was left at the end of World War I that it is futile to try to discover who destroyed a village or when.

The destruction of property as the Armenians were in their final retreat follows the logic of war. If the Armenians could not have Van, they would do what they could to make sure that what was left was unliv-

TABLE 9.1. Villages in the Province of Van.

	BEFORE WAR	INTACT IN 1919
Muslim	1,373	350*
Armenian	112	200[†]
Mixed	187	—
Total	1,672	550

Source: "The Report of Niles and Sutherland," in Justin McCarthy, "American Commissions to Anatolia and the Report of Niles and Sutherland," in *Türk Tarih Kurumu Kongresi XI, Ankara: 5–9 Eylül 1990* (Ankara: Türk Tarih Kurumu, 1994), pp. 1809–53.
* "Repaired" (houses rebuilt).
[†] "Armenian and mixed."

able. This logic only applies to the destruction in the final Armenian retreat, however. The problem is that most of the destruction of government buildings, Muslim homes and villages, and religious buildings took place not when the Armenians were defeated but when they were triumphant. The city of Van provides a good example. When the Ottomans retreated and the Armenians took control of the entire city, their first action was to destroy the surviving Muslim houses. Those houses now in effect belonged to the Armenians, and they had need of them. Their own houses had suffered extensive bombardment during the rebellion. Yet instead of occupying the Muslim houses, they destroyed them. The same type of destruction took place all over the province. The only somewhat logical reason given for the Armenian actions was the belief that the Muslims would not return if they had nowhere to return.[57] In fact, the cause for the destruction seems to have been irrational hatred of all things Muslim and Ottoman. Onnig Mukhitarian, who observed and approved of the burnings in Van, called the destruction "The Days of Sacred Folly." He stated: "No authority could have curbed the uncontrollable vengefulness that had seized the Armenians of Van."[58] The result was the demolition of all that was old and beautiful in Van Province, along with most of its houses.

The Ottoman lists of destroyed Muslim villages are long.[59] They demonstrate that the Americans Emory Niles and Arthur Sutherland were correct in stating that almost all the Muslim villages had been destroyed or badly damaged.

Virtually all the venerated tombs, holy sites, and Sufi monasteries (*tekke*) in the province, as well as most mosques, were destroyed by the Armenians, only occasionally by the Russians.[60] The pious foundation (vakıf) buildings that had been serving the poor for centuries were demolished.[61]

A larger proportion of the Armenian churches and monasteries survived; but without congregations they gradually fell into ruins.

MORTALITY

The mortality of the Van Armenians cannot be separated from that of the other Armenians of the East. No records were kept of the original home provinces of the Armenian migrants to the Southern Caucasus and elsewhere. It is thus only possible to compare the number of Armenian migrants who survived with those who originally lived in the Ottoman provinces of Van, Erzurum, and Bitlis and the Russian province of Kars. Those were the provinces from which almost all the refugees in the Southern Caucasus originated.[62] Of the original 575,000 Armenians in the four provinces, 339,000 survived when the fighting ended, a mortality rate of 41 percent. The Kars and Erzurum Armenians, however, did not undergo the same level of hardship as did the Van and Bitlis Armenians. The mortality rate of the Van Armenians, therefore, must have been over 50 percent.

Perhaps half the deaths of the Van Armenians came during the rebellion and especially during the disastrous forced march to the north in 1916. Once the Armenians reached Russian Georgia, Azerbaijan, and Armenia, their death toll from starvation and disease was tremendous. The British consul in Batum reported that Armenian refugees in the Russian Caucasus were dying at the rate of 350–400 deaths a day from dysentery, spotted fever, typhoid, measles, diphtheria, and cholera.[63] The Russians surely contributed to the Armenian mortality by refusing to allow most of them to return to Van. Those who went back to the Armenian Republic after their brief return to Van found conditions even worse than they had been in 1916. They came to an Armenia that did not have enough food for its own residents, much less for refugees.[64] Only foreign assistance from American Near East Relief fed the Armenians.[65]

Muslim mortality was statistically worse, although the disaster for both peoples was so great that such comparisons have little meaning. Of the 313,000 Muslims who had lived in Van before the rebellion and war, only 119,000 were present at war's end. The other 194,000 (62 percent, nearly two-thirds) had died.[66]

The majority of both Armenian and Muslim deaths came while they were refugees. The Ottoman Refugees Commission recorded 868,962 Muslim refugees from the area of Russian conquest, but these official counts did not include many people. It is impossible to separate the Van refugees from the others completely, but the government figures indicate that the numbers of refugees were great. A very rough estimate is that perhaps 130,000–140,000 of the Van refugees survived to October 1916.[67] Unlike the Armenian refugees, the Muslims received no help from America or any other country. The Ottoman Refugee Commission distributed what food was available, but it was little enough. There were no medicines. Cholera, typhus, and typhoid took a terrible toll.

The Armenian refugees had no homes and had to start afresh in the Armenian Republic. This was just as true of Van's Muslims. Two-thirds of the villages in Van Province had been destroyed by the Armenians and Russians, and almost all of the remaining Muslim villages had been badly damaged.[68] In most places only the Armenian houses remained. Just as the Armenians in the Armenian Republic were occupying the houses and farms of the 181,000 Muslims killed there or evicted from the republic,[69] so the Muslims of Van began to live in the houses of the Armenians. Again, unlike the Armenians, no one helped the Muslims.

THE TESTIMONY OF İBRAHIM SARGIN

Although he was only eleven years old when the events he describes took place and was obviously told much of what he relates by his parents and others, İbrahim Sargın's account of the events in Zeve village is corroborated by wartime records by both officials and villagers, who name the same villages and describe the murders of the villagers.[70] His story is illustrative of much that befell the villagers of Van. The villagers had no control over their fate, but they were willing to resist.[71] In the end, all was futile, and they died.

> A soldier who had heard that the Russians had come to Çaldıran went to Derebey village and told the muhtar [village headman], "Why are you plowing in the fields? The Russians have come to Çaldıran. They will be in your village tomorrow, if not today. Leave now, or everyone will be killed." The village gathered together. Taking only a little food and their bedding, they set out for Van City. They passed through Zorava village. It was a Circassian village. The Derebey villagers answered their questions by saying, "The Russians have entered Çaldıran. The have marched on Muradiye [Bargiri]. We are going to Van." The Zorava villagers said, "If that is true, we had better go also." Soon there was a caravan of villagers from Hakis, Zorava, Derebey, Şıh Ömer, Şıhkara, Şıhayne, Hıdır, and Göllü on the way to Van. By this time, Van had been evacuated, but the villagers knew nothing of the flight from the city.

When the villagers came to the Everek Plain, Armenians appeared. They called to them, "Hey, fools! Where do you think you are going?" They answered, "Refugees are going to Van from all over. We are going there too." The Armenians swore at them and called: "You fools. Van was lost six or seven days ago. The Turks have fled. Cevdet Paşa's rule is long gone. Aram Paşa has formed a government. In Van the wounded, the Muslims in the hospitals, the women, and the children have all been cut down. The mosques were burned down. The barracks were burned down. All the Muslims who remained in Van were killed. Only twenty to thirty women remained. They were handed over to Aram Paşa." Çerkez İbo said, "We will all be made slaves. We must go to Zeve village. (Zeve was my village.) Zeve is very close to the lake. We will be able to find boats there. Our families can escape by boat. Otherwise, we will be captured."[72]

The caravan came to our village. There were more than 2,000 people. "What is going on?" we asked. "We were moving to Van. Armenians blocked our way. They told us that Van had been lost. We came here to try and find boats, so our families can escape."

It was springtime. Because of that it was not easy to supply what the refugees needed. Homes, straw barns, and tents were used to house them. There were more than 2,000, of whom 500 were settled in some fashion in our village. Defeated soldiers, carrying their weapons, also came to our village. They were in terrible shape. Their hair had grown down into their beards; their clothes were ragged; each one was full of lice on his head and ticks on his body. These we also took in. Among them was my older brother Necip, my paternal uncle's son Mustafa, my sister's husband Mehmet, my maternal aunt's son İlyas, Şaban Ağa's son Sergeant Recep, Acemoğlu Mustafa's son Corporal Seyyat, and Acemoğlu Emrah's son Sergeant Şükrü. They were emaciated, only skin and bones. We had to pluck the lice from the loins and the backs of the burned ones with fingernails. My uncle Yunus, a fine barber, took his razor in hand. He washed them in warm water, then shaved them. Believe me, the blood flowed from the lice on their faces as they were shaved. Thus did they begin to become themselves once again.

Two days passed in this way. On the third day, our hoca [religious teacher and religious leader of the village], Server Hoca, recited the morning prayer. Some went to pray, the others tried with difficulty to do their work. A river ran through the middle of our village. It came from the Iranian border, and in spring the flood made it look more like a lake than a river. (None of us knew then where the water came from.) We heard a woman's voice from the other side of the wild river. A woman called from the meadow over there, "For the love of God, is there no one who will bring me across?" My uncle got on his horse and crossed over. What did he see but Acemoğlu Ahmet Ağa's daughter, Esma. "Esma, my girl, what is happening?" he asked. Esma had gone as a bride to Molla Kasım village. She answered him, "Sir, first take me across, then I will explain." He took her up on his horse and crossed the river.

Those who were leaving their prayers gathered together to hear Esma. She told them: "Protect yourselves. They have burned down Hamid. They have burned down Molla Kasım and Ayanos. Either today or tomorrow they will be here. Protect yourselves." Hearing this, Server Hoca said: "Brothers, we are Muslims. Our religion tells us to die rather than submit to evil. We have sixty guns and twenty cases of ammunition. Eight or nine soldiers have come to us with their weapons and ammunition. Let us resist. The militia leader, Hoca Osman Efendi, the son of my father's uncle, sent us those weapons and ammunition [for this purpose]."

You do not know the area. There are hills above the village. The high area overlooks a bridge and a green meadow [where the Armenians would come]. Those who knew the hills were positioned in defensive positions. They waited for the Armenians. Finally the moment arrived. Armenians surrounded the village on three sides and began to attack. Our men returned fire. They fought with the Armenians until noon, calling on God. They made an assault on the Armenians, who broke and ran. One group of them fled to the Mermit village, another to Vadar village. They were no longer seen on the battlefield.

There was a very large Armenian village of 400 houses, Alay. The Armenians gathered their forces together there and renewed the fighting. After the afternoon prayer, we saw a force of 100 mounted men riding quickly toward us on the road from Van. Our men said, "By God, they have come." We found out later that these were Russian Armenians. They had heard the sound of fighting and had hurried here. They had waited until the afternoon, then began the fight. We ran out of ammunition soon after. The enemy took advantage of this and entered the village, making martyrs of the Muslims. The human sea of 2,000–3,000 began to run back and forth in panic. The Armenians burned the village. They threw small children in the air, catching them on the points of their bayonets. Bayonets were plunged into children's bellies. Children fell to the ground, screaming. Some women and girls threw themselves into the river or into grass fields that had been set afire [trying to escape]....

Some innocent women and children were put into straw barns that were burned. Others had their throats cut like sheep. Only one child survived [İbrahim himself]. Of course I asked them later to tell me how I escaped.

The Armenians worked to completely annihilate the villagers. They killed until darkness fell, intending no one to survive. They grabbed Corporal Seyyat, struck him down, peeled off his clothes, cut open his shoulder, then began to flay him alive. They said they were pinning a medal to the shoulders that held the promotion given him by Sultan Reşat. They cut off both his arms and made a purse out of skin they cut from his side. After they had killed the men, they killed six beautiful girls from the village, including my uncle's daughter Seher, the village mayor's wife Esma, my father's brother-in-law's bride Hayriye, my uncle İsmail's wife Ayşe, and Güllü.

As the Armenians were leaving, one named Asvador, the son of Kırbe, found us. My father was well-known and well-liked in Asvador's village, Bardakçi. He had saved Kırbe's life. He told the Armenians, "Do not touch them," and prevented our deaths. (My father then was serving in the reserves on the Iranian front.) When the Armenians were done with the village they left. We came out of our hiding place. We heard the hideous moans and groans of the injured: "For the love of God, will no one bind my wounds? Will no one give me a drop of water?"

This Armenian brought us to Bardakçi village. For a time we remained there. In that village my cousin told us what had happened there, swearing an oath that it was all true. "It had turned evening when the Armenians came. They selected ten or eleven women from our 150. They raped and assaulted these women until morning, leaving them covered in blood in horrible condition." My cousin continued to tell us the sad events in that village. "A woman was making bread. An Armenian came up to her and asked, 'What are you doing?' 'As you can see, I'm making bread.' 'Don't you need kebab as well?' he said. He then cut open a child with his bayonet and threw him in the oven. The child began to burn fiercely. The woman could only watch as the child was burned alive."

At that time the Russian Government had been created in Van, with Aram Paşa still at its head. A little later, the government sent out a notice, "Let everyone come to Van. In Van food and drink are free for everyone." My father had come at this time with Halil Paşa's army to my maternal uncles' village, Hacik. From there they went to a village in Hoşap District. When they heard the announcement he and my uncles went to Van. They saw a city burned down. The buildings, mosques, baths, and government buildings were all destroyed. My father came to the Haçboğan neighborhood. There were Armenian houses there. By chance, Asvador saw my father there.

"Good morning, Halil Ağa," he said. My father also wished him a good morning and asked, "What news from the village?" Asvador answered: "What news! Zeve is completely destroyed. Only your young wife, your son, and your daughter survived. I saved them. I will give them over to you whenever you wish." My father answered this by saying: "You have been very good to me. But if I go there the Armenians will kill me. Bring them to me, then I will take them away."

Asvador came to us that evening. "Get ready," he said. "Today I saw Halil Ağa. I will take you to him." The next morning Asvador put us in an ox-drawn cart and took us to Van. I will never forget that day. My father brought us from Van to Hoşap. We did not stay there long, because the Armenians were attacking a village every day. [They became refugees.] Many went toward Iran, many toward Mardin, many toward Diyarbakır. They struggled to stay alive.

Notes

1. We have made the decision not to give or quote detailed descriptions of torture, rape, and murder, although such descriptions are contained in abundance in the sources. There is no need for them; the evidence of their existence is plain enough. The only exception is the "Testimony of İbrahim Sargın." His words have been left as he spoke them and contain a limited number of such descriptions.

Although most of those who suffered in the villages and the refugees from Van were in no position to forward reports on their sufferings, as they lay dying on the roads from Van, an effort was made by an Ottoman commission to collect reports of the travails in Van and elsewhere. Ottoman officials also sent reports of massacres by Armenians to Istanbul. A small percentage of these were published at the time (*Documents sur les atrocités Arméno-Russes* [Istanbul: Société Anonyme de Papeterie et d'Imprimerie, 1917]; Kara Schemsi, *Turcs et Arméniens devant l'histoire* [Geneva: Imprimerie Nationale, 1919]; Ahmet Rustem, *La Guerre Mondiale et la Question Turco-Arménienne* [Berne: Staempfli, 1918]). The last two of these were written by government officials, who collected and printed documents in their books. Many more have been printed recently. The most detailed of these is *Ermeniler Tarafından Yapılan Katliam Belgeleri (1914–1919)* (hereafter *Ermeniler Belgeleri*) (Ankara: Başbakanlık Devlet Arşivleri Genel Müdürlüğü, Osmanlı Arşivi Daire Başkanlığı, 2001). References to these sources here are to depositions of survivors, not to commentaries or analyses in the books.

2. *Ermeniler Belgeleri*, pp. 5–10.

3. *Documents sur les Atrocités*, pp. 18–19, 24–27.

4. Rustem, *La Guerre Mondiale*, p. 100; Kara Schemsi, *Turcs et Arméniens*, pp. 44–45; Ermeniler Belgeleri, p. 7; BOA HR SYS. 2872/2, Belge No. 9.

5. Kara Schemsi, *Turcs et Arméniens,* pp. 41–42; Rustem, *La Guerre Mondiale,* pp. 11–13, 31, 97–98; *Ermeniler Belgeleri,* pp. 7, 10–11.

6. Başkale, not Van, was actually the seat of the first Armenian government in Van Province, but it had an even shorter life. See *Documents sur les Atrocités,* p. 12.

7. Kara Schemsi, *Turcs et Arméniens,* p. 41.

8. Mukhitarian—who makes no mention of the first attacks, by Armenians on Muslims—contends that "the entire Armenian community of Başkale was massacred immediately following the retreat of the Russian army" (*An Account of the Glorious Struggle of Van-Vasbouragan,* translated by Samuels S. Tarpinian [Detroit: General Society of Vasbouragan, 1967], p. 3). Had he said "the entire remaining Armenian population," it is possible he might have been correct. The Armenians were, in fact, too intelligent to remain. Contradicting himself immediately after that statement, Mukhitarian says that not all the Armenians were massacred: "The good looking women and girls were brought to the Shamiram Turkish ward in Van to be auctioned off and to serve their bestial lust" (p. 3). This is such an astounding statement that it probably should simply be ignored, but one might mention that none of the Ottoman officials, American missionaries, or foreigners (Italians, Germans, Nogales, and others) make any mention of such an auction, which would surely have drawn their attention. Statements such as these indicate that the other assertions of Mukhitarian and similar writers are more than questionable.

9. Kara Schemsi, *Turcs et Arméniens,* p. 41.

10. Rustem, *La Guerre Mondiale,* pp. 98–99; *Documents sur les Atrocités,* pp. 15–16; Kara Schemsi, *Turcs et Arméniens,* pp. 42–43.

11. Kara Schemsi, *Turcs et Arméniens,* p. 59; *Ermeniler Belgeleri,* p. 18.

12. Ter Minassian ("Van, 1915," pp. 218–23), for example, describes the Ottoman actions as "ethnic cleansing" and does not mention any revolts.

13. *Documents sur les Atrocités,* pp. 49–51.

14. Adding up the Armenian estimates of living Armenian refugees and estimates of the dead produces a number greater than the number of Armenians who were in the region. Unlike their figures for later refugees, the Ottomans left no clear data on Muslim refugees of the earlier period.

15. *Documents sur les Atrocités,* pp. 15–16, 30–32, 52–53; Kara Schemsi, *Turcs et Arméniens,* pp. 42–43.

16. *Ermeniler Belgeleri,* pp. 52–54.

17. Rustem, *La Guerre Mondiale,* pp. 98–99.

18. No discussion of the murders of noncombatants in Van City during the fighting of the rebellion, for which there is only limited evidence, is included here. See Kara Schemsi, *Turcs et Arméniens,* pp. 60–62.

19. For the structure and officials of the government, see Mukhitarian, *An Account,* pp. 124–25.

20. Ibid., pp. 116–18. The American missionary Mrs. George C. (Martha) Raynolds wrote that only the "Armenian protected" area was not burned down (ABC 16.9.8, Eastern Turkey Mission, Woman's Board, vol. 2, Eastern Turkey, 1915–1920, Documents and Reports, Letters A–Z, "From Mrs. Clarence Ussher, Van, to Her Home in Connecticut, May 30, 1915").

21. The American missionaries Mrs. G. C. Raynolds and Clarence Ussher made some small admission of the murders of Muslims. Mrs. Raynolds said: "The Armenians seem perfectly debauched—plundering and revenge the only thought of the day, and we

might as well talk to the wall. The Armenians have suffered awfully and the massacring was done so cruelly it is no wonder perhaps that they are swept away now they have a chance to avenge themselves. I think too the thought of Armenians is to make this a purely Armenian province" (ABC 16.9.8, Eastern Turkey Mission, Woman's Board, vol. 1, Eastern Turkey, 1909–1914, Documents and Reports, Letters, A–Z). She was the most honest of the missionaries but made her comments only in a report to the American Board, not publicly. Ussher's statements were more public. He admitted that the Muslim males were murdered, though he was less than forthright about the women and children: "The men they put to death. The women and children they spared" (*An American Physician in Turkey*, p. 285). Strangely for a missionary, he excuses the Armenian behavior. Unless, as in this case, he was forced by the enormity of events to speak against the Armenians, Ussher was in no sense a reliable witness. Dr. Ussher's book has been used so often to describe the events in Van, however, even including a movie based on the book, that it is important to consider his testimony briefly. The flaws in Ussher's work are also an indictment of missionary reports in general.

Ussher plays upon all the prejudices of the time. According to him the Germans were responsible for the Armenians' troubles; Muslims hated Christians and routinely beat and persecuted Armenians; once defeated, the Muslims would convert to Christianity. Rather than simply question Ussher's statements on the Van rebellion, it is perhaps more instructive to consider his reports on other matters. The number of glaring factual errors in the book is astounding: despite his assertions, Germans were never in command in Van. Ussher stated that Ottoman army regiments made up of Armenians "hurled the Russians across the border, capturing one of their cities" (p. 217). No such event took place, of course, and there were no such regiments. Ussher writes that Van governor Ali's policy was to encourage Armenian revolutionary societies to import arms and secure recruits (p. 126), a statement too absurd to need further comment. In one place Ussher holds that Ottoman civil law was the Code Napoléon, which was used to oppress Christians (pp. 156–58)—untrue on both counts. In another place he writes absolute nonsense about the application of Muslim law to Christians (p. 157). According to Ussher, it was Sultan Abdülhamit II's emissaries who "encouraged revolutionary activities" among the Armenians (p. 161). He states that the CUP decided to keep the Capitulations because they were to its own advantage (p. 168). The list of errors goes on.

The British consul in Van in 1905, Captain Tyrrell, knew Dr. Ussher well. Commenting on a letter from Ussher printed in the *London Times,* Tyrrell wrote: "I myself know by experience that Dr. Ussher's statements are unreliable, and I never accept any of them without careful personal enquiry." Tyrrell understand the missionary's impulse to vilify the government: "The key to all this missionary correspondence is found in the last paragraph of Dr. Ussher's letter, 'to stir public opinion by anything that we write'; and nothing is ever written by them to show the other side—how far the Armenians are themselves to blame; outrages by the revolutionists; the difficulties with which the local authorities have to contend; any good work done by Turkish officials, &c." British ambassador O'Conor added, "The United States Minister, whom I spoke to, informed me that he regarded Dr. Ussher as most unreliable, and given to gross exaggeration owing to his innate dislike of Turks and his inordinate fanaticism."

Ussher, in short, is not to be trusted wherever Turks were concerned. His work is only used here in the few areas where his prejudices and outright lies are not evident, such as the comments above and mentions of typhus and starvation.

22. See, for example, *Ermeniler Belgeleri,* pp. 19–22. Most of the reports cited here contain descriptions of individuals killed and sometimes detailed lists.

23. The Armenian sources do not mention this, stating instead that all were delivered to the missionaries. One Muslim woman, however, comments on the Armenian who helped her, gave her money, and hid her in his house (*Ermeniler Belgeleri,* pp. 140–43). Sandık Emini Rupen Efendi is also mentioned as saving the lives of Muslim women by stopping other Armenians from murdering them (*Ermeniler Belgeleri,* pp. 11–12).

24. *Ermeniler Belgeleri,* pp. 11–12, 33–34, 36–38, 52–53, 140–44; Kara Schemsi, *Turcs et Arméniens,* pp. 46–48, 64–65; *Documents sur les Atrocités,* pp. 38–39. The American missionary authors Knapp (*Mission at Van,* pp. 41–42) and Ussher (*An American Physician in Turkey,* pp. 289–91) say that the refugees were completely safe but were thoroughly nasty people. The refugees themselves contradict such statements, and their accounts are completely consistent with each other, even describing the same number of loaves of bread distributed. The missionaries are simply not to be trusted. Mukhitarian (*An Account,* p. 117) states: "A large number of prisoners were taken, mostly unarmed men, women, old men, and even deserted children. None of these were killed." All the survivor statements contradict this, and they give names and details of the murders. Knapp (pp. 41–42) states that 1,000 Muslims were given to the care of the missionaries for protection. According to her, they were sent out to villages "for their safety." The survivors do not mention any order to leave for the countryside, although they do report women leaving on their own. If Knapp was correct, given the fate of Muslim villagers in Van Province (see below), that safety was doubtful.

25. *Documents sur les Atrocités,* p. 10.

26. Many Kurds were excused from military service because they were members of irregular units or were needed to perform agricultural duties and thus were present in their villages.

27. *Ermeniler Belgeleri,* pp. 140–43.

28. See "The Testimony of İbrahim Sargın" in this chapter.

29. Kara Schemsi, *Turcs et Arméniens,* pp. 60–61; *Documents sur les Atrocités,* pp. 10–11, 32–33, 50; *Ermeniler Belgeleri,* p. 10. Some of the names may be misspelled, because they were read in French transliterations of Turkish and Kurdish names. Some also appeared in various forms (e.g., Zeve and Zive). The sources listed contain the names of numerous other destroyed villages, but the informants obviously only listed villages that were close to their homes. Many of them were villagers themselves and probably knew no others beyond their own territory. Reports mention "Aram Paşa" as leading attacks on Muslim villages. This seems unlikely but not impossible. It may be that the attackers said they represented Aram (*Documents sur les Atrocités,* pp. 16, 20).

30. A relatively small number went to Iran. Western Iran was also in the control of the Russians and Armenians, so only members of tribes could have found much safety there. The situation in Iran was fluid, as always. The Russians controlled the cities, the roads, and most border areas. Armenians controlled Salmas and other areas. Nestorian refugees arrived when they were defeated by Kurds and troops early in the war. Kurdish tribes in Iran were never subdued. As seen in the previous chapter, they were a disruptive element, again as always. They were largely neutral in the war, but some took either the Russian or the Russian side, depending on who seemed to be winning.

31. *Ermeniler Belgeleri,* pp. 13–14. Pack animals were limited, having been requisitioned by the army.

32. Kara Schemsi, *Turcs et Arméniens,* p. 61; Justin McCarthy, *Muslims and Minorities* (New York: New York University Press, 1983), pp. 104, 108.

33. *Ermeniler Belgeleri,* pp. 13–14, 34–36, 53–54, 144–45; *Documents sur les Atrocités,* pp. 33–35.

34. *Ermeniler Belgeleri,* p. 24.

35. Some escaped from Van Province to Bitlis Province by boat across Lake Van. Armenian boatmen, who made up most of the boat owners and sailors, took rich refugees across the lake for large sums. This must have appeared to be an easy way to flee, but many never made it to the other shore. Those who did were often at the mercy of partisan bands and Russian soldiers who later moved down the western shore of the lake (Kara Schemsi, *Turcs et Arméniens,* p. 62).

36. Gevaş and Havasor were in themselves areas of considerable partisan attacks on Muslim villages. See *Ermeniler Belgeleri,* pp. 144–45; *Documents sur les Atrocités,* p. 35.

37. *Documents sur les Atrocités,* pp. 20–21; Korganoff, *La participation des Arméniens à la Guerre Mondiale,* p. 26, describes this southern region as "occupée exclusivement par les légions arméniennes et par des formations de volontaires arméniens de la région [occupied exclusively by Armenian legions and by volunteer Armenian units of the region]."

38. The Ottomans estimated that three hundred Russian cavalry and up to a thousand Armenians were in pursuit (*Documents sur les Atrocités,* p. 38).

39. ATASE Arşivi, I. Dünya Harbi Kolleksiyonu, K-2950, D-14, F-1-62.

40. See the many entries on Armenian attacks in Bitlis in Documents 1 and 2 and *Ermeniler Belgeleri.*

41. The complicated troop movements and battles of this period are beyond the scope of this study. See *Türk Harbi,* pp. 688–874; Allen and Muratoff, *Caucasian Battlefields,* pp. 302–63.

42. ATASE Arşivi, I. Dünya Harbi Kolleksiyonu, K-5240, D-6, F-1-14.

43. ATASE Arşivi, I. Dünya Harbi Kolleksiyonu, K-2950, D-26, F-1-39.

44. Ussher (*An American Physician in Turkey,* pp. 311–12) is one of the few sources on these events and is, as always, unreliable. He stated that seven thousand died, as judged by later observation of bones (!), and that Armenians threw themselves over cliffs and murdered their own children rather than have them captured, which seem to be unlikely actions by parents. Ussher also described the attackers as "Turks," although no regular military units were in the area, and said that no refugees were able to pass beyond Bargiri after the missionaries passed, which was also demonstrably untrue. Mukhitarian described the attackers correctly and made no untrue statements on closed avenues of escape, although his estimate of deaths seems incredibly high: "In the mountain passes at Bergery, tens of thousands were killed by Kurds" (Mukhitarian, *An Account,* p. 126). See Ter Minassian, "Van, 1915," p. 242, for Armenian sources on the refugee exodus.

45. See also appendix 3.

46. *Türk Harbi,* pp. 842–52, 857–69; Allen and Muratoff, *Caucasian Battlefields,* pp. 319–22; Korganoff, *La participation des Arméniens à la Guerre Mondiale,* pp. 31–36.

47. Richard G. Hovannisian, *Armenia on the Road to Independence, 1918* (Berkeley: University of California Press, 1967), pp. 58–62.

48. Minister of Agriculture A. V. Krivoshein, quoted in ibid., p. 58.

49. Ibid., pp. 62–64. In fact, purely honorific titles of governor were awarded to Kurds who had rebelled against the Ottomans. See "Siding with the Russians" in chapter 7.

50. A. Hulki Saral, *Vatan nasıl kurtarıldı; Nur Dağları (Amanoslar), Toroslar, Adana, Maraş, Gaziantep ve Urfa'da yapılan kuvayı milliye savaşları* (Ankara: Türkiye İş Bankası Kültür Yayınları, 1970), p. 210.

51. Esat Uras, The Armenians in History and the Armenian Question (Istanbul: Documentary Publications, 1988), pp. 631–33. Korganoff, *La participation des Arméniens à la Guerre Mondiale,* pp. 29–30, mentions only the "reorganization" of the Armenian units, not the problems that necessitated it.

52. *Birinci Dünya Harbinde Türk Harbi, Kafkas Cephesi, 3üncü Ordu Harekâtı* (Ankara: Genelkurmay Basımevi, 1993), vol. 2, p. 428; Allen and Muratoff, *Caucasian Battlefields,* p. 449.

53. The description of what may have been very flexible borders is drawn from A. Marsapetyan, "The Administration of Van," in *Van-Vaspurakani herosamarte 75,* ed. H. M. Poghosyan and H. D. Papazyan (Erevan: Hayastan, 1990) (translated for this study by Birsen Karaca), pp. 115–26. The area described may not have been under complete Armenian control. Marsapetyan gives much detail on the structure of the second Van Armenian government.

54. Richard G. Hovannisian, *The Republic of Armenia,* vol. 1 (Berkeley: University of California Press, 1971), p. 16. Hovannisian earlier wrote that 150,000 had come to Van, Bitlis, Erzurum, and Trabzon by the spring of 1917 (*Armenia on the Road to Independence,* p. 79), but the cited estimate seems more accurate.

55. *Birinci Dünya Harbinde Türk Harbi,* vol. 2, pp. 483, 491–92.

56. See "Political Preparations for Armenian Rebellion" in chapter 8 and appendix 4.

57. "It was necessary to despoil and destroy all Turkish quarters so they could not nurture any hopes of returning" (Mukhitarian, *An Account,* p. 117).

58. Ibid., pp. 116–17. "Everything that carried the signature of the despotic Turkish Government was burned in a few days, torn down, and was shattered under the feet of the Armenian people who were filled with centuries-long feelings of revenge" (Poharyan, "The Legendary Clash in Van," pp. 34–44).

59. There is no need to give long lists of village names here. For examples, see the descriptions in Kara Schemsi, *Turcs et Arméniens devant l'histoire,* pp. 61, 65–68.

60. For detailed lists, see ibid., pp. 67–68 (Bitlis). See also *Documents sur les Atrocités,* p. 24.

61. The Ottomans kept detailed lists of the destruction of the foundations in the various regions. For example, one of many partial lists: "In Gevaş Hacıhanı, Ağdad, Perkuri, Zive ve Hacızive, Pirkal, Mirhasanveli ve Arvas in Müküs, In Şatak [Çatak] kaza Kurandeşt, In Van Vanzivesi, Mollakasım, Van'da Hindibaba, Şeyhabdurrahmangazi, Şeyhgazali, In Gevar kaza Alilan, Yaplan" (*Ermeniler Belgeleri,* p. 11).

62. See appendix 3 for explanations on refugee numbers.

63. FO 371/2768, Stevens to H.M. Principal Secretary of State for Foreign Affairs, Batoum, January 3, 1916.

64. On the conditions in the Armenian Republic, see Hovanissian, *The Republic of Armenia,* pp. 126–33. Hovannisian writes: "Almost 20% of the Republic's population had perished by midyear [1919]" (p. 30).

65. For the considerable aid provided to the Armenians, see James L. Barton, *The Story of Near East Relief* (New York: Macmillan, 1930).

66. McCarthy, *Muslims and Minorities,* pp. 112, 133–37, 159. More precisely, the figure of 194,000 is "population loss," not mortality. It is the number of Muslims in 1922

Destruction and Murder in Van

subtracted from the number in 1912. If anything, these figures underestimate Muslim mortality, because they do not include the proportionately small number of Kurdish migrants known to have left the Armenian Republic for Anatolia. These would have been included in the 1922 figures, making the population loss appear smaller than it was. See *Muslims and Minorities* for precise numbers and calculations.

67. See Justin McCarthy, *Death and Exile: The Ethnic Cleansing of Ottoman Muslims* (Princeton: Darwin, 1995), pp. 222–23, for more details and sources. The 868,962 figure has only been found in summary form. In more detailed, more preliminary, figures for October 1916, the Refugee Commission estimated 200,000 refugees from Van and Bitlis Provinces, but stated that the count surely represented an undercount of 20 percent. In reality the undercount was much greater than 20 percent. For a detailed document of the Ottoman response to the refugee crisis, see *Documents on Ottoman Armenians,* 3 vols. (Ankara: Prime Ministry Directorate General of Press and Information, 1982, 1983, 1986), vol. 1, pp. 118–24.

68. The Report of Niles and Sutherland in Justin McCarthy, "American Commissions to Anatolia and the Report of Niles and Sutherland," *Türk Tarih Kurumu Kongresi XI, Ankara: 5–9 Eylül 1990* (Ankara: Türk Tarih Kurumu, 1994), pp. 1809–53.

69. McCarthy, *Death and Exile,* p. 217.

70. See, for example, Documents sur les Atrocités, pp. 51–52; Ermeniler Belgeleri, p. 23; Kara Schemsi, Turcs et Arméniens devant l'histoire, p. 40. Justin McCarthy met İbrahim Sargın on two occasions and traveled with him to the site of Zeve village, now an empty valley with a monument dedicated to the dead. Though by that time seventy years had passed since the events, Sargın's memories were clear and detailed. He spoke in much greater detail than in the testimony quoted here. This account is a translation of Sargın's testimony as printed in A. Süslü, G. Öğün, and T. Serdar, Van, Bitlis, Muş ve Kars'taki Ermeni Katliamları (Ankara: Van Yüzüncü Yıl Üniversitesi, 1994), pp. 34–39.

71. Other Muslim villages were sometimes armed and resisted, but they could not stand against both the local Armenians and those from Russia (see, for example, *Documents sur les Atrocités,* pp. 19–20). The government had distributed guns to some villages, as Sargın notes. The weapons were given to both Armenian and Muslim villages, as described in chapter 8.

72. The term translated here as "captured," *esir kaldık,* implies "enslavement."

CHAPTER 10

Conclusion

The Armenian revolutionaries lost. Decades of preparation only led them to ultimate disaster. Yet it is hard to fault the Armenian revolutionaries' tactical plan or its implementation. Aram Manukian must be counted as one of the geniuses of guerrilla warfare. Long before more modern revolutionaries coined phrases such as "rely on the peasants," Manukian realized that rural organization should be the cornerstone of the rebels' program. Arming, training, and organizing the Armenian peasantry was the basis of his most critical success. The capture of Van City from the Ottomans may have been the most visible feature of the Dashnak triumph, but it was the Armenian actions in the countryside that most damaged the Ottoman war effort—and that was the work of the villagers organized by Aram Manukian. In World War I the Armenians did exactly what was needed to aid Russian victory: holding down Ottoman units many times the size of the rebel forces, crippling military communications, forcing hundreds of thousand of refugees onto the roads to hinder army movements, and ultimately making the Ottomans abandon strategies that might have won the war in the East.

The problem with the Armenian rebellion was that it was necessarily dependent on others. The rebellion could never have triumphed on its own, because Armenians were such a small minority in the territory they claimed. They were dependent on intervention from a European power. These powers, however, never were willing to do what had to be done to create an Armenia on Ottoman soil. England and France were unwilling to commit the great number of troops that would be needed to create such a state and then to keep an Armenian minority in power. Their own diplomats and military leaders counseled against it. Moreover, there was always Russia to consider. Russia would never countenance an Armenia that was dependent on another power. Russia wanted Eastern Anatolia for itself. It did not hesitate to betray the Armenians once they were no longer of use. Instead of allowing, much less assisting, the Armenians to return to Van and create their Armenia, the Russians let them starve in the Southern Caucasus. The Dashnaks and their followers had done all that could be expected of them, but they failed because they trusted the Russians.

The Armenian revolution was always a futile endeavor. Armenian rebels might aid in destroying the Ottoman Empire, but they would never gain their state. With hindsight it seems that the revolutionaries should have known this, but nationalism is seldom rational.

After decades of preparation for revolution it probably would have been impossible for the Dashnaks to have done anything but oppose the Ottomans in World War I. One cannot help believing, though, that the fate of the Armenian people of Van would have been much better if they had kept their allegiance to the Ottomans. At worst they, and Van's Muslims, would have survived under Ottoman or Russian rule—a much better fate than the one the revolutionaries brought upon themselves.

Could the Ottomans have stopped the Armenian revolutionaries and escaped the destruction of Van? The Ottomans fought what is today called a guerrilla war in Eastern Anatolia. To understand the Ottoman failure in that war it is instructive to compare the Ottoman battle against the Armenian revolutionaries with the "five major mistakes in strategy and tactics" expounded by the expert in guerrilla warfare, Mao Tse-Tung. Mao described the errors that defeat a counterinsurgency campaign:

- Piecemeal Reinforcement. (Deploying a minimum number of troops and adding to them when needed.) Instead, a maximum amount of troops must be deployed to defeat the guerrillas in a decisive attack.
- Lack of Strategic Coordination. (A number of commanders each pursuing his own strategy and not cooperating fully with the others.) Forces must all follow a central plan and be directed by a central authority.
- Absence of a Main Direction of Attack. (Fighting the insurgents in a number of places at once and allowing them to set the conditions of battle.) Forces should not be divided to fight in a number of places. They should be massed to attack in one area, then move on to the next fight.
- Encirclement of Large But Annihilation of Small Numbers. (Winning battles, but allowing the enemy to escape.) The enemy must be destroyed or captured, not only engaged in battle and let escape.
- Failure to Grasp Strategic Opportunities. (Not following up victories

over insurgents.) Rebels should be pressed and never allowed to re-group.[1]

The Ottomans violated each of these principles. It is hard to see how they could have done otherwise.

Ottoman reinforcement against the revolutionary enemy was indeed piecemeal. In each of the major disruptions in Van the troops on hand were never sufficient. In 1896, 1908, and 1915 reinforcements had to be brought in. The troops available in 1896 were more than enough to stop the rebellion in Van but insufficient to capture the rebels or stop Kurdish reprisals, as was also the case in 1908. In 1915 not only were the forces in Van insufficient, but reinforcements could not arrive to save the city or the province. The reason was not military ignorance. There were never enough soldiers. The same condition was seen in Ottoman battles against guerrillas in Macedonia and Crete. It must also be said the Abdülhamit II's military policies contributed to the problem. Always justifiably fearful of his own military, he did not develop it sufficiently. It is doubtful, however, that the sultan could have done enough, even if he spent every available lira on the army. The Ottoman population was too small to face enemies on all sides and patrol often indefensible borders.

"Strategic Coordination" may have been an alien concept to the Otto-mans. The traditional Ottoman system of rule in the provinces was based on a very different concept—the division of power. For centuries the gov-ernor, the general (ferik), and the head of the judiciary (kadı) in each province were expected to watch over and check the power of each other. The power of the judiciary waned in the late nineteenth century, but the military and civilian leaders were as often at odds as they were cooperat-ing. The governor might build up a cadre of supporters in the military, just as the ferik would count on supporters in the bureaucracy. Both appealed to friends in the palace in Istanbul. When the general and the governor saw eye-to-eye all went well, but they often did not agree. The situation was complicated by the authority structure of one part of the military, the Hamidiye, which was under the control of a general in Erzurum, not of anyone in Van. The first sign that the Ottomans recognized that this disunity was hampering effective governance came in the time of Ali Rıza, arguably too late.

There was no "main direction of attack" in the fight against the Armenian rebels, and Ottoman forces fighting the rebels were always di-vided. This study has only considered the provinces of Van and, to a lesser extent, Bitlis, but Ottoman forces fought Armenian rebels in all the provinces of Eastern Anatolia, in Cilicia, in Trabzon, and even sometimes in Western Anatolia and Istanbul itself. The Ottomans never truly brought the attack to the Armenian rebels. It is easy to see what should have been done: Western Iran should have been invaded by a major force that destroyed the Armenian base in the Salmas region. The villages on the arms-smuggling routes should have been occupied. But again, where would the manpower for such a venture have come from? And what would the Ottomans have done in the resulting war with Russia, which had its own interests in Western Iran and never would have tolerated an Ottoman invasion there? Indeed, the optimum strategy for defeating the revolutionaries necessarily would have included war with Russia and the permanent closure of Armenian infiltration routes to the north as well as the east. These are absurd thoughts for an empire that had lost its wars to the Russians and had been invaded by Russia three times in the nineteenth century.

The Ottomans surely won battles and lost the war in Van. They defeated the revolutionaries in 1896 and 1908. Each time the real enemy escaped. That enemy was not the relative few who managed to flee across the Iranian border. The enemy was the revolutionaries who were allowed to stay behind, especially the Dashnak leaders and cadres in Van. The military victories in 1896 and 1908 were never followed by measures that might actually win the war. The attack against the revolutionaries should have been internal and political. Allowing one's enemies to propagandize and freely to organize military cadres inside one's country has all the appearances of political suicide. Yet this is exactly what the Ottomans allowed the revolutionaries to do. Being caught while distributing revolutionary literature might result in a trial and perhaps imprisonment. Running guns was an offense for which people would be tried, if they survived the firefight at the border. But European intervention and imperial amnesties freed those who were demonstrably guilty of treason. Operating a school for revolutionaries under the guise of religion on the Island of Akhtamar was not prosecuted.

The most direct attack on the revolutionaries, and one of which Chairman Mao would surely have approved, would have been to kill them. In most countries fighting an insurrection, captured guerrillas were summarily executed. Spreading the message of the revolution or transporting arms was also cause for execution, or at least a long sentence in a deep dungeon. Why did the Ottomans not exterminate the Dashnaks? Why was a rebel like Aram Manukian, a subject of an unfriendly power, allowed to walk the streets of Van freely, hold a position in the Armenian Church, and organize a revolution when everyone—Armenians, Turks,

Kurds, European consuls, Ottoman officials—knew that he was plotting the overthrow of the government? How did Ishkhan, a Dashnak leader known to be guilty of murdering the deputy of the catholicos, escape the hangman? Why were Aram, Ishkhan, and the others who were guilty of storing thousands of weapons in preparation for revolution pardoned?

To some extent the survival of the leaders of the Dashnaks and other revolutionaries was a relic of the Ottoman system of government. Although seldom recognized as such by their critics, the Ottomans were decidedly lenient in punishing political dissent. To see this, one need only compare the Ottoman record to the punishments imposed on those who opposed foreign rule in European colonies or to the political executions in many states in modern times. In the Ottoman Empire it was not only the Dashnaks and Hunchaks who usually escaped execution. Abdülhamit seldom executed his enemies among the Young Turks either; he bought them off or exiled them. Also, religious communities (*millets*) had been allowed to govern their own affairs since the earliest days of the empire. The tradition of religious separatism conditioned the Ottomans to avoid intervening in millet business whenever possible. Armenians were left to run their own affairs, even when this had become a dangerous policy.

It was not only Ottoman tolerance that allowed the Armenian revolutionaries to operate so openly and successfully. The Ottomans might well have forgotten their traditions and fought the rebels forcefully and violently were it not for European intervention. The Ottomans knew that any prosecution of Armenian rebels, no matter how guilty of treason, could result in a public outcry in Europe that would force, or allow, the European states finally to dismember the empire. The Ottomans knew that they would never receive a sympathetic hearing in Europe. European newspapers only reported the sufferings of Armenians, never Muslims, partly because the real story was suppressed. European consuls in the Ottoman East reported the activities of the revolutionaries in detail. Many of them accurately described the destruction that the rebels were bringing to the land. When newspapers reported highly exaggerated accounts of the suffering of Armenians or printed outright lies about events in provinces such as Van, consuls repeatedly pointed out the falsehoods. No retractions were printed. A strange thing had happened as this information went on its way to European capitals—as far as the European public was concerned, it never arrived. Ambassadors considerably toned down reports on the Armenian revolutionaries before forwarding them to their capitals. Politicians neglected such reports altogether. By the time information on the rebels reached "Prime Minister's Question Time" or the *Times* hardly a bad word was to be heard of any Armenian.

The place of the European powers in the destruction of Van and much of the rest of Eastern Anatolia is one of self-interest, religious prejudice, and hypocrisy. They directly intervened in Ottoman governance and justice. They demanded and received privileges for the revolutionaries. Not the least of these was the protection that extraterritoriality afforded the Russian subjects who led the revolution in Van. European actions can only have encouraged the revolutionaries in their belief that their plan of massacre and reprisal would indeed lead to European intervention in their favor.

What the Ottomans most needed to reform Eastern Anatolia, as attested by the Europeans' own representatives, was money. Soldiers were necessary to enforce civil security, yet not even the minimal number of soldiers available could be properly paid. Taxes needed to be remitted for those too poor to pay. Development projects were essential, even small projects such as providing seed to farmers so that they could feed themselves. Yet the Ottoman government could not even provide the minimal sums set out in its budgets for the province. Much of the problem was the poor economic ability of the Ottoman government, but the Ottomans were also kept from putting their economy in order by the Capitulations and other laws that completely favored Europeans, enforced by European military power. Worse than any cause of state poverty, though, was the effect of Russian military action against the Ottomans. The Russians invaded the Ottoman Empire in 1806, 1828, 1853, and 1877–78. They left behind destruction, a much weakened tax base, and the loss of territories such as Bulgaria, in which the Ottomans had spent much of their limited capital for development. Then the Russians demanded, and received, reparations from those they had attacked.

Failure to grasp strategic opportunities was most evident in 1896. That would have been the time to destroy the revolutionaries. Their hold on the Armenian population, especially in the villages, was still tenuous. The church and the merchants were still largely opposed to them. Their revolutionary intentions were obvious. They never should have been allowed back into the city of Van.

The arms discoveries of 1908 were perhaps the last chance to oppose the revolutionaries' control of the Armenian populace. Here, once again, politics intervened, this time the politics of the Committee of Union and Progress. A coalition of politically naïve military men and political idealists pardoned the 1908 rebels and allowed them to complete their organization under the banner of political democracy. The Dashnak Party was, in effect, recognized by the new government as the proper representative of the empire's Armenians. The traditional centers of power in the Armenian community—the merchants and the church—were cast off. All could see that it was the Dashnaks who were in power. The CUP had accepted the situation for its own political purposes, because Young Turk ideologues firmly believed that a measure of ethnic autonomy would bring the rebels into the Ottoman fold. They were as naïve in their own way as were the Armenians who believed they could trust Russia. Some of the Armenian revolutionaries may have thought that by cooperation with the CUP they would gain their goals. The creation of the inspectorates in Eastern Anatolia indicates they may have been correct. But the revolutionaries also continued to build up their arms stockpiles. When war came, they showed that their allegiance had never been to the Ottoman state.

Revolutions are most often judged by their outcomes. A successful revolution hails its champions as freedom fighters who created the new nation. A failed revolution leaves behind "terrorists" or "idealistic failures," usually hung by those whom they tried to unseat. The Armenian revolution was an even deeper failure than other lost revolutions. Not only were its warriors ultimately defeated, but the entire Armenian population of the Ottoman East was exiled from its homeland. Rather than create a New Armenia, the revolutionaries created a land without Armenians.

Failure, of course, does not necessarily mean that revolutionaries are wrong to revolt. The moral quality of any revolution is difficult to evaluate. In Ottoman terms, the rebels were traitors to a state that, while imperfect, had allowed them to live with their religion and customs intact for many centuries. The revolutionaries, their followers, and ultimately most of the Armenian population of the East had sided with the enemies of their own state, attacked their fellow subjects, and greatly aided in the downfall of the empire. To the Armenian revolutionaries, all these activities were justified by their goal. They had long believed that the lives of both Muslims and Armenians, including their own, were expendable. Their political ethics were the ethics of radical nationalism.

Only by the peculiar logic of radical nationalism could an Armenian revolution in the Ottoman Empire ever have been justified. It could only be considered just by those who believed that their people deserved to rule their own nation-state, no matter who was living on the land they claimed. For those whose ideology is majority rule, "one person, one vote," the at-

McCarthe et. al

p. 265 — 6

tempt by a minority to rule over a majority through force can never be justified. And the Armenians were a distinct minority in what they called Armenia. They made up less than 20 percent of the inhabitants of the so-called Six Vilayets, the region claimed as Armenia. Muslims were nearly 80 percent.

This does not mean that there could not have been a moral justification for revolution in the Ottoman domains. Ignoring the dangers inherent in any armed revolt, lack of democracy can be seen as cause enough for revolution. Indeed, that was the justification for the Ottoman Revolution of 1908–9. The difference between the revolt of 1908 and the revolution planned by the Armenians lay in its aims. Most of the 1908 revolutionaries wanted an empire containing many ethnic groups and religions. Most wanted a democracy, although they were not quite able to attain it. The Armenian revolutionaries wanted neither a unified empire nor a democracy, at least not a democracy of one person, one vote.

The Armenian revolt was an integral part of the great disaster that overcame the people of the Ottoman East. The slaughter of Muslims that accompanied the Armenian revolt in Van Province inexorably led first to Kurdish reprisals on the Armenians then to a general and mutual massacre of the peoples of the East. The Armenian revolt began an intercommunal war in which both sides, fearing for their own survival, killed those who, given the chance, would have killed them. The result was unprecedented horror. History records few examples of mortality as great as that suffered in Van Province: perhaps some regions during the Black Death, deaths in parts of eastern Iran during the Mongol invasion, disease mortality among Native Americans in North America, the attrition of Africans during slave deportation. German losses during the Thirty Years War or Russian losses in the Revolution cannot compare to the suffering and deaths in Van.

Judged by its own goals—the creation of an Armenian state and justice and freedom for the Armenians—the rebellion was in every sense a failure. Before World War I and the final Armenian revolt, the Armenians of the Ottoman East had been part of a troubled but slowly improving polity—economically better off than their fellow subjects and with considerable political power. Within the Russian Empire, Armenian political life and personal freedom were restricted but existent. After the wars, all had become worse for the Armenians. The Armenians of Eastern Anatolia were largely gone—emigrated or dead. The Soviets had put the Armenians of the Armenian Republic, including the refugees from Anatolia, under a domination that was far more complete and oppressive than that of the tsar or the sultan. Despite all the difficulties of life in the Ottoman East, remaining loyal to the Ottoman Empire would have been the better choice.

NOTE

1. Mao Tse-Tung, "On Protracted War," in Jay Mallin, ed., *Strategy for Conquest: Communist Documents on Guerilla Warfare* (Coral Gables, Fla.: University of Miami, 1970), pp. 108–11. The order of the errors has been changed.

APPENDIX I

Place Names

The list includes names as used in this book, variants seen on contemporary maps and in documents and books, and modern spellings. Names that have remained as they were in the nineteenth century (e.g., Van, Bitlis) do not appear in the list. Variant spellings not listed here are sometimes seen, especially in older maps. These names are usually easy to recognize, however: most commonly, umlauts are omitted and where the modern spelling uses *h* the old map uses *kh,* following Arabic usage. *D* and *t* and *b* and *p* are often interchanged. The Turkish characters *ş* and *ç* appear as *sh* and *ch,* respectively. Examples of these changes can be seen in the list below.

THIS VOLUME	VARIANTS	MODERN NAME
Abak Plain	Abaak, Abagha, Abağa	Çaldıran Plain
Adilcevaz	Adeljivaz, Adiljevas, Adil Jevaz	Adilcevaz
Ahlat	Akhlat	Ahlat
Akhtamar Island	Aghtamar, Aq Damar	Akdamar Island
Amadiya	Amadia	Al Amadiyeh
Bargiri	Beigir Kaleh, Begri, Aghbak	Muradiye
Başkale	Bash Kaleh	Başkale
Bayazıt	Bayazid, Beyazit	Doğuayazıt
Çatak	Şatak, Shadakh, Shataq, Shattakh	Çatak
Çölemerik	Hakkâri, Julamerk	Hakkâri
Dilman		Shapur
Dir	Der	Albayrak
Diyadin	Diadin	Diyadin
Diyarbakır	Diarbekr	Diyarbakır

267

Echmiadzin	Etchmiadind	Echmiadzin
Edremit	Atremid, Adremid	Sarmansuyu
Erçek	Arshak, Arshag, Archag, Archek	Erçek
Erciş	Ardjish, Arjish, Arjesh	Erciş
Erek, Mount	Varak, Varag, Varagavank	Erek
Erivan	Erevan, Yerevan	Yerevan
Erzincan	Erzingan	Erzincan
Erzurum	Erzerum, Erzeroum	Erzurum
Gevar	Gavar	Yüksekova
Gevaş	Vostan, Vastan, Kavash	Gevaş
Hakkâri	Hekkiari	Hakkâri
Hınıs	Khanus, Hinis	Hınıs
Hizan	Khisan, Khizan	Hizan
Hoşap	Hoşab, Koshab, Khoshab, Khushab	Güzelsu
Iğdır	Igdir, Ighdir	Iğdır
Kağızman	Kaghizman, Kaghisman	Kağızman
Karakilise	Kara Kilise, Kara Kilissa	Karaköse
Khoy	Hoy, Khoi	Khowy
Koçanis	Kochannes, Kocanis	Konak
Kop	Bulanik, Kop Bulanik	Bulanık
Lim Island		Yaka Island
Malazgirt	Melasgird, Manzikert	Malazgirt
Müküs	Meuks, Moks, Mukus	Bahçesaray
Nahçıvan	Nakhichewan, Nakhitchevan, Nakhichevan	Naxçıvan
Neri	Nehri	Bağlar
Patnos	Patnotz	Patnos
Saray	Serai, Mahmudie, Mahmudiye	Saray
Sasun	Sassun, Sasson	Sason
Savuçbulak	Sauj Bulak, Suj Bulak, Soujbulak	Mahabad
Şemdinan	Shemsdin	Şemdinli
Siirt	Sairt, Sert	Siirt
Tatvan	Tadvan	Tatvan
Urmia	Rumiye, Rezaieh	Urumiyeh
Zeytun	Zeitun	Süleymanlı

Armenians in the Van Government

1871

Van Sancak Administrative Council (Meclis-i İdare)	Şiran Bey, Agop Ağa
Provincial Council of Notables (Meclis-i Mütemeyyiz)	Kirkor Ağa, Karabet Ağa
City Council (Meclis-i Belediye)	Mığırdıç Ağa, Kivork Ağa
Menfaat Sandığı	Ohannes Ağa, Vartan Ağa
Provincial Council Administration Treasurer (Meclis-i Liva Kalemi Sandık Emini)	Agop Ağa
Among the Land Registration Officials (Tahrir Dairesi Memurin-i Seyyare Arasında)	Mığırdıç Ağa
Elbak Kaza Treasurer	Hacik Ağa
Çölemerik Kaza Treasurer	Simon Ağa
Gevar Kaza Treasurer	Mığırdıç Ağa
Gevar Administrative Council	Avadis Ağa
Gevar Council of Justice Member (Meclis-i Deavi Üyesi)	Ohannes Ağa, Yasef Ağa
Mahmudi Administrative Council Member	Nasturi Keto Ağa, Karabet Ağa
Mahmudi Council of Justice Member	Nasturi Yasef Ağa, Mardirus Ağa
Erciş Kaza Treasurer	David Ağa
Erciş Council of Justice Member	Mülkun Ağa, Simon Ağa
Adilcevaz Kaza Council of Justice Member	Manok Ağa, Avanos Ağa
Müküs Kaza Treasurer	Cevher Ağa
Müküs Administrative Council Member	Kirkor Ağa
Müküs Council of Justice Member	Kilos Ağa

Gevaş Kaza Treasurer	Ağas Ağa
Gevaş Administrative Council Member	Karabet Ağa
Gevaş Council of Justice Member	Artin Ağa
Şatak Kaza Treasurer	Azis Ağa
Şatak Council of Justice Member	Artin Ağa
Van Customs Administration Treasurer (Rüsumat Müdüriyeti'nde Sandık Emini)	Simon Ağa
Van Commercial Court Member (Ticaret Mahkemesi'nde)	Mıgırdıç Ağa, Mıgırdıç Ağa, Panos Ağa

Source: Salname-i Vilâyet-i Erzurum, 1288 Hicri Senesi (Erzurum: Erzurum Vilâyeti Matbaası, 1289), pp. 58–68, 124, 133.

1876

Van Sancak Administrative Council Member	Agop Ağa
Provincial Council of Appeals Member	Kevork Ağa
City Council Member	Mıgırdıç Ağa, Kevork Ağa
Auditor's Office Treasurer (Muhasebe Kaleminde Sandık Emini)	Karabet Efendi
Land Registration Commission Member (Tahrir Komisyonu'nda)	Mıgırdıç Ağa, Kevork Ağa, Karabet Ağa
Benefits Fund (Menfaat Sandığı)	Hayrabet Ağa, Karabet Ağa
Commercial Court Member	Panos Ağa, Mıgırdıç Ağa, another Mıgırdıç Ağa
Elbak Kaza Finance Office Treasurer (Mal Müdürlüğü'nün Sandık Emini)	Kevork Ağa
Elbak Administrative Council Member	Papa Ağa, Artin Ağa
Çölemerik Kaza Finance Office Treasurer	Agop Ağa
Çölemerik Administrative Council Member	Barut Ağa, Balon Ağa
Gevar Kaza Administrative Council Member	Üydis Ağa, Milyin Ağa
Gevar Council of Justice Member	David Ağa, Osmaset Ağa
Erciş Kaza Administrative Council Member	Sitran Ağa, Agob Ağa
Erciş Council of Justice Member	Melyin Ağa
Mahmudi Kaza Finance Office Treasurer	Agop Ağa
Mahmudi Administrative Council Member	Agop Ağa, Kirkor Ağa
Gevaş Kaza Finance Office Treasurer	Agop Ağa
Gevaş Administrative Council Member	Kazer Ağa, Sehak Ağa
Müküs Kaza Administrative Council Member	Vartan Ağa, Kilos Ağa

Müküs Council of Justice Member	Kilos Ağa
Şatak Kaza Administrative Council Member	Artin Ağa, Serkes Ağa
Şatak Council of Justice Member	Artin Ağa

Source: Salname-i Vilâyet-i Erzurum, 1293 Hicri Senesi (Erzurum: Erzurum Vilâyeti Matbaası, 1293), pp. 101–8.

1897

Van Province Governor's Deputy (Vali Yardımcısı)	Ohannes Ferid Efendi
Van Province Administrative Council Member (İdare Meclisi Üyesi)	Patriarch's Representative Arsen Efendi, Artin Efendi, Avidis Efendi
Van and Bitlis Justice Inspector (Adliye Müfettişi)	Viçin Efendi
Monopolies Director (Reji Müdürü)	Nikolaki Efendi
Chief Engineer (Sermühendis)	Sister Efendi
Provincial Accounting Office, Assistant Registrar (Vilâyet Muhasebe Kalemi Mukayyid Muavini)	Abdah Efendi
Treasurer	Mardirus Efendi
Taxation Official (Vergi Memuru)	Abdah Efendi
Cadastral Survey Official (Tahrir Memuru)	Keşişyan Dikran Ağa
Police Organization Third Commissioner (Polis Teşkilatında Üçüncü Komiser)	Agop Efendi
Police Officer (Polis Memuru)	Manok Efendi, Haçiyen Efendi, Ohannes Efendi, Teşan Efendi
Matbaa İdaresi'nde Mürettip	Ohannes Vartan Efendi
Makinesi Printing Machinist	Blozyan Ohannes Efendi
Assistant Lithography Official (Litografya Memuru Muavini)	Abdah Efendi
Court of Appeals Member (Mahkeme-i İstinaf Üyesi)	Gabriyel Efendi, Markar Efendi
Court of Appeals Penalties Division Member (İstinaf Mahkemesi Ceza Dairesi Üyesi)	Kirkor Efendi, Bogos Efendi
Public Prosecutor Accounts Clerk (Müdde-i Umumisi Hesap Katibi)	Vartan Efendi
Grand Jury Member (Heyet-i İttihamiyesi Bidayet Azası)	Agop Efendi
Grand Jury Legal Division Member (Bidayet Mahkemesi Hukuk Dairesi Üyesi)	Panos Efendi
Grand Jury Penalties Division Member (Bidayet Mahkemesi Ceza Dairesi Üyesi)	Agop Efendi

Commercial Court Member (Ticaret Mahkemesi Üyesi)	Bogos Ağa
City Council Member (Belediye Meclisi Üyesi)	Agop Ağa
Municipal Secretariat Inspector (Belediye Kalemi Müfettişi)	Markar Efendi
Agricultural Bank Office, Deputy Head of Section (Ziraat Bankası Dairesi Şube Muavini)	Abdah Efendi
Agricultural Bank Council (Ziraat Bankası Meclisi)	Agop Ağa
Monopolies Office Director (Reji Dairesi Müdürü)	Nikolay Efendi
Accountant (Muhasebe Memuru)	Mıgırdıç Efendi
Warehouse Official (Anbar Memuru)	Antuvan Efendi
Factory Official (Fabrika Memuru)	Mıgırdıç Ağa
Quarantine Office Doctor (Karantina Dairesi Doktoru)	Blavu Efendi

Source: Van Vilâyeti, *Van Vilâyeti Salnamesi, 1315* (Van: Matbaa-i Vilâyet, 1315), pp. 134–49.

These tables, covering three years, are representative of a much larger number of Armenians in Ottoman service in Van Province. Others are given by Mesrob Krikorian in his survey of Armenians in the Ottoman government.[1] For example, Markos Aghabekian was the assistant to the governor of Van in 1896, Tigran Amirdjanian was the head of the education council of Van from 1893 to 1897, Armenak Boyadjian was the assistant of the deputy-governor of Gevaş Kaza from 1905 to 1906, Ferit Yovhannes Boyadjian was the assistant of the governor of Van from 1896 to 1907, Karabet Efendi was the assistant to the deputy-governor of Çatak Kaza in 1902 and 1903, Stephan Melikian was the assistant of the provincial governor of Van in 1896, Nazareth Tcharukhdjian was a police superintendent in Van in 1908, and Vardan Efendi was the assistant to the deputy-governor of Gevaş Kaza in 1902 and 1903. There were many others.

Note that the coverage in the tables is different. The first two consider bureaucrats and advisors in districts, but not many in the Van administrative center, presumably because Van was a part of Erzurum Province in 1871 and 1876. The 1897 table does not list district officials.

NOTE

1. Mesrob K. Krikorian, *Armenians in the Service of the Ottoman Empire 1860–1908* (London: Routledge and Kegan Paul, 1977), p. 38.

APPENDIX 3

Armenian Refugees

Armenian refugees from Van went to the Southern Caucasus in three waves. They first arrived when the Ottomans began to conscript Armenians in earnest and increased when the empire mobilized. That wave included men of draft age and many of their families. The second wave came in July–August 1915, when the Russians evacuated Van. It included virtually the entire Armenian population of the province. Only a relatively small number of Armenians were allowed to return to Van after that. Their numbers increased when the Russian army dissolved and Armenian refugees returned briefly to Van. These fled when the Turks retook the province.

Figures on Armenian refugees from Anatolia were often very unreliable. One compilation used by the Allies was made "according to information obtained by Mr. Sarebey, the Dragoman of the Vice-Consulate at Van, from the Armenian bishop at Erivan, etc." That list (December 1915) included 173,000 Armenian refugees from the Ottoman Empire residing in the Caucasus: 105,000 from Van Province, 48,000 from Erzurum Province, and 20,000 from Bitlis Province.[1] Various sources estimated 150,000 in July 1915, but more were known to have come later.[2] Armenians offered an estimate of "more than 100,000" refugees at that time from Van Province alone.[3] This was obviously a very rough estimate, but it seems only slightly inflated, because it represents 77 percent of the prewar Armenian population of Van.[4] The estimate did not include the smaller number who would have gone from Van to the Armenian settlements in Iran or any of the refugees from Bitlis and Erzurum Provinces.

No one seems to have made a census of the number of Armenian refugees in the Southern Caucasus after World War I and the Turkish War of Independence. British intelligence did create one table based on Armenian sources, but it was accompanied by a note from the brigadier-general in

charge, stating that the statistics were unreliable. In any case, the data were
not for refugees but for refugees in need of assistance.[5]

The number of Armenian refugees waiting to return to Anatolia in
1919 was usually given by Armenian sources as "300,000."[6] These figures
generally seem to include refugees from Kars Province in Russia, which
had not been part of the Ottoman Empire. It is often impossible to tell
who was included in estimates of the number of refugees. One statement
of "refugees who await return" might include the Kars refugees, another
might not; and neither would identify the inclusion or exclusion of the
Kars Armenians.

Despite the confusion in the sources, analysis indicates that there were
indeed at least 300,000 Armenian refugees in the Caucasus.

Armenians in the Russian Caucasus, 1917

Total Population	1,783,000
Native Population	1,444,000
Difference (Refugees)	339,000

Armenians in Ottoman Anatolia, 1912

Erzurum	163,000
Van	131,000
Bitlis	191,000
Total	485,000

The 1897 Russian census recorded 1,161,909 Armenians in the Caucasus
region, which included Azerbaijan, Erivan, Georgia, Kars-Ardahan, and
nearby areas.[7] This population would have increased naturally to 1,444,000
by 1914.[8] The Armenian population could not have increased during wartime. Many of the potential fathers were gone, and births would only have
canceled out deaths, so the native Armenian population in the Russian
South Caucasus in 1917 can be assumed to have been the same 1,444,000.
Richard Hovannisian has quoted figures from "an official Russian source"
for the Armenian population of the Caucasus in 1917: 1,783,000.[9] Sub-
tracting the 1,444,000 natives from the 1,783,000 leaves 339,000. Those
339,000 must have been refugees from Eastern Anatolia.

The "extra" 339,000 Armenians can only have been refugees from the
Ottoman Empire. They would have included some refugees from Iran and
a small number of Armenians who returned from the United States and

elsewhere to fight on the Russian side, but these small numbers would have had little effect. Hovannisian estimates: "By the end of 1916, nearly three hundred thousand Ottoman Armenians had sought safety in Transcaucasia, where nearly half were destined to die from famine and disease."[10] Many of these refugees died (as seen in chapter 9), but more refugees came later.

The refugees from Ottoman Anatolia can only have come from three provinces—Erzurum, Van, and Bitlis, which together held 485,000 Armenians before the war.[11] It is unthinkable that many might successfully have made the journey from farther afield. If Hovannisian's figures for 1917 are correct, then 70 percent of the Armenians from Erzurum, Van, and Bitlis must have fled to the Russian Empire. Of course, his figures for 1917 are probably overestimates of the Armenian population. If half the refugees had died, however, lower estimates of the 1917 population would still have yielded a figure near 339,000.[12]

NOTES

1. FO 371/2768, Stevens to H.M. Principal Secretary of State for Foreign Affairs, Batoum, December 29, 1916. Stevens states that earlier Russian official figures listed 140,000.

2. FO 371/2768, Stevens to H.M. Principal Secretary of State for Foreign Affairs, Batoum, January 3, 1916.

3. Anahide Ter Minassian, "Van, 1915," in *Armenian Van/Vaspurakan,* ed. Richard G. Hovannisian (Costa Mesa, Calif.: Mazda Publishers), p. 242.

4. On Ottoman Armenian population, see Justin McCarthy, *Muslims and Minorities* (New York: New York University Press, 1983), pp. 70–78; Justin McCarthy, "The Population of the Ottoman Armenians," in *The Armenians in the Late Ottoman Period,* ed. Türkkaya Ataöv (Ankara: Turkish Historical Society/Grand National Assembly of Turkey, 2001), pp. 65–86; Hikmet Özdemir, Kemal Çiçek, Ömer Turan, Ramazan Çalık, and Yusuf Halaçoğlu, *Ermeniler: Sürgün ve Göç* (Ankara: Türk Tarih Kurumu, 2004). The calculations in this appendix are by Justin McCarthy. Ömer Turan's calculations (based on the volume by Özdemir et al.) would result in a higher number of surviving Armenian refugees and thus a lower Armenian mortality.

5. The table listed 133,850 refugees requiring assistance to be repatriated to "Turkish Armenia," 118,500 to Kars (more Armenians than there had been in Kars before the war, according to the Russian census), 83,710 to somewhere else, and 318,714 Russian Armenians who needed assistance (FO 608/79, Calthorpe to H.M. Principal Secretary of State for Foreign Affairs, Constantinople, April 19, 1919). Both high and low estimates abounded, always given without sources. General W. H. Beach (Staff Intelligence), who doubted the Armenian estimates, gave his own estimates: "Total requiring relief [including nonrefugees from Russian Armenia]: somewhere up to 500,000, of whom a total of from 200,000 to 300,000 are actually in danger of death by starvation" (ibid.). There were numerous uninformed estimates at the time. See, for example, FO 608/79, Dr. C. D.

Ussher, A.C.R.N.E., "A Plea for the Repatriation of the Armenians and the Kurds," which is typical of Ussher—estimates created from whole cloth. For a very complete description of various estimates of Armenian refugees and different calculations, see Özdemir et al., *Ermeniler: Sürgün ve Göç,* pp. 89–174.

6. Boghos Nubar Paşa and Avetis Aharonian, who represented Western Armenian interests at the Peace Conference, gave the figure of 300,000 (FO 608/79, no. 3999, "Proposed dispatch of troops for protection of Armenian Refugees," March 11, 1919).

7. Erivan, Kars, Tiflis, Elisavetpol, Baku, Batum, Kutais, and Daghestan.

8. At a rate of 0.012 per year. For explanations, see McCarthy, *Muslims and Minorities,* pp. 126–30. The resulting population is 1,425,000, but one must add the approximately 19,000 Armenians who migrated from Ottoman Anatolia between 1897 and 1914 and their descendants, calculated at a natural increase of .012 per year and an in-migration of 1,000 per year. For explanations, see McCarthy, "The Population of the Ottoman Armenians," pp. 74–75.

9. Richard G. Hovannisian, *Armenia on the Road to Independence* (Berkeley: University of California Press, 1967), pp. 14–15.

10. Ibid., p. 67.

11. Trabzon Province is sometimes given as a source for refugees, but no evidence suggests that many refugees came from there. There were 68,000 Armenians in Trabzon in 1912: 4,800 were deported; an unknown number died (McCarthy, *Muslims and Minorities,* p. 112; Yusuf Halaçoğlu, "Realities behind the Relocation," in *The Armenians in the Late Ottoman Period,* ed. Türkkaya Ataöv [Ankara: Turkish Historical Society/Grand National Assembly of Turkey, 2001], pp. 131, 132).

12. Two factors must be considered. First, the 1917 figures, like other such wartime figures, were likely exaggerations of the Armenian population. They are only estimates, because the Russians took no census during the war. Second, the native Armenian population of the Russian Caucasus must also have died of starvation and disease, although surely not in as great numbers as the refugee population. The following is speculation but is probably a more accurate, though very imperfect, picture: 1,444,000 (native population in 1914) minus 144,000 (native population loss from starvation, combat losses, and disease by 1917) plus 340,000 (refugees from Anatolia) minus 85,000 (population loss among refugees: 25 percent) equals 1,555,000 (approximate Armenian population of the Russian Caucasus in 1917).

Extract from the "Instructions for Personal Defense" (1910)

THE VILLAGES

We have three kinds of villages:

1) Those situated between other Armenian villages and exclusively inhabited by Armenians;

2) Those situated in non-Armenian zones, but nevertheless exclusively inhabited by Armenians;

3) Those inhabited at the same time by Armenians and non-Armenians.

From the organization point of view, there is no difference between these three kinds of villages. Each of them will organize a special detachment, and all existing forces will join it with their weapons. Each detachment will be divided into two sections: "the stationary force," and the "active force." Each section shall have a chief and an assistant chief. In each village, the stationary force and the active force will jointly select their leader among the most experienced. This leader shall hold the highest authority in the village and all the forces in the place will be under his orders. He will be at the same time the representative of the zone command and of the general staff.

The chiefs of villages situated in the same zone shall assemble and elect among them a provisional staff composed of three members. On days of battle, the staff, or the commander of the zone, may, under their own responsibility, take their weapons from those who would not be able to use them and give them to more experienced men. Villages attacked by surprise shall immediately send messengers to neighboring localities asking for assistance. Armenians inhabiting mixed villages and who, being a minority, cannot expect assistance from neighboring villages, must at once join the Armenian zones, taking with them their lightest chattels.

In mixed villages, where the enemies would be in [sic] minority in relation to Armenians, the enemies must be kept as hostages if they have previously fled, or requested to leave the village, according to the attitude adopted by them or by their Government.

During battle, the doors of houses must be left open to assist combatants fleeing before regular troops or policemen. In those circumstances, unarmed people must absolutely remain indoors. All the village must pay the price of any weapons that might fall into the hands of the enemy. Arms taken from the enemy belong to those who have captured them.

TO ATTACK VILLAGES.
In order to attack villages, it is necessary:
1) To know the fortified sections of enemy villages;
2) To select beforehand the line of retreat and have it guarded by sentries;
3) To ascertain from where the enemy may receive reinforcements and prevent their arrival.
4) To attack the village only on three sides, leaving a side free for the besieged to make good their escape. (If the village is attacked on all sides, the enemy may fight with desperation and compromise victory.) However, on the side left free, a section of attackers must conceal themselves in order to pursue the enemy and cause him as much damage as possible. Furthermore, the object of leaving a side free is, rather than favor the retreat of the enemy, to break up his force of resistance and thus hasten victory;
5) In order to disturb the enemy, the time of attack should be fixed at the early dawn. If begun sooner, it might stop fighting owing to darkness, which would uselessly cause victims;
6) In order to provoke a panic in the adversary's camp, fire should be set and kindled in several places at the same time. All that is necessary for this should be provided before beginning the attack;
7) If the detachment delivering the attack is not mounted, several horses will have to be held in reserve to transport the dead and wounded to Armenian villages, and thus prevent their being recognized.

A few days before the attack, several capable and trustworthy men, chosen and appointed by the staff, must be sent to the village without disclosing their identity; each one of them will remain in the assigned zone as long as necessary, and after having completed his investigation, will send his report upon the basis of which the attack will be prepared.[1]

NOTE

1. The "Instructions" were issued in 1910 and widely distributed: "in tens of thousands of copies," according to the Ottomans. They were printed in the National Congress of Turkey, *The Turco-Armenian Question: The Turkish Point of View* (Constantinople, Société Anonyme de Papeterie et de l'Imprimerie, 1919), Annex Number 1.

APPENDIX 5

An Example of Attacks on Villagers

Inhabitants of Mergehu village "murdered or annihilated with the utmost savagery by local Armenians who joined Armenian gangs strengthening the Russian Forces":

REPORT OF MARCH 15, 1915

NAMES	METHOD OF ANNIHILATION
Haci Ibrahim, son of Abdi	Bullets and bayonet
Abdi, son of Haci Ibrahim	Bullets and bayonet
Reso, son of Abdi	Beaten and cut into pieces
Sado, son of Omer	Beaten and cut into pieces
Aso, son of Reso	Beaten and cut into pieces
Kulu, son of Canko	Stabbed in the eye with a bayonet
Musa, son of Canko	Bayonet in his eye
Emin, son of Molla Hamit	Bayonet in his eye
Molla Abdullah, son of Hamit	Bayonet in his eye
Ibo, son of Haci	Bayonet in his eye
Sado, son of Haci	Bayonet in his eye
Abdullah, son of Canko	Slaughtered
Ibo, son of Ahmet	Abdomen ripped open
Ismail, son of Ibo	Burnt in fire
Musto, son of Ozii	Bullets
Mahmut, son of Seyyo	Slaughtered
Kocak, son of Birro	Bullets

Musto, son of Husnu	Bullets
Uso, son of Alo	Bullets
Maksut, son of Peri	Bullets
Haci, son of Peri	Bullets
Mehmet, son of Hasanali	Bayonet
Ibo, son of Hasanali	Bayonet
Abdo, son of Mehmed	Bayonet
Molla Suleyman	Burnt in oven
Mazgi, son of Abdullah	Stabbed in abdomen by bayonet
Sulis, son of Hasan	Bullets
Mahmo, son of Mehmet	Stabbed with a dagger
Murat, son of Hasan	Stabbed with a dagger
Uso, son of Avci	Blinded by bayonet
Lesko, son of Mehmet	Stabbed with a dagger
Abdullah, son of Kasim	Bullets
Shepherd Abdullah	Bullets
Seymo, son of Mumin	Bullets
Muammer, son of Reso	Bullets
Paso, son of Merzi	Bullets
Gülü, son of Bitor	Bullets
Murat, son of Yusuf	Bullets and bayonet
Cedo, son of Haci Ibrahim	Bullets and bayonet
Faki Mehmet	Bullets and bayonet
Silo, son of Abdulcebbar	Bullets and bayonet
Kasi, daughter of Huso and wife of Haci Ibrahim	Bullets
Fati, daughter of Isa, wife of Aduz	Bullets
Zeresan, daughter of Amat, wife of Reso	Bayonet
Güllü, daughter of Iyso	Cutting off her breasts
Sülnü, daughter of Sülo, wife of Ibo	Ripping open her abdomen and burning her baby in oven
Fatma, daughter of Ibo	Slaughtered and burnt in oven
Fidan hatun	Burnt in oven
Gulfizar, daughter of Hacihan, wife of Musto	Slaughtered
Rahime, daughter of Mehmet, wife of Halil	Bullets

Binefs, daughter of Haci Kerim, wife of Suleyman	Burnt in oven
Mahiye, daughter of Ali, wife of Sivno	Slaughtered
Hati, daughter of Haci, wife of Ahmet	Slaughtered
Hacer, daughter of Meho	Bullets and bayonet
Nadire, daughter of Haci, wife of Suvis	Raped and murdered
Hani, daughter of Kulu, wife of Zerko	Raped and murdered
Zaliha, daughter of Telli, wife of Silo	Raped and murdered
Arap, daughter of Sami, wife of Hilo	Raped and murdered
Beki, daughter of Hamit, wife of Amo	Bullet wound
Hasan, son of Haci	Bullet wound
Zeyni, daughter of Abbasa, wife of Canko	Bullet wound
Alo, son of Hasan	Bayonet wounds in arms and in abdomen
Ebu, daughter of Fatih (virgin)	Bullet wound

Source: ATASE Archives, Archive No. 1/2, Cabin No. 113, Drawer No. 3, File No. 520, Contents No. 11, Documents 1, no. 15.

APPENDIX 6

The Manifesto of Abdürrezzak

The Kurdish movement

The Pamphlet of Abdur-Rézzak

Help oh Seyid, oh prophet of God…

The Turkish Government, after being compelled to give Tripoli to Italy, was defeated by the four Balkan powers, and lost seven millions of population, lost all the European Vilayets, down to the neighbourhood of Constantinople, lost all the Aegean Islands and Crete, the resources of which places are far larger than those of Anatolia.

Besides the above the Government has given privileges to the Lebanon, and to two ports in Syria in the Damascus Vilayet, and Hussein Hilmi Pasha has been appointed to carry out these reforms.

The questions of Koweit, Shat-el-Arab and the railways in the neighbourhood of Baghdad have been settled in favour of England, and in order to please Syria (sic) the Turkish frontier question is to be settled in favour of Persia. Then the partition of Turkey in Asia was discussed among the powers and, the Ottoman army and treasury having been ruined, the Government under the protection of England accepted the following conditions in order to preserve the independence of the remaining countries.

1. All the internal affairs will be mainly under the control of England and the other great powers.
2. The Ottoman army will be under German officers.
3. The law courts, the income and expenditure, the police, gendarmerie, and all other organizations will be in charge of officials from Europe.
4. The six Vilayets of Van, Bitlis, Erzeroum, Sivas, Kharput and Diarbekir, under the name of Armenia, will have special privileges for Armenians.
5. The council of Ambassadors in London and Paris who examined and decided the situations of the four victorious Balkan powers, will examine and decide the question of reorganizing Armenia and the Armenian privileges, treating Armenia as a fifth power.[1]

The above articles have already been accepted by the Turkish Government. Europe is also considering the question of giving Jaffa, the port of Jerusalem, to France and also of giving similar compensation to each of the other powers, and it is evident that besides America the fate of the other parts of the world is in the hand of Europe.

The Armenians being considered as the fifth victorious power, if their privileges are sanctioned by the council (of London), then weeping will be the share of the Kurds.

The Ottoman Government who put an army of 7 to 800,000 in the field, lost 350,000 persons dead and wounded; 300,000 persons were prisoners; four fifths of the guns and ammunition are gone; the treasury has been emptied; no means of self defense were left; and seeing that the remainder of the countries left would also be divided, Turkey has become like Morocco and Persia and been compelled to prefer to undergo the protection of England and accept a privileged Armenia rather than be altogether ruined.

Should the Government not sacrifice the Kurds, Constantinople and Asia Minor would go out of its hands. As the proverb says "Is it possible to commit another fault in order to conceal the one already done?" Therefore Turkey drew back her hands from Kurdistan and gave herself up to the wishes of Europe.

We Kurds who are known to the majority of Europeans and in all enlightened circles, and even in dictionaries as half savage tribes living by robberies and as shepherds are not recognized as a nation entitled to claim the rights of civilization as the Armenians are. It is evident that no one will listen to our telegrams, speeches, or representations, and under the circumstance we will say as the Persian proverb says "Sword in hand the nation will be protected." We do not however say that we will not accept the decision of the six powers, but the population of the Vilayets placed under the name of Armenia, and those of other places are four fifths Kurdish, and the Kurds own most of the Lands, and therefore their rights and interests come first. Now as the Government has forsaken us it must be considered that if there is a nation worthy of receiving privileges it is the Kurdish one. Moreover the Assyrian Christians who have the same habits, manners and tribal fitness as the Kurds, and who have joined us and are our allies, will never consent that privileges should be given to Armenians and the Kurds and Assyrians be left uncared for.

This time in order to attain our object and to obtain our lawful rights we will not pillage or take revenge (as hitherto), but will do no harm to any Moslem, Christian, Armenian or Jew. We will get armed with our Assyrian fellow-countrymen and will say to the great powers that "We do not say that we do not accept your decisions, as the Ottoman Government which was up to now one of the Great Powers has now become like Morocco and Persia; by the decree of God we will undergo the control of Europe, but as the Kurds and Assyrians are each a nation, their interests should be taken into consideration and when we agree we will ourselves help Europe to carry out its decision."

If the Kurds do not succeed in establishing their rights and privileges, I tell you from now that the first thing will be the collection of arms, disarming the Kurds and the ruin of Sheikhs, Ulemas, Beys, and Aghas, and then how will the ignorant Kurds be able to protect their rights against the rich but immoral Armenians.

Oh Kurds! do you wish your courage to be despised, your religion, nation and fatherland to be ruined? If not, know that now the Kurds, Seyids, Ulemas, Sheikhs, noblemen, learned people, statesmen, beys and aghas, rich and poor have formed a committee and have sworn to protect the religion, nation and the fatherland with their blood. In order not to be "rayas" to Armenians we must do the following. Those who love their religion and fatherland should get armed and help the fighters. Besides, the Kurds, Moslems and Christians and all other fellow countrymen of our opinion, and especially the military officers and officials are invited to join our committee. Take into consideration that 65,000 officers and officials are without work in Roumelie, and if we hand the six Vilayets to Armenians, you officers and officials will remain hungry in the streets with your families, the nation will be ruined by emigration, and as in Roumelie, Crete and other lost Islam provinces, our praying places and habitations will be ruined and polluted.

(follows a prayer in Persian)

The decision of the Kurdish committee.

1. As the Ottoman Government has unwillingly consented that the six Vilayets should be sacrificed to the benefit of Armenians under the name of Armenian reforms, it is necessary to protest against these decisions from now, and until all the other nationalities in the country besides the Armenians consent to the above decision, let us by force of arms turn out all the Ottoman officials of the Vilayets, livas, cazas, nahies and form a new Government to be governed by men elected by the nation.

2. To behave as brothers with the officers and the officials who join our fighting men, but to fight and kill those who act against us, looking upon them as traitors to religion, fatherland and nation.

3. The Kurds who help the traitors will be killed and their property seized.

4. A representative from each tribe and neighbourhood should be sent to the principal revolutionary centre which is to be chosen.

5. To form a temporary Government to decide on our claims and, considering the situation of the country, to settle every question and to govern the nation.

6. To send a deputation to political circles and to the Council of Ambassadors in order to introduce to the Great Powers the temporary Government of Kurdistan.[2]

Notes

1. That is, Armenia will be treated like Greece, Bulgaria, Serbia, and Montenegro, as if Armenia won the Balkan War.

2. FO 195/2450, Monahan to His Britannic Majesty's Ambassador, Erzurum, October 31, 1913, enclosure, "A summary translation from the Armenian newspaper 'Haratch.'"

Bibliography

Ahmet Rustem. *La Guerre Mondiale et la Question Turco-Arménienne*. Berne: Staempfli, 1918.

Akçora, Ergünöz. *Van ve Çevresinde Ermeni İsyanları (1896–1916)*. Istanbul: Türk Dünyası Araştırmaları Vakfı, 1994.

———. "Yaşayanların Diliyle Van ve Çevresinde Ermeni Mezalimi." In *Yakın Tarihimizde Van Uluslararası Sempozyumu*, pp. 87–116. Van: Van Yüzüncü Yıl Üniversitesi, 1990.

Allen, W. E. D., and Paul Muratoff. *Caucasian Battlefields*. Cambridge: Cambridge University Press, 1953.

Arslan, Esat. "Çanakkale'de Günceler Işığında Cephenin İki Tarafı." *Silahlı Kuvvetler Dergisi* (April 1997).

Askeri Tarih Belgeleri Dergisi 83 (March 1983).

Ataöv, Türkkaya. "Ermeni Terörizminde silah Sağlanması: Osmanlı Belgelerine Dayalı Gerçekler." In *Uluslararası Terörizm ve Uyuşturucu Madde Kaçakçılığı Sempozyumu*, pp. 163–71. Ankara: Ankara Üniversitesi, 1984.

Barton, James L. *The Story of Near East Relief*. New York: Macmillan, 1930.

Bayur, Y. Hikmet. *Türk İnkilâbı Tarihi*. Vol. 2, section 3. Ankara: Türk Tarih Kurumu, 1983.

Birinci Dünya Harbinde Türk Harbi, Kafkas Cephesi, 3üncü Ordu Harekâtı. Vols. 1 and 2. Ankara: Genelkurmay Basımevi, 1993.

Çark, Y. *Türk Devleti Hizmetinde Ermeniler*. Istanbul: Yeni Matbaa, 1953.

Çelik, Hüseyin. "Ali Paşayı Vurdular." In *Van Turizm ve İş Rehberi*. Istanbul: İhlâl Finans, 1998.

———. *Görenlerin Gözüyle Van'da Ermeni Mezalimi*. Van: Van Yüzüncü Yıl Üniversitesi, 1996.

Cemal Paşa. *Hatıralar*. Ankara: Atatürk Üniversitesi, 1978.

Cuinet, Vital. *La Turquie d'Asie*. Vol. 2. Paris: E. Leroux, 1891.

Cumhuriyetin Ellinci Yılında Van. Istanbul: n.p., 1973.

Dahiliye Nezâreti, Sicil-i Nüfus İdare-yi Umumiyesi Müdüriyeti. *Memalik-i Osmaniye'nin 1330 Senesi Nüfus İstatistiği*. Istanbul, 1336 Mali.

Dasnabedian, Hratch. *History of the Armenian Revolution Federation, Dashnaktsutiun*. Translated by Bryan Fleming and Vaha Habeshian. Milan: GEMME Edizione, 1989.

———. "The Hnchakian Party." Translated by Mariné A. Arakelians. *Armenian Review* 41, no. 4 (Winter 1988): 17–39.

Deliorman, Altan. *Türklere Karşı Ermeni Komitecileri*. Istanbul: Boğaziçi Üniversitesi, 1975.

Demirel, Muammer. *Ermeniler Hakkında İngiliz Belgeleri (1896–1918)/British Documents on Armenians.* Ankara: Yeni Türkiye, 2002.

Demiroğlu, Faiz. *Van'da Ermeni mezâlimi, 1895–1920.* Ankara: Türk Kültürü Araştırma Enstitüsü, 1985.

de Nogales, Rafael. *Four Years beneath the Crescent.* New York: Scribner's, 1926.

Documents on Ottoman Armenians. Vols. 1, 2, and 3. Ankara: Prime Ministry Directorate General of Press and Information, 1982, 1983, 1986.

Documents sur les Atrocités Arméno-Russes. Istanbul: Société Anonyme de Papeterie et d'Imprimerie, 1917.

Ermeni Komitelerinin Amal ve Harekât-ı İhtilâliyesi. Istanbul: Matbaa-i Amire, 1332. Reprinted, Ankara: Başbakanlık Basımevi, 1983.

Ermeniler Tarafından Yapılan Katliam Belgeleri (1914–1919). Vol. 1. Ankara: Başbakanlık Devlet Arşivleri Genel Müdürlüğü, Osmanlı Arşivi Daire Başkanlığı, 2001.

Farah, Irmgard. *Die deutsche Pressepolitik und Propagandatätigkeit im Osmanischen Reich von 1908–1918 unter besonderer Berücksichtigung des "Osmanischen Lloyd."* Stuttgart: Steiner, 1993.

Gökaçtı, Mehmet Ali. *Dünyada ve Türkiye'de Belediyecilik.* Istanbul: Ozan, 1996.

Gossoian, Haig. *The Epic Story of the Self Defense of Armenians in the Historic City of Van.* Translated by Samuels S. Tarpinian. Detroit: General Society of Vasbouragan, Raven Publishers—AKA, 1967.

Great Britain, Imperial War Museum. *Handbook of the Turkish Army: Eighth Provisional Edition, February, 1916.* Nashville and Skokie: Imperial War Museum, 1996.

Great Britain, Parliament. Misc. No. 31, 1916. *The Treatment of Armenians in the Ottoman Empire 1915–16.* London: HMSO, 1916.

Gülsoy, Ufuk. *Gayri Müslimlerin Askerlik Macerası.* Istanbul: Simurg Yayınları, 2002.

Günay, S. Selçuk. "Hamidiye Hafif Süvari Alayları ve Erzurum." *Türk Dunyası Araştımalları* 53 (1988): 81–85.

Gürün, Kamuran. *The Armenian File.* London: Rustem and Weidenfeld and Nicolson, 1985.

Halaçoğlu, Yusuf. *Ermeni Tehciri ve Gerçekler/1914–1918.* Ankara: Türk Tarih Kurumu, 2001.

———. "Realities behind the Relocation." In *The Armenians in the Late Ottoman Period,* edited by Türkkaya Ataöv, pp. 109–42. Ankara: Turkish Historical Society/Grand National Assembly of Turkey, 2001.

Hampikian, Nairy. "The Architectural Heritage of Vaspurakan and the Preservation of Memory Layers." In *Armenian Van/Vaspurakan,* edited by Richard G. Hovannisian, pp. 87–116. Costa Mesa, Calif.: Mazda Publishers, 2000.

Hanioğlu, M. Şükrü. *Preparation for a Revolution: The Young Turks, 1902–1908.* Oxford: Oxford University Press, 2001.

———. *The Young Turks in Opposition.* Oxford: Oxford University Press, 1995.

Heller, Joseph. *British Policy towards the Ottoman Empire.* London: Cass, 1983.

Hewsen, Robert H. " 'Van in This World; Paradise in the Next': The Historical Geography of Van/Vaspurakan." In *Armenian Van/Vaspurakan,* edited by Richard G. Hovannisian, pp. 13–42. Costa Mesa, Calif.: Mazda Publishers, 2000.

Hocaoğlu, Mehmed. *Arşiv Vesikalarıyla Tarihte Ermeni Mezâlimi ve Ermeniler.* Ankara: Anda, 1976.

Hovannisian, Richard G. "The Armenian Question in the Ottoman Empire, 1876–1914." In his *The Armenian People,* vol. 2, pp. 218–26. New York: St. Martin's, 1997.

———, ed. *Armenian Van/Vaspurakan.* Costa Mesa, Calif.: Mazda, 2000.

———. *Armenia on the Road to Independence, 1918.* Berkeley: University of California Press, 1967.

———. *The Republic of Armenia.* Vol. 1. Berkeley: University of California Press, 1971.

Hüseyin Nâzım Paşa. *Ermeni Olayları Tarihi.* 2 vols. Ankara: Başbakanlık Devlet Arşivleri Genel Müdürlüğü, Osmanlı Arşivi Daire Başkanlığı, 1994.

Işık, Hüseyin. *Şehitlerimiz ve Gazilerimiz.* Ankara: Jandarma Matbaası, 1995.

Kaligian, Dikran Mesrob. "The Armenian Revolutionary Federation under Ottoman Constitutional Rule, 1908–1914." Ph.D. dissertation, Boston College, 2003.

Kalman, M. *Batı Ermenistan Kürt İlişkileri ve Jenosit.* Istanbul: Zel, 1994.

Kansu, Aykut. *The Revolution of 1908 in Turkey.* Leiden: Brill, 1997. Turkish edition also cited: *1908 Devrimi.* Istanbul: İletişim, 1995.

Karaca, Ali, ed. *Anadolu Islahatı ve Ahmet Şâkir Paşa.* Istanbul: Eren, 1993.

———. "Tehcire Giden Yolda Ermeni Meselesine Bir Çözüm Projesi ve Reform Müfettişliği (1878–1915)." In *Ermeni Meselesi Üzerine Araştırmalar,* pp. 9–90. Istanbul: Tatav, 2001.

———. "Türkiye'de Ermeniler İçin Yapılan Reformlar (Örtülü Bir İşgale Doğru) ve Tehcir Gerçeği (1878–1915)." In *Uluslar arası Türk-Ermeni İlişkileri Sempozyumu,* pp. 107–70. Istanbul: Tarih ve Tabiat Vakfı, 2001.

Kara Schemsi. *Turcs et Arméniens devant l'histoire.* Geneva: Imprimerie Nationale, 1919.

Katchaznouni, Hovhannes. *The Armenian Revolutionary Federation (Dashnagtzoutiun) Has Nothing to Do Anymore: The Manifesto of Havhannes Katchaznouni, First Prime Minister of the Independent Armenian Republic.* Translated by Matthew A. Callendar. Edited by John Roy Carlson (Arthur A. Derounian). New York: Armenian Information Service, 1955.

Kayalı, Hasan. "Elections and the Electoral Process in the Ottoman Empire, 1876–1919." *International Journal of Middle East Studies* 27, no. 3 (August 1995): 265–86.

Kévorkian, Raymond H., and Paul B. Paboudjian. *Les Arméniens dans l'Empire Ottoman à la veille du génocide.* Paris: Editions d'Art et d'Histoire, 1992.

Khatanassian, Yervant. "Two Glossaries for the Assistance of Researchers." *Armenian Review* 32, no. 3 (September 1979): 267–79.

Kılıç, Orhan. *XVI. ve XVII. Yüzyıllarda Van, 1548–1648.* Van: Van Belediye Başkanlığı, 1997.

Klein, Janet. "Power in the Periphery: The Hamidiye Light Cavalry and the Struggle over Ottoman Kurdistan." Ph.D. dissertation, Princeton University, 2002.

Kley, Otto. "Der Deutsche Bildungseinfluss in der Türkei." *Beiträge zur Kenntnis des Orients* 14 (1917).

Knapp, Grace H. *Mission at Van.* Privately published in 1916. Also in Great Britain, Parliament, Misc. No. 31, 1916, *The Treatment of Armenians in the Ottoman Empire 1915–16,* pp. 32–47. London: HMSO, 1916.

Koçaş, M. Sadi. *Tarihte Ermeniler ve Türk Ermeni İlişkileri.* Istanbul: Kastaş, 1990.

Kodaman, Bayram. "Hamidiye Hafif Süvari Alaylar: II. Abdülhamid ve Doğu-Anadolu Aşiretleri." *Tarih Dergisi* 32 (1979): 427–80.

Korganoff, Général G. *La participation des Arméniens à la Guerre Mondiale sur le Front du Caucase (1914–1918).* Paris: Massis, 1927.

Kouymjian, Dickran. "Visual Accounts of Van through Travel Accounts." In *Armenian Van/ Vaspurakan,* edited by Richard G. Hovannisian, pp. 153–70. Costa Mesa, Calif.: Mazda Publishers, 2000,

Krikorian, Mesrob K. *Armenians in the Service of the Ottoman Empire 1860–1908.* London: Routledge and Kegan Paul, 1977.

Kuneralp, Sinan. "İkinci Meşrutiyet Döneminde Gayrimüslimlerin Askerlik Meselesi." *Toplumsal Tarih* (December 1999).

Kurat, Akdes Nimet. *Türkiye ve Rusya*. Ankara: Ankara Üniversitesi, 1970.

Langer, William. *The Diplomacy of Imperialism*. New York: Knopf, 1960.

Larcher, Commandant M. *La Guerre Turque dans la Guerre Mondiale*. Paris: E. Chiron, 1926.

Mao Tse-Tung. "On Protracted War." In *Strategy for Conquest: Communist Documents on Guerilla Warfare*, edited by Jay Mallin, pp. 108–11. Coral Gables, Fla.: University of Miami, 1970.

Marsapetyan, A. "The Administration of Van." In *Van-Vaspurakani herosamarte 75*, edited by H. M. Poghosyan and H. D. Papazyan, pp. 115–26. Erevan: Hayastan, 1990.

Maslovski, E. V. *Umumi Harpte Kafkas Cephesi, Eserinin Tenkidi*. Ankara: Genelkurmay Matbaası, 1931.

Maunsell, F. R. *Military Report on Eastern Turkey in Asia: Compiled for the Intelligence Division of the War Office*. London: War Office, 1894.

Mayewsky. *Van, Bitlis Vilâyetleri Askerî İstatistiği*. Istanbul: Matbaa-i Askeriyye, 1330.

McCarthy, Justin. "American Commissions to Anatolia and the Report of Niles and Sutherland." In *Türk Tarih Kurumu Kongresi XI, Ankara: 5–9 Eylül 1990*, pp. 1809–53. Ankara: Türk Tarih Kurumu, 1994.

———. *Death and Exile: The Ethnic Cleansing of Ottoman Muslims*. Princeton: Darwin, 1995.

———. *Muslims and Minorities*. New York: New York University Press, 1983.

———. "The Population of the Ottoman Armenians." In *The Armenians in the Late Ottoman Period*, edited by Türkkaya Ataöv, pp. 65–86. Ankara: Turkish Historical Society/Grand National Assembly of Turkey, 2001.

McDowall, David. *A Modern History of the Kurds*. London: I. B. Tauris, 2000.

Menteşe, Halil. *Halil Menteşe'nin Anıları*. Istanbul: Hürriyet Vakfı Yayınları, 1986.

Mukhitarian, Onnig. *An Account of the Glorious Struggle of Van-Vasbouragan*. Translated by Samuels S. Tarpinian. Detroit: General Society of Vasbouragan, 1967.

Nalbandian, Louise. *The Armenian Revolutionary Movement*. Berkeley: University of California Press, 1963.

National Congress of Turkey. *The Turco-Armenian Question: The Turkish Point Of View*. Constantinople: Société Anonyme de Papeterie et de l'Imprimerie, 1919.

The Ninety-fourth Annual Report of ABCFM Presented at the Meeting Held at Grinnell, Iowa, Oct. 11–13, 1904. Boston: American Board, 1905.

The Ninety-seventh Annual Report of ABCFM Presented at the Meeting Held at Cleveland, Ohio, Oct. 9–11, 1907. Boston: American Board, 1908.

The Ninety-ninth Annual Report of the ABCFM Presented at the Meeting Held at Minneapolis, Minnesota, Oct. 13–15, 1909. Boston: American Board, 1910.

Oktay, Hasan. "Ermeni Komitecilerini Katlettiği Van Valisi Ali Rıza Paşa ve Türküsü." *Yeni Türkiye Dergisi* 38 (2001): 832–38.

———. "Ermeniler ve Van İhtilal Örgütü 1896–1915." *Ermeni Araştırmaları Dergisi* 5 (2002): 84–137.

———. "On the Assassination of Van Mayor Kapamacıyan by the Tashnak Committee." *Review of Armenian Studies* 1, no. 1 (2002): 79–89.

———. "Taşnak Partisinin Van Şubesinin V. Kongresi (Varparugan Ermeni ihtilal Komitesi Meclis-i Meşveretinin Müzâkerât Fezlekesi)." *Yeni Türkiye Dergisi* 38 (2001): 822–31.

Önal, Sami. *Sadettin Paşa'nın Anıları*. Istanbul: Remzi Kitapevi, 2003.

The One Hundredth Annual Report of ABCFM Together with the Minutes of the Centenary Meeting Held at Boston Oct. 11–14, 1910. Boston: American Board, 1911.

The One Hundred and First Annual Report of ABCFM Together with the Minutes of the Meeting Held at Milwaukee, Oct. 10–13, 1911. Boston: American Board, 1912.

The One Hundred and Fourth Annual Report of ABCFM, Together with the Minutes of the Meeting Held at Detroit, Michigan, Oct. 13–16, 1914. Boston: American Board, 1915.

The One Hundred and Fifth Annual Report of the ABCFM Together with the Minutes of the Meeting Held at New Haven, Connecticut, Oct. 26, 1915. Boston: American Board, 1916.

Ormanian, Malachia. *The Church of Armenia.* Edited by Terenig Poladian. 2nd ed. London: Mowbray, 1955.

Orman ve Maden ve Ziraat Nezâreti, Kalem-i Mahsus Müdüriyeti İstatistik Şübesi. *1325 Senesi Asya ve Afrika-yı Osmanı Ziraat İstatistiği.* Istanbul: Matbaa-yı Osmani, 1327 Mali.

Ortaylı, İlber. *Tanzimattan Cumhuriyete Yerel Yönetim Geleneği.* Istanbul: Hil, 1985.

Ottoman Empire. *Aspirations et agissements révolutionnaires des Comités Arméniens avant et après la proclamation de la Constitution Ottomane.* Istanbul: n.p., 1917.

Özdemir, Hikmet, Kemal Çiçek, Ömer Turan, Ramazan Çalık, and Yusuf Halaçoğlu. *Ermeniler: Sürgün ve Göç.* Ankara: Türk Tarih Kurumu, 2004.

Özoğlu, Hakan. *Kurdish Notables and the Ottoman State: Evolving Identities, Competing Loyalties, and Shifting Boundaries.* Albany: State University of New York Press, 2004.

Papazian, K. S. *Patriotism Perverted.* Boston: Baikar Press, 1934.

Peroomian, Rubina. "The Heritage of Van Provincial Literature." In *Armenian Van/Vaspurakan,* edited by Richard G. Hovannisian, pp. 133–52. Costa Mesa, Calif.: Mazda Publishers, 2000.

Poghosyan, H. M., and H. D. Papazyan, eds. *Van-Vaspurakani herosamarte 75.* Erevan: Hayastan, 1990.

Poharyan, A. "The Legendary Clash in Van." In *Van-Vaspurakani herosamarte 75,* edited by H. M. Poghosyan and H. D. Papazyan. Erevan: Hayastan, 1990.

Rawlinson, A. *Adventures in the Near East.* London: Melrose, 1924.

Salname-i Devlet-i Aliyye-i Osmaniyye. Istanbul: Matbaa-i Âmire, 1306.

Salname-i Nezaret-i Maarif-i Umumiye, 1316 sene-i hicriyesine mahsustur (also 1317, 1318, 1319, 1321). Istanbul: Matbaa-i Âmire, 1316–21.

Salname-i Vilâyet-i Erzurum, 1288 Hicri Senesi. Erzurum: Erzurum Vilâyeti Matbaası, 1289.

Salname-i Vilâyet-i Erzurum, 1293 Hicri Senesi. Erzurum: Erzurum Vilâyeti Matbaası, 1293.

Sami Bey (Frasheri). *Kamusülalam.* Vol. 6. Istanbul: Mihran, 1316.

Saral, A. Hulki. *Vatan nasıl kurtarıldı; Nur Dağları (Amanoslar), Toroslar, Adana, Maraş, Gaziantep ve Urfa'da yapılan kuvayı milliye savaşları.* Ankara: Türkiye İş Bankası Kültür Yayınları, 1970.

Sasuni, Garo. *Kürt Ulusal Hareketleri ve 15. Yüzyıl'dan Günümüze Ermeni Kürt İlişkileri.* Istanbul: Peri/Med, 1992.

Selvi, Haluk. "Hangi Antranik?" *2023 Dergisi* 12 (April 2002): 30–35.

Seyfeli, Canan. *İstanbul Ermeni Patrikliği kuruluş ve tarihten günümüze idari yapısı.* Ankara: Aziz Andaç Yayınları, 2005.

Shaw, Stanford J., and Ezel Kural Shaw. *History of the Ottoman Empire and Modern Turkey.* Vol. 2. Cambridge: Cambridge University Press, 1977.

Sonyel, Salahi. *The Ottoman Armenians.* London: Rustem, 1987.

———. "The Turco-Armenian 'Adana Incidents' in the Light of Secret British Documents." *Belleten* 201 (December 1987): 1291–1338.

Stieve, F., ed. *Der diplomatische Schriftwechsel Iswolskis 1911–1914.* Vol. 3. Berlin: Deutsche Verlagsgesellschaft für Politik und Geschichte, 1924.

Suny, Ronald Grigor. "Eastern Armenia under Tsarist Rule." In *The Armenian People from Ancient to Modern Times,* edited by Richard G. Hovannisian, vol. 2, pp. 109–37. New York: Palgrave/St. Martin's, 1997.

Süslü, Azmi, Fahrettin Kırzıoğlu, Refet Yinanç, and Yusuf Halaçoğlu. *Türk Tarihinde Ermeniler.* Ankara: Württemberg Türk Dernekleri Koordinasyon Kurulu, 2001.

Süslü, A., G. Öğün, and T. Serdar. *Van, Bitlis, Muş ve Kars'taki Ermeni Katliamları.* Ankara: Van Yüzüncü Yıl Üniversitesi, 1994.

Sykes, Mark. "The Kurdish Tribes of the Ottoman Empire." *Journal of the Royal Anthropological Institute of Great Britain and Ireland* 38 (July to December 1908): 451–86.

Talay, Aydın. *Yıkılan Bir Şehrin Anatomisi.* Van: Van Belediye Başkanlığı, 1996.

Tekeli, İlhan. *Türkiye'de Belediyeciliğin Gelişimi.* Ankara: n.p., 1982.

Teotik Salnamesi. Istanbul: Dahiliye Nezâreti, 1911.

Ter Minassian, Anahide. "The City of Van at the Turn of the Twentieth Century." In *Armenian Van/Vaspurakan,* edited by Richard G. Hovannisian, pp. 171–93. Costa Mesa, Calif.: Mazda Publishers, 2000.

———. "Ermeni Kaynaklarına Göre Yüzyıl Başında Van." In *Modernleşme Sürecinde Osmanlı Kentleri,* edited by Paul Dumont and François Georgeon, translated by Ali Berktay. Istanbul: Tarih Vakfı Yurt Yayınları, 1992.

———. *Nationalism and Socialism in the Armenian Revolutionary Movement.* Translated by A. M. Berrett. Cambridge, Mass.: Zoryan, 1984.

———. "Van, 1915." In *Armenian Van/Vaspurakan,* edited by Richard G. Hovannisian, pp. 209–44. Costa Mesa, Calif.: Mazda Publishers, 2000.

Turan, Ömer. *The Turkish Minority in Bulgaria (1878–1908).* Ankara: Türk Tarih Kurumu, 1998.

Türkmen, Zekeriya. "Birinci Dünya Savaşı Öncesinde İttihat ve Terakki Hükümetinin Doğu Anadolu Islahat Projesi ve Uygulamaları." In *Yedinci Askerî Tarih Semineri Bildirileri,* pp. 239–68. Vol. 2. Ankara: Genelkurmay Basımevi, 2001.

Uras, Esat. *The Armenians in History and the Armenian Question.* Istanbul: Documentary Publications, 1988.

Ussher, Clarence D. *An American Physician in Turkey.* Boston and New York: Houghton Mifflin Company, 1917.

van Bruinessen, Martin. *Agha, Shaikh, and State: The Social and Political Structures of Kurdistan.* London: Zed Books, 1992.

———. "Kurdish Tribes and the State of Iran: The Case of Simko's Revolt." In *The Conflict of Tribe and State in Iran and Afghanistan,* edited by Richard Tapper, pp. 364–400. New York: St. Martin's, 1983.

van der Dussen, W. J. "The Question of Armenian Reforms in 1913–1914." *Armenian Review* 39 (Spring 1986): 11–28.

Van Vilâyeti. *Van Vilâyeti Salnamesi, 1315.* Van: Matbaa-i Vilâyet, 1315.

Westenenk, L. C. "Diary concerning the Armenian Mission." *Armenian Review* 39, no. 1 (Spring 1986): 29–89.

Wiessner, Gunnar. *Hayoths Dzor—Xavasor.* Wiesbaden: Reichert, 1997.

Yavuz, Celalettin. "Ermenilerin Arkasında Hep Birileri mi Olacak?" *KÖK Araştırmalar* 3, no. 1 (Spring 2001): 3–25.

Yıldırım, Hüsamettin. *Rus-Türk Ermeni Münasebetleri 1914–1918.* Ankara: Kök, 1990.

Index

Numbers in *italics* refer to maps